FORTUNE AND MEN'S EYES

DEWEY GANZEL

FORTUNE AND MEN'S EYES

The Career of John Payne Collier

Oxford New York Toronto Melbourne

OXFORD UNIVERSITY PRESS

1982

Oxford University Press, Walton Street, Oxford OX2 6DP

London Glasgow New York Toronto
Delhi Bombay Calcutta Madras Karachi
Kuala Lumpur Singapore Hong Kong Tokyo
Nairobi Dar es Salaam Cape Town
Melbourne Auckland

and associate companies in
Beirut Berlin Ibadan Mexico City

British Library Catalogue in Publication Data
Ganzel, Dewey
Fortune and men's eyes: the career of John Payne Collier
1. Collier, John Payne
2. Scholars—Great Britain—Biography
I. Title
001.2'092'4   CT788.C/
ISBN 0-19-212231-2

Library of Congress Cataloging in Publication Data
Ganzel, Dewey, 1927—Fortune and men's eyes.
Includes bibliographical references and index.
1. Collier, John Payne, 1789–1883.
2. Shakespeare, William, 1564–1616—Forgeries—Collier.
3. Shakespeare, William, 1564–1616—Editors.
4. Editors—Great Britain—Biography.   I. Title.
PR2951.G36 1982   822.3'3   81-22326
ISBN 0-19-212231-2   AACR2

Set by Burgess & Son (Abingdon) Ltd
Printed in Great Britain
at the University Press, Oxford
by Eric Buckley
Printer to the University

*This book is for my wife Carol and
for my daughters Rebecca, Catherine, and Emily*

Preface and Acknowledgements

This book began with a very different subject. I initially intended to compare the careers of John Payne Collier and John Forster, two nineteenth-century 'men of letters' which suggested to me an interesting paradigm of similarity and contrast, but I learned that someone else was writing a full-scale biography of Forster, and I therefore decided to consider Collier alone. I was not unhappy with this change; I was intrigued by the enigma of the scholar-forger which Collier presented. Why, I wondered, should a man who had discovered and published hundreds of *bona fide* documents of great literary and historical value succumb to passing off bogus and, apparently, not very well executed fabrications of little or no importance? It seemed to me there was a significant story there – possibly a cautionary tale.

As it turned out, there was, but not the one I was looking for. When I began my work, I was convinced of Collier's guilt – that, indeed, was the core of the subject – but as my research progressed, I was increasingly aware that the traditional history of John Payne Collier was not the true one, and with misgivings I saw my original subject slip away. No reader of this book, accustomed to the conventional judgement against Collier, will be more sceptical than I was of the conclusions to which my study pointed. For a time the *raison d'être* of the project seemed to have disappeared; it was no longer an enigma I was describing, but a whodunit, a much more involved and complex story that, at least initially, I was not prepared to tell. What was to have been a two-year sprint stretched into a ten-year marathon.

The result is not the modest book I planned, but, I hope, a more valid one. Its conclusions are, of course, my own, but others have helped me to arrive at them. Without a grant in aid from Oberlin College, the initial research could not have been undertaken; without the generosity of many correspondents and libraries, that research would have been fruitless;

without the support of my family and colleagues, the project might have been abandoned when its outlines loomed increasingly large.

My study is based on unpublished manuscripts in several public and private collections. Specific acknowledgements are in my notes, but something more than a bibliographical citation is due to:

the Trustees and Director of the Folger Shakespeare Library, Washington, D.C., for permission to use and to publish items from the largest collection of extant letters and manuscripts of John Payne Collier;

the Trustees of Alleyn's College of God's Gift, Dulwich, for allowing me to consult the Henslowe and Alleyn manuscripts in their possession;

the Trustees of Dr. Williams's Library, London, for granting permission to read and to publish excerpts from Henry Crabb Robinson's manuscript correspondence, diary and reminiscences;

the Trustees of the Henry E. Huntington Library, San Marino, California, for permission to use and to publish excerpts from the Perkins Folio, manuscripts formerly in the Bridgewater and Devonshire Collections, and unpublished correspondence concerning Collier and his associates;

the Trustees of the Chatsworth Settlement who allowed me to consult and to quote from the diary and correspondence of the Sixth Duke of Devonshire, in the Devonshire Collections at Chatsworth;

the Department of Western Manuscripts, Bodleian Library, Oxford, for access to the papers of Edmond Malone and for permission to publish items from the manuscript diary, papers and correspondence of Frederic Madden;

and, finally, the Department of Printed Books of the British Library, for extended use of its facilities and to the Department of Manuscripts of the same institution for permission to use and to publish documents in its collections. In this as in other projects, the British Library has been my primary source of information and satisfaction.

The staff of each of these repositories gave me continuous assistance throughout weeks – sometimes months – of research in their collections and always with unflagging courtesy and patience with my ignorance.

For permission to conduct research of shorter duration, for subsequent correspondence, and for permission to quote from unpublished manuscripts, I wish to thank the Director and Trustees of the Henry W. and Albert A. Berg Collection of the New York Public Library, Astor, Lenox and Tilden Foundations; the Curator of Manuscripts and the Trustees of the Houghton Library, Harvard University; the Dyce Collection of the Library of the Victoria and Albert Museum; and the Keeper and Trustees of the National Library of Scotland, Edinburgh.

One of the happy results of this work has been my acquaintance with Collier's great grand-daughter, the late Mrs Violet Cornelia Koop and her daughters, Diana Rees and Wendy Gillett. I met Mrs Koop when I still posited Collier's guilt, and although this view contradicted her own belief in Collier's innocence (a conviction she admitted was based on familial pride rather than fact), she helped me in innumerable ways, filling in details of family history, allowing me to use letters and manuscripts in her possession, and discussing, in friendly disagreement, our views of 'the old man'. Her death has denied me the opportunity to let her know that, in the end, the evidence supported her predilection. It is some compensation that her daughters have seen her belief vindicated, and I am grateful to them for their continued interest and for their permission to publish the photograph of Collier and excerpts from his manuscript correspondence.

My initial work was encouraged by Giles Dawson, Emeritus Curator of Books and Manuscripts at the Folger, whose interest in Collier predates my own. I profited greatly from Professor Dawson's generous conversation and correspondence. As readers of my Appendix will know, my conclusions, drawn from evidence he has not seen, differ from his, but that in no way diminishes my gratitude for his assistance and encouragement at a time when such support mattered a great deal. I am also pleased to be able to express my thanks to June Lines who typed the manuscript, and to David Young who as friend and colleague was generous in his support. My continuing debt is to my wife who has been my most demanding reader and my most penetrating critic.

The faults of this book are my own; I share whatever virtues it may have with all of the above.

DEWEY GANZEL

Oberlin, Ohio
11 January 1982

Contents

List of Illustrations

DISGRACE

The only surviving portrait of John Payne Collier is a photograph taken in 1861 when he was seventy-two. It is a disconcerting picture; at first it might seem to reflect good-humoured satisfaction with a life well-lived and talent well-spent, but on second glance the subject loses its air of composure, its decorum seems counterfeit and the gentle demeanour of the old man seems to mask a bitter imagination. Confined by age, engulfed by suspicion, he appears to be waiting, somewhat impatiently, for death. Collier called the portrait 'a disappointment'. He might have said the same of his life.

Had he died ten years before the picture, Collier's reputation would have been secure. In 1850, he was acclaimed as a man of prodigious learning, widely recognized as the foremost literary scholar of his generation, the author of over forty books, the first historian of English drama, and a pre-eminent editor of Shakespeare. A decade later, he was almost universally despised, a pathetic object of contempt and execration, a man accused of outrageous crimes and deceptions, condemned to live another twenty years in disgrace and unremitting self-recrimination. He would outlive his accusers but not his dishonour. At the age of ninety-four, virtually blind, his hand an arthritic knot scarcely able to hold the pen, he would write: 'I am bitterly and most sincerely grieved that in every way I am such a despicable offender. I am ashamed of almost every act of my life.'[1] When death came at last to release him from his long confinement, he found it easier to think himself a sinner than a fool.

The calamity of Collier's life was caused by an event which when it occurred was widely acclaimed. On 31 January, 1852, the London *Athenaeum* announced the discovery of a curious treasure, a copy of the Second Folio of Shakespeare that, according to those who had examined it, contained thousands of corrections, in ink, in a hand which appeared to be almost contemporary with the book, alterations so comprehensive and valuable they seemed to have an authority greater than mere conjecture. Virtually every page of the volume had corrections and emendations – occasionally whole lines were inserted – and as a result some of the most confusing parts of Shakespeare's text were made intelligible for the first time. The book appeared to be the most valuable Shakespeare discovery ever made, and the man who made it was John Payne Collier.

The announcement caused a sensation. As most students knew, the only authoritative collection of Shakespeare's plays was the First Folio of 1623, but that edition contained hundreds of errors of omission, transcription and printing, and 'making sense' of the folio had been the chief occupation of Shakespeare scholars for over a century and a half. Hundreds of errors continued to baffle readers, awaiting correction, an authoritative source, some new manuscript evidence, perhaps, which might return the text to what Shakespeare had written. Collier's discovery, soon to be called the Perkins Folio from the words 'Tho. Perkins his Booke' written on its cover, seemed to many to be this long sought authority.

Collier made only modest claims for the book – some of the 'emendations', he declared, seemed 'purely arbitrary or conjectural' – but taken as a whole the corrections were significant. To illustrate his claim, he published eleven of them ('only a few out of hundreds, – and by no means the most striking') and announced his intention to publish the rest in a 'suitable form'. Within a week or two of his announcement, Collier showed the book to the Council of the Shakespeare Society and shortly thereafter to the Society of Antiquaries. 'My desire,' he said, 'is that all who are interested should be gratified as far as possible, and enjoy the means of judging for themselves the value and curiosity of the book.'[2] All who saw the Perkins Folio agreed without exception that it was a discovery of paramount importance, and although a few rival editors grumbled that some of the emendations were not new, their caveat was ignored. To most of the literary world the Perkins Folio quickly became the literary discovery of the century.

It is difficult for modern scholars to understand how the corrections of the Perkins Folio could have created such excitement. The fact that they were universally considered authoritative emendations to Shakespeare's text – that they should have been considered subjects of literary rather than antiquarian interest – suggests that textual criticism in 1852 was still entangled in the antiquarianism from which it derived and that the literary artefact was not yet sharply differentiated from other historical remains. The old was still assumed to be more valuable than the new, the past to have more authority than the present. It was, moreover, believed to be recapturable, and reverence for the authority of the past was usually coupled with a passion for its reconstruction. The past was unknown only insofar as its historical remains were missing, and it was assumed that diligent exploration would eventually uncover the rosetta stones of history and that with intelligent scrutiny they would be deciphered.

This search for the unrecaptured past was particularly frustrating to the Shakespeare scholar. Early printers had corrupted Shakespeare's text with demonstrable errors, and the means for reconstructing his texts were lost: for over a hundred and fifty years there had been an intensive search for Shakespeare's manuscripts (the alacrity with which the literary public had accepted the Ireland forgeries at the end of the eighteenth century suggests the keenness of its desire for such evidence), but none had been found and it was increasingly evident that none would be. This fact did not diminish the desire to recover Shakespeare's text, it merely encouraged new ways to satisfy that appetite. The absence of authorial manuscripts gave seventeenth-century emendations an importance they would not otherwise have deserved. The Perkins emendations were thus merely the latest and, to many who saw them, the best examples of a textual tradition that had flourished for a century.

Nevertheless, the Perkins Folio would not have created the sensation it did had it not been for the reputation of the man who discovered it. For over thirty years John Payne Collier had been a prolific editor of early English drama and the most redoubtable of a score of Shakespeare editors. None of his peers and not-so-gentle competitors had matched his industry, and few his achievements. At sixty-two his reputation was unimpeachable: his twenty-year-old *History of English Dramatic*

Poetry was a landmark in literary historiography, his research into Shakespeare's sources was brilliant, and he had published a score of books containing important documentary discoveries of the late sixteenth and early seventeenth centuries. Most significant of all, his edition of Shakespeare, completed in 1844, was a work of significant revisionist scholarship. In a decision which reversed the editorial practices of a century, Collier took the text of the early printed versions of the play, removing hundreds of 'accepted' conjectural emendations by eighteenth-century editors. It was his reputation for conservative editorial scholarship which made Collier's announcement of the Perkins Folio a sensation. If Collier, the most restrictive of editors, had been converted by the Perkins emendations, they *had* to be remarkable!

And valuable, too. Collier's competitors soon learned that, contrary to usual scholarly practice, he intended to keep the Perkins corrections firmly under his control. Although he unhesitatingly let others see the book, he made it clear that he considered the new emendations to be his property, subject to his copyright, and to be published only under his aegis. The Perkins Folio emendations were accepted – not merely accepted, revered – and Collier was quick to respond to a rising demand for their publication. Within a few weeks he produced *Notes and Emendations to the Text of Shakespeare's Plays,* a selection of the more important corrections, and this was followed in short order by a second edition 'revised and enlarged'. The initial curiosity which the Folio had inspired soon turned to veneration. 'I think Collier has stumbled on a very precious bundle of restorations,' William Charles Macready, the great Shakespearian actor, wrote to a friend. 'I think the discovery a great boon to the readers of Shakespeare.'[3]

It was also a great boon to John Payne Collier. Public interest in anything concerning Shakespeare had been intense for five generations, and it would not abate for two more. (Over thirty editions of Shakespeare would appear in the nineteenth century.) Obviously publishing Shakespeare could be profitable, but it was very competitive. For example, although Collier's 1844 edition was still standard in 1852, there were at least four new editions in the making whose publication would seriously challenge its pre-eminence. By claiming a copyright over the new readings, Collier placed all these ventures at a commercial disadvantage. The announcement that new 'manuscript' evidence was to be available only to Collier was bound to forestall interest in editions other than his own. This advantage was enough to make other editors and their publishers hesitate. Moreover, Collier managed his discovery shrewdly: he published *Notes and Emendations* in a volume uniform with his edition of 1844, and the new emendations could be read with ease only in conjunction with that edition. A few months after this 'supplement', he brought out a one-volume edition of the plays without notes which incorporated the best of the Perkins readings, and this, too, was very successful. (It was almost immediately pirated in the United States.) Three years later, in 1856, Collier published yet another volume which purported to contain a list of 'all the corrections' in the Perkins Folio, and in 1858 he published a second edition of his multi-volume Shakespeare which incorporated many of the Perkins Folio emendations in a more elaborate annotated form. In a period of six years, then, Collier published four separate works based on the folio, each one successful, and for all that time his able competitors were kept from the field. It was one of the most remarkable publishing coups of the nineteenth century.

But though the procedure was commercially remunerative, the bitterness it created was ultimately to make the Perkins Folio the most notorious book in Shakespeare criticism and Collier the centre of the most shocking literary scandal of the century. What most puzzled his friends and angered his enemies was the fact that Collier, although initially generous in showing the folio to interested persons, became secretive with the volume when the emendations began to appear in print. The folio had never been examined out of his sight and after *Notes and Emendations* appeared Collier never displayed it at all. His reporting of the emendations began to seem eccentric: despite the demand and his own announced intent, the full contents of the book were never revealed, and yet he was able to pull remarkable treasures from it as occasion demanded. In consequence, the book which had inspired veneration began to acquire mystery.

For seven years, despite his antagonists' growing animosity, the book remained unexamined and Collier's competitive position impregnable. The Folio became the property of the sixth Duke of Devonshire, Collier's long-time friend and patron. One rumour said Collier had received an enormous price for the book and a promise that His Grace would keep it locked away in the great library at Chatsworth, Derbyshire, far from the eyes of would-be competitors. However, in 1858, Devonshire died, and his successor, the seventh duke, a man unknown to Collier, succeeded to possession of the dukedom and its properties that included Chatsworth, its library – and the Perkins Folio. Collier's antagonists now saw an opportunity. Within a few months the book was delivered to the Manuscript Department of the British Museum where for the first time it was minutely examined by someone other than John Payne Collier.

The results of this 'inquisition' were astounding. Within hours of the Folio's arrival at the Museum, Sir Frederic Madden, Keeper of the Manuscripts and the foremost paleographer in England, privately declared the emendations were not in 'a genuine hand of the 17th century'.[4] Subsequent examination confirmed his belief. Although the writing was apparently all in a single hand, Madden declared that it looked artificial, as though it had been 'drawn', and showed gross inconsistencies in certain capital letters which would not have existed if the hand were genuine. Moreover, the ink was unlike anything he had seen on genuine seventeenth-century documents. But an even more remarkable discovery followed: some of the emendations contained the faint remains of pencil marks 'in a bold hand of the present century' which corresponded exactly to the ink writing and some of these modern pencil equivalents it appeared were directly *under* the ink. The modern pencil notations preceded the ink although the latter was written to suggest that it was at least two hundred years older. The emendations, Madden declared, were forgeries.

On the morning of 2 July, 1859, *The Times* contained a letter from Nicolas S. E. A. Hamilton, Assistant Keeper of Manuscripts of the British Museum, declaring the Perkins Folio a fraud. 'I conceive it positively established that the emendations, as they are called, of this folio copy of *Shakespeare* have been made within the present century', he wrote. Although Hamilton's letter made no public accusation, Madden privately stated that he recognized the handwriting of the pencil notations as belonging to John Payne Collier. What the letter to *The Times* clearly implied was that Collier himself had forged the Perkins Folio emendations and methodically perpetrated the fraud for his private financial gain.

Almost overnight the reputation of the Folio fell from the most revered of books to the most condemned, and Collier's reputation fell with it, from the most influential to the most disreputable and ignominious of the age. His crime seemed the more shocking because it had been concealed for so long and so successfully. Now Collier's literary prosecutors began to examine his earlier publications and to assert that some of his most important works were based on forged manuscripts. Twenty years before, he had printed half a dozen documents pertaining to Shakespeare and the early English theatre which he claimed to have found in the Ellesmere Papers of the Bridgewater library; now all of these were declared to be forged. In the Alleyn manuscripts at Dulwich College, Collier had unearthed documents which were among the most valuable extant concerning Elizabethan and Jacobean theatre practice, and he had published them in three of his most famous books: *Henslowe's Diary, The Alleyn Papers,* and the *Life of Edward Alleyn*; now the manuscripts on which these monumental works were based were declared to be shot through with forged insertions. The list of fabrications grew almost daily, and in every case it appeared that the forged document had been discovered and published by Collier. For over a quarter of a century one of the country's most respected scholars had had unrestricted access to the greatest manuscript collections in England, and now it appeared that he had betrayed that trust by systematically planting forgeries in them. It was a monstrous crime and a pernicious one, for Collier's great learning would have enabled him to insinuate the forgeries into places where no ordinary scholar would suspect them. No other man had the knowledge and few had had the opportunity to carry out such subversion. The crime had no parallel in literary history.

The accusations created a controversy which raged for two and a half years. Collier stubbornly declared his innocence, and a few staunch friends fought beside him, but the outcome was apparent almost as soon as the charges were made. To most of his contemporaries and virtually all subsequent historians, Collier's defence was too weak to be accepted: forgery is a crime of which one is more easily accused than acquitted, and Collier's defence seemed disingenuous. In any case, he lost the support he most needed: the public, usually deferential to established authority, was quite ready to believe the worst. Cast doubt on any reputation, no matter how esteemed or unblemished, and something is taken from it, if only the assumption that it is unimpeachable, and in Collier's case the apparently irrefutable evidence was presented by the most important authorities in the field. The Perkins Folio which had been greeted with nearly universal acclaim less than a decade before was now universally damned. Collier's punishment was severe. For the next thirty years his was a life dishonoured, and successive ages have been even harsher than his own in excoriating his memory. For over a century his reputation has been the blackest in the history of scholarship.

In the face of this universal condemnation, it may seem quixotic to argue that history's judgement is wrong, that the evidence presented against Collier in the Perkins Folio controversy was incomplete, misconstrued, or falsified, to declare, in short, that John Payne Collier was an innocent victim of malicious ignorance. Yet this is the conclusion to which I have come after re-examining the case. I am sure some of my readers will find this an unlikely conclusion and perhaps a disturbing one. How, one might ask, could so many scholars be mistaken? Certainly it would be foolish to pretend that Collier's character and career were without blemish: he was often careless; his critical judgement was not impeccable; he was mildly paranoic and sometimes vindictive; he was unnecessarily secretive and intolerably jealous, vain of his accomplishment and guilty of deliberately obscuring facts to hide his errors and incapacities. These are serious faults and they are in no way palliated by the fact that all of his adversaries shared them. But I think the evidence demonstrates that he was not guilty of forging the emendations in the Perkins Folio or of fabricating the disputed documents in the Alleyn and Bridgewater papers. Insofar as the judgement of history is founded on the distorted accounts which his accusers left behind,[5] it is wrong.

To correct that judgement, it is necessary to recount part of Collier's life and career and to describe the events which followed his discovery of the Perkins Folio, a sequence which has never been fully examined before. The crime as recorded was outrageous: what actually happened was even more outrageous. The destruction of John Payne Collier may have been the most successful conspiracy in literary history.

I

FORTUNE

'Do you mean to breed him up to authorship?'

1

One of the Collier family legends was its descent from Jeremy Collier, the seventeenth-century theologian and iconoclast. John Payne Collier often repeated the story although he admitted he could find no evidence for it. The known history of the family began in the mid-eighteenth century when Payne's grandfather, John Collier, left Stoke Newington in Oxfordshire to study medicine at Edinburgh. In 1756 he journeyed to London, set up shop in Newgate and immediately began to rise in his profession. He became Yeoman in the Society of Apothecaries and, as the years passed, moved to increasingly fashionable residences: from Newgate to Cheapside, where John Dyer Collier, Payne's father, was born in 1762, and from there to Aldermanbury, where, in partnership with Dewaynes, he became chemist to the royal family in 1786, a lucrative honour which he held for twenty-six years. From Aldermanbury he moved to Charterhouse Square, where Dyer and his older brother Joshua attended Charterhouse School, and from there to an even larger house in Islington. Around 1785 John sold his practice and retired to Theobalds Park, Hertfordshire, and busied himself writing lengthy tracts on Jewish History, the life of Christ, and the possibility of 'reanimation' after death.[1] At his most affluent, he possessed a fortune in excess of £50,000. The chemist's business, said John Collier, 'is quite 11^d in every shilling.'[2]

Payne's father, John Dyer Collier, therefore spent his childhood and youth in comparative luxury. At Charterhouse he became proficient in Latin and Greek and he wanted to proceed to Oxford but his father decreed that his sons were to be merchants, and at his retirement he gave each £10,000 to establish a trade. Dyer quickly invested his capital in Spanish Merino wool, and the venture prospered. Something of a dandy, he enjoyed his affluence; a miniature painted about this time attests to his blue-eyed good looks and to his vanity. Intelligent, robust and wealthy, Dyer at twenty-four was a marital 'catch', and it is not surprising that he married well. Jane Payne, who became his wife in 1786, was in every way his equal, by all accounts a remarkably beautiful woman with wit and taste at least as cultivated as Dyer's own. She was the eldest daughter of a successful sugar refiner who at his death some years before had left her £7,000 in Chancery and at the time of her marriage this earned £120 per year. The newly-weds took an imposing house on Broad Street, and when their first child, Jane, was born in January 1787, their future was bright.

When John Payne Collier arrived two years later, it was beginning to dim. He was born at Broad Street on 11 January, 1789, the year of the French Revolution. 'Nonsensical as it may seem', he was to write many years later, 'it gives me some pleasure to think that the period at which I was born was marked by some extraordinary occurrence.'[3] So far as the Colliers were concerned, a concurrent event was more catastrophic: a sudden shift in the English commodity market brought a rise in the value of Saxony wool and a decline in Spanish Merino. John Payne Collier's birth therefore coincided with the collapse of his father's fortune. Within six months, Dyer was forced to give up his fine house in London and to move to Leeds in a vain attempt to salvage his wool shares. In spite of frantic effort, Dyer was bankrupt, with a wife and, now, three children, a second daughter, Mary, having been born shortly after their arrival in Leeds.

Payne's early childhood was warped by poverty, insecurity, and vague fears of disaster and early death. His earliest and most vivid recollection was of an injury to his foot which made him lame. Dyer had got the idea ('from some French writer,' Payne surmised) that good health was impaired by over-protection, and he forced his children to go barefoot in winter. As a result, Payne got a chilblain in his right foot and the big toe became infected. Payne's earliest memory was of sitting on a kitchen table, sucking an orange and, in spite of great pain,

uttering no sound, while an overzealous doctor amputated the
toe. His father, he recalled, was very proud of him and
commended his 'spartan' stoicism. 'I have ever since tried
more or less to keep up the character,' Payne was to declare.[4]

Another event was even more traumatic. Teased into a
tantrum by one of Dyer's friends, Payne, barely three years
old, threatened to cut his own throat. Told to 'cut away
Master Johnny', he seized a carving knife and actually sliced
into the skin of his neck before he was disarmed by the
horrified man. Payne carried a scar for the rest of his life.
These events were strange portents of a life which was to be
perilously balanced between stoicism and self-destruction.

After months of hapless uncertainty, Dyer decided to
prepare for the bar, a popular and not very demanding
occupation which seemed compatible with his social pretensions. The family moved to a tiny house in Thames Ditton,
next to the river and opposite the wall of Hampton Court,
where they lived for two desperate years while Dyer read
Blackstone and the commentaries. Surprisingly, Payne's
memories of Thames Ditton were happy ones. They lacked
furniture (the children slept on the floor), but they had books,
and Payne was intellectually precocious. At three, reading was
his greatest pleasure; at four, his father began to teach him
Latin.

Life was more difficult for Jane, an imaginative woman cut
off from the city life she had been born to. The principal of her
inheritance was fortunately beyond the reach of Dyer or his
creditors, but it was a pitifully small annuity to support her
family. The birth of their fourth child, Richard, increased her
anxiety and when Dyer became seriously ill during their
second winter at Thames Ditton, she begged her sister, Mary
Field, for help. Mary's husband, a successful leather manufacturer, owned a run-down soap factory in Southwark which
had been surety on a bad debt. Field's attempts to sell the
business had been unsuccessful, and since he didn't want to
run the factory himself, he offered to turn it over to Dyer,
promising that any profits from the sale of soap would be
Dyer's. His only stipulation was that Dyer continue to
purchase as much tallow as the former owner had. Dyer
thought the position beneath him and would have refused but

for Jane's insistence. As Payne later recalled, 'as usual she was right and our poor dear misjudging father in the wrong.'[5] The agreement was struck, the factory repaired, the family moved to Great Suffolk Street, Southwark – and Dyer became a soap maker. To the astonishment of everyone, including Field and probably Dyer himself, he was very successful. Within two years he doubled the amount of tallow he bought from Field. In less than four, he sent £2,500 to his bankers.

This return to affluence meant the Colliers could once again attend the theatre regularly (Payne's earliest recollection of the stage was of Mrs Siddons), and frequent the clubs they had left so abruptly four years before. It was at a club that the Colliers met the man who was to become the confidant of their oldest son. Henry Crabb Robinson was newly arrived in London to read law. At twenty, he was still more boy than man, impressionable and lonely, grieving for his mother who had died two years before and somewhat estranged from his father who had remarried. Since his mother's death, Robinson had sought the friendship of women who might fill her place, and it was not surprising that Jane, vivacious, beautiful and seven years his senior, attracted him. One evening in July, 1797, Jane, unaccompanied, attended the Westminster Forum, a popular debating club, and in the course of the evening she struck up a conversation with Robinson. 'It seemed she knew me', he recalled afterwards. This was introduction enough. Later when she was unable to find a carriage to Southwark, Robinson escorted her home, and a few days later Dyer called on Robinson to thank him. A friendship thus began which, Robinson declared, changed the course of his life.[6] Robinson thought Jane the most beautiful woman he had ever seen, and her affection for him encouraged his love which was always honourably – if sometimes painfully – platonic. He was soon a regular guest at Southwark, virtually a member of the family, and he took a particular liking to Payne, then a bookish boy of eight, who, like Crabb, was an intellectual loner whose vulnerability the older youth recognized and understood.

The Colliers' prosperity ended suddenly when Field, jealous of Dyer's unexpected success with the soap factory, announced that henceforth the factory's profits were to come to him and

that Dyer would be on salary. Dyer, stung by an affront to his
sense of fair play as well as his social pretensions, quit the
business, drew his £2,500 from the bank, bought a 250-acre
farm at Hydes Bridge near Epping, and set himself up as a
gentleman farmer. The result was catastrophic. Within a
couple of years the soap business was again bankrupt and
Dyer's adventure in agriculture, founded apparently on no
more knowledge than might be had from reading a book or
two, had wiped out his savings and dragged his family back
into poverty. Worst of all, Dyer, confident of success, imposed
on his new friendship with Robinson by borrowing £400 at
five per cent from the young man's own small savings. For
three bitter, fruitless seasons, Dyer tried to produce a crop
which would feed himself, his wife and – now – five children
(William Field Collier had been born shortly before his uncle
dispossessed them all). The Colliers were hopelessly ill-suited
to the demands of farm life, and Dyer finally admitted failure.
In 1801 the family was back in London, worse off than it had
ever been.

With the help of friends Dyer became, in Robinson's words;
a 'bookseller's fag', a hack-writer, facile, adept, ready to write
whatever would sell for whomever would pay. His range was
wide: he wrote 'fill' for periodicals and penny-a-line copy for
newspapers. He translated French travel accounts for cheap
English editions and longer 'serious' works of popular history.
He wrote much of the text for a book of contemporary
biographies, and he even tried his hand at a novel. It was
drudge work but he was good at it. He was in demand and
eventually he learned shorthand and acquired a reputation
for speed. 'Short order' jobs were his forte; on one occasion he
wrote a 200-page biography on commission in less than a
week.[7] He called it 'literature' but it was not work which
supported his intellectual pretensions, and his success was
marred by self-contempt.

Payne had to help. When they first returned to London, he
spent the daylight hours colouring engravings with his
mother, but when Dyer's commissions increased, the boy
learned shorthand to transcribe his father's notes, and before
long, he was doing some of the composition himself. He had
no friends; his brothers and sisters, less precocious than he,

were of little help to their father and no company for Payne.
He was forced to give up childhood early. He, too, became
adept.

Much of their work was for newspapers. Despite Dyer's
enthusiasm for reform while the Tories were in power, he
learned to carry his politics in his purse, and his employers
were not much concerned about his personal opinions so long
as what he wrote matched theirs. For a year or two he was
'editor' of the *Monthly Register and Encyclopedia* for Richard
Phillips, a Whig famous as the 'great master of literary hacks',
and at the same time a contributor to Peter Stuart's Tory
newspaper, the *Oracle and Daily Advertiser,* at a guinea per
column. The *Monthly Register* was less remunerative, but more
regular because in addition to the magazine, Phillips published twopenny books and with Payne's help, Dyer wrote
many of them.

In the spring of 1803, Stuart hired Dyer as a 'regular' for
three guineas per week, and about the same time Dyer began
to write two galleys of agricultural news for another magazine
for five guineas a month. 'This to John is play', Jane reported
to Robinson.[8] He had apparently learned enough among the
barren fields of Epping to guide others – presumably down a
more satisfactory path. Over and above his salary at the
Oracle, Dyer earned £110 in the first nine months of 1803.
With this return to relative prosperity, the Colliers moved to a
larger house at 3 Little Smith Street, Westminster, and Dyer
proposed that in lieu of £20 annual interest, Robinson should
be their lodger. 'You have a rascally debtor', he wrote to
Robinson, 'and you might conveniently contrive to put
yourself under his roof and set his Beef and Pudding at work
to rub off a little of the score.'[9] Robinson liked the idea, and
when he returned from Germany early in 1806, he began a
sojourn with the family which was to last seven and a half
years.

Dyer's work at the *Oracle* was parliamentary reporting (he
was probably the first to use shorthand to report the debates),
and Payne regularly assisted him in the gallery, learning the
job literally at his father's knee. Parliamentary reporting was
not a despised vocation (many of the best writers of the age
served a term in the gallery at one time or another) and it was

the best paid among newspaper jobs; with Payne's assistance, Dyer was soon earning over £300 a year at the *Oracle*. But the work was arduous and parliamentary reporters were vulnerable to political reprisal: they could be punished at the bar of the House for 'libel', that is, for reporting events a powerful member of the House might wish to conceal. In addition, the work was physically exhausting. The public gallery in the old House of Commons was small, and reporters from twelve or fifteen London papers had to share it with the general public; not until 1803 was a section reserved for the press and even then there was scarcely room to sit, let alone to write. The evening sessions often lasted over eight hours, and the usual procedure when Dyer began in 1802, was to alternate two-hour turns with another reporter, a severe test of stamina and skill.

Although he was to become very good at it, Payne never liked parliamentary reporting, and in later life he would realize how much he had been deprived by being sent into the lists so early. At fourteen he was tall and awkward, with a slight limp and a shock of unruly brown hair. He was inordinately shy; he had no taste for camaraderie and no time for it in any case. His intellectual interests were literary and imaginative, incipient tastes rather than developed appetites, no less real for being inchoate and no less powerful for being private. His real vocation – although he could not have defined it himself – was scholarship. On one occasion Payne accompanied his father to Montague House, the musty mansion which then housed the British Museum, and standing at the doorway of the reading room, he was overwhelmed by an almost palpable sense of the past: the crowded shelves towered above him, dead scholars stared from the blackened portraits on the walls, and over all there was silence, reverent, oppressive, expectant, a hush broken only by the scratch of pens. In that moment he glimpsed his vocation and, perhaps, his fate: to be half-victim, half-acolyte, a successor to those grey pedants who looked up, annoyed by the presence of a boy in the chamber. He wanted to be one of them. It was a desire which would shape his imagination for the next eight years, his introduction to a world which, for good and ill, was ultimately to be his own.

He would enter that world, but he would do so late and unprepared. At fourteen, Payne's education was directed to other ends. Robinson, who alone recognized the boy's promise, protested that Dyer had not given 'due reflection' to Payne's career, that Payne might become, by default, a mere literary hack. 'I fear this', he wrote Dyer from Germany shortly before Payne's fifteenth birthday. 'Do you mean to breed him up to authorship?'[10] For a short time there were plans for Payne to join Joshua's sons at Westminster School, but they were forgotten as Payne became increasingly necessary to Dyer's livelihood, and as a result Payne was never to attend school or university. He was to be, in his bitter phrase, a 'captive of newspapers', forever shamed by his lack of formal education. He never learned mathematics and he had only a smattering of philosophy; he read the major Latin authors, but he never mastered Greek. In the view of those scholars with whom he would try, unsuccessfully, to claim fraternity, he was hopelessly 'unprepared', and although he would eventually achieve literary eminence, he would never lose the sense of being out of place, intellectually incomplete and culturally shabby. 'I never became a good scholar', he wrote in the last years of his life. 'To this day I am very ignorant.'[11]

Payne did not go to Westminster School – he went to *The Times*. John Walter II, who had recently taken control of that newspaper, read Dyer's accounts in the *Oracle*, liked them, and hired him to report the proceedings of the King's Bench. In addition, Walter agreed to hire Payne as Dyer's assistant at a guinea for each session he attended. It was Payne's first regular, paid employment. Dyer had yet another job for his oldest son, that of writing 'letters' for provincial papers. Over a period of four or five years, Dyer was to assemble a dozen clients in Dublin, Edinburgh, York, Newcastle, Bristol and elsewhere to whom Payne sent regular dispatches. Payne's work at court and Parliament gave him more knowledge of politics and social issues than any ordinary fifteen-year-old was likely to have, and the provincial correspondence taught him how to market what he knew. At its peak, the service brought the family over £700 a year. He was being bred up to authorship, no doubt of it.

His work for *The Times* gave him money of his own, and he began to indulge what he was later to call 'a strong, and even greedy, desire' to own books. He became an avid frequenter of bookstalls and book auctions and developed a particular interest in works of the sixteenth and seventeenth centuries. It was a specialized taste and an unusual one, and there is no way of knowing how he acquired it. Initially he may have been attracted by the age of the books, by the quaintness of their type or their archaic format, but his passion for them soon went beyond mere antiquarianism. He felt the thrill of their possession, to be sure, but he had, as well, the desire to know what they said, and in the course of buying, selling and trading books he would acquire a remarkable first-hand knowledge of rare and ephemeral tracts.

His bibliomania was abetted by Thomas Amyot, an old friend of Robinson who had risen through the ranks of the civil service to a position of power and financial independence. To Collier, Amyot was 'one of the first friends that literature procured me'; he was unquestionably the best.[12] He, too, was a regular at the Evans and Sotheby book auctions, and he had assembled a valuable library. With Amyot's assistance Payne was admitted to the library of the Society of Antiquaries as well as to that of George III at Buckingham House. Still later Amyot introduced the young man to Sir Henry Ellis, then Principal Librarian of the British Museum who, in spite of Payne's youth, gave him a reader's ticket to the national library. Payne's interest in these collections was what today would be called 'bibliography', the history and description of books, but in 1805 there were no accepted methods to guide his study, and he was therefore compelled to develop his own procedures by fortuitous discovery, a process which, coupled with intelligence and a retentive memory, was to make him, in the course of two decades, one of the foremost bibliographers in England.

In December 1806, the Colliers moved to a larger house at 56 Hatton Garden, and Robinson, their lodger for six months, went along. Robinson had been engaged, somewhat reluctantly, as a theatrical reporter for *The Times,* and Payne frequently accompanied him to performances, a practice which sharpened his appetite for the theatre. Other influences

were shaping the boy's literary taste: the Colliers were close
friends of Charles and Mary Lamb, and through Robinson
they met Wordsworth, Southey, and Flaxman. Coleridge, too,
was a frequent guest at Hatton Garden for supper and
conversation, and when he came, Payne was to recall many
years later, 'people were generally content that he should have
much of the talk to himself.'[13] For a youth in his 'teens, these
evenings had a powerful influence and Payne was an excellent
listener. The family's friendship with Coleridge was close.
When the critic planned a series of fifteen lectures on
Shakespeare in the fall of 1811, he sent a special invitation to
the Colliers urging them to attend. Payne went to all of them
and took verbatim shorthand notes – a circumstance which
was later to be of great importance when they were found to
be the only surviving record of what Coleridge said.[14]

Dyer had worked on *The Times* for four years when he
quarrelled with Walter and left the paper for the *Morning
Chronicle*. His departure was not unexpected, but Walter's
reactions were: he fired Robinson and gave Dyer's job to
Payne. As a result, Robinson, at thirty-four, began serious
preparation for the bar, and Payne, at twenty-one, became the
youngest full-time reporter (albeit, one with over five years'
experience) in the gallery. Within a year he was earning as
much as his father had, a success which was as exhilarating as
it was unsettling. 'I believe I have a large portion of Vanity',
he wrote in a diary about this time. 'And yet . . . praise when I
do not deserve it, and when I know that I do not, has been
always disgusting to me. Even in making this journal I shew it
for I have empty folly enough to imagine (for it is nothing but
mere fleeting imagination) that at some time or other, even
my history, and as connected with it this Diary, may be
interesting to others as well as to myself. . . . From what I have
already observed it may be gathered that I have to add to
Vanity and the love of praise a dubiously valuable quantity
which is Ambition.'[15]

He was soon to realize how pride – the inevitable concomitant of ambition – can lead one to self-destructive competition. Shortly after Payne joined *The Times*, Walter had hired
Thomas Barnes, and an amicable but intense rivalry for
Walter's attention developed between the two young men.

Barnes, only four years Payne's senior, was not his intellectual superior, perhaps not even his equal, but he had attended Pembroke College, Cambridge, and Payne was convinced that Walter preferred Barnes for this reason alone. A more secure and less proud man might have accepted Barnes's 'advantage', but Collier was pitifully dependent on the opinion of others, and a successful competitor was a cause for self-reproach. Certain that Walter was about to appoint Barnes editor of the paper, Collier squandered his own success and quit *The Times*. It was a reckless act which he almost immediately repented, for Walter appointed not Barnes but a man named Stoddard to the post and Payne was now unemployed. It would not be the last time that he allowed jealousy and pride to overwhelm good sense. Shortly after Payne quit *The Times*, he spoke at one of the debating clubs concerning 'the evils of ambition to Society'. The speech was, apparently, wretched. 'He attempted imagery', Robinson reported, 'but very unsuccessfully.'[16] No doubt his heart wasn't in it. For a time he assuaged his pride pretending to 'prepare' for the bar. He entered his name in the Middle Temple register, but that was about *all* he did; eighteen years would pass before he was called and he never practised.

After several months he found more practical employment: James Perry, the proprietor of the *Morning Chronicle*, a man of intelligence and taste who has been credited with 'inventing' modern parliamentary reporting,[17] hired Payne for his paper. The new job was better than the old in every way but one: Payne was again working with his father, and it was not a happy reunion. As he grew older, Dyer became increasingly unstable. He assumed that since Payne was under his roof, he was, thereby, under his control as well, and Payne, now twenty-three and able to assert a will of his own, disagreed. Living together became intolerable when they began to work together also, and after Robinson was admitted to the bar in May 1813 and left the Colliers to take chambers at the Inns of Court, there was no one to referee their quarrels. Dyer was humiliated that his modest reputation had been eclipsed by his son's and bitter that the writers who now visited his home came to see Payne rather than himself.[18] For two years their disagreement continued and got worse until at last Dyer

ordered Payne to move. In January 1815, Payne carted his belongings, which now included a large collection of books, to new lodgings at Smith Square, Westminster, close to Parliament, two miles from the *Chronicle* office and comfortably distant from Hatton Garden. For his mother's sake, he continued to take his meals with the family, but thereafter his relationship with his father was cool.

'Nothing could exceed my industry and application ... after I quitted my father's house', he declared many years later.[19] He would remember this period of his life as debonair and romantic, but at twenty-six Payne was no Lothario. His appetites were domestic, more readily satisfied in a family circle than in the taverns and brothels frequented by his brothers. He was glad to be freed from his father's domineering jealousy, but he missed the domestic comforts, and since he was a conventional man, he soon took conventional means to secure them. He was good-looking, his professional prospects were better than average, and by modest standards he was an 'eligible' young man who ought to have had some matrimonial choice among the ladies of his family's acquaintance. But apparently he was undemanding. His choice was his cousin, Mary Louisa Pycroft, the youngest of five daughters of Jane's sister and her husband William Pycroft of Putney, a singularly plain woman two years his senior, with no fortune, few social accomplishments and none of Payne's literary interests or taste. She lacked, in fact, all the intellectual and romantic qualifications which Payne might have sought, but she had important practical ones: she lived nearby and she was available. She could be wooed and won with little emotional strain and with only the physical exertion required to row, more or less regularly, up the Thames to Putney. None of his family saw much merit in the union and his friends criticized it. 'This is not a splendid marriage', Robinson declared. 'M:P: is not handsome, her fortune is but small.... John is doing a bold act in marrying with prospects of affluence so little chearing.'[20]

Custom demanded a year's engagement, and in the interim there were to be significant changes in Collier's life. About four months after he moved to Smith Square, Payne left the *Chronicle* for his old job at *The Times*. Barnes had pressed

Walter to rehire him at an increase in salary, and Payne, eager to be freed from working with Dyer, accepted at once. The rivalry between the two papers was at its peak, and Perry, incensed that Payne should have left him for his chief competitor, retaliated by firing Dyer. This ultimate demonstration of Payne's pre-eminence would almost certainly have created a permanent rupture between Payne and Dyer had not old John Collier unexpectedly died and left his two sons over £11,000 in various investments and another seven or eight hundred pounds in banknotes and gold. Dyer's share easily compensated for his loss of employment and – briefly – restored his bonhomie. He repaid his debt to Robinson, a gesture which renewed their former friendship, and five days after John Collier was buried in Bunhill Fields, the Colliers, Robinson and Mary Lamb attended the theatre to see, appropriately enough, *A New Way to Pay Old Debts* starring Edmund Kean.

The Collier inheritance had another less fortunate consequence: in the spring of 1816, Dyer used part of it to purchase the *Critical Review,* a defunct journal of no reputation. It was a foolish purchase: he might, that is, have failed under a title of his own invention as well as another's, but in the brief period of good feeling engendered by the bequest, Dyer's optimism flourished and he even prevailed on Payne to supply articles for the publication. From May 1816 until the demise of the journal a year later, Payne wrote sixteen essays which appeared under the heading 'Bibliotheca Antiqua'. These concerned tracts by such little known seventeenth-century authors as Greene, Churchyard, Heywood, Shirley, Stubs, and Nashe, and were the beginning of what was to be an almost uninterrupted half century of scholarship. They were a labour of love, and the chance to see them in print probably accounted for Payne's unexpected willingness to join Dyer's ill-conceived venture. When it was clear that the journal was headed for oblivion, Payne doubled the number of essays published in the final issues. He was proud of them; of all the many pieces he published in 1816 and 1817 he chose to sign and save only these.[21]

2

The wedding of Payne and Louisa occurred, as scheduled, at Putney Church on 20 August 1816. After a six-week trip to France, the couple took up residence at a small, neatly furnished house at 27 Vincent Square, and Collier's marriage quickly moved into an unremarkable pattern of domesticity which it would follow for forty years. Even Robinson, the unregenerate bachelor, declared that 'the situation of married man' suited Payne and made him 'enviable'. Payne's domestic life was tranquil, but his professional life continued to be unsatisfactory. In spite of his apparent success at *The Times*, he continued to seek more literary employment. He briefly replaced an old friend, Frederick Shoberl,[22] as editor of Rudolph Ackermann's *Repository*, a newly revived monthly art magazine notable for its lithographic reproductions. Shoberl had planned to leave London for good, but he changed his mind and reclaimed his job, and Payne lost his place. Walter, increasingly jealous of the time Payne spent on his extra-curricular activities, demanded that he make himself more accessible by living closer to *The Times'* office, suggesting, somewhat ominously, that however much Walter valued his talent, Payne should not think himself indispensable to *The Times*. When the *Critical Review* failed, therefore, Payne gave in to Walter's demand and took a house in Bouverie Street, off Fleet Street and around the corner from the newspaper.

Here Payne's first child, Mary Frances Collier, was born on 27 May 1817, almost nine months to the day after the wedding, and Mary Louisa, in failing health, was bedridden for several months thereafter. Her illness was of great concern to Payne and he had to contend with other family matters. He was intermittently forced to mediate between his sisters and their on-again off-again fiancés, and Dyer was newly obstreperous: with the collapse of the *Critical Review* in the summer of 1817, he had turned once again to farming. With his future son-in-law, Robert Proctor, Dyer leased a 300-acre farm, Smallfield, in Essex, and it was soon apparent that his second attempt at agriculture would go the way of the first. 'Twice the money and twice the stock of cattle, houses, etc. could not have made it profitable', Payne was later to declare.[23] Dyer

bullied Proctor and Jane was increasingly wretched. Eventually Proctor quit the farm, married Mary, and in a display of
daring which alarmed the family, set off with his new bride to
seek better fortune in Peru. Their departure made Smallfields
totally repugnant to Jane, and when Dyer adamantly refused
to give up the farm, she left him, asking Robinson to draw up
a legal separation. For several years, the family was sadly
divided. Payne's sympathies were, of course, with his mother,
and he was all too ready to leave any attempts at reconciliation to Robinson whose patience appears to have been
unlimited.

In Payne's defence, he was inordinately busy during the first
year of his marriage. In addition to his parliamentary and
court reports for *The Times,* he wrote many columns for other
papers and magazines, ephemera quickly composed, sold and
soon forgotten. One group of articles was an exception to this
pattern. In the Autumn of 1818, under the pseudonym
'Amicus Curiae', Payne sold the *Examiner* a series of thirty
vignettes of famous barristers whom he had observed in the
courts he had covered. Few periodicals paid so well as the
Examiner, and Payne received £100 for the initial publication
plus another £100 in the spring of 1819 when the series was
collected into a book, *Criticisms on the Bar.*[24] The essays revealed
a prejudice against lawyers strange in a man who aspired to be
one. ('There is no class of persons, from various causes, so
difficult of persuasion', he wrote in the Preface.) But the book
was not vicious so much as pretentious and condescending.
Payne had been a longtime observer of the men he criticized,
but he was not an ideal arbiter of judicial intelligence or of
oratorical skill, and when it became known that he was the
author he was damned for his effrontery. Crabb Robinson,
who had nominated Payne for entrance in the Middle
Temple, was appalled by the critiques of men who were his
personal friends. It was not, Robinson wrote, 'that they were
ill done, but that they ought not to have been done at all. It
seems an impertinent obtrusion of public censure without any
right to play the critic.'[25] Payne came to regret having written
the series and to view the book as 'altogether a very foolish
piece of business'.[26] But shorn of its venal comments, Collier's
criticism treated real grievances which a quarter of a century

later would be exposed and addressed by a parliamentary commission. Collier correctly described a system overburdened with 'forms, processes and pleadings' in which justice was delayed by an 'accumulation of business', a process in which admission to the bar was based on flattery and bribery, and a system which bred lawyers who, in Collier's words, would 'rather abandon a man to a dungeon, than abandon their own hopes of success in their profession.'[27] Had he avoided personalities, he might have made a more influential case; but then, of course, had it been less personal and outrageous, the series would never have been sold at all.

Two or three months after *Criticisms on the Bar* appeared, Collier was guilty of a lesser indiscretion which at first seemed far more serious. In *The Times* account of the House of Commons debate of Tuesday, 8 June 1819, Joseph Hume, a radical member of the opposition from Aberdeen, was quoted as saying that George Canning, then an M.P. for Liverpool and a cabinet minister, had 'been able to place himself... far above [the] unhappy conditions' of the poor 'by habitually turning' their 'sufferings' into 'ridicule'. Actually, although Hume was attacking Canning's view, he made no reference to Canning's career, and the report was therefore a misstatement, but a comparison of the report with Hansard[28] suggests that the newspaper version was compatible with the tone of the remark. As it happened, Canning and Walter were engaged in a long-standing personal feud, and the reporter caught between them was John Payne Collier, who, by ill chance, had reported the segment in question. The paper printed a retraction, but Canning seized the occasion to take vengeance upon Walter. He demanded that the 'persons responsible' be punished, and Collier was brought before the bar of the House on Tuesday 15 June 1819. By all accounts, Payne acquitted himself well of the charge of malice, but the government was determined to punish *The Times,* and Collier was remanded to the custody of the Sergeant at Arms. His incarceration caused great distress. Mary Louisa had not yet fully recovered from the birth of their second child, John Pycroft Collier, five weeks before, and he was separated from his family when it most needed him. Moreover, for the first few hours he had every reason to believe that he would be jailed for the rest of the parliamentary session which still had some weeks to run. As it turned out, his imprisonment was short and the affair was turned to his advantage: a day after he was taken into custody a private bill was passed unanimously which effected his release. Walter, recognizing that Payne had been the victim of his own disagreement with Canning, gave him £50 to 'cover costs', which came to less than a third that amount. 'This is very generous certainly', Robinson wrote in his diary. Collier's 'manly behaviour' before the House had raised him in Walter's opinion.[29] But the effect of the incident was nonetheless bitter: he had been reminded once again that his livelihood was dependent upon the whims of powerful men. He had been intimidated, unjustly accused, and humiliated to satisfy the ambitions of others – and not for the last time.

The incident increased Payne's 'pining to get clear of newspapers', and for a time he thought he had found a way to do so. Among the publishers to whom he sold free-lance articles was Archibald Constable. Payne had been contributing articles on parliamentary subjects to Constable's *Edinburgh Review*. The editor liked his work and promised to 'cheerfully receive' anything Payne cared to send – in particular, 'spirited articles on the Drama'.[30] Constable published books as well as periodicals, and Payne, with his *Critical Review* essays in mind, proposed a book on the subject of poetry and drama of the Elizabethan and Jacobean period. Constable was initially unenthusiastic. He doubted that such a work would be 'suited to a widely extended class of readers'.[31] But Collier, promising to treat his antiquarian subject in a 'popular way', persuaded Constable, and *The Poetical Decameron, or, Ten Conversations on English Poets and Poetry* was published in two volumes in 1820. The book was only a modest success. Collier's attempt to popularize his arcane subjects encouraged a style more dilettante than scholarly and more arch than informal. The form he chose, a 'conversation' among three good friends, was archaic in 1820: Bourne, the first speaker, who 'pursues the lives and productions' of Shakespeare's contemporaries, is Payne himself; Elliot, the second, an admirer of Byron and Southey who 'had been much abroad' in Germany, is the counterpart of Crabb Robinson; and Morton, the third, 'with

relations near Dorchester', has great similarity to Thomas
Amyot. Despite these trappings, the opinions they express are
invariably Collier's, and the subjects they discuss are his
special interests only.

Though these 'conversations' lacked informality, they
nevertheless demonstrated a remarkable knowledge of early
English literature, and they illuminated subjects which would
thereafter engage Collier. The history of the English stage,
Shakespeare's plays, anonymous satires and ballads, and rare
editions of Elizabethan and Jacobean tracts – these subjects
would constitute Collier's research and publication for the
next sixty years, and *The Poetical Decameron* revealed that at
thirty-one Collier had studied them as comprehensively as
anyone of his generation.

The book also illustrated the amalgam which would
characterize his critical style: a significant discovery (e.g., that
Barnabe Riche's 'Apolonius and Silla' was the principal
source for *Twelfth Night*[32]) is coupled with unsupported and
provocative conjecture (e.g., that *A Yorkshire Tragedy* was
'probably' written by Thomas Nashe), and effete antiquarianism (e.g., whether Thomas Lodge was or was not the 'second
English satirist'). More disturbing, the book reveals a fault
which would be all too common in his subsequent work: a
disputatious manner coupled with a penchant for belittling
the work of other scholars. In this, his first book of literary
comment, Collier announced a dictum which, unfortunately,
would guide him throughout his career: it was a principle
with him, he said, to 'avail' himself 'as little as possible of
other men's labours'.[33] His presumed self-sufficiency would
seriously limit the quality and the continuing value of his later
achievements and it would feed the intense animosity of many
of his contemporaries. This misguided view of his vocation
was the result of circumstance. He worked alone, against great
odds and with small hope of financial reward, and he did so
without a university degree to validate his talent and without
personal wealth or political sinecure to support his study. As a
result he had an emotional stake in the historical facts he
discovered and in the critical conclusions they supported.
There is in the *Poetical Decameron* and in most of the books
which followed it the implication that Collier's information

was his personal possession, that it belonged to him by right of discovery and that other scholars could use his information only with his permission.

Of course, Collier was not unique in this regard. His was a time of scholarly pretension and professional distrust; intellectual paranoia was common among his contemporaries; disagreement was often taken as personal affront, and contradiction as a cause for recrimination. Few of his colleagues revealed these failings so often as John Payne Collier. His successes – which were real – were almost always presented in the context of another's failures. He had, he declared in the *Poetical Decameron*, 'gained a knowledge of not a few facts of importance and books of value, that had escaped the researches of some of the most indefatigable antiquaries' (p. xii), and he is harsh in condemning his predecessors whom, he declared, were 'puerile and incompetent'. 'I could find [it] in my heart to hack and hew every one of them', he wrote. He was contemptuous of Malone (a 'punctilious puny'), of Theobald ('a dull dust-raking drudge'), and of George Steevens ('an uninformed mass . . . a chaos of confused quotations and pedantic allusion'). 'If they are dead', he declared, 'that is all the good that can be said of them' (xxiv–xxvii). This pugnaciousness almost swamped the valuable information the book contained. In fact, the only praise Collier could muster was for a bookseller, Thomas Rodd, who at twenty-five had only recently taken over his father's shop. Collier was a regular customer of both father and son and the puff was therefore self-serving. (For the next thirty years Rodd would be one of the best known booksellers in London, and Collier, as we shall see hereafter, would be closely associated with him.)

The success of the *Poetical Decameron* was small. It recouped its costs and Collier was paid £200, but it was not widely noticed – it was ignored by the *Edinburgh Review* itself! When Payne sent a copy to Charles Lamb, the letter of thanks suggested only guarded praise: 'I have not such a gentleman's-book in my collection', Lamb wrote. '. . . I take less pleasure in books than heretofore, but I like books about books.'[34] The comment describes a fault. It was a 'gentleman's book', not a scholar's, a 'book about books' for a dilettante audience. Moreover, its presentation, including the gratuitous reference to the Middle Temple after Collier's name on the title page, was pretentious. That Collier missed his mark is apparent in Robinson's diary: after taking nearly three years to fulfil his 'duty to look over' the book, he declared that it was 'thoroughly uninteresting and unreadable – talk about old books valuable only for their antiquity and scarcity, soon fatigues'.[35] Since Robinson represented the audience Payne had been trying to interest, this was a significant condemnation.

Despite its minimal reception, Collier was exhilarated by the publication of the *Poetical Decameron*. Increasingly, the time he spent in the gallery seemed time stolen from scholarly research. His disaffection did not go unnoticed by Walter who told Robinson he thought Payne was 'shirking', but Collier ignored Walter's displeasure and in the fall of 1821 moved out of Bouverie Street, away from the stench of the city and Walter's surveillance, into a pleasant cottage on the river at Hammersmith. There, surrounded by his books and his family (his third child, William, had been born the previous May, about the time the book appeared) he spent what he would remember as the happiest time of his life. Robinson, on a visit of reprimand, found Hammersmith delightful, but he feared that Collier was treating Walter too casually.

In fact, Collier *was* shirking his duties at the paper. His disaffection with the grimy office of *The Times* was increased by his attraction to the elegant, high ceilinged rooms of the British Museum library. Whenever possible he would mumble a plausible excuse, secure his desk, grab his coat and slip down the stairs and across the city to Bloomsbury. The *Decameron* had been composed in the Museum reading room at Montague House, and much of the information it contained had been gleaned from its vast and disorganized conglomeration of manuscripts and printed books. Charles Lamb's *Specimens of English Dramatic Poetry* had initiated Payne's interest in the drama, and now it was Lamb who introduced him to the riches of the David Garrick collection of printed plays which had lain in the Museum virtually untouched for fifty years. Lamb was systematically reading through this trove ('rich and exhaustless beyond what I then imagined', he was to say of it) and Collier followed his lead, collecting information and examples he would use for the rest of his life.

The £200 Collier received for the *Decameron* allowed him to indulge himself even further. In 1810, about the time he began his aborted diary with the admission of 'a large portion of vanity', he had composed an epic inspired by Spenser and infused with Wordsworthian romanticism. It was a bad poem, but Collier was proud of it, and now he had the money to have it printed. Its original plan was grandiose: three books, 'The Poet's Pilgrimage', 'The Poet's Purgatory', and 'The Poet's Paradise', to be divided into twelve cantos. Collier finished only the pilgrimage; purgatory and paradise were not apparently within the grasp of his imagination in 1810, and after toying with the poem for a year or two, he became vexed with it and destroyed all but the first four cantos. Now, twelve years later, mesmerized by the fustian of his youth, he prepared them for the press.

He prepared them again and again. In later years he declared he printed the poem only to give work to a poor typesetter, but if that is true, Collier was generous beyond his means. Much of the poem was printed not once but twice: he tinkered endlessly with the text while it went through the press. He put his name on the title page and then, in a wave of uncertainty, he took it off; he rewrote his introductory poem several times and dedicated the work to various people at various times (he settled at last on Wordsworth). Nevertheless, Payne was proud of the result. 'Unless I am silly with vanity or mad with self-conceit', he wrote in very old age, 'I assert that it is good, both in design and execution.'[36]

He was not mad, but he was mistaken. The poem is a dodo epic; constantly stretching its wings for flight, it remains grotesquely pedestrian, a paean to imagination rather than its embodiment: a poet wanting 'a deathless name' meets a Pilgrim who tries to dissuade him from seeking mere fame by invoking the memory of Dante, Tasso, Aeschylus, and Ovid, all of whom he claims were scorned by their contemporaries. The search for fame alone, he declares, will come to a bad end. The point is made painfully particular by a visit to the Court of Queen Fortune where the Poet finally meets Fame, who blows his horn 'to the thickening mass/Of awe-struck slaves below – the baseborn crowd – /Not up to highest heaven' and discovers that this is 'Broad Rumour', not true Fame. Subsequently separated from the Pilgrim in the vale of Disappointment and Despair, the poet meets another youth, Ignoto, who is the Poet's companion to the Cave of Neglect:

> Here rare inventions of mechanic skill
>   Were register'd as uselessly invented,
> To perfect which, enduring every ill,
>   The ruin'd author died, yet ne'er repented.
> And here were high achievements deep indented,
> Which mighty nations happy made and free
>   But th' achiever, with the deed contented
> Died unrewarded: here again I see
> The vanity of wit and wisdom's misery!
>
> Canto III, xlviii

It is, apparently, a salutary experience, and the Poet learns that 'well could his lofty soul the world's contempt despise!' and that, finally, 'to be a poet is enough reward!'

At length the Poet leaves the Cave of Neglect, finds his Muse who will dwell with him in Poverty, i.e., in The Poet's Purgatory which was to come. However, the arrival of his Muse notwithstanding, Collier's inspiration ended at this point and, in a glut of scholarly notes invoking Dante, Wordsworth, Chaucer, Spenser, and others, so did his poem.

Collier had a hundred copies printed and put them up for sale. 'It was once advertised to be published', he wrote on the flyleaf of what is, apparently, the only surviving copy of the 1822 edition, 'and 3 copies were sold before I recalled it. In this way it got to Oxford, Cambridge, and the Brit.Mus.'[37] There is no evidence that copies were ever in those libraries, but assuming they once were, their acquisition was probably not by purchase but by author's gift. Collier presented copies of the poem to several of his friends (the printing was conveniently completed just before Christmas, 1822) and, the market for anonymous allegories being what it was, the remaining copies were ultimately used to light fires.

The reaction of his friends was what one might have expected. Charles Lamb got his copy of the poem from Payne about the same time he got the present of a pig from Dyer. He preferred the pig, but praised the poem: 'John Collier Jun? has sent me a Poem', he wrote Dyer, 'which (without the smallest bias from the aforesaid present, believe me) I pronounce *sterling*.'[38] Robinson was more circumspect: 'I envy J.C.'s power in doing this', he declared, 'but with so much power, would rather have translated a masterpiece.'[39] Robinson may have passed along this advice, for Payne's next book was a translation of Schiller.

3

The failure of *The Poet's Pilgrimage* cooled Collier's poetic ambition. Like many another failed artist, he blamed his lack of success on an obtuse public and on an 'age' unpropitious to the man of literary genius. 'The only authors who, as a class, are not starving, are periodical essayists', he wrote, 'as almost the only writers who can keep their reputation above water are anonymous critics.' The author, he declared, must look to the public for support. 'We must please to live, and therefore should live to please.' Moreover, he knew that, notwithstanding his intelligence and imagination, he would always be handicapped in a society which equated literary success with social class. 'A professional man, who should come into the world, relying on his genius or learning for his success, without other advantages, would be looked upon as a pedant, a barbarian, or a poor creature', he declared.[40] He knew his position in Queen Fortune's Court, and he scorned his newspaper occupation.

He revealed his antipathy in an anonymous article 'The Periodical Press', which appeared in the *Edinburgh Review* in May 1823. At Constable's request, he wrote what was supposed to be a critique of London's journals, but it became an exposé of *The Times* which, Collier thought, demanded too much and paid him too little.[41] Collier disliked Alsager, Walter's new editor, whereas Black, who had become editor of the *Chronicle* at Perry's death in 1821, was his good friend, and a return to that paper looked increasingly attractive. Collier's essay was thus a panegyric for the *Morning Chronicle* and a sharp attack on the pretensions of *The Times*, which, he declared, was crude and 'not to our taste – either in matter or manner', a pompous journal which 'might be imagined to be composed as well as printed with a steam-engine'. The *Chronicle,* on the other hand, was a model paper, 'the best, both for amusement and instruction, that issued from the daily press'.[42] The long-standing competition between the two papers made the contrast particularly invidious, the more so since Collier went out of his way to contrast the professionalism of the recently deceased Perry with that of Walter, whom he described as sacrificing the principles of good reporting to make money.

The article was a severe critique, but not a bitter one. Its chief fault was its source: professional propriety ought to have kept Collier from making a sharp anonymous criticism while in the pay of *The Times.* As he must have expected, Walter quickly discovered the identity of the author and fired him on the spot. There was, however, no public scandal. Even such a gossip as Robinson got no whiff of the true controversy. Although he noted in his diary that Payne was dismissed and, he suspected, 'not without reason', he didn't know why. Since Collier was immediately hired by the *Chronicle* at a salary of £270 per annum, his motives in writing the article were suspect, but his judgement was honest. *The Times* had actively discouraged his literary ambitions; the *Chronicle,* he hoped, would support them. At thirty-four, Collier was well embarked on a career of literary scholarship; in the next twenty years he would establish his reputation, and throughout that period his chief source of income was to be the *Morning Chronicle.*

The Collier family circumstances were improved about this time by two events. First, Robert and Mary Proctor, having found Peru inhospitable, returned to England and with the inheritance from the elder Proctor's estate, purchased what remained of the Smallfield lease from Dyer and energetically set about recouping the losses of that calamitous venture. (They were only partially successful and a year later gave up the farm and invested their capital in the Aldermanbury Dairy in London which, at least initially, prospered.) Dyer, freed at last from the agricultural débâcle he had brought upon himself, returned to London and with the help of Robinson was reconciled to Jane. The reunion was a convenience rather than a return to former affection; living together was cheaper than living apart, and Dyer was ill. This reunion coincided with a second event, the death of Dyer's ninety-year-old mother, whose £300 annuity now came to him. As a result, Dyer was able once again to pay his debt to Robinson, restoring what Robinson called 'the comfort and enjoyment' of their friendship.

Dyer's health worsened. Jane and Robinson took him to Switzerland in hope of a cure, but when they returned in early November, 1825, Dyer was dying. Richard begged to be reconciled with his father, but Dyer refused and within a few days he was dead. When Dyer was buried near his father at Bunhill Fields, there were only eight mourners, among them his three sons and Robinson. Only Richard showed grief, sobbing throughout the service.

In spite of his dying wish, Dyer's will provided equally for his five children – Robinson had seen to that. He had also made sure that Jane would be, as he reported to Dorothy Wordsworth, 'not rich but in comfortable circumstances'. By agreement she was to divide her residence between her daughters, with Jane at Lewes where George Proctor had become headmaster of a school, and with Mary at the Aldermanbury Dairy. The children's inheritance was small, only £100 a year a piece – not nearly enough to satisfy Richard's debts, but enough to give William for the first time an income of his own. He began diligently to read law, and soon fell in love with (or, as Jane would have it, was 'entangled by') a girl named Emily Phillips, and despite his mother's disapproval they were married.[43]

Payne received an extra 100 guineas as his father's executor, and he celebrated his new resources in characteristic fashion by moving from his modest Hammersmith cottage to 23 Hunter Street, a much larger and more impressive house in a new development. They had needed more room: the Colliers now had five children; William had been born at Hammersmith in May, 1821, Jane Emma in February, 1824, and Emma Letitia, in May, 1826, shortly after the family moved to Hunter Street. The new house was very close to the British Museum where Collier continued to spend most afternoons, but the establishment was more fashionable than he could

afford, and to supplement his income he tried his hand at
translation. He sold two, Schiller's ballads *Fridolin*[44] and *The
Fight with the Dragon*,[45] to Edward and Septimus Prowett,
Strand booksellers, who issued them in handsome folio
editions with Schiller's text on one page facing Collier's rather
prosy English verse on the other. Each was illustrated with
steel engravings by Henry Moses, and Collier was identified
on the title pages as the author of *The Poetical Decamerone* (sic),
a bow to his literary pretensions. The Prowetts were shrewd
dealers and the editions probably made money, but they did
not help Collier's reputation as a poet. Apparently, as part of
the agreement, the Prowetts issued a new edition of *The Poet's
Pilgrimage*. That youthful effusion had gained nothing by
being put aside for three years. The poem Prowett published
was virtually identical to the earlier one except for a new
dedication to Charles Lamb, who had rashly told Collier he
liked it. Collier hoped for fame and profit; he got neither, and
he blamed his publisher. He was to write many years later
that Prowett – surely one of the shrewdest bookdealers of his
generation – 'didn't understand business', whereas the truth
was that Collier was a bad poet whom even Prowett couldn't
sell.

Nevertheless, Payne became an associate of the Prowetts
who were prolific publishers. Among the books passing
through their presses in early 1824 was a new edition of
Dodsley's Old Plays, a collection of Elizabethan and Jacobean
drama first published in 1744, subsequently taken through a
second edition by Isaac Reed in 1780 and partly reprinted in
an aborted third edition by Octavius Gilchrist in 1814.
Having acquired Reed's notes and Gilchrist's addenda,
Septimus Prowett had printed about half the collection when
he hired Collier to prepare the remainder of the plays for
publication. The edition was to be in twelve volumes,[46] and on
taking over the job in late 1825 Collier's work, anonymous and
minimal, was limited to the last six. Had Collier been given
editorial control from the beginning of the project, he would
certainly have chosen to re-edit the whole of the anthology,
but Prowett intended only to reprint the old text, and before
Collier was taken on the only alteration of the earlier text was
to omit the plays of Ford and Shirley which were then being

newly edited by William Gifford.[47] This meant that Ford's *'Tis Pity She's a Whore* and Shirley's *The Bird in a Cage* and *The Gamester* had been taken out along with *Andromana* (which the earlier editors had erroneously ascribed to Shirley). When Collier began his job he saw that these omissions created a gap and an opportunity, and he urged Prowett to add four plays, one each by Thomas Lodge, Robert Greene, Thomas Nashe, and George Peele, and two interludes[48] which he proposed to edit from unique copies of the first editions never before reprinted. It was a good plan, but it failed. The set was expensive (over £5) and in the financial panic of 1826–27 few were sold. 'I was to have had £20 per volume', Collier recalled later, 'but the failure of Prowett caused me to be rewarded with a mere trifle, and I could not work for nothing; so the book was mangled.'[49] The plays were published without Collier having a chance to read the proofs and as a result the edition was replete with errors which were to embarrass him for the rest of his life.

Despite Collier's dissatisfaction, the new plays demonstrated a clear advance over the prevailing practices of the time. His introductions were concise and informative, a sharp contrast to the displays of arcane knowledge with which editors commonly barred a reader's entry to a text. His notes were precise, shorn of gratuitous analogues, and his texts were faithful to the originals. (Some of them, in fact, would not be superseded for a century.) Collier's work was marred by editorial practices which modern scholars condemn – he 'regularized' punctuation and altered spelling inconsistently, and largely because of these faults, his late nineteenth-century successors would be quick to damn his 'carelessness'. But he was, in fact, more consistent and exact than his age demanded. His editorial intentions floundered on the choice between an exact reproduction of the original printing on the one hand and a lucid intelligible text for unsophisticated readers on the other, and if his choices between these alternatives were often inconsistent, he was less arbitrary than almost all editors before him and many since.

The historical significance of the Dodsley edition of 1825 therefore does not rest on the quality of its text but rather on Collier's rediscovery of Lodge, Greene, Nashe and Peele. In

1825, these dramatists had been forgotten and their plays virtually unread for two hundred years. Collier's selection marked their revival and initiated a new interest in the minor Elizabethan drama: within a decade there were new collected editions of the works of both Peele (1828) and Greene (1831). Had the Dodsley edition been successful, the scope of this revival might have been even broader, for Collier had initially proposed including six more plays by Anthony Munday, Henry Chettle, Thomas Hughes, and Nathaniel Field, all unknown at the time, in a supplementary volume. When that plan was aborted, Collier edited these plays[50] individually and in 1828 he cajoled Prowett into publishing them in individual cheap editions. Unfortunately, this was as ill-starred as the edition which preceded it.

The failure of the Dodsley edition was made more bitter by the success of Collier's next book for Prowett. *Punch and Judy,* a history of the puppet play in England illustrated by George Cruikshank, was to have the greatest continuing sale of any Collier work. It appeared in dozens of editions during the next hundred years and earned thousands of pounds profit – none of it Collier's. Fearing a reprise of the Dodsley débâcle, he had sold his manuscript outright to Prowett for a mere £50.[51]

In 1827, Collier was again in need of money. He was intermittently ill, and since the *Chronicle* paid him only when he worked, his salary declined. Even worse, illness deprived him of the energy he needed to turn out the hack articles that now provided the larger part of his income. His mother accused him of being 'impractical', and in want of 'worldly Wisdom', a comment which showed little understanding of his difficulties; Collier knew the world too well. Robinson was more sympathetic and wrote to his friend John Murray, the publisher, to urge that Payne be hired to complete the edition of Shirley's plays which Gifford's death had left unfinished. That project, however, was turned over to Alexander Dyce, a young Scots divine nine years Collier's junior whose editorial reputation was even less distinguished than Collier's, but whose advantages Collier could not match: he had an independent income and a degree from Exeter College, Oxford. Collier and Dyce would vie with one another for the next forty years, first as friendly adversaries and, in the end, as bitter enemies, and throughout their competition the Scot's advantages were to be crucial.

By midsummer 1827, Collier had borrowed from his aunt, Emma Pycroft, and when that was insufficient he appealed to Robinson to arrange a £100 advance from the funds in Dyer's estate. His anger at having to beg such help was matched only by his shame in having to accept it when it came. 'Since I have been substantially useful to him', Robinson ruefully remarked, 'he does not seem to have pleasure in my company.'[52] Even in the face of obvious disqualification, Payne wished to appear the leisured man of letters. His pride was overweening and his self-knowledge painfully real. He knew the chasm between his pretension and his prospects, and he could not live with the dissatisfactions of failure. The will to win extended to petty activities. When Mary Louisa's genial cousin John Pycroft defeated him in a game of chess, Payne was in anguish, and after a sleepless night swore he would never again play the game – and he didn't. Defeat was too bitter. 'No game was worth it', he declared. His wife desperately wished him to devote himself to preparing for the bar, which consistently pursued might have brought him a modest but regular income. 'It is a pity', Robinson wrote in January 1828, 'that he has just so much little talent as he has – with more he might obtain fame and that with skill may draw after it profit and comfort – With less he might be content to be a lawyer or a man of business – As it is – !'[53]

In the spring of 1828 Payne began to 'report' the theatre for the *Chronicle*. The work came easily to him. He had attended the theatre since childhood, and whereas most theatrical reporters were handicapped by the deadlines imposed on reviewers, Collier, conditioned by his early training with Dyer, wrote best under pressure. 'A first impression, what is struck off at a blow', he declared, 'is in many respects better than what is produced on reflection, and at several heats.'[54] The increased income was useful, but it did not promise a long-term solution to Collier's indigence. The fact was, at thirty-eight, he had no assured livelihood. Mary Louisa continued to demand that he prepare for the bar, and in November, 1828,

he finally agreed to be called. 'I am very sure he will never
have the perseverance necessary to success', Robinson wrote in
his diary, 'and he has no connections to give him business of
favour.'[55] Robinson's pessimism was matched by Collier's
ambivalence. He would be called, he wrote his mother, but
'whether I shall do any good is another question.'[56] Despite ill
health and disaffection, Payne spent the next ten weeks taking
his meals 'in term' at the Middle Temple, and on 6 February
1828, he was called to the bar.

That, however, was more or less *that*. Although he often
declared a great desire to 'put on his wig', to give up
newspapers and follow the profession, Collier never practised
law, and his failure to do so infuriated his wife and mother.
Mary Louisa's anxiety was increased by the arrival of their
sixth (and last) child, Henrietta Anna Robinson Collier. The
boys were shipped off to the tutelage of their uncle, now *Dr.*
George Proctor, newly installed as the President of Guernsey
College (at £700 a year! Jane gleefully reported to Robinson),
and this reduced the family's expenses somewhat, but not
Jane's concern.

Collier's reputation as a reporter and theatre reviewer
thrived. The *Chronicle* carried more theatrical news than any
other daily, and since the London theatre audience contained
many visitors to the city who relied on newspaper reports to
guide them, Collier was sought out by theatre managers and
aspiring playwrights who subtly or blatantly requested him to
puff a play. There is no evidence he was suborned, but he was
certainly flattered. His circle of acquaintances grew. Through
Robinson he met Thomas Campbell, editor of the *New
Monthly Magazine*, to whom he subsequently sold several
miscellaneous articles, and in the spring of 1828 Amyot
introduced him to Robert Peel, then Home Secretary, who
gave him access to the State Paper Office. In 1828, Amyot
sponsored his membership in the Society of Antiquaries, a
venerable almost moribund organization. Robinson, another
fellow of the Society, complained that it did 'nothing at all'
and was mired in 'precious foolery',[57] but Robinson had little
sympathy for the arcane subjects which filled the Society's
meetings and its publication *Archaeologica*. The 'merely' old
was inevitably inane to one who, like him, wanted demon-

strable value for his money. To the true antiquarian – and Collier was surely one of these – the past and the possibility of its recreation were inherently fascinating, and the Society of Antiquaries was to be a great stimulus to his career. From the beginning of his membership he was one of the organization's most active fellows, and he would be one of its most influential directors as well.

As this might suggest, Collier's scholarly ambition was keen during the late 1820s. He had large projects in mind that would need these and still other resources. In particular, he had long planned a history of English drama, a subject never fully assayed by earlier scholars who had seen the genre as an adjunct to poetry and who had considered the theatre itself beneath notice. Collier's research among the Garrick plays in the British Museum had revealed how much was still to be discovered about early English drama and how much, despite its treasures, was missing from the Museum's collection. To complete his research he needed other resources.

Chief among these was the cache of printed plays assembled by John Philip Kemble, the actor. This collection had never been catalogued and had rarely been seen, and its riches were, therefore, truly fabulous. In 1828 the Kemble plays were part of the great Chatsworth Library of William Cavendish, the sixth Duke of Devonshire, who had purchased the collection, in 1821, for what had been a near record price of £2,000. The purchase was characteristic of Devonshire who was then intent on creating the finest private library in England. He had succeeded to the dukedom in 1811, a particularly propitious time for a man with that ambition, for during the next two decades there were at least a dozen great private libraries put up for auction, and Devonshire bought much of the best of all of them. In 1812, for example, he purchased most of the late Duke of Roxburghe's unrivalled collection of Caxtons. In the same year he acquired Thomas Dampier's unique collection of incunabula at the sale of the Bishop of Ely, and in 1825 he bought the recently discovered and (then) unique First Quarto of *Hamlet* (1603). He continued to add to his holdings, buying whole libraries and carting them off to Chatsworth where he converted a former painting gallery into a huge two-level library and filled it. As this suggests, the

Kemble plays were only a small part of a collection almost unparalleled in England. Collier was determined to use this treasure, and early in 1830 Amyot arranged an introduction to the Duke.

The result of this meeting was access to the collection and financial support for Collier's work for the next fifty years. By all accounts, Devonshire was an intelligent, sympathetic patron, but he was also changeable. He seldom held any interest for long.[58] (For example, having amassed one of the greatest coin and medal collections in Europe, he lost interest and sold it for a small fraction of its cost.) As it happened, Collier's introduction to the Chatsworth library came at a time when Devonshire himself was becoming jaded with it, and Payne's enthusiasm had the effect of rekindling the Duke's own. At Collier's request, Devonshire had the whole of the drama collection (much larger than the Garrick collection, Collier discovered) brought from Chatsworth, where it was inaccessible, to Devonshire House in London. There, each morning, Collier would pore over the quartos, occasionally with the Duke at his shoulder taking a vicarious pleasure in Collier's activity.

Their relationship was mutually rewarding. Collier had carte blanche to a superb collection of books and manuscripts and the pleasure of being associated with one of the great families of England. How gratifying this must have been to one forced to spend his afternoons in the *Chronicle* office or in a cramped parliamentary reporter's pew! Devonshire for his part had the benefit of Collier's expert assistance in adding to his collection. Collier assumed this rôle with gusto, taking a special pride in the discovery and purchase of items which Devonshire unassisted would have missed. But the relationship had its well defined limits. William Cavendish, one year younger than Collier, was in all other respects his 'superior' and it was never suggested that the tall, slightly stooped savant who limped back and forth among the elegant cases at Devonshire House was the equal of his patron. Only once did Collier forget his place. When Devonshire invited him to Chatsworth for a month to catalogue a part of his collection, Payne was overwhelmed by the luxury and appalled by the state of the library and his manner became officious.

Devonshire was irritated. Having Collier around, the Duke wrote in his diary, 'is very well in London, but here it's impossible. He is so simple and vulgar.' Collier's initial excitement abated and as the days passed he became 'a shade better', but Devonshire was convinced that he 'could never submit to his society, poor man'.[59] Collier, properly chastened, was careful thereafter to make certain the Duke would never need to worry on that account. The Duke was 'always cheerful, friendly, and encouraging, never touchy with me', Collier candidly declared many years later, 'for, as he kindly said, I knew how far I ought to go, and he never feared, let him introduce me to whom he would . . . that I should over step the line.'[60]

II

THE HISTORY OF
ENGLISH DRAMATIC POETRY

*'I have sometimes picked up curiosities in the
most beaten paths.'*

4

The History of English Dramatic Poetry[1] was a milestone in
literary historiography. It is not too much to say that the
systematic study of English drama as a genre began with its
publication: before Collier, drama was thought to be 'serious'
literature only when it was written in verse and it was usually
considered as poetry, not as drama. English drama, it was
assumed, began with Shakespeare and apparently ended with
him too. Collier's book changed that. It declared that drama
was a distinct literary genre with a history of its own. 'The
dramatic poetry of this country form[s] of itself a department
so important and interesting as to demand to be separated
and systematically examined', he wrote in his Preface to the
book. 'For England to possess the greatest dramatic poets of
the world, and to be without a history of her dramatic poetry,
seem[s] an extraordinary solecism in letters' (I,vi). Collier's
knowledge of pre-Shakespearian drama was unparalleled, for
he had read virtually all the extant English plays – in print
and in manuscript – in the British Museum, and with this
knowledge he could see what others had missed. He traced the
earliest English drama to its French sources, articulated the
differences between the miracle play and the morality play,
and, by close textual comparison and historical association,
clearly described the evolution of religious drama into
conventional English 'comedy' and 'tragedy'. Shakespeare's
plays, Collier declared, were a part – a pre-eminent part to be
sure, but only one part – of a continuum of theatrical
convention which began long before Shakespeare arrived in

London. In effect, he established the modern view that Shakespeare must be read in the context of his predecessors and contemporaries. Among these were at least a dozen dramatists – Marlowe, Greene, Lyly, Peele, Nashe, Lodge, to name only the most notable – who had been virtually forgotten until Collier revived them.

Collier's historical account contained two valuable addenda: the 'Annals of the Stage', which reconstructed a chronology of English stage performances to the Restoration; and 'An Account of Theatres and their Appurtenances', which described the evolution of the physical theatre building and the devices of theatrical production. These subjects had been surveyed by other commentators, notably the great eighteenth-century scholars Edmond Malone, George Steevens, Isaac Reed, and George Chalmers, but these accounts were long out-of-date. Chalmers, the most recent, had published his work nearly thirty years before, and since then several great collections had become available to scholars, most notably the Landsdowne manuscripts acquired by the British Museum in 1807 containing among other riches the papers of William Cecil, Lord Burghley, chief minister to Queen Elizabeth. Collier was the first to use these papers systematically, and they were his greatest resource in compiling the 'Annals'. He found new treasure in well-known collections, too. For example, for nearly half a century the Harleian manuscripts had been read by scholars and it was assumed that nothing new remained to be unearthed in that collection. But it was there that Collier made one of his most notable discoveries: the diary of a seventeenth-century barrister named Manningham,[2] a 'table book' of cases at law described at stultifying length in an almost indecipherable hand, which contained, buried among notes of arcane legal description, a brief eye witness account of the first performance of *Twelfth Night* at the Middle Temple in 1602. Prior to this discovery, it had been believed that Shakespeare wrote the play at the end of his career whereas Manningham's account proved it to have been composed much earlier, a fact of great importance in establishing the order of Shakespeare's plays and hence in understanding the development of his talent. Among the Royal Manuscripts in the Museum Collier discovered two previously unknown masques by Ben Jonson,[3] and the State Paper Office, long used by scholars, was a mine of details for Collier. The collection at the Chapter House, Westminster, was even more useful; among the thousands of seals, warrants, and other documents, Collier found unique information concerning sixteenth-century theatre history in the household expense books and correspondence of Lord Thomas Cromwell.

When he began his *History,* Collier had been using these well-known repositories for several years, but there was one out-of-the way collection he had never seen, and before his book went to press he arranged to have a look at the Alleyn Papers at Dulwich College. In the light of Collier's subsequent career, this was a significant, not to say fateful, event. The Dulwich manuscripts had been known to Edmond Malone who, shortly before the final volume of his *Shakespeare* appeared in 1790, had been given more or less permanent possession of many of them. Malone's 'discovery' (actually, the papers had been consulted by scholars for at least fifty years before he got them) was untimely, and he was able to publish only a few details from the Alleyn papers in a hastily composed addendum to his work, but his information was remarkable.[4] Malone quoted at length and, it was assumed, exhaustively, from the 'Diary' of Philip Henslowe, a manuscript account book of theatrical transactions at the Fortune Theatre from 1592 to 1609. Collier had used Malone's quotations from the diary in his notes to *Dodsley's Old Plays* in 1825, and now as he was finishing his *History* he wanted to examine the original. Although it seemed highly unlikely that Dulwich contained much that Malone and his successor, James Boswell the Younger, had not found and published, Collier was curious. 'I have sometimes picked up curiosities in the most beaten paths', he declared,[5] and through Amyot he obtained an introduction to John Allen, Master of Dulwich. In the Spring of 1830 he visited the College for the first time.

There, in a small, very cold and virtually unused library, Collier found a welter of uncatalogued sixteenth- and seventeenth-century manuscripts whose value no one – not Malone nor Boswell nor the Dulwich authorities themselves – had fully realized. The collection had been poorly maintained, and over the years much of it had been given away or traded for less valuable books. What remained at Dulwich had been mixed with other manuscripts, dispersed and incompletely reassembled. Collier discovered that several of the Dulwich papers Malone had printed were no longer there, but since Malone had never made even a rudimentary catalogue of the papers he took from Dulwich, there was no way to determine what had been lost. (Malone had treated the manuscripts as his own while they were in his possession, on occasion cutting autographs from their pages to embellish his books.) Nevertheless, though much was missing, much more remained. In his haste to print some of the Alleyn manuscripts in his edition of 1790, Malone had had to pass over many of equal importance. Collier was similarly pressed. When he journeyed to Dulwich his *History* was virtually complete, and since it would take months to examine all of the Alleyn papers he was forced to limit his scrutiny, in the first instance, to Henslowe's diary which, he declared, was 'by far the most curious existing record connected with our old stage and its performance'.[6]

Most of the information in Henslowe's accounts had not been suggested, let alone accurately recorded, by Malone. He had used the book primarily to discover titles of lost plays, and his references to Henslowe's accounts were therefore sketchy. Collier's examination of the manuscript was comprehensive, and it was therefore left for him to discover new and valuable information concerning building contracts, accounts of day-to-day expenses, the court and country performances of the company, references to extra-theatrical events which affected the theatre's operation, and so on, all of it information Malone had passed over. These details provided Collier with significant last minute additions to his account of theatres, including a new section on the payment of actors and authors, previously a matter for conjecture only, and a new chapter concerning the 'Intermediate Precursors of Shakespeare' based on Henslowe's accounts of transactions with various playwrights. Among these Collier discovered an entry recording a payment of five shillings to 'Thomas Dikkers' for 'a prolog to Marloes Tamberlen'. The authorship of *Tamburlaine* had been disputed (Malone, for example, thought it by Nashe), and this was the first contemporary evidence to support the assumption that it was by Marlowe.[7] Collier's *History* was the culmination of many years' research to which the Dulwich manuscripts supplied only supplemental last minute addenda, but their importance was to outweigh much of the rest of the book. Many years later some of them would become, as we shall see, notorious.

In June 1830, Collier made an agreement with Murray, the publisher: upon delivery of the manuscript he would receive £300, an agreement Robinson (who would have known) declared a 'good bargain'. Almost immediately the book was advertised as 'forthcoming', and Collier worked feverishly to meet Murray's early September deadline. His work was constantly interrupted. His health was poor and the daily demands of the *Chronicle* did not abate much that summer. Moreover, as he was finishing his work, his younger brother William developed a brain tumour, and Collier moved to Putney to care for him during the last weeks of his life. Somehow, despite these difficulties, Collier kept his part of the contract. Murray, unfortunately, did not keep his. Collier was to have been paid on delivery, but Murray took the manuscript, put it in production and went on vacation. It was months before Collier received anything from him.

In June 1831, the *History of English Dramatic Poetry* was published in three volumes. 'Every man interested in literature *ought* to own the book', Collier declared half-facetiously to Robinson. 'If it be not very lively, as antiquarian subjects treated antiquarily only can seldom be', he declared, 'it will contain a good deal of information and matter...'[8] He knew it had a rather specialized appeal ('too much for antiquarians to be fit for the general taste', was the way Jane put it to Robinson[9]) but the book had an excellent press. The *Quarterly Review*, for example, carried a forty-page résumé and review of almost unqualified commendation,[10] and the *New Monthly Magazine* declared it an important departure in literary history.[11] But the times were not propitious for literary history; politics had driven almost all other subjects from the public mind. As the *Gentleman's Magazine*, in a long, laudatory review summed it up, 'We know not what success this excellent work will find, for there seems now to be no taste left for any amusements, only for studying the newspapers about Reform.'[12]

The critical response nevertheless buoyed Collier and made him gloss over his difficulties. His burdens had been great, but Collier had had help in shouldering them. Amyot in particular had been a great support, and in gratitude Collier intended to dedicate the book to his friend, but Amyot counselled him to choose Devonshire instead. This politic gesture so gratified the Duke that he gave his new protégé a stipend of £100 per year. Other largess seemed likely: William IV had come to the throne the previous June, and in November 1830 Devonshire was named Lord Chamberlain.[13] Among other functions, the Lord Chamberlain licensed theatres in London and censored the dramas they performed. This rather considerable power was delegated to a 'licenser', appointed – for life – by the Lord Chamberlain, who received not only a £400 stipend from the Crown but also all of the licensing fees which the theatres were required to pay. The post was a coveted political plum.

In the spring of 1831, the office of licenser seemed likely to become vacant, and if it did, Collier seemed likely to be asked to fill it. The incumbent was George Colman the Younger, who having made a reputation of sorts with several coarse and vulgar dramas had acquired, long with the censor's power, a flagrant moral scrupulosity which astonished those who knew him. Under the long tenure of his predecessor, John Larpent (an ardent Methodist), the stage had been rid of impropriety; under Colman, it seemed about to lose good sense. Larpent had banned representation of heavenly beings; Colman, going one better, banished any *mention* of heaven. 'Angel' became a taboo word, and 'God' could not be mentioned even in prayer on the London stage. Colman's quixotic dicta amounted to harassment of theatre owners, and it was not surprising that there were many who nourished the hope that Colman, sixty-nine years old and ill with gout and other maladies, might resign his office or, barring that unlikely possibility, might be taken down to his reward, leaving the post of licenser to another. Collier lived in expectation.

In August 1831, Colman went abroad to take the waters, planning to continue his labours by mail, but Devonshire demurred and appointed Collier licenser *pro tempore*. The general expectation was that Colman would not return to the post and that Collier would soon hold it in his own right. Unfortunately, that is not the way it turned out. After two months abroad, Colman returned, apparently revived. He was to live – in office – another five years.

Despite this disappointment, Collier's reputation had been enhanced by his sojourn in public service and Devonshire's open support. Increasingly, theatre managers sought his advice or favours. He was flattered by the deference of Charles Kemble, and Kemble's daughter Fanny, the darling of the theatre after her recent triumph as Juliet, asked his advice concerning a play she was writing. He was in regular correspondence with literary lions, he was invited to join the Garrick Club (Devonshire sponsored him and paid his way), and he was frequently consulted by Parliamentarians with a special interest in drama and the theatre. After so many years of grubbing anonymity, this new-found recognition was gratifying. But it brought a backlash of professional jealousy, notably from Alexander Dyce. Dyce shared Collier's passion for Elizabethan dramatists and book collecting, and the two often met at sales and in Rodd's shop, their mutual interest made stronger by the knowledge that, as Dyce put it, they were 'kindred souls' with an interest few others could share.[14] There was, at least initially, real friendship between them ('I like you better than any one in London', Dyce was once moved to declare),[15] but their admiration was always mixed with professional envy. They shared information – who else knew as much as they? – but they were jealous of it, too. Dyce was nine years younger than Collier, could not match Collier's experience and practical knowledge; Collier lacked Dyce's university degree and independent income. Dyce, an intimate and frequent guest of many of the landed aristocracy, might confess to being 'jealous' of Collier's 'intimacy at Devonshire house' where there were 'volumes I cannot finger'. Collier might parry the implication with an offhand reference to the treasures he had, indeed, found in Devonshire's collection – had he told Dyce about the Inigo Jones sketchbook he uncovered at Chiswick? Sometimes they teased with offers made only to be withdrawn. Dyce entreated Collier to join him in editing Greene's works and, when Collier agreed, peremptorily withdrew the offer. 'Don't be offended', he wrote, well aware of giving offence, 'an association with any one would fidget me to death, and I should be unable to fiddle faddle with it in my own peculiar Dycean style.'[16] So it went, an intellectual sparring match in Payne's dark backroom study or over sherry in Dyce's chambers or at bookstalls – an amusing, stimulating, irritating association.

Or so it seemed until the good reception of Collier's *History* changed the nature of the game and put Dyce at an apparent disadvantage. Collier had several large paper editions of the book struck off for special friends and when Dyce received his copy his admiration was mixed with envy. Acknowledging the gift, he suggested that the book was dull and unlikely to have much sale. When Collier, bitterly offended, chided Dyce for his lack of civility, Dyce 'apologized' in an even more churlish reply. 'I only meant', he wrote, 'that it [the *History*] was excellent in its kind, but that I could not help thinking the style a little heavy.... I have in my eyes, as an opposite to yours, the very elegant but not too ornate style of Warton in his H.E.P., which I agree with Mitford in thinking the most agreeable book (at least in modern times) of factual criticism.' Having brushed aside Collier's past work he proceeded to polish off his present and possible future occupations. 'The prospect ... is of your succeeding G. Colman as Licenser', he wrote alluding to the current gossip. 'I suppose the office is attended with considerable emolument: at least it should be, for I conceive nothing more disgusting than the necessity of reading over all the dramatic trash daily hashed up, except being obliged to see it acted.'[17] It was, perhaps, characteristic of their relationship that, having cruelly insulted his friend, Dyce could fill three more pages with casual literary and social chitchat.

Dyce's jealousy was more than counterbalanced by Amyot's unselfish delight in Collier's success. Amyot was, in fact, a partner in one of Collier's most important purchases. With the money from the *History*, Collier joined Amyot in buying a collection of over two thousand manuscript plays from the widow of John Larpent, the former Licenser. These scripts, many of them unique, were the examination copies submitted to the licenser of plays from the imposition of the Licensing Act in 1737 until Larpent's death in 1824; in addition, the collection contained hundreds of letters and memoranda pertaining to the plays' performances. When he left office Larpent had claimed all of the documents as his personal property and he subsequently bequeathed them to his wife. Collier recognized the importance of the collection. 'It is out of the question', he was to write later, 'for anybody to pretend to write a history of theatres, actors, and authors, during that period, without resort to these authorities.'[18] He thought he could make a series of marketable magazine articles out of the scripts, and Amyot believed some of the plays might be profitably revived. The purchase price was £180 and the collection, bound up in six or eight immense bundles, soon crowded Collier's tiny backroom.[19]

A hundred years later, the Larpent collection would be recognized as a priceless manuscript source of eighteenth-century drama and the £180 purchase price an unbelievable bargain, but Collier and Amyot soon regretted their purchase. Two of the plays in the collection were revived at Covent Garden in 1831 but with no apparent profit to the partners,[20] and, in fact, the only financial return seems to have been two signed articles Collier sold to the *New Monthly Magazine*[21] and several untraceable pieces for which he received twelve guineas a page. Amyot hoped this publicity would make the collection easier to sell for a profit, but no new buyer was attracted. At first the collection was kept together in Collier's study, but eventually it was divided between the owners – and ignored for twenty years.

5

Nearly three years would pass before Collier published another book. Scholarship paid little or nothing, and he could not afford the luxury of unremunerated publication. In the fall of 1831 the issues of Reform continued to dominate the public imagination and politics filled the papers. The *Chronicle* was less liberal under Clement than it had been under Perry, but it was the chief organ of the Whigs, and Collier was one of its chief political writers. Although he had never been (and never would be) particularly political, he had been exposed to the 'reformist' Whig doctrines of his father, and his political commentary therefore was based on personal conviction as well as professional necessity. In particular, he hoped the winds of change would regenerate the drama which, it was generally agreed, had reached its nadir: new plays were trash; productions, trumpery; and theatrical economics, ruinous. Collier was convinced that this sorry state was the result of parliamentary confusion and that Reform would produce necessary changes.

The drama was poor because although it was popular it had an uncertain base derived in large part from legal confusion concerning theatrical 'monopoly'. For two hundred years the 'Theatres Royal' of Covent Garden and Drury Lane had claimed an exclusive 'royal patent' to perform the legitimate drama in London, but this presumed right was virtually impossible to exercise. Over the years dozens of minor theatres had been licensed by London magistrates to perform 'burlettas', a genre rather loosely defined as 'plays with music', and by 1832, the distinction between the 'burletta' and the 'legitimate drama' was indiscernible. As a result, the patents gave no economic advantage to the majors but only an ambiguous means to harass the minors, and in the resulting conflict both suffered. This difficulty was exacerbated by the lack of dramatic copyright to protect a playwright from unauthorized performance of his work. Copyright had long given protection against unauthorized *printed* publication, but theatrical 'performance' was not construed to be 'publication', and once performed a play could be revived without royalty. As a result, would-be playwrights found drama unprofitable. They were, moreover, constrained by theatrical censorship. For nearly a century, the drama had been subject to the personal crotchets of the likes of John Larpent and George Colman. No other form of literature was so hampered.

These problems – monopoly, the lack of copyright, and censorship – were caused by Acts of Parliament. To Collier, Reform meant legal change and chief among those who sought to effect that change was Edward Bulwer, later Bulwer-Lytton, a popular novelist who entered Parliament in 1831 calling for reform of the theatre. On 31 May 1832, the

House created a Select Committee on Dramatic Literature with Bulwer as its chairman, and from the middle of June to the middle of July, 1832, the Committee conducted an exhaustive examination of drama and theatrical production.[22] Collier was the only literary historian asked to testify before the Committee, an indication of the prestige he had acquired from his *History*. The Committee put several hundred questions to him, and his answers contrasted sharply with those of George Colman who succeeded him on the stand. Collier discounted the exclusive right of the Theatres Royal to perform legitimate drama (Colman staunchly defended it) and blamed the failure of the patent houses on prodigious managerial ineptitude and cavernous theatre buildings in which it was difficult either to see or to hear. Collier said that the minor theatres, smaller, more comfortable and better run, performed drama as well as the 'majors' and should be made legitimate.

This call for abolishing the monopoly indicates the extent of Collier's radical reformism; his response to questions concerning censorship suggest narrow self-interest. Collier still hoped to be Colman's successor and with admirable lucidity – if somewhat faulty logic – he presented arguments for maintaining censorship of the drama, arguments which were to be heard again and again during the next century. 'I think there ought to be no more control over the purchase of amusements than over the purchase of the common provisions of life', he said, 'provided we take care, in the case of amusement, that what is given is wholesome, as we take care in the case of food what is bought is wholesome....'[23] The fundamental difference between food and art was lost on Collier as on many of his contemporaries, and what is 'wholesome' has certainly not been a matter of agreement among his successors. The purpose of censorship, as Collier must have realized, was not to preserve public morals – only *new* plays were censored (any bawdy play of the Restoration could be played without the Licenser's approval) –but to curb political dissent. Collier had no brief for *that* sort of thing. When Francis Place, a later witness, declared there should be political plays, Collier and the Committee were, apparently, shocked. 'When he concluded', Collier reported in the *Morning Chronicle* of 16 July

1832, 'the room was cleared of strangers; and some expectation was felt that the Committee would order the evidence of
Mr. Place to be expunged: but those who wished it (and none
wished it more than the true friends of the Minor Theatres)
were disappointed.'

Collier not only testified before the Committee but also
reported the proceedings in the *Chronicle* – at length and with
great effect. He was, moreover, Bulwer's confidant and when
Bulwer's bill appeared, Collier carried the fight for its
adoption in the columns of the newspaper. Bulwer's reform
was to be modest at best. Although he had earlier indicated a
desire to abolish censorship, he gave it up, perhaps as a result
of Collier's influence, and his draft bill initiated only dramatic
copyright and the right of 'minor' theatres to perform the
legitimate drama. By the time it got to Commons the licensing
provision was struck out, and ultimately only dramatic
copyright was enacted. Nevertheless, Collier's testimony
against the monopoly had been widely publicized, and there
remained little historical support for the 'exclusive' claims of
the patents. Almost immediately there was a boom in 'minor
theatre' building, and abolition of the monopoly twelve years
later was to be an anticlimax.

The *Report* of the Committee contained a verbatim transcript of expert testimony and Collier's influence did not go
unremarked. Jane confided to Robinson that she had read the
Report 'and like an old fool, I am pleased with what John said
and so is John's Duke.'[24] Devonshire's good opinion was of
great importance to Collier. He had not given up the
possibility that 'his Duke' would release him from daily
drudgery by appointing him to political office. There was
always the chance that what the scorn of peers could not
accomplish, Colman's poor health might effect, and the Old
Licenser's retirement was a month to month expectation for
Collier. So long as Devonshire remained Lord Chamberlain,
his chances seemed good.

In the summer of 1832, the Duke had an accident which
injured his knee, and as a result planned to resign his post. If
that occurred, Collier knew his chance was lost, and in
desperation he proposed to Colman that if the old man would
resign, Collier, as his successor, would give him all the

licensing fees during Colman's lifetime! It was a rash proposal, and Colman turned it down. Two years passed without change, but events finally came to an unhappy conclusion. In November 1834, William IV unexpectedly called on Robert Peel to form a new Tory administration, and in December the Duke of Devonshire resigned his office. Apparently he could have remained in the post despite the change of government; his friendship with William was close and he had no enemies in Peel's administration, but his ill health had made the job burdensome. For Collier, the resignation was a disaster. He petitioned the new government through every possible avenue to establish his claim to. the job of licenser, but to no avail. Shortly thereafter, a new Lord Chamberlain was appointed – and George Colman promptly died. Almost immediately, Charles Kemble, the actor, a good Tory and Collier's sometime friend, was appointed Licenser of Plays, a post which he held for the next twenty years. Political mischance had denied Collier a place, and he learned anew and with some bitterness the danger of fixing one's hopes on the political career of another.

The pathetic drama of Collier's dashed hopes took several years to reach its climax, and in the meantime he was busy and increasingly well paid. His contract with the *Chronicle* required him to do theatrical reporting and to serve in the Reporters' Gallery at Parliament; for the latter, his pay was the highest among his peers. In addition to his *Chronicle* work, he reported on drama for some of the weekly papers, continued with the daily country letters, and wrote anonymous articles for several periodicals, the *New Monthly Magazine* and Leigh Hunt's *Tatler* among them. He also attempted to translate Boccaccio (it was never published) and composed a New Year's masque entitled 'The Contention of the Seasons' which he unsuccessfully tried to sell to the *Quarterly Review* for its January 1833 number.

In 1833, he produced an important bibliography, a printed catalogue of the early English books in the library of Richard Heber. When Heber died in 1833, his heirs put his library on the block and in preparation for this sale, one of the most spectacular of the decade, the auctioneer published a lengthy catalogue of the collection under the title of *Bibliotheca*

Heberiana. Collier compiled the section on poetry, drama, ballads, and broadsides, and after the sale this section, Part IV of the original, was published separately.[25] Since Heber's collection contained many unique works, Collier's bibliography was of great importance.

His reputation was rising and so were his fees. William Pickering, a prolific publisher, wanted to engage him for regular contributions to the *Gentleman's Magazine,* but Collier turned him down. ('While the New Monthly will pay me 12 guineas a sheet I cannot write even for you for £5', he wrote Pickering.[26]) About the same time Collier also turned down a proposal to edit Shakespeare. It was a tempting offer and Collier's reputation was almost strong enough to ensure success. ('I think him the only man to give us a *princeps* Shakespeare', Baron Field wrote to Robinson.[27]) But on the advice of Charles Lamb, Collier rejected the proposal. Lamb advised Coller to wait eight or ten years until he was ready to do the job right.

This profitable popularity coupled with Payne's continuing hope of government preferment, encouraged the Colliers to move once again. The house in Hunter Street, they decided, was too small and too vulgar, and in February 1833, the family resettled a few blocks away in more fashionable quarters near the new Euston Station. The house at Euston Square was expensive to maintain and Robinson severely censured Payne's 'extravagance'; he feared Payne was once again slipping into debt and rashly 'anticipating' his mother's inheritance.[28]

If that was the case, his anticipation was short-lived. Jane Collier died on 19 October 1833. In the eight years since her husband's death her friendship with Robinson had deepened. He had come to know her better than her children and to appreciate her more than her husband. 'No one else will ever feel for me the friendship she did', he wrote in his diary, and he confided to Dorothy Wordsworth that her passing was 'the severest loss I have sustained for many years'.[29] Jane's death materially changed Robinson's association with the Collier family. 'That connection', he wrote five months after her death, 'as far as it is one of friendship is at an end. It is now one of gratitude . . . a less pleasing feeling in every way.'[30]

Collier received £900 from his mother's estate, a boon which financed, among other things, a spate of scholarly publications, pamphlets, and several drama reprints. He later implied that the chief purpose of his labour was to help a printer, Frederick Shoberl, Jr., the son of Collier's old benefactor, and this may have been partly true, for none of the works had a large printing and the bibliography was not for sale. At any rate, from 1835 to 1837 Collier published eight titles which Shoberl printed: two pamphlets, one purporting to give *New Facts Regarding the Life of Shakespeare*,[31] the other promising *New Particulars Regarding the Works of Shakespeare*;[32] five miracle plays which Collier published on his own from manuscript copies in various collections; and *A Catalogue, Bibliographical and Critical, of Early English Literature; forming a portion of the library at Bridgewater House,* in effect a catalogue of a large part of the library of Sir Francis Egerton. (This was privately printed at Egerton's expense and distributed by him to friends.)

The impetus for these works, apart from the newly acquired funds to print some of them, was the superb collection announced in the last title. As an historical treasure, the Bridgewater Collection was the greatest resource Collier had yet been able to use, for unlike the collections amassed by Devonshire and Heber, it was a family repository well over three hundred years old which had been maintained with care and informed interest by several generations. It was in part a great collection of books, but more significant to Collier's purpose, and to subsequent literary historians as well, it contained family muniments of unique importance to literary history, most notably those of the founder of the dynasty, Sir Thomas Egerton, Baron Ellesmere and Viscount Brackley, who had been Lord Chancellor under James I. The Ellesmere manuscripts contained many papers treating Privy Council matters and myriad other subjects associated with Jacobean England. Throughout the eighteenth century the library was housed at Ashridge, the county seat of the Dukes of Bridgewater in Buckinghamshire, where it was regularly open to visitors. In 1802 the collection was transported to the

Duke's London residence, Cleveland House, for safer keeping and greater accessibility. As a result, when the library was inherited by George Leveson-Gower, the first Marquis of Stafford, in 1803, it was very well known and it was subsequently described in great detail in William Clarke's account of the most 'celebrated British libraries'. It received still further publicity when its former librarian, the Revd. Henry Todd, wrote about the collection in 1823.[33] Collier may have used the Bridgewater Collection while he was gathering information for his *History*, for he made several footnote references to it, but if he consulted the collection at Cleveland House before 1830, he could not have done so more than once or twice, for he made no acknowledgement to the Marquis of Stafford in the preface of his book, an opportunity he would not have ignored. In 1833, the Marquis (by then the first Duke of Sutherland) died, and the library passed to Francis Leveson-Gower who assumed with the bequest the family name of Egerton. (He later became the Earl of Ellesmere in his own right.)

This transfer of the Bridgewater manuscripts was of great importance to Collier's career, for Francis Egerton was to become a patron to Collier almost equal to Devonshire. He was introduced to his new patron by Charles Greville, Egerton's brother-in-law about the time the young heir gained possession of the Bridgewater Collection, and their friendship was, apparently, immediate and firm. Egerton's tastes were akin to Collier's own. He had a keen interest in the drama and had written several plays (one, *Catherine of Cleves,* had been successfully produced at Covent Garden). Moreover he shared Collier's pleasure in German literature; like Collier, Egerton had translated Schiller. He was a member of the Society of Antiquaries and a benefactor of the British Museum, on whose board of trustees he would soon serve. Egerton was almost as wealthy as Devonshire, with an income well over £90,000 a year and a commitment to sharing his wealth and collections with the public; It could not have been lost on Collier that Egerton, as a Liberal-Conservative of the Canning school, was more likely to have political influence in the years just ahead than would Devonshire, who had pretty much resigned his power with his Chamberlain's post. And, of course, there was the Bridgewater library itself. As Collier later described it, 'Lord Francis Egerton gave me instant and unrestrained access' to the collection 'with permission to make use of any literary or historical information I could discover.'[34] The uses Collier discovered were many. Although the manuscripts were famous, they were largely uncatalogued. In the first decade of the century, Henry Todd had made a class catalogue of some of them, but when he departed to become Keeper of Manuscripts at Lambeth Palace he left behind no one to continue his work, and no systematic survey of the Bridgewater Collection appears to have been undertaken before Collier used them.

Among the most valuable of the uncatalogued documents were many bundles of papers which ranged from 1581, when Sir Thomas Egerton was made Solicitor General, to 1616 when he retired from the office of Lord Chancellor. Many of these had never been examined and, as Collier noted, some packets had never been opened since Sir Thomas Egerton's 'own hands tied them together'.[35] As Collier was later to write of the circumstances in his pamphlet *New Facts Concerning the Life of Shakespeare,* within one such bundle, 'a most unpromising heap, chiefly of legal documents', he made an astounding discovery: seven manuscripts pertaining to the theatre, four of which contained the name of Shakespeare and one which referred to him indirectly.[36] The details of Shakespeare's biography were virtually unknown, only the barest kind of legal record survived to document his life; a manuscript which referred to Shakespeare, however remotely, was therefore a major historical discovery, and Collier announced that he had unearthed *five*!

One was a roll of members of the Blackfriars Theatre, part of a petition to the Privy Council dated November 1589, which listed Shakespeare as a sharer in the company. This document appeared to be the earliest reference to Shakespeare in London and, Collier believed, disproved once and for all the tale that Shakespeare began his theatrical career holding horses.

A second document was an undated record of the principal sharers in the company which Collier conjectured was made in 1608. It not only indicated that Shakespeare and Richard

Burbage each owned 'four shares' (which made them the largest owners at the time) but also placed a cash value on those shares from which one could calculate Shakespeare's yearly income from the theatre. Another document, an undated 'true copy' of a letter signed 'H.S.', purported to be an introduction of Burbage and Shakespeare to Lord Ellesmere. Collier believed its date to be about 1608, the signer Henry Southampton, and the purpose of the introduction a chance for Burbage and Shakespeare to argue against the persecution of the Blackfriars Players by the Corporation of London. (Another document suggested they were successful in their plea.) One more document mentioned Shakespeare by name: a warrant, dated January 1609 in the name of Robert Daborne, to organize a company, the Children of the Queen's Revels. This request apparently was never granted.

In addition to these, one other letter in the Bridgewater bundle referred to Shakespeare without naming him: in writing to Ellesmere, Samuel Daniel expressed his gratitude for the post of Master of the Queen's Revels (to which, by verified fact, he had been appointed in 1603) and suggested that Shakespeare had been an unsuccessful petitioner for the same position.

These documents collectively told more about Shakespeare's professional life than all previous discoveries put together. *New Facts Regarding the Life of Shakespeare* was therefore of singular importance to scholars and to the general readers who revered Shakespeare's plays. There were other less important details in *New Facts*: a comment in the Inigo Jones Sketchbook which Collier had discovered in Devonshire's collection describing the traditional costume of Falstaff, and a record from the Chapter House, Westminster, which apparently recorded Shakespeare's purchase of New Place in Stratford-upon-Avon.

New Facts, issued in a small edition in May 1835, was written in the somewhat archaic form of a 'letter' to Collier's friend Amyot (the usual practice followed in presenting papers at the Society of Antiquaries of which Amyot was then Treasurer). *New Particulars,* its companion issued seven months later, was addressed to Alexander Dyce, an indication of Collier's esteem for his younger rival. While it contained less startling information than its predecessor, the second pamphlet announced some notable discoveries, chief among them a manuscript Collier had unearthed in the Ashmolean Collection at Oxford, *The Bocke of Plaies and Notes Thereof* by Dr. Simon Forman, a contemporary of Shakespeare. The *Bocke of Plaies* was a series of memoranda concerning plays Forman had seen, among them four by Shakespeare: *The Winter's Tale, Cymbeline, Macbeth,* and one, untitled, which Collier conjectured was *Richard II.* The importance of the original staging in determining Shakespeare's text was obvious to Collier's predecessors, but until the Forman notes were discovered no eye witness account of an original Shakespeare production had been found. Forman's description of *Macbeth* seemed to differ from the First Folio version (the only extant text of the play), suggesting that there might have been another, 'lost' version closer to what Shakespeare actually wrote.

New Particulars contained two new discoveries from the Bridgewater manuscripts: the first was an item in Sir Arthur Mainwaring's Revels Accounts of expenses incurred when Egerton entertained Queen Elizabeth at Harefield in 1602. Under the date of 6 August, he noted a payment of £10 to 'Burbige's players for Othello'. This reference was significant because it seemed to establish the existence of the play two years prior to 1604, the date that Malone had given it in the order of Shakespeare's last great plays. The second was an undated manuscript copy of a poem, apparently part of a masque performed at Ashby, which was signed, as Collier read it, 'W.Sh.'. With 'some hesitation' Collier ascribed the poem to Shakespeare – although it was not, he concluded, in Shakespeare's handwriting. As such, it was a curious work, for as Collier admitted, Shakespeare 'appears from early life to have devoted himself to the theatre only, and not to have sought employment in the preparation of masques, shows, or entertainments for private societies.' Whether by Shakespeare or not, the poem was 'certainly worth preserving', he concluded.[37] Finally, two lesser 'particulars' were featured in the pamphlet: a reprint of an elegy on Richard Burbage which listed twenty parts he had played – twelve of them Shakespearean – and the contents of a manuscript book of thirty ballads he had earlier mentioned in *New Facts*. From the latter he quoted excerpts from two ballads. One, 'The Atheist's Tragedy', concerned Christopher Marlowe; it declared the poet had been a player and described his death.[38] The other ballad was 'The Tragedie of Othello the Moore', a curiosity composed after 1625 and based on Shakespeare's play.

The discoveries Collier announced in *New Facts* and *New Particulars* were the fruits of several years' research (he had discovered Forman's accounts at least three years before he announced them in *New Facts*[39]), and they might have been subjects for profitable periodical essays, but Collier chose to present them in privately printed pamphlets in issues so small they did not pay printing costs. Moreover, about the same time he produced a private edition of five miracle plays[40] which he bestowed as 'gifts of the editor'. It might seem foolish for one in his circumstances to have been so extravagant, but his discoveries received more notice published in pamphlets than in periodical essays, and private publication had more cachet than commercial. More than money Collier wanted recognition. In particular, he wanted to be a member of the Athenaeum, since 1823 the most important literary club in London. The Garrick Club, to which Collier had been admitted within a year of its founding in 1831, was only slightly less distinguished than the Athenaeum, but Collier wanted the higher pretensions of the latter. At its founding, membership was fixed at a thousand 'men of letters', artists, or men of science – what Robinson, himself an early choice of the club, called 'producers' of culture and 'lovers of literature'. (Robinson had gained entry through Amyot and Richard Heber, the book-collector, and Collier, no less their friend, could count on their support. Collier courted other influential club members, in particular Sir Walter Scott, a founder, to whom he sent a copy of his *History* with a particularly obsequious letter.) Collier's private publications in the mid-1830s were part of his campaign to establish his *bona fides* as a 'producer' and 'lover' of literature, and by any fair standard they surely did so, but he never became one of 'the thousand'. By the time his name was submitted in 1836, some of those who might have carried the day for him were no longer members – Heber and Scott were dead – and the club's criteria had become increasingly aristocratic. Moreover, Robinson, his champion, was at odds with John Wilson Croker, the club panjandrum, and this disaffection made any Robinson protégé unacceptable to Croker and his friends. Collier was blackballed in March 1836 'on the ground', Robinson later reported, 'that only first rate men ought to be brought in by the Committee – a scrupulosity that annoys me on the present occasion and I think absurd.'[41] Such a rejection was not uncommon, and names of famous men of literature who were denied membership in the Athenaeum are legion, but for Collier the rejection was a personal and professional blow. He informed Robinson that he did not want his name brought in again.[42]

Collier's pride was partially restored by an advancement on the *Morning Chronicle*. Two years earlier, John Easthope and two associates had purchased the ailing paper from Clement and had begun changes which were designed to bring it back to its former prominence. Easthope, a wealthy manufacturer and liberal politician, intended to advance his political career, and at the price he paid the paper was a cheap means to that end. He hired new staff and reassigned the remainder, and as a result, in September 1836, Payne was made sub-editor, virtually second in command to Black. In this new post, Payne wrote leading articles, 'founded', as he later described them, 'upon closely watched public and private events', at the rate of some fifty columns every three months.[43] With the new duties came a good increase in salary to £450 per year. 'They have found out', he wrote to Robinson, 'that I can write a little, and in a style not very usual in the papers, and accordingly my business is daily (when a fit subject offers), to give them something of my penmanship.'[44] For the most part, his columns were unsigned 'editorial comments' on political events which were printed immediately after the masthead of the paper. Collier was allowed to choose his subjects so long as they were politically in line with Easthope's Whig liberalism, and since those views were close to Collier's own he had no difficulty in maintaining them with vigour. With Easthope's interest and financial support, the circulation of the paper nearly doubled.

For several years Collier's newspaper career was ascendant. He was now a confidant of Easthope (he canvassed with him during the latter's successful run for the seat of Leicester in Parliament) and was so 'in favour' that Robinson was sure Collier would soon succeed Black as editor. His older son, John Pycroft Collier, now eighteen, was hired for the gallery at £100 a year, proud to be the third generation of parliamentary reporters in the family. Easthope had further arranged to have Collier's younger son, William, apprenticed to the Great Western Railway in training for a civil engineer, and although William was more laconic than his brother, his career too seemed well established.

The only difficulty which Collier foresaw in his advancement at the *Chronicle* was the possibility that it might discourage the special interest Egerton was beginning to show him. 'My position is an odd one', he wrote to Robinson in November 1837, 'writing as I do for the M.C. (though under some trammels which "cramp my genius") and going in and out of such a high Tory's house as Lord Francis Egerton.' He resolved to confess to Egerton that he wrote political leaders for the paper, and to his surprise the news made the peer 'rather more cordial than before'; the privately printed catalogue of the Bridgewater Collection of early English Literature continued and was published on schedule,[45] and Collier's friendship with Egerton actually became warmer in the years that followed. However, after the bibliography appeared, Collier's scholarly publications ceased for a time, and it looked as though Robinson was to have his wish, that Collier was about to turn away from his 'unprofitable literary' avocation and devote himself entirely to a career in journalism.

Collier's intimacy with Easthope was well known. For example, when the paper sought a foreign correspondent in Constantinople, Thackeray asked Collier's support in getting the job. 'A word from you will be, I am sure, all powerful', he wrote.[46] (Thackeray was not hired for Constantinople, but he later became a *Chronicle* 'regular'.) Collier was often a go-between when the strong-willed Easthope tangled with his employees. Charles Dickens had been hired (with some assistance from Collier) as a parliamentary reporter for the paper, and when Dickens suddenly left the paper in November 1836 to edit *Bentley's Miscellany* Easthope was bitter. Collier managed to insert a good notice of Dickens's first *Miscellany* when it appeared, but he otherwise failed to mollify the irascible proprietor. Collier's influence was limited.

It was also to be short-lived. Ironically, as the fortunes of the paper improved, Collier's relations which Easthope deteriorated. The proprietor demanded more and more control over Collier's columns and Collier became restive. 'I am ashamed always of my newspaper criticism', he wrote to Leigh Hunt, 'but many are fathered upon me for which I am not responsible. . . . I am obliged often to keep other people's illegitimates.'[47] The immediate cause of the break between Collier and Easthope is not known. Collier later declared that he was not politically radical enough for his superior, but other considerations were probably as important. There were strong differences among Easthope's co-proprietors who gradually restrained his control; as Dickens remarked, there were 'half a dozen Proprietors and agents . . . pulling different ways – each for himself.'[48] In such a situation, Collier's relations with Easthope became uncertain, and within a few years they were strained. Easthope was strong-willed and ambitious, and unlikely to allow much independence to a subordinate. 'I foresee that I shall have no easy task of it', Collier confided to Robinson. 'I wish to Heaven he would either not think for himself or think better.'[49] Inevitably, they fell out. In the latter part of 1839, Collier ceased to be a sub-editor and became, once again, merely a reporter. The loss of favour severely wounded both his professional pride and his financial standing, for his salary dropped to the 'Fleet Street minimum'. It was, as Robinson noted, 'both a loss and a humiliation. He is reduced to a clerical office – from eight to five guineas a week – and is forced to go into the gallery again . . .'[50]

Collier anticipated his demotion. Several months earlier he had moved out of the elaborate establishment in Euston and into a more modest house at 24 Brompton Square. He also began to look for other employment, but the search was unfruitful. Another newspaper was unlikely to have him. *The Times* did not want the chief political writer of its bitterest rival, and no other paper would be willing or able to offer him more than he made at the *Chronicle*. It was a sad circumstance: after nearly thirty-five years of writing for the daily press, Collier had no more security and little more salary than the most recently hired novice. There was, he knew, little hope of climbing back up the treadmill he had tumbled from. He had been close, but he had lost his chance, and he knew it wouldn't come again.

One alternative to journalism was a government appointment. Melbourne was well established in his second administration, and Collier thought it possible that his political articles for the *Chronicle* might have earned him some credit with the government. He had also continued his minimal duties to the Duke of Devonshire who still had some influence in government circles. In the spring of 1840, therefore, Collier once again sought the aid of his Whig patron. He was not successful. Devonshire, who had paid Collier £100 annually for nearly a decade, was not eager to do more, and in friendly fashion he refused Collier's new request. Collier answered with ill-advised petulance. He had not asked Devonshire for aid since he left office, he declared, and the Whigs owed him something, although they were, perhaps, more interested in buying off enemies than in rewarding friends. 'I say it in all humility, that I have deserved something of literature: I forsook it to support Ministers with my pen, and I did so for two or three years. I only ceased because my writings were not sufficiently *radical.* This ought rather to have recommended me, than otherwise. Your Grace would not believe me if I said that I was not disappointed – Yet what had I to expect?'[51]

Devonshire was irritated by this further appeal. He had no personal stake in Melbourne's ministry and the editorial policy of the *Morning Chronicle* could in no sense be taken as his. The request was strident and the argument ill-conceived to win his assistance. He put Collier's request aside.

It is a sign of Collier's desperation that three weeks later he wrote yet again to Devonshire, and the obsequious manner he now adopted was as obnoxious to the Duke as stridency had been. Collier asked for preferment on the list of barristers who might be appointed to Police Magistrates, noting that Devonshire had power through family and friends to bring it about. 'The only question is whether your Grace thinks it worth while to exercise your power for me? I wish I could answer the question.' His appeal was, he declared, not for himself but for his wife and six children. 'I do most humbly entreat your Grace to excuse my apparent importunacy, or importunity, and to be assured, that were I only concerned, I would fight my way through the world without the slightest obligation to anybody but myself.'[52] This appeal was also denied. There was to be, Collier realized, no assistance from Devonshire or the government. He was fixed as a journalist and any release from that confinement would come, as it always had in the past, solely by his own exertions.

The one advantage to his change of status was that it freed him once again for non-journalistic work. For nearly three years his writing had been almost solely for the *Chronicle*. The forced vacation from literature had, if anything, increased his desire to return to scholarship, and he now hoped to combine pleasure with profit. He laid plans, quite methodically, to edit Shakespeare.

Collier's credentials for the undertaking were as good or better than any of his potential competitors. *The History of English Dramatic Poetry* had established his reputation as the pre-eminent historian of English drama, and *New Facts* and *New Particulars* had made him an authority on Shakespeare as well. But Shakespeare had heretofore been a secondary interest. Collier's perspective was the reverse of his distinguished predecessors: their interest in dramatic history derived from their devotion to the bard; his interest in Shakespeare came as an adjunct to dramatic history. His real love was the drama of lesser known Elizabethan playwrights, but editing them would not be profitable whereas an edition of Shakespeare's plays might be.

In December 1839, Collier published *Farther Particulars Regarding Shakespeare and His Works*,[53] a collection of analogues to Shakespeare's plays. Although it did not bear comparison with its predecessors, this pamphlet was highly successful in staking Collier's professional claims. In a postscript, he attacked all former editors of Shakespeare who, he declared, had quixotically ignored the First Folio and created a confusion where none should exist. He called for a new 'pure' text, and made it clear that he was about to produce it. His words seemed to announce a proposal, but they were actually intended to attract one, and they did. A month or two after the pamphlet appeared, Collier contracted with George Whittaker, a successful London bookseller, to edit the plays of Shakespeare, with notes, commentary, biography, and historical survey. The work was to be in eight volumes and Collier was to be paid £500.

III

THE WORKS OF WILLIAM SHAKESPEARE
'Few know what it was, and fewer what I have made it.'

6

Collier took four years to complete this edition of Shakespeare (the first volume appeared in February 1842, two years after his agreement with Whittaker, and the last two years later), but he did not work on it exclusively during that time, for he had other commitments which antedated his agreement with Whittaker. In the next ten years he was to publish nearly forty separate titles. Over thirty of these would be issued by three book clubs in which he had a special, not to say a proprietary, interest. In the spring of 1838, Collier had joined other members of the Society of Antiquaries in founding the Camden Society. In the summer of 1840, he and Amyot were leaders in establishing the Percy Society, and a year later he was the chief organizer of the Shakespeare Society. These were separate organizations, but they share a common interest in what later scholars would call historiography, and they had similar programmes to reprint rare works of literary or historical importance in inexpensive editions. The idea was not new. For twenty years the Roxburghe Club, founded in 1813 by a group of wealthy bibliophiles, had required each of its members to print a volume for distribution among his colleagues. Less affluent scholars had occasionally printed literary rarities and shared the cost of publication among those who received copies, and Collier himself had produced half a dozen books in this cooperative fashion. The Camden, Percy and Shakespeare Societies were the first to do collectively and regularly what had previously been done piecemeal.

What Collier and his co-founders envisioned in each case was an organization of several hundred subscribers who would pay a fixed sum, usually a guinea, to receive six to eight books a year in well-printed, well-bound editions. The cost of the books would be low because the officers of the society and the individual editors themselves would work without remuneration, but the 'market' value of the books would be high because their number would be limited. This was a key consideration: to maintain this advantage, a society's membership had to be smaller than the number who wanted to join. Collier was particularly aware of this necessity and he argued to restrict the enrolment in each case.

The societies had many overlapping members (Robinson, for example, belonged to all of them), but they were quite distinct from one another, and only Collier was on the governing council of all three. The Camden Society, more strictly 'historical' than the other two, was named for William Camden, the Elizabethan historian and topographer; it promoted the publication of 'early historical and literary remains', particularly inaccessible or little known historical documents, letters, and ancient poems.[1] It was the most popular and longest lived of the book clubs. (It merged with the Royal Historical Society in 1897 and continues to exist under that aegis.) Its membership, first limited to five hundred persons, was increased (over Collier's objections) to one thousand, in response to the pressure of applications. Significantly, most of the influential officers of the Camden Society were Collier's close associates. Egerton was its first President, Devonshire a charter member, and Robinson, one of its three auditors, was soon its director, a position he held until his death. Collier himself served on the first Council and produced the second work issued by the Society, *Kynge Johan* by John Bale, edited from a unique manuscript he had discovered in Devonshire's library.[2] Several years later he edited another important work for the Society, a selection of Egerton manuscripts from the collection at Bridgewater House.[3]

Like the bishop after whom it was named, the Percy Society had a formative interest in early ballads, songs, plays, minor pieces of poetry, and 'popular literature'. Its first council included Alexander Dyce and James Orchard Halliwell as well as John Payne Collier, who was elected its first director. Moreover, Collier edited its first publication, a collection of twenty-five ballads printed from early broadsides,[4] and he prepared two more works among the five offered by the Society in its first year.[5]

The Shakespeare Society, organized in 1841, followed closely on Collier's contract with Whittaker, and it was for him a natural extension of the Shakespeare edition. 'It is remarkable', he wrote in the 'Prospectus' of the Society, 'that all that has hitherto been done for the illustration of Shakespeare has been accomplished by individuals, and that no literary association has yet been formed for the purpose of collecting materials, or of circulating information, by which he may be thoroughly understood and fully appreciated.'[6] The Shakespeare Society was the first co-operative venture in a study which had long been characterized by jealous men working alone. The Society's first publication was a series of little known fifteenth- and sixteenth-century pamphlets, and it was no coincidence that these were the tracts which Collier had discussed in the *Critical Review* nearly twenty-five years before. Although he would have preferred it otherwise, Collier himself finally edited most of them for the Society's subscribers.

Although he was already serving as Director of the Percy Society, Collier became Director of the Shakespeare Society as well. His function in each case was to find suitable works for publication, engage editors to prepare the copy, present these projects to the council for its approval and, when a work was approved, to supervise its printing and distribution to the membership. The societies' councils were often contentious, and Collier had to cope with many problems. He had some help from Frederick Shoberl, Jr., the son of his old friend, who printed all the Shakespeare Society books, and from Thomas Rodd the publisher, who assisted in their distribution, but caring for the day-to-day minutiae devolved on Collier alone, and he was rewarded with small thanks and no pay.

His chief difficulty – and these were to be duties not of months but of years – was persuading scholars to edit the works for publication. Everyone was gratified to receive the publications – they were bargains – but only a few were willing to prepare them. The reasons for this lack of co-operation were various. Professional jealousy may have deterred some from contributing, and Collier's directorial manner, honed to a sharp edge over the years, did little to assuage it. The announced intention of the Shakespeare Society was to issue one book a month, but this proved to be much too ambitious, and only six were produced in the first year. The number was no larger thereafter, and to maintain even that number Collier himself had to prepare many of the manuscripts. His letters to friends during the years of his directorship were usually pleas for assistance. A letter to Dyce only a few months after the Shakespeare Society was founded was typical: Would Dyce edit Gosson's *School of Abuse* for the Society? 'I would do it myself', he wrote, '... were it not objectionable to see the same name over and over again as editor. Variety gives confidence.'⁷ But even though Collier promised to provide the transcript of Gosson's work and assured Dyce his labours would be of a day or two only, Dyce refused, and Collier was forced to edit the manuscript himself. This sequence occurred many times: in the eleven years' life of the Shakespeare Society, over half of its forty-five publications were edited by Collier and many of these were published without his name on the title page. The same problem obtained with the Percy Society: while he was Director, Collier edited far more texts than any other member.

His energy was inexhaustible. During the four years he was editing Shakespeare for Whittaker (1840–1844), he produced no fewer than nine works for the Percy Society and ten for the Shakespeare Society. While some of these, like the edition of Gosson just mentioned, called for only an introduction and a few explanatory notes to accompany a transcript made by another, several of them were substantial works of scholarship requiring extended research and composition. That he should have completed all these labours concurrently with editing Shakespeare is remarkable; that he should have done most of them well is astonishing. And when one remembers that for a good part of each year, while Parliament was sitting, he was busy many nights taking dictation in the Gallery, his accomplishment is almost beyond belief.

Collier's rewards were never commensurate with his labour: few of his contemporaries praised him for the productions of these years, and his successors have damned him for some of them; several of the works Collier published for the societies derive a special importance from later controversies. For example, the *Egerton Papers,* issued in 1840 as the twelfth volume of the Camden Society, was the result of a monumental undertaking. It consisted of documents selected from among the thousands in the Bridgewater Collection. Collier had come to know that repository well, and as previously noted, had published important discoveries from it. Since Egerton served as President of the Camden Society, it was perhaps inevitable that Collier should suggest editing more of the collection for its members. Over several years, he had collected documents pursuant to writing the biography of Sir Thomas Egerton (he never wrote it) and he decided that some of these manuscripts, grants, warrants, patents and letters of various kinds, could be printed without preempting the other project. In the *Egerton Papers* he reproduced over a hundred – documents on a wide range of subjects, and with an explanatory introduction.[8]

For the Shakespeare Society Collier edited a work of even greater importance. The *Memoirs of Edward Alleyn* was the first of three volumes which would derive from the Alleyn manuscripts preserved at Dulwich College. Collier it will be remembered had first seen the welter of documents in this collection in the spring of 1830, as his *History of English Dramatic Poetry* was about to be printed, and in the ten years which followed he had often wanted to examine the rest of the collection. In 1840 he returned to Dulwich to prepare Henslowe's diary for publication,[9] but what he found there radically altered his plans. He had assumed like everybody else that Edmond Malone had gleaned everything of literary value from the Dulwich manuscripts, but he discovered that Malone had used only a few of them; while these (e.g. Henslowe's diary) were among the most important, there were many more of almost equal value he had missed, documents which revealed important details of Edward Alleyn's life and career and the history of early seventeenth-century English theatre. Among these were Edward Alleyn's script for Greene's *Orlando Furioso* (it remains the only extant Elizabethan manuscript 'part'); a lease of shares in the Fortune Theatre; articles of agreements between Henslowe and his company of actors; a Privy Council warrant for reopening the Rose Theatre and another permitting the construction of the Fortune in 1600. Moreover, on re-reading Henslowe's diary, Collier discovered an entry Malone did not reprint, which revealed that, commencing in June 1594, and apparently continuing until November 1596, Henslowe's company, the Admiral's Men, played at Newington Butts Theatre with the Lord Chamberlain's Men, the company to which Shakespeare belonged, and that during this sojourn the Lord Admiral's Men performed ten plays with subjects corresponding to Shakespeare's, among them *Hamlet, The Taming of A Shrew, 'Andronicus',* and *'Harry the V'.* The obvious possibility was that these were Shakespeare's plays, and hence that some of his early plays were performed by the Admiral's Men. Collier made other notable discoveries: an inventory of costumes unnoticed by Malone, a cache of letters from Thomas Dekker, William Bird, Nathan Field, and other dramatists, to Alleyn or Henslowe, and more letters from Henslowe to Alleyn. One of the latter substantiated the account – previously only hearsay – of Ben Jonson's duel with Gabriel Spencer in which Spencer was killed.

Virtually the whole of the professional life of Edward Alleyn, with Burbage one of the two greatest actors of his age, lay before Collier, and he knew the importance of his discovery. Heretofore the careers of Shakespeare's professional contemporaries had been sketchy, mere anecdotal bits and gossip, but now the life of one of the most important was revealed in abundant detail. Collier put aside his plan to print Henslowe's diary – he would return to it later – and devoted himself immediately to composing the life of Edward Alleyn, linking the narrative events of Alleyn's life with transcriptions of over fifty of the most important of the manuscripts he had uncovered.

It must have been obvious to Collier that a biography of Edward Alleyn, based on new manuscript evidence, had commercial value which could have earned him substantial royalties from any one of several publishers. Alternatively, since dozens of the manuscripts which he discovered were unique primary documents to which every subsequent scholar would need access, he, like Malone, might have used them to embellish his forthcoming edition of Shakespeare. Collier chose neither of these profitable alternatives. Instead, he prepared the book for the Shakespeare Society without any remuneration at all, and *The Memoirs of Edward Alleyn* appeared as the fledgling society's first publication in January, 1841.

Among the many documents which Collier reproduced in the book were four which mentioned Shakespeare. These were incidental to the memoir, but in later years they were to become notorious. One was a poem, 'Sweet Nedde, now winne another wager', concerning a competition between Alleyn and actors at the Globe, and referred to 'Willes newe playe'. Another was a badly decayed letter to Alleyn from his wife, Joan, which incidentally mentioned 'Mr Shakespeare of the globe'. The third was a list, in the margin of a copy of a 1604 Privy Council warrant of the company of the King's Men, which included the name of Shakespeare; and the fourth was an assessment list of 1609 for residents of the Clink, an area in Southwark, which included, along with the names of Henslowe and Alleyn, that of 'Mr Shakespeare'. Only the last two were of any historical significance, for they seemed to establish Shakespeare's connection with the King's Men in 1604 and to identify his last London residence before he returned to Stratford. These 'facts' were not particularly startling – they had been suggested before and were widely accepted – but any reference to Shakespeare, no matter how minor, immediately acquired an interest disproportionate to its intrinsic worth. The importance of Collier's discovery was widely recognized. 'It has been the fortune of few, however zealously they have laboured, to contribute so much as Mr. Collier to the illustration of our early dramatic literature and the history of the English stage', the *Athenaeum* declared, 'and these Memoirs of Alleyn are assuredly not among the least valuable of his services.'[10] As might be expected, the publication was a boon to the Shakespeare Society.

While at Dulwich, Collier sought Alleyn's manuscript memorandum book from which Malone had quoted some intriguing comments concerning the Fortune Theatre, but the manuscript could not be found, and Collier assumed it was lost. But shortly after the biography of Alleyn was published, the memorandum book turned up and Collier described it in a long article in the *Athenaeum*,[11] and soon thereafter, James Orchard Halliwell announced that he owned twenty-eight Alleyn manuscripts that presumably had once been among the documents in Malone's possession. Halliwell, a member of the Council of the Shakespeare Society, presented the manuscripts to Dulwich in March 1843, and Collier immediately undertook to publish them, with long extracts from the memorandum book, as a supplement to his earlier volume. *The Alleyn Papers*[12] was completed in September 1843, and issued as number 18 of the Shakespeare Society publications. Since Malone had seen all of these documents and had printed some of them, the book was not so important or valuable as its predecessor, but it contained dozens of documents selected by Collier from the hundreds at Dulwich. Moreover, he wrote an introduction and commentary which linked the disparate items into a single coherent narrative.

Collier had now printed two volumes of Alleyn manuscripts, but Henslowe's diary, the prize which had taken him back to Dulwich in the first place, still remained unpublished. He had obtained permission to transcribe the book on 13 October 1840[13] but the actual editing was delayed, and the book was announced as 'in preparation' for several years. Given the many works Collier had in hand during the first three years of the decade, this is not surprising. The manuscript was in a very confused and mutilated state and putting it in proper order was a complex job which Collier could not undertake whilst fulfilling his contract with Whittaker. Nevertheless, he took time to edit for the Shakespeare Society seven rare tracts by Heywood, Gosson, Nashe and Ford, among others, and Dekker's *Patient Grissil,* whose sources he then edited for the Percy Society. In addition, he reprinted six other texts for the Percy Society and privately published four additional tracts. Two of these[14] were intended for gifts, but two, *Pleasant Quippes for upstart newfangled gentlewomen,* by Stephen Gosson, and *A Treatise, shewing... the pryde and abuse of women,* by Charles Bansley were edited for the Percy Society and rejected for unknown reasons. The incident serves to disprove any assumption that Collier had absolute control over the societies he directed.[15] In addition, before he completed his Shakespeare, Collier reprinted three other tracts which he distributed privately,[16] and in 1843, Thomas Rodd engaged him to edit *Shakespeare's Library,* a collection of seventeen 'romances, novels, poems, and histories, used by Shakespeare as the foundation of his dramas'. Rodd chose the works to be reprinted and supervised the details of printing; Collier's sole responsibility was to write short introductions to each selection. It was a very successful venture.[17]

Unfortunately, the dilettantes who constituted most of the membership of the Percy and Shakespeare Societies did not appreciate Collier's labours. Even Robinson confided to his diary that he didn't like what he was receiving for his membership fees. After finishing the biography of Alleyn, he declared it 'a very dull book indeed'. It made him 'fear this society will not be much better than the Percy Society, whose first year's publications are very unpleasant books – not one do I recollect that has given me any pleasure.'[18]

This was a sad comment, and it foreshadowed the ultimate fate of Collier's work for these societies. By twentieth-century standards Collier's editing was poor, but it was qualitatively better than that of his contemporaries; his faults were commonplace, but in his time whereas his achievements were unique: he resurrected and preserved dozens of rare works essential to the study of early English drama which might otherwise have been lost. Moreover, he was the first scholar, and for many years the only one who recognized the need to make primary manuscript resources available in *comprehensive* printed form. Others before him had used the Alleyn manuscripts and presumably had appreciated their value, but none of these precursors, not even Malone, had recognized the importance of publishing them *in extenso* for the use of other scholars. The importance of this fact can hardly be exaggerated. One of the essential prerequisites for modern literary scholarship was to be the accessibility of unique manuscript resources; until scholars everywhere could consult primary evidence, the systematic study of early English literature was restricted to the very few who could examine the originals. Collier was the first to publish not only the Alleyn manuscripts (1841, 1843) but also *Henslowe's Diary* (1845) and the Stationers' *Register* (1848, 1861–63), works which are essential to every student of Elizabethan-Jacobean drama. For a generation these were the only editions, but they were not appreciated when they appeared and they have been denigrated since. It is one of the ironies of his career that whereas Collier's contemporaries criticized him for being too interested in esoterica, his successors have belittled him for announcing the obvious.

7

Notwithstanding his commitment to the book clubs, Collier's chief concern between 1840 and 1844 was to complete his contract with Whittaker, and thus most of the time he could wrest from his job at the *Chronicle* was devoted to editing the plays of Shakespeare. 'I wish to cut myself adrift from my other uncongenial drudgery and devote my time and attention more to this one purpose', he wrote to Devonshire,[19] but he could not afford to give up his livelihood, and he therefore had to work fifteen hours a day: for Shakespeare from dawn until noon and for Easthope from noon until late at night. Despite poor health, he continued this regimen for five years. Only someone driven by extraordinary ambition could have done so.

Editing Shakespeare in the mid-nineteenth century was professionally frustrating. The plays had been so worked and reworked, so vigorously threshed and gleaned by eighteenth-century editors, that it seemed futile to hope that anything new or valuable could still be written about them. Moreover, the critical groundwork laid by Collier's predecessors was shaky at best and often treacherous. There was much to lose and little to gain in the undertaking. It is difficult to understand Collier's editorial purpose, to appreciate the difficulties he encountered, or to judge the quality of his achievement without knowing something of the history of the transmission – and transmutation – of Shakespeare's text in the previous century and a half.

'Editing' Shakespeare was an eighteenth-century innovation, a response to the desire for a better text than the seventeenth-century printers had produced. The First Folio was prepared seven years after Shakespeare's death by John Heminge and Henry Condell, actor-proprietors of Shakespeare's company, in 1623, and although they did not 'edit' the plays in any modern sense of that word, the book they produced was a great success. The First Folio led to a second in 1632, a third in 1663, and a fourth in 1685, each printed from the text of its predecessor. By standards then prevailing, the text of the First Folio was good, but it contained hundreds of misprints that were repeated and compounded in subsequent folios, and as a result, the Fourth Folio text was clogged with accumulated errors. In the first decade of the eighteenth century, it was decided that these faults should be removed, and the Shakespeare Editor was born.

Nicholas Rowe, the man who first took the role, was a poet, translator and playwright, but the editorial problem which confronted him was overwhelming. In the first place, none of Shakespeare's manuscripts survived, and the copy texts from which the early editions were set were lost or destroyed. This lacuna would have been less significant if Shakespeare, like Ben Jonson, had himself published his works, but there is no proof that he had a hand in – or even approved of – any of the various quarto editions of his plays which appeared in his lifetime. Without auctorial manuscripts or authorized printed versions, the job of editing Shakespeare has been extremely difficult. Rowe's response to this problem was straightforward but naive:

I must not pretend to have restor'd this Work to the Exactness of the Author's Original Manuscripts: [he declared] those are lost, or, at least, are gone beyond any Inquiry I could make; so that there was nothing left, but to compare the several Editions, and give the true Reading as well as I could from thence.[20]

In practice, this process was more difficult than Rowe's words imply. What were the 'several Editions'? How were they to be 'compared'? And how could Rowe determine the 'true Reading . . . from thence'? As the first man on the job, Rowe's opportunities were overshadowed by the handicap of having to invent complicated editorial procedures on his own. He did 'as well as he could' and he corrected some of the obvious errors in the folio text, but he ignored many others and created hundreds of new corruptions in flagrant attempts at 'improvement'.

Rowe's most serious blunder was in restricting his comparison to the folio editions of the plays and, except in very rare instances, ignoring the quarto texts. He compounded this error by starting his work with the Fourth Folio, the last and most corrupt of the seventeenth-century versions. His choice of the last folio was probably one of convenience rather than conscious selection, but deliberate or not, it implied that the 'true' test was to be determined by the editor's preference rather than the author's intention. At least nineteen[21] of the thirty-six plays of the First Folio were published in quarto editions before 1623, and some of these versions differ significantly from the folio text. It is obvious that when more than one version of a play exists, an editor must choose between the alternatives. To be ignorant of the choice and to accept the folio reading by default, as Rowe did, is nonetheless a 'choice' – and a bad one. His method – or rather the lack of it – has been almost universally condemned. In the words of one of his successors, he 'neither received much praise, nor seems to have expected it'.[22]

The editors who followed Rowe faced up to the quarto-folio problem, but they did not solve it. In 1723, Alexander Pope declared the quartos were, with one or two exceptions, Shakespeare's 'original' versions, and hence of prime authority; ten years later, Lewis Theobald argued for the folio. The quartos, Theobald declared, were pirated, 'taken down in Shorthand, and imperfectly copied by Ear, from a Representation' or 'printed from piece-meal Parts surreptitiously obtain'd, from the Theatres, uncorrect, and without the Poet's Knowledge'.[23] They were, therefore, not to be trusted, whereas the folio, although frequently obscure, had the authority of the theatre manuscripts from which, Theobald assumed, it was derived. Pope and Theobald rather neatly illustrated the two editorial alternatives – rather too neatly, perhaps, since theory is one thing whereas in Shakespeare scholarship practice is often another. The announced intentions of Pope and Theobald were sharply opposed, but their procedures did

not differ very much at all: in practice, Pope did not begin
with the quarto texts but, like Rowe before him, with the
Fourth Folio – or rather, Rowe's version of the Fourth
Folio – and when he diverged from that text, he showed no
clear preference for the quartos. Theobald was more consistent in keeping to his announced preference for the folio, but
he too repeated Rowe's error in taking the corrupt Fourth
Folio as his base text – or rather, Pope's version of Rowe's
version of the Fourth Folio – and although he did not often
defer to the quartos, he regularly changed the folio reading for
new emendations of his own.

With such ambiguous precedents, it is no surprise that the
successors of Pope and Theobald were uncertain and inconsistent. Like Pope, most would declare in principle the authority
of the quartos, but like Theobald, most in practice would
follow the folio and emend it with abandon. For example, in
1766, George Steevens published all the extant Shakespeare
quartos which, he declared, 'preserved' Shakespeare's 'first
thoughts' and provided the most correct versions of the plays
they represented. However, when Steevens edited his edition
of all the plays in 1773, he regularly ignored the language of
the quartos and printed the folio text or his own 'corrections'
with no apparent justification other than personal preference.
An even more remarkable example of this ambivalence was
Edward Capell, perhaps the most discriminating of the
eighteenth-century editors, who published an edition in 1768
in which, he announced, he 'adhered to' thirteen quarto texts,
most significantly the 1604 quarto of *Hamlet,* which he judged
to be more authoritative than their folio counterparts. Capell
supported his judgement by publishing the first collation of
textual variants in all the early copies – a remarkable innovation. But despite his care and declared intention, Capell
frequently and silently chose the folio over the quartos – even
in the case of *Hamlet.* These glaring inconsistencies do not
mean that Pope and Theobald or Steevens and Capell were
liars or incompetents but merely that throughout the eighteenth and most of the nineteenth century the question of
auctorial intention was qualified – and frequently displaced –
by editorial 'taste'. In theory the quarto texts were 'authoritative', in practice they were often ignored. The result was an

eclectic text, part-quarto, part-folio, with no clear editorial rationale for the mixture.

The early editors altered the text even when the quarto and folio agreed. For all their avowed respect for the early printed versions, whenever they spied an 'error' in the text which they thought they could 'correct', they did so without hesitation and frequently without good reason. The rationale governing emendation was therefore another problem confronting the early editors. What constituted an 'error' in the text and what criteria should control its 'correction'? Pope freely emended passages which were intelligible but offensive to his personal taste; for Pope the quality of an edition derived not from textual fidelity to the old copies but from the poetic sensibilities of the editor in replacing the often obscure and uneven brick walks of the early texts with marble passages of his own. Theobald was quick to denounce Pope for his interpolations, declaring that his predecessor had butchered Shakespeare ('He has attacked him like an unhandy Slaughterman; and not lopp'd off the *Errors* but the *Poet*').[24] But Theobald's own practice was hardly less destructive and much more fervid. For him, the editor's sole purpose was to 'restore sense' to the text; residual obscurity was a mark of failure. 'Wherever [an editor] finds the Reading suspected, manifestly corrupted, deficient in Sense and unintelligible,' Theobald declared, 'he ought to exert every Power and Faculty of the Mind to supply such a Defect, to give Light and restore Sense to the Passage, and, by a reasonable emendation, to make that satisfactory and consistent with the Context, which before was so absurd, unintelligible, and intricate.'[25] As Pope was arbitrary in defining 'taste', so Theobald was arbitrary in defining 'sense'. His theoretical objective was admirable, but his threshold of non-sense and unintelligibility was apparently very low. He had misgivings about the provenance of *both* the quartos and the folio, and this encouraged his tendency to find confusion or nonsense, whch he took to be the results of errors of transmission, in passages which others thought intelligible as they stood.

To satisfy his predilection for change, Theobald was the first editor to use the 'secondary sources' which a growing number of Shakespeare enthusiasts had been collecting and creating. His knowledge of Shakespeare's contemporaries was phenomenal (he claimed to have read over eight hundred early plays in preparing the glossary of obsolete or unusual words which accompanied his edition) and he used the suggestions of other scholars as well. There were, for example, many copies of the old folios with manuscript notes which imaginative readers had written in their margins, and the absence of author's manuscripts gave an importance to this sort of 'collateral evidence' which it otherwise would not have had. Perhaps the most famous of all Shakespeare emendations, Theobald's alteration of Mistress Quickly's description of the dying Falstaff (*Henry V,* II, iii) from 'a Table of Greenfields' to ''a babbled of green fields', was derived from a manuscript note in the margin of an old copy.[26] After Theobald, all eighteenth-century editors used emended folios and many of the corrections they found were inserted into the text.

The core of the problem was the lack of agreed criteria for identifying and correcting 'errors'. The belief that the First Folio was botched by ignorant printers was to become an editorial shibboleth: the worse the received text, the more justified arbitrary emendations became. In Capell's words, 'the bad printing of the folio made it proper and necessary to look into the other old editions, and to *select* from thence whatever *improves* the Author. . . . that they do improve him, was with the editor an argument in their favour; and a presumption of genuineness . . . [emphasis added]'.[27] This view was common throughout the eighteenth and well into the nineteenth century: the editor's purpose was to 'improve' the text of Shakespeare – sometimes the word was 'restore' – and the presumed aesthetic value of an emendation was proof of its legitimacy. From this point it was an easy step to argue, as for example Steevens did, that the Second Folio was frequently to be preferred to the first because it contained variants which are qualitatively 'better' than its predecessor; and the final step was only slightly more difficult: to argue that any emendation that seemed to 'improve' the text – whether the original was comprehensible or not – had 'authority'. In short, if the text could be made 'better', it ought to be, for Shakespeare must have intended it so and to make the change was to 'restore' his intention. In various guises, this was the dominant attitude until Collier's edition.

Rivalry and the penchant for innovation frequently swamped editorial discretion and logical method. The absence of manuscript authority coupled with rudimentary bibliographical methods turned emendations into mere conjecture; there was no way to distinguish idiosyncratic preference from scholarly reconstruction, or *amour propre* from historical fact. As a result, the competition among editors of Shakespeare was often intense and personal, vituperative and irreconcilable, the start of a tradition of critical querulousness which was to continue among Collier's contemporaries and on into our own day. The celebrated quarrel between Pope and Theobald which culminated in Pope's brilliant – and unjust – characterization of his competitor in *The Dunciad* was only the first of many bitter feuds which have been waged over minutiae. In 1747, William Warburton, Theobald's successor, produced an edition in which he went out of his way to insult his former colleague, and so it was to continue. It was as though the only way an editor could justify a new edition of the plays was to accuse his predecessors of stupidity and misfeasance – or worse. Edward Capell was the first editor to decry this professional competition; he chided Pope and Theobald for their public quarrel, but the contagion was so pervasive that, having identified the disease, Capell himself became its victim by reviling *his* predecessor, Hanmer, whose edition, he declared, 'excites an indignation that will be thought by some to vent itself too strongly; but terms weaker would do injustice to my feelings . . .'.[28] Perhaps the most insidious quarrel was that between George Steevens and Edmond Malone, the last important editors before Collier, close friends and collaborators who became bitter antagonists. Their quarrel was as tawdry as that of Warburton and Theobald and as vindictive as that of Theobald and Pope, but it was more vicious than either because it was carried out in secrecy and, on Steevens's part, with occasional treachery: Steevens, sometimes called the Puck of Commentators, went so far as to plant misinformation in Malone's path in order to mislead him into making judgements which Steevens would then disprove.[29]

Steevens and Malone were part of the 'third generation' of

Shakespeare critics. Over half a century had passed since Rowe's edition, and in the ensuing years the emphasis of Shakespeare scholarship had shifted slightly: Capell's collation of the early texts was a culmination of the concern with textual verification through comparison. Hereafter editors would continue to make nice distinctions between quarto and folio readings and to emend 'errors' with conjectural alternatives, but there was a growing interest in the historical circumstances of Shakespeare's composition and early theatre practices. The 1780 *Supplement* to Steevens and Johnson's *Shakespeare* (1778) marked the beginning of a special interest in dating Shakespeare's plays and in discovering details of his biography. Steevens's contribution was a pioneering interest in his sources and contemporary analogues to his plays. Between them, Malone and Steevens were the first to suggest reconstructing Shakespeare's text by using contemporary analogy and historical-biographical data, and their discoveries were to direct Shakespeare scholarship for the next fifty years – until Collier's time and after.

8

In the context of its eighteenth-century predecessors, Collier's edition of Shakespeare has an importance which might otherwise be overlooked. His career paralleled the development of methodology in literary study: the perspectives that emerged with Malone were beginning to lead to new standards of textual documentation, and Collier's edition can be seen as the first based, however intermittently, on recognizably 'modern' criteria. It was not a revolutionary work, but it illustrates a redirected editorial practice. As the Malone–Boswell edition of 1821 (the so-called Third Variorum) was the culmination of eighteenth-century procedure, so Collier's edition twenty years later was the first to demonstrate a new editorial taste.

Collier's treatment of the early printed texts is illustrative: when he began work on his edition, the prevailing critical opinion of the quartos and folio editions was still that of Capell and Malone. In 1845, the Revd. Joseph Hunter summarized this consensus: the early texts could not be

trusted. 'There never were books more carelessly superintended through the press', he wrote. 'The first and most
important duty of an editor is to take care that there is not
palmed upon us something as Shakespeare's which he would
have disdained to write, or something which, though not
absolutely unintelligible and bad, is yet not so good as that
which he had actually written. An editor ought to regard
himself as the protector of our poetical inheritance.'[30]

This was essentially a restatement of Capell's assertion of
the fallibility of the First Folio and the editorial 'responsibility' to 'improve' the text, or, in Hunter's new terminology, to
'protect' the poetical inheritance from the ravages of careless
early printers. Whether the editorial intention was to 'improve' or to 'protect', the effect on the text was the same.

Collier's edition was based on the opposite opinion. 'The
First Folio', he declared in his prospectus, 'is more correctly
printed than any other dramatic production of the time, with
the exception perhaps of the folio edition of Ben Jonson's
Works in 1616. . . . Let anybody compare the typographical
execution of the folio of 1623 with that of any plays printed or
reprinted between the years 1600 and 1630, and they will be
aware of the laudable pains that must have been bestowed
upon it.'[31] None of Collier's predecessors had made that
comparison, but Collier's knowledge of early seventeenth-
century texts was unsurpassed. Moreover, as a newspaper man
he knew the techniques of printing which had changed little
since Shakespeare's day; he was the first Shakespeare editor to
relate textual problems to printing procedures from which
many of them derived. He respected the skill of early
compositors and studied the typographical features of the
quarto and folio copies which he assumed were more likely to
be accurate transcriptions of authoritative manuscripts than
the errors of ignorant typesetters. This respect for the printing
idiosyncrasies of the early editions has become a tenet of
modern scholarship and Collier was the first to declare it
without qualification. He was not blind to the faults of the
early copies but he felt constrained to follow them unless there
was an overriding necessity – obvious error or complete
unintelligibility, for example – to emend. 'It is not the
province of an editor to attempt to *improve* Shakespeare', he

declared. Others had said this before him, of course, but Collier was the first to follow its implications in practice as well as in theory, and as a result, his edition was a dramatic return to the texts of the early quartos and the First Folio. He paid careful attention to the spelling, punctuation and typographical variations that most former editors had ignored or altered. Previous editions had 'regularized' the versification of the Folio, for example, but Collier was meticulous in maintaining the metre of the early printed copies, believing 'that many passages, now considered defective, were purposely left so by the poet.'[32]

Collier's answer to the 'problem of the quartos' was characteristic. As we have seen, editors since Pope had granted the authority of the quartos, but used them as points of departure apparently uncertain as to how they could be reconciled to the folio versions. Collier recognized that, despite the implications of their collection in the First Folio, the plays were not a single corpus but an accumulation of diverse individual works, that each play had an individual provenance, a textual history of its own. Other editors, notably Capell, had suggested this obvious fact, but Collier was the first to trace the progression of each play by 'minute and patient accuracy of comparison of the old copies, quarto and folio' and to base his text on the result. This, he declared, was 'indispensable'[33] and his scrutiny of the quartos was more searching than that of any of his predecessors. No editor had been able to use as many quartos as Collier had at his disposal. He was able to use all the early copies of his eminent predecessors: most of Steevens's copies were in the British Museum, Malone had bequeathed his collection to the Bodleian Library at Oxford, and Capell's collection was at Trinity College, Cambridge. Collier used them all, and in addition to these, he had the two magnificent collections of Devonshire and Ellesmere which contained quartos Steevens, Malone and Capell did not know. Of the forty-one pre-1623 quartos of Shakespeare's plays which were known to be extant in 1841, Collier had the unlimited use of twenty-nine in the collections of his patrons. Of all the quartos known to have been published in Shakespeare's lifetime, Collier lacked only one of significance, *Much Ado About Nothing* (1600). All the rest were available to him including the unique *Hamlet* (1603), which had been discovered in 1825, and subsequently purchased by Devonshire.

The Devonshire and Ellesmere quartos duplicated one another slightly, and this proved to be an unexpected boon. Since Rowe, editors has assumed that all copies of a given quarto were identical, but no one had had the opportunity (or taken the trouble) to test this assumption. Collier did. In collating the duplications between the Ellesmere and Devonshire collections, he discovered substantive textual variants in two quartos (*Love's Labour's Lost* and *The Merchant of Venice*) which he concluded derived from 'stop press corrections' – that is, editorial changes made in the type after printing had commenced. Collier believed that these suggested copyediting and possible 'auctorial' correction. At the very least, they showed a greater care in quarto publication than had been previously supposed. Following this lead, Collier collated copies of the First Folio and discovered substantive variants in that text as well,[34] and subsequently he found similar differences in copies of the early editions of Shakespeare's poems.[35]

In pursuing this line of research, Collier revealed a 'modern' understanding of the connection between printing and textual emendation. He even presaged twentieth-century bibliographers in suggesting that the idiosyncrasies of otherwise unknown compositors might alter the text in predictable ways.[36] He did not pursue the implications of his discovery and his conclusions were therefore rudimentary, but his insights were brilliantly suggestive. Although some of his contemporaries scorned his interest[37] twentieth-century scholars have pursued similar lines to remarkable discoveries.

Collier's respect for the early printed texts encouraged a concomitant distaste for the emendations of his predecessors. His text was very conservative – virtually a return to the original editions. He discarded scores of emendations, many of which had been accepted by several generations of scholars, and rigorously reinstated the text of the early printed texts. He was not slavish in his adherence to the old copies; when a traditional emendation restored sense to an otherwise unintelligible passage he retained it, but such instances were relatively few. The effect was salutary but shocking to readers who had long accepted the effusions of Rowe, Pope, Theobald, Capell, Hamner, Steevens, Malone *et al.* as Shakespeare's own.

His treatment of *Hamlet* is illustrative. There are three different early texts of the play: the 'bad' first quarto of 1603, the 'good' second quarto of 1604 and the First Folio text of 1623. Collier was the first editor to sort out the relationships among these texts and to describe what has become the prevailing modern view of them, that despite their differences, all were derived from a single play; that Q^1 had no textual authority and was derived from a memorial reconstruction, possibly taken from actors, which may have been supplemented with shorthand copies; that Q^2, the most complete version, was closest to Shakespeare's original text, 'at least as authentic a copy ... as any of Shakespeare's plays that came from the press in his lifetime'; and that the folio version was printed either from some 'unknown quarto' or a 'manuscript obtained by Heminge and Condell from the theatre' which had been shortened for performance. As a result, Collier based his text of *Hamlet* on Q^2 and he adhered to that text more closely than any of his predecessors – even more closely than Capell (who had announced the Q^2 as his base text and then proceeded to ignore many of its readings).[38] It is commonly supposed that the distinction between the 'good' and 'bad' Shakespeare quartos was a twentieth-century discovery; actually it was described by Collier in 1842.

Collier's textual notes broke with tradition, too. He omitted virtually all reference to analogues from Shakespeare's contemporaries with which five editorial generations had encumbered the text. His descriptive comments were brief and generally modest, and similarly the introduction with which he prefaced each play was short (rarely more than three pages), factual and succinct, with little of the display of self-gratifying pedantry that had cluttered earlier editions.

Collier restricted his historical compendia to Volume I (the last published) in which he presented a history of the stage to the time of Shakespeare founded largely on his own *History of English Dramatic Poetry* of a decade before. In addition, he included the obligatory *Life of Shakespeare* which was essentially an amalgam of documents he had previously published either in his own pamphlets (in particular, *New Facts*) or those he had produced for the Shakespeare Society (notably the *Memoirs of Edward Alleyn*), and he drew on his research in editing *Henslowe's Diary* which was to appear shortly after his Shakespeare was completed. He had some satisfaction in this task of bringing together isolated details of Shakespeare's life and period that had hitherto been published only in unrelated and fragmentary form, and he added new manuscript information from various collections that bore directly on Shakespeare's career and the chronology of his plays.

It would be a gross error to suggest that the result of Collier's labour was, as one reviewer suggested, 'a Shakespeare approaching as nearly to perfection as his text is capable of being brought by the mere exertion of skill and labour in collation of old copies.'[39] It wasn't, and later editions following the same lines made it obsolete, which was and is the pattern in scholarly publication. What is significant is the methodology he employed (subtly belittled even in favourable reviews like the one just quoted), which was perhaps the first coherent example of modern scholarship in Shakespeare textual criticism. This is not to argue that he 'fathered' modern critical method (no one man did that), but rather to reassert a fact often ignored in our enthusiasm for the brilliant textual critics of the present century: that the so-called 'modern bibliographical method' was not a creation of the twentieth century but the result of discoveries and innovation of the nineteenth. If the subsequent attack on Collier had not occurred, he might have been recognized as the first editor to perceive, however dimly, the lines of modern bibliographic method. He was fallible and often inconsistent, but he carried on his work with great care and discrimination. 'My endeavour has been', he wrote to Robinson shortly after the first two volumes appeared, '... to take as little as I can to or upon myself. Nobody can do me justice for the labour and pains I bestow upon the text: few know what it was, and fewer what I have made it. ... However, all this I care not much about, as in due time [credit] will come of itself and unsought and in the meantime I strive to produce a good book.'[40]

9

Collier's Shakespeare prospectus, *Reasons for a New Edition of Shakespeare*, quickly went through two printings and created high expectations. Charles Dickens wrote to Collier immediately after reading the pamphlet that he thought it made 'a good case' and he was eager for the new text – 'although', he declared, 'I am the proprietor of a Boswell's Malone.'[41] Robinson, who had a limited appetite for purely 'literary' facts even when fished up by his friends, proclaimed the prospectus to be 'sensible'. The first volume was published on schedule in February 1842, the second in April, and the succeeding six at regular intervals until April 1844. They sold well, but Collier's payment was fixed, and the success of the venture added to his reputation rather than his income.

Meanwhile, Collier continued his arduous work on the *Chronicle*, his chief means of support. His salary from the paper had been reduced by half and his editorial authority to almost nothing. He had become essentially a clerk, coping with the daily grind of assembling the middle pages of the paper, of dunning better paid writers – among them Dickens – for late reviews and sketches, and when they did not respond on time of turning out hack replacements of his own. And once again he was forced to take his turn in the Reporters' Gallery.

His two occupations created constant conflict: his scholarly editing was actively discouraged by Easthope and Black, who believed it reduced the *Chronicle*'s claim on him, and his newspaper livelihood was scorned by his literary friends, men of private means and insufferable snobbery. He 'passed' among them as their peer, but he was always vulnerable to gratuitous insult. Robinson records that one evening at the Society of Antiquaries, after Collier had 'talked well without pretence or effort', he was casually insulted by John Bruce, his close associate in the Shakespeare Society, who referred to newspaper writers as 'enemies of the human race'. It was an insult, Robinson noted with characteristic understatement, 'which Collier seemed to feel',[42] and only one of many.

Still he kept it up, meeting the daily bouts at the *Chronicle*, editing with care and on schedule, and – incredible though it seems – directing publication for three societies[43] and preparing some of the texts, notably *Henslowe's Diary,* himself. Not incidentally, he continued to be librarian for the Duke of Devonshire, making purchases and answering queries about the Devonshire collection.

While he struggled, Collier had no relief from family worries. As usual, his financial need was great. His fee from Whittaker was to be paid in full only when the Shakespeare edition was complete, and his reduced newspaper salary demanded new economies. He moved once again, this time to a more distant and less expensive house in Victoria Road, Kensington. His wife was again ill and bedridden, and his brother-in-law Robert Proctor, perhaps his closest family confidant, suffered a series of catastrophes in his once profitable London dairy which ultimately forced him to give it up, leave London and move to Bray near Maidenhead, Berkshire. Under this stress, Collier's own health faltered. The quinsy which he had suffered since childhood returned with new severity, and at times his throat became so swollen he had to force a passage through it to keep from suffocating. The pain was excruciating, but he was unable to stop work. And so he continued, with few complaints, striving to 'make a good book' of his Shakespeare.

In the opinion of most of the public, he succeeded. Despite a high price (£4.16*s*), the edition sold well, singly and as a set, and quickly became the standard text, a position it held for over a decade. However, the jealousy that had marked Shakespeare criticism from the beginning flared up again, and some of the attacks against Collier were unexpectedly acrimonious. The first came almost casually from the Revd. Joseph Hunter, whose comments on 'protecting' Shakespeare's words were quoted earlier. Hunter, six years older than Collier, was a man for whom Collier had great respect – *Farther Particulars* had, in fact, been addressed to him. He had been a Presbyterian minister at Bath for a quarter of a century before his interest in searching out historical facts and artifacts brought him to London as a commissioner in the Public Records Office, to which he was named Assistant Keeper in 1838. Although most of his antiquarian interest concerned church and county history, he had followed many by-ways. (One of his better known books was entitled *Golden*

Sentences. A Manual that May be Used by All who Desire to be Moral and Religious, 1826. Hunter prided himself on being both.) Along the way he had developed a great interest in Shakespeare, and in 1839 he published a 'disquisition' on *The Tempest* which attempted to prove, among other things, that Prospero's island was really Lampedusa and that the play was one of Shakespeare's first rather than one of his last. This view was generally ignored, and Hunter's lack of success may have exacerbated his jealousy of Collier's increasing reputation. What particularly annoyed Hunter was Collier's coup in unearthing several important manuscripts, notably the Man-ningham Diary and the Forman *Bocke of Plaies*. (See pp. 44, 61 above.) These unique eye-witness accounts of contemporary performances of Shakespeare's plays were great discoveries. Half a dozen years after Collier published them, Hunter suddenly declared that he had used the manuscripts long before Collier. This assertion was quickly discounted, along with Hunter's opinions about *The Tempest*; rebuffed, he devoted himself to writing yet another defence of his opinions, *New Illustrations of . . . Shakespeare*, intended to be the last word on the playwright and his plays, and in Hunter's words, 'supplementary to all editions'.

Hunter's chief interest lay in the details of Shakespeare's life and in the defence of his interpretation of *The Tempest*. Thus, when Collier's last volume (containing both his text of the play and Shakespeare's biography) was about to come from the press, Hunter was warmed once again by the heat of competition. Although his book was not yet finished, he published the completed biographical section as a pamphlet (*The First Part of New Illustrations . . . of Shakespeare*),[44] which appeared simultaneously with Collier's edition.

Hunter's pamphlet was, in fact, deferential to Collier and complementary to his early works. He wrote, for example, that Collier's edition of *Shakespeare's Library* 'ought to accompany every edition of these plays', and he called the *Poetical Decameron* 'a work abounding in valuable information'. He even praised Collier's *Shakespeare*, calling it an 'elegant edition'.[45] But he reasserted his prior knowledge of Collier's discoveries, and in addition propounded, at some length, a genealogical tree which rescued the poet from the line of

Richard Shakespeare whom he called 'a tenant farmer at Snitterfield near Stratford' and placed him safely among the monied heirs of 'Richard Shakspar of Wroxhall'.

Hunter's claims to prior knowledge were ignored by reviewers and his arguments for Shakespeare's gentle birth were left moot. In that respect his pamphlet was unsuccessful, but it got wide notice because of incidental comments he made concerning documents Collier had published years before in *New Facts*. Hunter believed four of these were 'modern fabrications'. It will be recalled (see pp. 59–60 above) that Collier claimed to have found these now-disputed manuscripts among the papers of Sir Thomas Egerton, afterward Master of the Rolls to Elizabeth I and still later Lord Chancellor to James I. They were among hundreds he had printed from the Bridgewater Collection, and none had been questioned heretofore. Except for the petition to the Privy Council, which listed Shakespeare as an actor and shareholder at Blackfriars in 1589, a date earlier than had been previously assumed, these documents were of no great intrinsic importance, but merely supported generally accepted facts of Shakespeare's life. But any suggestion of 'fabrication' in a collection as important as the Bridgewater library was cause for alarm. Moreover, Hunter said he had been refused permission to see the originals, and the implication was that Collier had requested Ellesmere to sequester the manuscripts because they were doubtful.

It was a strange charge. In the eight years since the papers had been published, Hunter had neither publicly questioned their authenticity nor pressed to see them. He raised his question only after the conspicuous failure of his disquisition on *The Tempest* and the appearance of Collier's *Shakespeare*. Of course, Hunter hastened to absolve Collier of any implications of wrong doing: 'No one who knows Mr. Collier', he wrote, 'can for a moment doubt that they were found by him there; the question only is, *How came they there?*' His own conjecture was that they were deliberately planted by George Steevens to catch an unwary scholar. Steevens, dead forty years, had been a notoriously quixotic man, Hunter claimed, who 'in the perversity of his humour, was accustomed to abuse the enthusiasm of his Shakespearian friends, and to perplex the judgement of the more knowing. I speak with as much confidence as a person ought to do who depends solely on memory (for my note, if one was ever made, is lost), when I say that I have somewhere seen that Steevens had access to the Egerton Papers.'[46]

These animadversions about the Bridgewater manuscripts became a subject of gossip. At first Hunter was singularly deferential to Collier and claiming only greater knowledge as an historiographer, but among their mutual friends the controversy was provocative and disagreeable. In his diary, Robinson noted that Hunter 'imputed nothing to Collier' but Robinson was puzzled as to why Hunter was not allowed to see the bundle of manuscripts. 'Why Collier did not procure a sight of it I cannot guess. He must take notice of this charge now and I fear it will lead to an unpleasantness between them.' Nevertheless, Collier ignored Hunter's book and this, in Robinson's eyes, showed 'a want of confidence or a want of candour'.[47] Collier probably lacked both, but he also knew that defending questionable documents could only draw him into a morass of unprofitable competition. He could not have been happy at the thought that documents he had accepted so wholeheartedly and reprinted in the comprehensive biography of his edition were fabrications, but he remained silent.

Hunter's charge seemed to have little effect on the public. The response of a review in the *Gentleman's Magazine* was typical: after discussing the 1589 document citing Shakespeare as a part owner in Blackfriars it declared that Hunter's case was unconvincing. 'His objections, are not in our opinion, sufficient to invalidate it.'[48] This public response deeply embittered Hunter.

Significantly, when Hunter later examined the manuscripts he had condemned, he privately reconsidered his judgement: Ellesmere wrote to Collier that Hunter's original doubts were removed by comparing them with others of a similar date.[49] But Hunter never publicly admitted to having examined the papers or to changing his mind, and when he brought out his *New Illustrations* a year or so later, he omitted the reference to being denied access but reiterated his disbelief. By the time his book appeared, the controversy had so angered him that he would allow no deference to Collier's view. The tone of his remarks had become decidedly personal and led to a full scale attack on Collier's *Shakespeare* on 'textual' grounds:

Mr Collier cannot have been a long and critical student in these writings. . . . It is to be hoped that this edition will not be taken, either as to text or illustration, as an exhibition of the state of Shakespearian knowledge in the reign of Her Majesty Queen Victoria, although the circumstance of Mr Collier being the Director of the Shakespeare Society, in which so many respectable names are found, may seem to give it that degree of consequence.[50]

Hunter's assault on Collier's work was more irritating than damaging, but a more serious attack, one particularly distressing to Collier because it was motivated by personal animus, came from a man whom he had considered a good friend. In May 1844, a little over a month after Collier's edition was completed, Alexander Dyce published his *Remarks on Mr. J. P. Collier's and Mr. C. Knight's Editions of Shakespeare,* a scathing critique of Collier and, to a lesser degree, of Knight (whose 'Pictorial Shakespeare' of several years before was reissued in a cheap edition about the same time that Collier's last volume appeared). Heretofore the rivalry between Dyce and Collier, while keen, had been without acrimony. They were close associates: together they had founded the Shakespeare Society and co-operated in publishing its tracts. For over a decade they had given one another continuous editorial assistance – their correspondence was full of bibliographical questions asked and answered and each had publicly acknowledged his debt to the other: Collier's pamphlet *New Particulars* had been addressed to Dyce, and in 1840 Dyce had dedicated his five-volume edition of Middleton to Collier; one of the first copies of Collier's Shakespeare prospectus had been sent to Dyce, and one of the half dozen 'large paper' editions of his *Shakespeare* (which he had had printed at his own large expense) was presented to his 'good friend, Alexander Dyce'. In the light of this association, Collier was astonished by Dyce's attack.

He ought not to have been. In so far as their common interest led to personal association, it had been, for Dyce, a source of disaffection. Collier perhaps pushed himself too hard, and Dyce was annoyed when Collier assumed intimacy between them. Collier for his part refused to be patronized by one he considered his intellectual peer, and he was, apparently, oblivious to Dyce's irritation. He frequently invited Dyce to casual dinners: 'Come if you like (us or boiled beef)', he might write, and Dyce, annoyed at the presumption, seldom responded in kind. If Collier needled him ('Observe the address', Collier wrote on the bottom of one letter. 'You may have forgotten it.'[51]), Dyce became stiff. He did not wish to become the close friend of a man he privately disdained, a Fleet Street scribbler below his own social class. In his eyes their friendship was too one-sided and Collier too eager to maintain it.

Dyce's attack was presaged by a cryptic note acknowledging the gift of Collier's *Shakespeare*. 'Many thanks,' Dyce had written, 'for the concluding volume of a work which I wish most heartily that you never had begun. Yours always, A.Dyce.'[52] This insult was followed by a book which characterized his friend's work as 'prodigious absurdity' (79), 'beyond measure injudicious' (99), and 'piteous' (158). The book must have taken Dyce several months to prepare and compose, yet it appeared almost immediately after Collier's last volume was published; for several months he had nurtured his intention in secret and maintained a façade of friendship until he was ready to strike. Collier had worked with energy and care over his text for four years, seeking Dyce's opinion and assistance (as he concurrently helped Dyce in the latter's edition of Beaumont and Fletcher), and now, virtually without warning, the irascible Scot published a scornful critique. In his preface Dyce sneered at 'those who have thought themselves competent to become [Shakespeare's] editors' and he dedicated the book to the Revd. John Mitford who, he said, 'will read it with a conviction that it originated in pure love to Shakespeare'.[53] If Mitford had such a conviction, he was the only reader in England who did.

Dyce's motivation was professional jealousy. He had intended to edit Shakespeare himself, and the success of Collier's edition made his own less likely. Moreover, he was angered by the way Collier had ruthlessly excised eighteenth-century emendations and reinstated the original quarto and folio readings. Dyce strongly condemned the early printed

texts and generally preferred the 'improvements' of eighteenth-century editors. In almost every passage that Dyce
singled out for sarcasm, Collier had removed an early editor's
emendation and reinstated a quarto or folio reading. Dyce's
book was, therefore, an attempt to justify the old order of
editorial conjecture which Collier had repudiated. When
Collier noted that a folio reading in *Much Ado About Nothing*
was 'probably right' in substituting 'dumb' for the quarto
reading 'dead', Dyce was contemptuous: '"Probably right!"'
he wrote. 'Why even if *all* the old eds. had "dead", the rhyme
would be sufficient to prove that Shakespeare must have
written "dumb"' (p. 34). 'Did Mr. Collier really believe that
"sounded" could be used in the sense of "having, or giving
forth, a sound"?' he asked sardonically about a note on *A
Midsummer Night's Dream* (p. 49). 'If Mr. Collier had wished to
prove beyond all possibility of dispute that the reading which
he gives is the wrong one', he remarked about a line in *All's
Well That Ends Well,* 'he could not have done so more
effectually ...' (p. 71). 'Had Mr. Collier really *read* this speech,
when he sent his note to press?' he asked about a passage in
Macbeth (p. 200), and so on. Even in those few instances in
which Dyce *agreed* with Collier he did so in a patronizing
manner, and he seldom missed a chance to display what he
thought was his own greater learning ('Mr. Collier, who has
taken the trouble to chronicle a great many wretched
conjectures, does not even mention Theobald's emendation of
the present passage ...', p. 167). 'What can Mr. Collier mean by
"laudanum him" coming nearest to the sound?' he said in comment on a Collier note to *The Winter's Tale.* 'Those critics who
have been the most successful in conjectural emendation were
never guided by similarity of sound, but solely by the *ductus
literarum*' (p. 81). (Collier, more aware, perhaps, of the way
phonic differences might have altered the printed text would
disagree, as would many modern editors, but in any case
Collier was not in this instance suggesting a new emendation
but discarding an earlier one.) And while there is some truth
in Dyce's charge that 'Mr. Collier has read our early dramatic
literature rather as a searcher after facts than as a philologist'
(p.206), the criticism could have been applied to virtually all
Collier's contemporaries, Dyce chief among them. Dyce's

Remarks did not detract from the reception of Collier's Shakespeare. In fact, the critique was summarily dismissed – 'three hundred pages of additional trifling', the *Athenaeum* called it, declaring that its chief virtue lay in its being published 'apart from Shakespeare's works' to be 'squeezed' by those who have leisure, and then thrown into the fire.[54]

But if Dyce's comments did not succeed in provoking a reaction against Collier, they delighted a few who, for various personal reasons, were happy to see Collier attacked. Hunter, irritated by the even weaker reception of his own pamphlet, took some comfort from Dyce's words, which encouraged him to treat Collier with more severity himself. It was a strange union; neither had a very high opinion of the other's work. They were joined solely in opposition to Collier and for contrasting reasons: Hunter's quarrel with Collier was over the facts of Shakespeare's life and career and he initially praised the text, whereas Dyce condemned the text and applauded, however weakly, Collier's 'Life' and 'History of the Stage'. Nevertheless, something resembling a cabal formed among the close friends of Hunter and Dyce and, to his great discomfort, Robinson was sometimes on its fringe.

These and other competitors who were editing or making plans to edit new texts of their own found it difficult to applaud Collier's achievement, but others with less personal bias respected it.[55] Collier believed, rightly as it turned out, that his critics would be discounted in the end and that his edition would prevail on its own merits. Neither Dyce's nor Hunter's attacks provoked him to defend his editorial integrity, and he even superintended Dyce's edition of *Sir Thomas More* through the press for the Shakespeare Society in the spring of 1845. His position as the ranking editor of Shakespeare gave him new professional esteem, and he ignored his accuser, which rankled Dyce still more. However, Collier's determination to admit no breach between them merely hid the quarrel from public view. Dyce was chagrined that his broadside attack had failed; he hated to be bested by one he thought his inferior, and after a year of private enmity and public pretence, he complained to his close friend John Forster that Collier had unaccountably snubbed him, asking Forster to attempt a reconciliation. The reasons for Collier's disaffection ought to have been apparent to all and especially to Forster, who shared some of Dyce's disdain for him, but Forster, who served with Collier on the Council of the Shakespeare Society, responded to Dyce's request and invited both to dinner. Collier thought Dyce needed no intermediary, and he refused the invitation, declaring he could not understand the cause of Dyce's animosity. 'He chose to begin attacking me, and he has chosen to go on attacking me; and now for some reason or other he seems to want to be reconciled to a man who has never given offence to him or taken offence at him. . . . I am not his enemy: he is mine.'[56]

Forster was embarrassed, but he nevertheless asked Peter Cunningham, another member of the Shakespeare Council and good friend of Collier, to entreat him to meet Dyce, and Collier finally acquiesced, revealing, perhaps, his social vulnerability. Although ostensibly the injured party, Collier wrote Dyce suggesting a reconciliation, and enclosing, somewhat gratuitously, an anecdote for the Beaumont biography Dyce was then writing. Dyce replied immediately. 'Believe me that I am truly anxious that what has passed should be eternally forgotten', he wrote, 'but I cannot let the subject be dismissed without most fully and distinctly acknowledging, – that *I was the offending party*: you, indeed, mistook (as it was perhaps only natural that you should) *my feelings* towards you, but still *you were the injured person*.'[57] In closing he mentioned that he already had the anecdote in print *and* in manuscript of his own, 'but perhaps you may be able to give me some new information on other points'. In the final volume of his edition of Beaumont and Fletcher, Dyce gave special thanks for Collier's assistance and softened some of his earlier editorial criticism of Collier's works. Thus Collier and Dyce quieted the anxieties of their friends and satisfied their separate vanities, at least for the moment, but latent distrust remained to erupt, as we shall see, in later years.

10

The disagreement with Dyce was a distraction, not a crisis; Collier was too busy to spend much time quarrelling. The years between 1842 and 1845 were among the most prodigiously productive of his career: in addition to completing his edition of Shakespeare, editing a dozen texts for the Percy, Shakespeare, and Camden Societies, and publishing *Shakespeare's Library,* Collier produced a book for the Roxburghe Club, *The Household Books of John, Duke of Norfolk,*[58] and issued four privately printed pamphlets.[59] Collier's scholarly achievement during this period would have been remarkable had he done nothing else, and when it is remembered that until 1847 he worked 'full time' at the *Chronicle,* his industry becomes truly phenomenal. Newspaper writing, he later declared, trained him to write under pressure.

When the Shakespeare edition was finished, he immediately contracted with Thomas Longman to edit a selection of Roxburghe Ballads from the unique collection recently purchased for the British Museum library.[60] Collier himself was an authority on the subject. He had collected ballads for over forty years, and he knew as much about them as anyone in England. He persuaded Longman to publish a selection of fifty-five ballads from the Museum collection supplemented by several from his own. The edition was handsome, well printed on fine paper and profusely illustrated with facsimile woodcuts, and it quickly became a collector's item. The book scarcely tapped the unexplored riches of the Roxburghe Ballads and W. J. Thoms agreed to edit another selection related to old plays for the Shakespeare Society. When Thoms was unable to complete the job, Collier himself prepared the new edition.

Collier's interest in ballads inspired his work for the Society of Antiquaries during the 1840s. The Society had an unusually fine collection of broadside ballads, and under Collier's guidance this was augmented by discriminating purchases and gifts from his own collection, among them a unique black-letter ballad concerning the marriage of Henry VII and Elizabeth of York printed in Caxton's type and believed to be the oldest broadside in English.[61] Collier was Treasurer of the Society, and in March 1848 he was elected to succeed his old friend Amyot as Executive Vice President. Thereafter he presided at the regular meetings of the Society, secured papers for its programmes and supervised publication of the Society's *Proceedings.* It was an important office and

Collier held it for two four-year terms (until 1856), but as with many such positions, its prestige was greater than its power. He found, for example, that the Fellows of the Society of Antiquaries were no more willing to produce papers than were the members of the Shakespeare Society (indeed, the memberships overlapped considerably), and when papers were not forthcoming, Collier usually supplied the deficit with work of his own. The Society of Antiquaries heard papers by Collier on such diverse subjects as the life of Henry Algernon Percy, sixth Earl of Northumberland (gleaned from the Shrewsbury Papers in the library of Lambeth Palace); Sir John Hawkins, Elizabeth I's naval commander; Richard Hakluyt, the geographer; an ancient crosier of the Bishops of Waterford and Lismore (from Devonshire's collection); and Sir Walter Raleigh, concerning whom he wrote four long papers constituting, in toto, Raleigh's biography from 1576 to 1598.[62]

But Collier's most diligent and apparently thankless labour was for the Shakespeare Society. Between 1845 and the spring of 1850, he produced nine volumes for its membership. Two of these were issues of the Society's *Papers*, a periodic collection of short articles begun at Collier's suggestion in 1844: for Volumes III (1847) and IV (1849) Collier wrote at least nine articles, some of them anonymous, on a wide variety of historical and literary subjects. Of the other six books, two were editions of plays or tracts for which he wrote descriptive introductions and incidental notes,[63] and one, *Riche his Farewell to Militarie Profession* (1581), was a long and important source book which Collier edited and reprinted with great care from the only complete copy in the Bodleian Library.

The other four volumes he produced for the Shakespeare Society before 1850 were of greater historical significance. In July 1845, Collier published, at last, his edition of *The Diary of Philip Henslowe*, the first complete transcription of the manuscript in the Dulwich College library. The diary (really an account book) was probably the most important publication to be issued by the Society. The manuscript was in a very confused state, often illegible, incomplete and jumbled. Amyot and Cunningham made the initial transcript (according to Collier's later account, they proceeded by comparing the original with a transcript made for Chalmers sometime during the late eighteenth century), but Collier was to provide the final copy for the printers as well as an index to the printed text.

Even before Henslowe's diary was distributed Collier had begun yet another book for the Society, a collection of biographies of the twenty-six players listed at the beginning of the First Folio as 'the Principal Actors' in Shakespeare's plays.[64] Collier's predecessors, notably Malone and Chalmers in the previous century, had done some of this work in piecemeal fashion, but Collier's discoveries among the Alleyn Papers had disclosed much new biographical information. Collier's sources were diverse (e.g., token books and church registers as well as the notes of Henslowe and Alleyn), many of which he himself had discovered. Moreover, this was not an edition of manuscript fragments but a book requiring composition and lengthy documentation. The section on Richard Burbage, for example, ran to over fifty pages. And once again, Collier compiled a long and detailed subject index to the text.

Two other books he published with the Shakespeare Society during this time were the first volumes of a planned three-volume edition of *Extracts from the Stationers' Register,* the record kept by the guild of printers in the sixteenth and seventeenth centuries to enforce copyright among its members. The Stationers' Company had been incorporated by royal charter in 1557 to have sole control of all printing in the Kingdom, and by its rules members were required to enter into the Company's *Register* the name of every book, pamphlet or broadside they printed. As a result these registers are the most complete record of works published between 1557 and 1640, a span which encompassed all Elizabethan and Jacobean poetry and drama. Despite their unique value, the *Registers* had been pretty much ignored until the last quarter of the eighteenth century when Thomas Warton referred to them in his *History of English Poetry* (1778); thereafter, Steevens and Malone consulted the registers but no one before Collier had undertaken to publish them.

Collier's plan was particularly ambitious because lack of money and a concern for accuracy forced him to make all the transcripts himself; the registers were frequently difficult to read and occasionally incomprehensible once deciphered. For months he pored over the volumes in Stationers' Hall and for months thereafter he indexed, annotated, and illustrated the entries he found. By the standards of the time, Collier's copies were good,[65] but making them took two years (1847–48), time stolen from other pressing responsibilities.

Collier's transcript was not complete (hence the title 'Extracts'), but it included all entries that related to popular poetry and prose, plays, tracts, voyages, travels, and lighter literature, and he expanded the text with esoteric and valuable information about printers, authors and their works, alternative readings, gloss words and so on. In addition, he illustrated many entries with ballads which, he declared, 'no doubt, once existed in print, but which have been lost, and are now only known from transcripts.'[66] Among the most significant of these were thirty-four ballads copied into a manuscript commonplace book in Collier's possession. 'They will be found to add materially to the attractiveness of the volume, and by their poetry, humour, and spirit, to relieve the dryness of the details into which elsewhere it has been necessary to enter',[67] he declared.

Collier transcribed all of 'Register A' and 'Register B' (as they were called in Stationers' Hall), but he was able to publish only part of these under the auspices of the Shakespeare Society. The first volume containing entries for the years 1557 to 1570 appeared in 1848, and the second volume continuing the serial to 1587, the year Shakespeare was traditionally assumed to have arrived in London, was published in 1849. The third volume covering the period from 1587 to 1607 was announced for publication in 1852, but although this volume ought to have been of greatest interest to the membership, the project was delayed, and the Society disbanded before it could be published. (Collier eventually completed his transcript to 1607 and published the entries for 1587 to 1595 in *Notes and Queries*.)[68]

The publication of the Stationers' *Register* was comparable in importance and difficulty to that of Henslowe's diary which Collier had produced three years before. Like the earlier work, it made readily available to the general reader records previously seen by only a few scholars, records which were among the most important in the study of early English literature. The publication of these sources was a milestone in literary historical research. To be sure, Collier's editions had serious errors in transcription and judgement, faults derived from incomplete or idiosyncratic method and the absence of standardized notation and consistent methodology, but they are nonetheless a remarkable scholarly achievement. If one compares them with later editions of the same texts (with Arber's edition of the Stationers' *Register* or Greg's of Henslowe's diary, for example) they demonstrate an accuracy far above the standard for the age.

It is a bitter irony that although Collier was now pre-eminent among the Shakespeare scholars of his time, his energies almost unlimited and his production without peer and almost without precedent, he was, nonetheless, on the edge of financial ruin. Although he still received the annuity from Devonshire and something more from Louisa's shares, his income was largely based – as it had been for twenty years – on his salary at the *Chronicle*. Scholarship did not pay, and Collier was committed to scholarship. His commercial publications added something to his income, but nothing commensurate with his labour (hack writing for the penny press would have paid him more) and his scholarly editing for the societies brought him nothing at all, not even the thanks of his fellow members. The publication of Henslowe's diary and the *Extracts from the Stationers' Register* were produced without much support from the lethargic membership of the Shake-speare Society. Few scholars fully appreciated the value of his work. He was *self*-driven; a kind of madness possessed him, madness mixed with pride intensified by a sense of virtue unrewarded. Against his own best interest, his health and his peace of mind, and at the loss of friends, family tranquillity, and financial reward, Collier worked to put the documents of early English literature into print. This self-immolation was beyond the understanding of his friends. Crabb Robinson, watching Collier's career from a distance, despaired that he would ever become financially secure. 'The truth is', Robinson wrote in his diary, 'that Collier so exclusively devotes himself to Shakespeare that he is indifferent to everything going on in the present day, however important.' Collier, he declared, was 'too . . . literary to know how to raise money.'[69] Collier's friends chided him for neglecting his responsibilities, forgetting that he had worked forty years in jobs he had detested in order to provide for his family, relegating the work he loved to hours snatched from a daily journalistic grind. His critical reputation had been achieved by twenty years of sacrifice, not self-indulgence.

Nevertheless, at fifty-eight Collier was not secure. His achievements were remarkable and his reputation high, but his financial state was as precarious as ever and he knew his work on the *Chronicle* was once again threatened. The paper had suffered great financial losses. Even Black had been forced to quit, and Collier knew that he, misused and ill-paid though he was, would be the next to go. He was therefore once again forced to beg favours. He could not petition Devonshire: the humiliating failure of six years before still burned in his memory. He turned therefore to Francis Egerton, now the first Earl of Ellesmere who, flattered by the discoveries Collier had made among the manuscripts in his Bridgewater Collection, had allowed Collier special and easy access to his library, and secured positions in the Stamp Office for Collier's sons. Surely the Earl had other largesse to bestow?

As it happened, he did. Ellesmere had just been appointed chairman of the Royal Commission to inquire into the management of the British Museum, and he responded to Collier's request by appointing him secretary to the commission at a stipend of £500 per year.[70] This was slightly more than Collier was earning at the *Chronicle,* and since the duties of the secretary took less time than newspaper reporting, Collier would be more free for other possibly profitable work. Ellesmere offered that, too; he engaged Collier to prepare a descriptive catalogue of works in the Bridgewater Collection associated with Shakespeare, precisely the kind of work Collier did best. Moreover, Ellesmere thought the secretaryship might lead to a more important appointment in the Museum itself.[71] He suggested that the commission's work would probably bring about a reorganization of the Museum and that the library might be divided into books in English and those in foreign languages, creating a new position of Keeper of

English Books. This, Ellesmere suggested, was a position for which Collier would be a likely candidate.

The plan to divide the collection was far-fetched, but Collier, driven by need and pride, clutched at the possibility. For twenty years he had worked hard and well for small return. Surely he had proved his qualifications? Surely he deserved the recognition and the security of a place in the national library? The public was notoriously ungrateful to its scholars, but wasn't it possible, just possible, that he would at last be given his due?

The commission itself was not expected to be long about its business and the secretary's post, all he really had to count on, was expected to continue for only a year or two. Nevertheless, it was a preferable alternative to Collier's precarious position at the *Chronicle*. He gratefully accepted Ellesmere's appointment, quit newspapers – he hoped forever – and plunged into what was to become one of the most fateful battles of his life.

IV

THE CATALOGUE CONTROVERSY

'I entirely, and from the first, misunderstood.'

11

To understand that battle, one must know something of the field on which it was fought. The British Museum which confronted the Royal Commission in 1847 was miserably housed and badly run by men who were, at best, dedicated amateurs. It always had been. Throughout its hundred-year history the Museum had been crowded and incorrigibly mismanaged. It had enormous riches – greater than anyone really knew, for what it owned was largely uncatalogued and carelessly preserved – and yet it was poverty-stricken, literally unable to keep a roof over its head. Parliament maintained it, in a manner of speaking, but with reluctance, and never with enough money. It limped along, a strange mass of contradictions: valuable beyond price yet mendicant, enfeebled by tradition yet downright adolescent in its prodigious growth, aimless and without apparent limit, almost monstrous in its headlong accumulation of the things of knowledge.

The situation was scandalous and probably inevitable. The Museum had been established by Parliament in 1757 on the gift of three great libraries, those of Sir Hans Sloane, Sir Robert Cotton, and Edward Harley, Earl of Oxford – it was no accident that the chief officer of the institution was titled 'Principal Librarian' – but although the library was central to the Museum's purpose, it was not all encompassing. Sloane's bequest included not only books and manuscripts but also antiquities and specimens of natural history, and the Museum was therefore divided into three parts: Printed Books, Manuscripts, and 'Natural and Artificial Productions' – which later became the Departments of Natural History and of Antiquities. These three divisions were intended to encompass and to integrate all knowledge into a single whole to be preserved, as the Museum's first *Statutes and Rules* declared, 'for the use of learned and studious men, both natives and foreigners, in their researches into the several parts of knowledge. . . .'[1] In the mid-eighteenth century it seemed possible to maintain this amalgam under one aegis, but in the following century, as scientific knowledge increased, the collections became diversified beyond recognition, the departments expanded and sub-divided, and the hope of synthesis faded. Conceived as co-operative and mutually sustaining parts of a whole, the departments soon became self-contained and strongly competitive, and by 1847 there was open warfare among them. The Department of Printed Books maintained a running battle with the Department of Manuscripts. They co-operated only in their fight against the Department of Natural History, which they both wanted thrown out of the Museum.

The great contention was over space or, rather, the lack of it, for nothing seems to have slowed acquisitions. The Museum was first established in Montagu House, one of the finest residences in London, but it was obvious almost immediately that although palatial the house was too small. By 1823 the crowding' had reached emergency proportions and Parliament belatedly authorized a new building, a huge quadrangle designed by Robert Smirke, intended to meet the needs of all the departments for many years. The proposed building seemed enormous to everyone at the time, but it ultimately proved to be too little and it came much too late. The building took thirty years – until 1852 – to complete and then it could not accommodate all that had to be put into it.

The library was the most crowded. The policy of the library had always been to allow readers to use books only within the Museum itself, and this necessitated space for readers. So long as the number of readers was small, there was no problem, and for the first seventy years or so, the library was used only by a fortunate few who obtained permission from a trustee. For example, in 1828, five years after Smirke's building was begun, only 750 readers' tickets were outstanding and only 100 new ones were issued. The reading rooms were still very much as they had been twenty years before (when Collier first visited them) – poorly ventilated and inconvenient but large enough to accommodate readers. In the 1830s, however, pressure from a better educated public and a partially reformed Parliament made readers' tickets easier to obtain with the result that by 1848, 32,000 tickets were outstanding; in that year alone, over 1,200 new ones were issued.[2] The coterie which had formerly used the library had given way to the crowd, but the means for serving them had not been proportionately increased.

Of course, the library was not the only department to expand so dramatically. The use of the Departments of Antiquities and of Natural History had grown too, and the competition for space and staff was increasingly angry and disruptive. Unfortunately, the governing structure of the Museum was unable to adjudicate these rival claims. With one or two important exceptions, the administrators of the Museum during the first century of its existence were ministers of religion and doctors of medicine who had little interest in adapting its organization to changing functions. Their chief concern seems to have been to preserve their individual hegemonies through a system of seniority and perquisites based on tenure rather than merit or institutional need. It was a system best characterized by a Museum functionary in 1837 as 'that alleviation of labour which ... is gained by promotion to a superior place.'[3] It was a doomed structure. By the 1840s there were signs that a new kind of professional was emerging within the Museum hierarchy, ambitious, highly contentious, dedicated to the ideal of a truly national and public institution, and confident of its ability to direct the Museum to that goal. The competition among these 'new men' was keen and often very public, and the animosity it created was exacerbated by the failure of the administrators of the Museum to understand or direct what were, after all, forces of healthful change.

The Principal Librarian in 1847 was Sir Henry Ellis, a product of the old system, a scholar and bibliographer of solid achievements who was, as one of his successors put it, 'as devoid as a man well can be of the combative spirit.'[4] He was not the best person to arbitrate among competing subordinates. As the chief officer of the institution he presided over the Board of Trustees, at least that was what the organizational structure called for, but he regularly avoided this responsibility and the void was filled by the Museum Secretary, the Revd. Josiah Forshall, formerly Keeper of the Manuscripts, as 'old guard' as Ellis but much less squeamish about executing his will throughout the Museum. He ran the institution to his own liking, sometimes without even bothering to inform Ellis of his administrative decisions. The Museum trustees who theoretically had ultimate control, were a large and unwieldy group of dilettantes who had only incidental knowledge of the work of the Museum, and they seemed quite willing to allow Forshall and the assenting Ellis to gloss over developing administrative crises. Thus a government of supernumeraries and venal or unresponsive administration attempted to direct an institution that was changing radically in size and function. The result of this mismanagement was confusion and, finally, public clamour.

In the spring of 1847 the British Association for the Advancement of Science formally protested to the Prime Minister that the Museum failed to provide 'proper guidance of the Natural History Department'.[5] Another petition signed by many prominent scholars complained that the library was almost impossible to use because the catalogue of the book collection was a quagmire and accession procedures were hopelessly in arrears; there was a backlog of over 100,000 uncatalogued books and a delay of two to five years in cataloguing new acquisitions. In addition, the petition deplored the fact that the printed catalogue, promised by the Department of Printed Books for nearly twenty years, had been suspended although huge sums had been appropriated for its completion.

The state of the catalogue had long been a subject of controversy. The Museum had a tradition of publishing a list of the books in its collection. The first printed catalogue had been compiled by Samuel Harper in 1787 and the second by Henry Ellis and Henry Baber in 1819, but this edition had no successor, and after thirty years one was desperately needed: the skeletal frame of the index in use in the Reading Room derived from the mutilated corpse of the old catalogue of 1819 many times expanded and rebound, with tens of thousands of manuscript insertions that vainly attempted to bring the list up to date. The result was a virtually illegible register, hopelessly confused and bulky beyond use. In 1835 a select committee of Parliament had emphatically recommended a new printed catalogue; Parliament had appropriated money for its completion, and the Museum Trustees had announced the intention to complete the work by 1845, but it took seven years to produce the first volume (comprising the letter 'A') and it was so filled with errors that no later volumes were prepared. Nevertheless, the Museum administration pretended the project was progressing on schedule and blandly declared that they expected a complete printed catalogue by 1845. To nobody's surprise, it never came. By 1847, several thousand readers used the library and they had had enough of delays and excuses. The petition was the formal public declaration of frustration (private comment was more angry and unprintable), and when the Prime Minister appointed the Royal Commission to examine the business of the Museum in June 1847, it was generally believed that the new inquiry would quickly reaffirm the conclusions of its predecessor and that a printed catalogue would at last be planned, fully financed and completed with dispatch. The selection of Ellesmere as the commission chairman encouraged this view because he had been an active member of the select committee of 1835, and when Collier was appointed secretary to the commission in July, the outcome seemed assured, for he had long been an outspoken advocate of a compendious, printed 'finding catalogue'.

This conclusion was premature. As it happened, the catalogue mess derived not from administrative ineptitude, but from the calculated intention of one man. Anthony Panizzi was Keeper of Printed Books in 1847 and he *kept* them – under his control and for his own ends. A printed catalogue was decidedly not one of these. He brushed off the complaints of the Reading Room regulars and he grandly ignored the directives from the trustees. The catalogue would take the form he chose – or none at all. True, he seemed to comply with the trustees' directives in issuing the abortive Volume A, but the real purpose of that inept publication was to prove that any printed catalogue would be inaccurate and incomplete. He wanted a new catalogue, but only if it contained a 'complete' bibliographical description following his own criteria, and only if it were kept in *manuscript*. The administration of the Museum was so divided and ineffectual that Panizzi was able to continue this policy for over a decade. It was a struggle for power, and what Collier and his friends didn't realize was that the Royal Commission of 1847 would determine not merely what the catalogue was to be but who would ultimately control the British Museum. Neither did they realize that the dominating figure in these deliberations was to be Panizzi himself.

Anthony Panizzi was the most unlikely person to be Keeper of Printed Books at the British Museum in 1847 or any other year. He was a foreigner, a fugitive revolutionary, and a Roman Catholic. Given contemporary prejudices, any one of these might have excluded him from the job even if training and experience had fitted him for it. Born fifty years earlier in the Italian duchy of Modena (then a part of the Cisalpine Republic), Panizzi had originally prepared for the law, but when the Republic was overthrown by Austria, he became a revolutionary, and when the revolution failed, a refugee, escaping to Switzerland, and thence to England. In May 1823, he had arrived in Liverpool, almost penniless, knowing virtually no English and carrying little more than a few clothes and letters of introduction to several eminent Liverpool Liberals.

His rise in the next fourteen years was one of the most remarkable success stories of nineteenth-century England. Panizzi remained in Liverpool five years, teaching himself English and cultivating his Liberal connections, through whom he made the friendship of Lord Brougham, then the greatest trial lawyer in England and one of the most powerful Whigs in Parliament. In 1827 Panizzi's knowledge of continental law helped Brougham to win a celebrated criminal prosecution, and the next year Brougham became Panizzi's assiduous patron, securing him the post of Professor of Italian at the newly established University of London, and entrée to Holland House, whose *habitués* were to dominate English politics for the next twenty years. When the Whigs came to power in 1831, Brougham, now Lord Chancellor, immediately exercised his power as an ex officio trustee of the British

Museum to have a place made for his protégé, and within a few weeks Panizzi was appointed an 'extra assistant librarian' in the Department of Printed Books and assigned to the catalogue project.

Panizzi was not a professional bibliographer; in fact, he had had virtually no experience in preparing a catalogue or in organizing a library. Moreover, his immediate superiors in the Museum were Sir Henry Ellis, then Principal Librarian, and Henry Baber, Keeper of Printed Books, who had compiled the 1819 catalogue. This presented a problem for Panizzi because his own good sense quickly satisfied him that the rules Ellis and Baber had used in compiling their catalogue were inconsistent and erroneous and that to continue to follow them would be a long-term disaster. In characteristic fashion, he secretly began creating a new bibliographical order out of the chaos of their rules. His patterns were European and his method was ultimately much more sophisticated and exact than that of Ellis and Baber, but his objective differed from theirs: they had produced a *catalogue*; he wanted a *descriptive bibliography* of the collection, a much more grandiose and difficult objective and one less immediately useful to the readers who used the library.

Panizzi necessarily kept this resolve to himself; any attempt in 1833 to bring about the changes he sought would certainly have provoked his dismissal by Ellis or Baber, not only because it would, in effect, discredit their earlier work but also because it would require scrapping most of the entries already completed on the revised edition and rewriting the titles in the old 1819 catalogue as well. Panizzi was then in no position to challenge the judgement of his superiors. It was a difficult role for a man with so much ambition, brilliance, and mercurial temperament, but he bided his time, hid his intransigence, and waited for his chance.

It wasn't long in coming. When the complaints of an employee fired from the Department of Manuscripts brought about the select committee inquiry of 1835, Panizzi recognized his opportunity: four years in the Museum had shown him how sorely it needed reorganization and redirection, and he used his testimony before the committee to advocate new procedures, particularly for the Department of Printed Books.

To the committee, as well as to the much wider and ultimately more important public which was to read his testimony in the final parliamentary report, Panizzi made the most thorough-going and astute analysis of the problems and future goals of the library that anyone in or out of the institution had attempted, and he supported his conclusions with impressive knowledge. This performance was to make Panizzi pre-eminent among the junior members of the Museum staff. It also provoked jealousy among his peers.

Panizzi's new repute was soon to be rewarded: one of the recommendations of the select committee of 1835 was a regulation that Museum staff members could not hold offices outside the Museum, and Baber gave up his post as Keeper of the Printed Books in order to retain a lucrative church living outside London. By long-established tradition the 'next man in line' was the Assistant Keeper, the Revd. Henry Cary, but Panizzi challenged that succession, and a classic confrontation of traditional sinecure and powerful political patronage quickly developed. Cary was a much respected functionary, twenty-four years Panizzi's senior, who had worked in the Museum for nearly two decades. Panizzi was an inexperienced newcomer who owed his place to political connections outside the Museum. Cary was a Tory English protestant divine; Panizzi was a revolutionary Italian Roman Catholic. By all traditional criteria, the appointment was Cary's, but by all the practical political ones, it was Panizzi's, and politics prevailed. Given the administrative vacuum in the Museum itself, the appointment was left to the three principal ex-officio trustees of the Museum – the Lord Chancellor (Brougham), the Speaker of the House of Commons, and the Archbishop of Canterbury. Canterbury was strongly opposed to Panizzi, but in the last days of Parliament he was briefly out of London, and in his absence Brougham and the Speaker quickly signed the certificate of Panizzi's appointment and the Archbishop was presented with a *fait accompli* on his return. Cary and his supporters were furious, and letters to *The Times* made Panizzi's selection a subject for public outrage, but the appointment was made and Cary resigned. As a result, the first years of Panizzi's tenure as Keeper of the Printed Books were marked by quarrels as venomous as any in the history of the Museum.

For all his cleverness and vitality, Panizzi really didn't know very much about his job. He saw the gross mistakes of his predecessors, but he had, at first, little besides ambition and intelligence to correct them. The public who used the library and virtually all the hierarchy of the Museum staff had opposed his appointment, and this initial distrust quickly turned to animosity. But Panizzi was not above using his political influence outside the Museum to effect his wishes within it, and the general decay of the governance of the institution made it vulnerable to such an attack. Henry Ellis, although an early friend, was increasingly suspicious of Panizzi and became incapable of exercising the administrative control which, as Principal Librarian, he should have had over the Department of Printed Books. He refused to speak officially or unofficially against Panizzi, but he could not bring himself to the point of supporting him either. The conflict undoubtedly intensified Ellis's distaste for controversy and led him to the general abdication of responsibility which, as much as anything, brought on the collapse of administrative authority and resulted in the investigation of 1847. Forshall, for his part, became a strong and outspoken opponent of Panizzi, recognizing in him a counterpart to his own appetite for power and sensing, perhaps, a potential competitor for the Principal Librarianship when Ellis retired.

If Panizzi evoked fear and distrust in his superiors, he incensed his peers. Edward Hawkins, Keeper of Antiquities, took an intense dislike to him and strongly opposed his appointment. John Edward Gray, head of the Department of Natural History, was another enemy. (Panizzi had declared to the select committee in 1836 that scientists were 'all crotchety ... I never saw scientific men go right, or view things as other people do.')[6] But his most bitter adversary was Frederic Madden. Madden's appointment as Keeper of Manuscripts was to have been concurrent with Panizzi's as Keeper of Printed Books, but Panizzi's had been arbitrarily predated (to meet the legal requirement of the Speaker's parliamentary tenure) and hence Panizzi had acquired several days' seniority which gave him precedence over Madden in housing and other perquisites. Madden developed a cankered hatred of Panizzi. His capacity for vindictiveness was almost boundless and, as his diaries suggest, paranoid. Panizzi, Madden declared in his diary, was 'a scoundrel Italian, whose proper sphere is, not to be at the head of the national library, but to fill the odious post of a political spy; to lye, to cozen, to humbug, and to execute every other dirty and vile office, which no *gentleman* could be found to do.'[7] There was to be no reconciliation – they were blood enemies for thirty years.

And yet, despite Panizzi's effrontery, and in spite of his remarkable ability to provoke the worst passions in his adversaries, he was ultimately successful. He had two overriding objectives: first, to make the British Museum the greatest national collection of books and manuscripts in the world, and second, to make this collection accessible to scholars. With great energy and shrewdness, he went far toward achieving both. The first was abetted by an intensive acquisitions policy supported by large new government appropriations that he almost single-handedly extracted from Parliament. In 1845, for example, he went over the heads of his superiors in the Museum and persuaded Parliament to pledge an annual grant of £10,000 – an enormous sum for the time – exclusively for the acquisition of printed books. It was a coup his predecessors would have envied. Some of his detractors grumbled that the money might have been better spent bringing the catalogue up to date, but Panizzi grandly ignored all critics and began to buy heavily in England and abroad, making the British Museum the most aggressive book-buyer in the world. Panizzi also brought about a stricter enforcement of the legal copyright requirement that copies of all books published in Great Britain be given to the Museum, and the library immediately began to grow. It was to quintuple before he retired thirty years later.

To achieve his second objective, making the books accessible, Panizzi reorganized the collection and introduced useful procedures, many of which are still followed today, but he was blind to the need for a short printed catalogue, and as soon as he became Keeper all work on that project virtually ceased. In Panizzi's view, the catalogue was properly a complete bibliographical description in manuscript of the books of the collection, nothing more and nothing less. Although he was prescient in establishing modern rules for accurate and consistent bibliographical description, he failed to see that readers who wanted the book itself needed another sort of catalogue, not a detailed description but an index containing the minimum reference necessary to identify the volume they required. Panizzi's failure to appreciate this distinction created chaos when he imposed another innovation, a change in the method which had been used to retrieve books since the library was opened in 1759: heretofore, a reader had asked a library assistant for the volume he wanted and the assistant had found the book on the shelves and had delivered it to the reader. In this process, the reader did not have to consult the catalogue; all he needed to know was the title of the book (or its approximation) or its author, and the assistant did the rest. This procedure worked well enough while the collection was small, readers few and assistants knowledgeable, but as the number of volumes in the collection grew it became necessary to shelve new acquisitions in remote and arbitrary places, and to find them a system was evolved in which each book was given a 'press mark', a code identifying its 'press' or shelf in the storage area. Thereafter, when an assistant received a request, he had to consult a shelf index in order to find the book, and as the numbers of readers grew the assistants spent an increasing amount of time looking up press marks. Panizzi's innovation was to make the press marks the readers' responsibility. The shelf index was incorporated with the general reading room catalogue and readers were thereafter required to supply the press mark as well as the author and title of the work sought. It was a reasonable regulation and an efficient one, but it dramatically altered the function of the catalogue which became, in effect, an index to the collection rather than a bibliographical description of it, a procedural necessity rather than a scholarly convenience. Panizzi either did not understand or refused to recognize this result. Previously readers had consulted the general catalogue only rarely to determine if the library owned a book they wanted; now the catalogue had to be consulted every time a book was requested. The use of the catalogue increased enormously and the inappropriate form of its entries, their unnecessary length, their near illegibility, their complex and confusing rules of order and so on, frustrated readers who felt victimized. For reasons he failed to justify, Panizzi refused to separate the bibliographical and index functions of the catalogue. He insisted that the two files be one and the same, and as a result the reading room catalogue became increasingly unusable for either purpose. All the acrimony that Panizzi's unorthodox promotion had engendered was kept alive by partisans who were sure that this state of affairs would not have occurred had Cary been appointed Keeper.

Panizzi was not surprised by the petitions of 1847; neither was he displeased by the announcement of the Royal Commission shortly thereafter. In fact, he had good reasons for wanting a full-scale investigation. His Whig friends in Parliament had no love for the Tory retinue at the Museum, and he hoped a public examination might reveal the incompetence of his superiors. Let his critics attack him in the press! His advocates would appoint the commission, and Panizzi would make sure that its membership would be friendly to his cause. His success is best illustrated by the fact that, although the complaint of the Department of Natural History had been one of the primary reasons for the investigation, no scientist was appointed to the commission. (Panizzi's prejudice against scientists was, apparently, shared by others in power.) It was 'Panizzi's Commission' from the start, and the investigation was to be dominated by his concerns, a vehicle to overwhelm his adversaries within the Museum and to disable his critics without. It is not too much to say that the final report of the Royal Commission of 1847–50 established Anthony Panizzi as the inevitable successor to Sir Henry Ellis as Principal Librarian.

12

No one was to be more surprised by this result or more damaged by it than John Payne Collier. Like nearly everyone else he expected the commission to clean up the 'mess' of the catalogue once and for all, but almost alone among the advocates of an index catalogue he was ultimately to stake his professional fortunes on that end. It was a losing cause, a battle fought in the wrong place and at the wrong time.

To those who had eyes to see it, the result of the inquiry was apparent from the outset. The commission's first session in July 1847 lasted only three days. The first witness, the Principal Librarian, Sir Henry Ellis, declared that there were no disagreements among the Museum staff that he was aware of. Since the Museum's internecine warfare had been a public entertainment for years, his remarks demonstrated his incompetence. Secretary Forshall followed Ellis and indirectly proved what Panizzi had privately declared, that the Secretary was deliberately obstructing Panizzi and his department. After Forshall's testimony the first session was adjourned for six months, but the point had been made to Panizzi's advantage. Panizzi himself would testify at the next session, but even before the commission reconvened in December 1847, the Museum trustees foresaw the outcome and passed a resolution which, in Panizzi's words, affirmed his 'views' concerning the organization of the Department of Printed Books and its catalogue.[8] Thus, in effect, when the testimony was barely begun and before the commission itself reported, the trustees acted to resolve the library issue in Panizzi's favour. In January 1848, to cement this advantage, Panizzi addressed a letter to Ellesmere, the commission's chairman, detailing his objections to a printed short-title index and outlining his plans for the new catalogue.[9] As a result, when the commission reconvened in February, Panizzi's opponents were on the defensive. Hawkins, the Keeper of Antiquities, briefly displayed his anger at the treatment of his department, and then Secretary Forshall was recalled for a severe cross-examination, largely directed by Panizzi. Finally, Frederic Madden gave his testimony, an outburst of anger, charging ill use and revealing a luminous hatred for Panizzi. Thus, even before he himself spoke, Panizzi's case had been made by his opponents: Ellis had revealed his incompetence, Forshall his malice, Hawkins his bitterness, and Madden his venomous jealousy. The effect was not lost on the commissioners.

Panizzi took the stand for the first time in the middle of May 1848, and testified for a total of seven days before the end of July. His testimony was not the brilliant exposition and defence some of his biographers have claimed but, given his opponents, brilliance was not required. Compared with the witnesses who preceded him, Panizzi sparkled. He was assured, precise, and articulate, and he was talking to judges who were, in the words of the *Athenaeum,* his 'friends beforehand and his partisans throughout'.[10] Ellis, Forshall and the rest had devoted most of their testimony to justifying the governance procedures of the Museum and to arguing against Panizzi's intransigence. Panizzi, making short work of these arguments, revealed in detail the defects of the management, some of them structural, but more of them caused by the incompetence of the Museum hierarchy. Yes, there were procedural delays in the business of his department, but they were inevitable when the Secretary denied him all direct, personal discourse with the trustees. Moreover, Panizzi complained, he had little control over appointment or assignment of personnel to his department; 'extra sub librarians' had been appointed without his approval, a procedure which undermined his control. (Sixteen years before, Panizzi's appointment had been of the same kind.) The organization of the Department of Printed Books, ostensibly in his charge, was out of his purview; he could not even ensure the safety of the collection since he knew at least 150 staff members had 'house keys' and could enter the library – with their friends – at any hour.

The disorder which Panizzi revealed in the running of the Museum quickly destroyed the credibility of the witnesses who had preceded him, and the rest of his testimony was given over almost entirely to a discussion of the catalogue, the subject that was to dominate the commission's remaining months. Panizzi's case was simple: he maintained he was following the orders of the trustees as he understood them – to complete a manuscript catalogue following a consistent and uniform plan of 'full and accurate' listings of works in the library. The crux of the controversy was the interpretation to be given to 'full and accurate'. If 'full' were construed to mean 'sufficient to use' as an index for readers in the library, the entries could be concise, quickly made and subsequently printed in small compass. If, however, 'full' meant a complete bibliographical description of a work the compilation must be voluminous, and any subsequent printing necessarily difficult and expensive. Panizzi insisted that the latter had always been the objective of the trustees, that he had pursued this goal consistently in enforcing his famous ninety-one rules for cataloguing, and that the plan to print the catalogue interfered with these objectives. It had been suggested that the process might be speeded and the results made more legible if the entries were set in type in the first instance and subsequently printed on slips to be pasted in the catalogue volumes, but Panizzi scorned the idea. It would be 'impossible to use or understand a catalogue prepared from such material', he declared. It would make the books too thick and there would be 'unknown difficulties'. The catalogue must be in manuscript. All the continental catalogues were in manuscript. So no printing. He had followed his plan and it was going forward; over 500,000 entries had already been made according to Panizzi's bibliographical principles: did anyone want that labour to be thrown away? What was needed was more support, and less criticism from outsiders so that he could get on with the job. When it was completed it would be, he declared, 'the best catalogue of a large collection ever compiled'.[11]

It was a forceful presentation, and when Panizzi finished his testimony, the committee recessed for another six months, pretty much convinced of the virtues of his cause and the small-mindedness of his detractors. This unexpected result enfuriated Panizzi's enemies within and outside the Museum. Panizzi, now doubly secure, went on the attack. He produced a list of persons who had been critical of procedures in the reading room and asked the commission to 'examine the complainers'. 'I want those gentlemen who make complaints anonymously, to come to this table and state the facts that they have to complain of and I pledge myself to answer their complaints; I shall be very sorry if they do not make their complaints here.'[12]

It was a shrewd move, for it seemed fair; Panizzi had testified and merely asked his accusers to do the same, but the challenge had a pernicious implication: any critic who did *not* come forward, who would not subject himself to a public grilling by Panizzi, would admit he had no case. Moreover, the unusual rules which the commission had adopted for its sessions placed most witnesses at a serious disadvantage. The commission meetings were closed to the public. Only the Museum administrators, the Museum trustees, and the commission and its staff were allowed to attend all the sessions, and witnesses who gave evidence were not allowed to hear the evidence of others or even to have a transcript of their own testimony. (The verbatim record was not published until several months after the commission produced its report some three years after the investigation began.) Witnesses could not question the statements of previous witnesses or qualify their remarks in the light of them. Panizzi, on the other hand, heard all the evidence and through friendly members of the commission, notably the Lord Advocate and Lord Seymour, was able to cross-examine witnesses. This procedure was not exactly the epitome of British fair play, and by taking advantage of it Panizzi was able to determine the substance of the evidence and to shape the final judgements of the commissioners. While other Museum administrators (Ellis, Forshall, Madden, Gray, *et al.*) might have exercised the same privilege, they avoided meeting Panizzi on his own ground.

John Payne Collier's name was on Panizzi's list and Ellesmere therefore asked him to testify. Collier had been outspoken in advocating a compendious index, he was aware of the drift of the commission, and he feared that, if Panizzi went unchallenged, he might succeed in circumventing the legitimate demand for an index catalogue. He was aware too that almost alone among those who advocated a change he could match Panizzi's advantage. As secretary to the commission he had heard all the testimony and could therefore confront Panizzi on equal terms. Nevertheless, Collier hesitated. It was now clear that the Commission was disposed to grant Panizzi almost everything he asked for. To oppose such an obvious favourite was to start with strong odds against him and to lose such a confrontation would be humiliating. On the other hand, Ellesmere clearly expected him to respond, and if Panizzi were successful in shaping the commission's report, Collier's own half-conceived hopes would be destroyed. In a real sense, then, Collier had no choice but to take up Panizzi's challenge, and he promised Ellesmere he would.

Once set on confrontation, Collier determined to make a strong fight of it. In January 1849, a month before the commission was to reconvene, he set forth his opinions in a short pamphlet. ('I penned it in two days [and] printed it in one', he later remarked.) He addressed it to Ellesmere and sent copies to all the commissioners, declaring himself 'quite willing to submit to any interrogatories, and to go through the order which Mr. Panizzi has required that persons, who are adverse to his views, should be subjected.'[13] It was a compelling response. Sir Robert Inglis, an M.P. who also testified before the commission, called it 'conclusive',[14] and the case which Panizzi had made over the previous eighteen months was put in serious jeopardy for the first time. Despite the fact that he had requested such comments, Panizzi was enfuriated by Collier's pamphlet, and accused Collier of acting improperly in his role of secretary of the commission. In reply, Collier declared that he saw no fault in addressing 'parties who had already had Panizzi's elaborate argument on the other side of the question under their consideration *for more than a twelvemonth.*'[15] Ellesmere agreed. The pamphlet was, he declared, 'just right': such matters could not be settled without controversy, and Collier was 'just the sort of reader who ought to be consulted about the catalogue.'[16]

Collier was not alone; over twenty witnesses answered Panizzi's challenge, all but three or four sharply critical of library procedures. But although it was apparent that a good many people were displeased by Panizzi, the criticism was general and unfocused before Collier spoke. His testimony was long – only Panizzi testified at greater length – and was essentially a recapitulation of the case he had made in his pamphlet against Panizzi's catalogue, but his elaboration was done with care and surprising tact. Sensitive, perhaps, at least in the beginning of his testimony, to the effect of his sometimes pugnacious style, he tried to stay on the issues of the catalogue and to avoid *ad hominem* arguments.[17] In fact, he went out of his way to praise Panizzi as a man of talent, 'acquirements', and civility. 'I speak of him only as the advocate of what I consider a bad system', he declared.[18] Moreover, in his opinion Panizzi was the 'most competent man' to be in charge of the catalogue. 'I would give him the entire superintendence of it. If it were necessary for him to have assistants in particular departments, I would take care that he had that assistance...'[19] The issue was not the man but the plan. The form of the catalogue should not be determined by Panizzi alone, but by those who used the library.[20]

'Very likely I am one of the most experienced readers in that room', Collier declared. 'For a period of 40 years I have been a frequenter of it, but all the readers have more or less experience of the deficiency of the present catalogue...'[21] The problem was, Panizzi's bibliography was of little use to any serious library reader, whereas a catalogue was a necessity to all. 'No bibliographer would be satisfied with any title that he found in a printed or a manuscript catalogue', he declared. 'A bibliographer is a person of such patient research, and such accurate detail, that he would not be content to take the word of any cataloguer as to the title, or any other portion of a book; he would not be satisfied with anything but an examination of the book itself.'[22] To be sure, the kind of catalogue Panizzi was producing would be of use to the administrators of the library, but making such a bibliographical description should be a secondary priority and to produce it the Museum should not 'delay an instant to give all literary men the immense advantage of a brief intelligible catalogue' such as he had described.[23]

It was also obvious, to Collier, that the catalogue should be printed. Typographical selection (the use of bold face or italic type, for example) would immediately distinguish important information in a way manuscript could not, and the order and compression which print afforded would allow a reader to take in many titles at once. Almost equally valuable would be the possibility of multiple copies for the use of readers not only in the British Museum reading room but in other libraries as well. He conjectured that the catalogue could be printed concisely in two columns and published in parts to allow its inexpensive piecemeal acquisition by the general public: 'it seems to me,' Collier declared, 'the Keeper of Printed Books in this institution, instead of considering what catalogue would be advantageous to the readers and to the literary world generally, has considered what catalogue would contribute the most to his own reputation...'[24]

To this point, Collier's testimony was a model presentation of his case; his facts were true, his arguments strong. By pamphlet and testimony he had clearly described the essential faults of the catalogue Panizzi was creating and suggested its long-term deleterious results. Had he stopped here and rested his case, it is possible he might have been successful in changing the course of the proceedings. But he did not stop. Encouraged, in part, by his success and led on by the shrewd questioning of some of the commissioners, he made a disastrous tactical error. In his testimony Collier had asserted that the ninety-one rules on which Panizzi had insisted unnecessarily cluttered the text and slowed down the cataloguing process. This statement was now picked up by Panizzi's advocate, Lord Seymour, who asked Collier how many rules he thought were necessary, and Collier allowed himself to be trapped into declaring that '20 rules would be sufficient'.[25] It was an arbitrary figure produced on the spur of the moment to suggest expertise that he did not really have. When Seymour pressed him as to what his rules would be, Collier was suddenly on the defensive. Instead of admitting the arbitrariness of his statement he promised to support it later. 'I am not prepared to do that at this moment,' he replied, 'but if the Commissioners will give me till another day I will be prepared with a statement of such rules as I consider indispensable for the catalogue, and such rules as I think ought to be left to the discretion of the cataloguer.'[26] It was a pretentious promise typical of Collier's overweening manner and it would be used to direct the argument away from the central point of Collier's earlier testimony. The pertinent question was not whether *Collier* could establish proper criteria, but whether Panizzi *had*. The subject should properly have been Panizzi's defence of the length and complexity of his rules, not Collier's skill in reducing them; but out of vanity, Collier accepted the burden of proof.

Four days later he produced not a list of rules but a series of sample catalogue entries which, he declared, he had made in a very short time at the rate of twenty-five to thirty an hour describing books taken at random from his own shelves. It was sheer bravado, an attempt to make the task look as simple as, perhaps, Collier thought it to be, and it was carelessly done.

Almost any other means would have served his cause better; he might, for example, have taken some of the over-long titles from the discredited 'A' Volume prepared and published under Panizzi's direction and shown how they could be reduced. Or he might have illustrated the many necessary exceptions to Panizzi's rules which produced organizational chaos in that book. Instead, he produced new entries of his own which, given his limited *cataloguing* experience, were certain to contain errors that would discredit his case.

The arguments Panizzi made in his testimony had been well refuted by Collier's letter to Ellesmere and by Collier's subsequent testimony before the commission.[27] Panizzi realized this and he refused to cross-examine Collier concerning the pamphlet (a procedure which would have put Collier's answers into the record). To regain the offensive, Panizzi needed to turn the argument away from *his* failures and toward those of his accusers, and Collier's gratuitous catalogue illustrations presented him with just such an opportunity. When Panizzi returned to testify before the commission in May, Collier's examples were his text and his weapon. They contained, he declared, 'almost every possible error which can be committed in cataloguing books.'[28] He compared them seriatim with entries which John Winter Jones, his chief cataloguer, had written and demonstrated that many of Collier's entries were incomplete or inaccurate, even for books that Collier himself had written. Panizzi produced his evidence with relish and increasing disdain: here Collier had omitted the first name of an author, there he had incorrectly quoted a title, this entry omitted the name of the editor, that the name of the annotator, and so on. The effect was devastating and Collier's argument against Panizzi was 'disposed of'. It was a masterful performance. 'I have observed in general', Panizzi announced in conclusion with withering hauteur, '... that the more ignorant people are, the more troublesome they are.'[29] The commission was his again.

It was an ironic outcome for Collier. His case, as contrasted with his tactics, was not disproved, merely discredited. What was not pointed out in subsequent testimony (Collier himself did not take the stand again) or in the ensuing report, was that in censuring Collier's entries, Jones had, in fact, produced

concise *index* entries of his own, that is, Panizzi's evidence, in
effect, demonstrated the truth of Collier's principal charge
that Panizzi's own preference and not the exigencies of
cataloguing had dictated lengthy descriptive entries. When so
directed, Jones could produce short catalogue titles and in far
less time than bibliographical ones. But though the principle
was inadvertently proved, the practice was damned and the
argument lost.[30]

Collier was now virtually excluded from the commission's
deliberations. As the commission secretary he might have
been expected to be instrumental in preparing its final report
(published in Parliament in March 1850), but he was allowed
no part in it. It was, he declared to a correspondent, 'prepared
solely by the Commissioners, and it merely passed through my
hands'.[31] It was just as well; writing the report could only have
been humiliating to him. The report, prepared under Ellesmere's direction, was delayed for several months. Ellesmere
was under great pressure to affirm Panizzi's case, and
although he apparently held back for a time, ill-health and
general weariness finally wore him down. The report emphatically rejected Collier's views. 'We unite in deprecating any
proposal for entering now on the preparation with a view to
publication, of a compendious catalogue', it stated, and
proceeded by indirection to snub Collier's testimony: only two
or three of the two dozen witnesses who testified supported
Panizzi's manuscript procedure, but the commission endorsed
it without question. We 'are disposed', they wrote, 'to attach
much weight to the evidence of some of our witnesses who, on
various grounds, are opposed to the scheme of a compendious
printed catalogue. Among these witnesses will be found some
by experience and pursuit highly qualified to judge of all
questions connected with the subject.' (So much for Collier's
qualifications!) 'With us,' the report concluded, 'the opinion
prevails that the principal advocates of a printed catalogue
have over-rated its utility, and underrated its difficulties.'[32]

Panizzi's victory could not have been more complete had he
written the report himself. Moreover, during the three years
the commission deliberated and in response to the trend of the
investigation, his position within the Museum had improved.
At the outset, he had complained that he had no control over

his staff; in his last testimony he declared that he had been given total direction of all employees and procedures in the Department of Printed Books. His attitude had changed as well. Initially he seemed as concerned as his readers about the compelling need for a better catalogue in the reading room; at the end, he flatly refused to make a new catalogue available to readers until the whole was completed at some unknown future time.

Panizzi's opponents did not accept the decision quietly. Newspapers and periodicals printed many letters of outrage and disapproval, and the cause was taken up in Parliament. In July, the report was debated at length, and in August, a new petition was presented to Parliament asking that it 'direct that a simple, concise Finding Catalogue of all the Printed Books in the National Library may be prepared, printed and published in the cheapest form and with the least possible delay.' 'We are as confident as men can be who are speculating on the future', the *Athenaeum* wrote, 'that no amount of opposition on the part of the officers of the Museum, indifference on the part of the Trustees, or misdirection on the part of the Commissioners will prevent the public from finally having a Printed Catalogue.'[33]

But it was not to be – at least not in the lifetimes of those who fought for it. The decision of 1850 stood for a generation. Panizzi succeeded in delaying the publication of the British Museum Catalogue, one of the great scholarly achievements of the nineteenth century, for nearly fifty years. In the meantime, users of the library had to make do with a catalogue which was illegible, over long and far in arrears. Panizzi's great achievements in reorganizing the library's procedures, building its collection and enlarging and redesign-ing its reading room, are blighted by this legacy of delay in the printed catalogue. The greatest irony of all is that after Panizzi's death, when the British Museum Catalogue finally resumed publication in 1881, it was a compendious index to the collection, printed in double column, published in parts – a catalogue of the kind, scope and form that Collier, to his disfavour and loss, had advocated over thirty years before.

But that, of course, was long after it made any difference to Collier or his reputation. He was crushed, not only by the report but also by its unanimous adoption. Ellesmere, too, at last had voted against a printed index catalogue. He had disowned, albeit with misgivings, the evidence which he himself had urged Collier to present. Even before the report was completed he wrote Collier a kind of apology for what was to come. 'Circumstances have certainly occurred in the course of the enquiry which have occasioned me considerable trouble, embarrassment and regret the more so because I consider them to have originated entirely in my own incaution and want of foresight', he said.[34] This could be only a small comfort to Collier, but he showed no lasting bitterness towards Ellesmere. 'The only fault of his character', he was to write many years later, 'was having too high an estimate of those who were interested in misguiding him, and too little reliance upon his own unswayed convictions. If Ellesmere had only been as firm as, in my opinion, he was right, we might possibly . . . have obtained the easiest mode of reference to every printed volume in the Library.'[35] Possibly. Possibly not.

The preferment Collier had hoped for was lost, and his desperation can be gauged by the hopeless gestures he made to save himself. The most painful of these was an appeal to John Campbell, his old acquaintance who had just been named Lord Chief Justice. Campbell had known the Collier family for nearly fifty years, ever since he had worked with Dyer on the *Oracle* and thereafter on the *Morning Chronicle*. Campbell, subsequently called to the bar, had had a highly successful legal career, a lucrative practice, a peerage and the bench. Their paths had long since diverged, and Campbell must have been surprised by the invitation he received for tea at the Payne Collier residence in Kensington, and even more surprised on his arrival when, after the shortest pause required by civility, Collier blurted out his anguish and asked – begged actually – Campbell to appoint him a police magistrate. It was a perquisite well within Campbell's power to bestow but Collier was deluded in thinking there was any chance that Campbell, one of the most cunning of political manipulators, would give it, without any personal advantage to himself, to a mere acquaintance, especially an acquaintance out of a slightly disreputable past. When he heard Collier's appeal,

Campbell burst out laughing. 'Impossible!' he cried, and, still laughing, immediately departed.

Collier's career was a shambles. He had worked without let-up for nearly half a century for low pay and in poor conditions. He had contributed in large measure to the learning of his generation; and he was ready to contribute more, but he was, nonetheless, a discarded man. He had no 'prospects' at all – not in newspaper work, government service, or remunerative scholarship. His merit had been denied, not for weakness or failure, but for candour. The injustice overwhelmed him, but as his anger subsided, he proceeded to set his life in order. With great mental suffering but almost no self-pity, he wrote to Robinson, his first and most stalwart friend, describing what he had resolved to do:

> Victoria Road
> Kensington
> 4 March 1850

My dear Robinson

As the Commission on the British Museum is now practically at an end, and as the result has been the disappointment of any hopes of further advantage to me from it, you will not be surprised (or at all accounts not much surprised) to hear that I am putting my affairs into as small a compass as I can, and that with my Wife and four daughters I am about to retire into the country.

The distance we are going is not great, and the friends and relations to whom we are going most kind and considerate. Robert Proctor and Polly, at Geys, have a larger house than they at all need, and they have agreed to take us in on such terms as offer them no benefit, but as will afford us a most agreeable and welcome asylum. In this way I shall be able, I think, to make my small income sufficient; and I am too old now to be able to increase it in the way in which, as you are well aware, I formerly managed to eke it out, and make both ends pretty nearly meet.

I shall employ my leisure, in my retirement, in writing to as much profit as I can, but my knowledge, I am sorry to say, is not of the most saleable kind. What I can do I will do; and however ill advised, on many accounts, has been my course, I do not believe that anybody can justly say of me that I have not been a willing and a hard-working man. At sixty, my health would not be equal to night-work upon newspapers, and unless I could do night-work, I do not know what employment I could obtain. If you happen to hear of any, consistent with my knowledge, abilities (such as they are) and health, you do not know a man more desirous of performing it.

I wish to make my change as easy and noiseless as I can upon all accounts; and it is not unnatural that at my age I should not object to retirement, though I may not like obscurity.

The truth of the matter is (but I do not wish it to go farther now) that the Commissioners will do nothing for me. In advocating, with more zeal than discretion, a short, but complete printed Catalogue of the books in the Museum, I opposed not only Mr. Panizzi, but the views of the great majority of the Commissioners, and instead of floating down the stream of good luck, I am left high and dry on the sand-bank of disappointment. Without a future, I took the honest but the unwelcome course; and for the sake of literature and poor literary men, I placed myself in a position rather to offend than to please those whom I served. I must take the consequences, though I cannot but feel them severely, and the more severely because I necessarily draw my dear old wife and my daughters into the scrape. However, they suffer so cheerfully, that they do much to reconcile me to the condition of my affairs. They believe it is no fault of mine, and on some accounts I rejoice in my comparative poverty.

I am troubling you too much at length upon these matters; but recollecting that you are the oldest friend of me and of my family, I will not make any apology.

Bob and Polly will do everything to make us comfortable, and, in the country, I shall at least get rid of the irritation and anxiety occasioned throughout by the adverse working of the Commission, the object in appointing which I entirely, and from the first, misunderstood. I am,

My dear Robinson,
Your always affectionate friend
J. Payne Collier

Do not speak of the subject of this letter excepting in general terms to any of our mutual friends. I wish, as much as I can, to keep up appearances.[36]

V

THE PERKINS FOLIO

'I at first repented my bargain . . .'

13

In late March 1850 Collier moved to Holyport near Maidenhead, a charming village scarcely thirty miles from London. The move should have been salutary. London was an unhealthy place for him to live; in winter, its soot-heavy air racked his lungs and brought on excruciating attacks of quinsy; in summer, the stench of the Thames made him ill. Collier ought to have been eager to leave it, but he wasn't. A Londoner born and bred, he could be truly at home nowhere else. The city encapsulated his past, and leaving it, even for a pleasant village nearby, was one of the saddest events of his life. He was well past the age when such a change could promise a new beginning; it was, rather, a step towards death, another of the bitter disappointments that punctuated his life. At sixty-one, John Payne Collier was an unhappy and distrustful man, brusque, supercilious and insecure. He had good cause to be bitter, but his manner was no less objectionable for that. He could not live easily with himself, and he was not an easy person to live with.

It was therefore fortunate that the Colliers moved in with Mary and Robert Proctor, the only members of the family who had enough patience and goodwill to get along with them. Collier's niece Mary (Polly) and her husband still had the spirit and imagination which took them to South America as well as the industry which enabled them to make a success of the Aldermanbury Dairy thereafter. The farm Robert Proctor had rented two years before was a tidy acreage with a charming house, 'Geys Cottage', an eighteenth-century villa which over the years had been expanded into a gentleman's country seat, surrounded by a large, well laid out garden and furnished in a manner that gave the place an air of casual elegance. ('Even bad family portraits when old have a good effect', Robinson remarked after a visit.)[1] It was a place that readily supported the pretensions of the Payne Colliers, a more congenial surrounding than they might have expected. The Proctors' invitation was not, however, prompted by family feeling alone; only three Proctor children lived at home (their eldest son was in London reading law) and good huswifery demanded that the empty rooms at Geys should be filled. Payne's family now numbered seven: he and Louisa, his four unmarried daughters and Louisa's sister, Emma Pycroft, and he was to pay a large share of the Proctors' rent.

Paying that share, however, was difficult. When his work for the commission ended, he had lost half his income, which dropped to something less than £400 per year, three-fourths of it from the Pycroft sisters' shares of the Pelican Life Insurance Company and the rest the £100 which the Duke of Devonshire continued to pay him for his duties as 'librarian'. It was soon apparent that even in Holyport £400 could not support the Collier family. Payne's two older daughters were mortally ill with pulmonary disease and required, with increasing frequency, expensive convalescence at Brighton or Torquay. His sons could not help him. John was well placed as the private secretary to the Chief Officer of the Exchequer, but his salary was small; he had married the previous October and had family responsibilities of his own. William, Payne's younger son, was worse off than his brother: his position in the Stamp Office paid scarcely enough to support a frugal bachelor, and yet he too had married and his wife had borne him four daughters in four years. Payne's sons were more likely to ask for money than to give it.

Payne had sold everything of value he possessed. Even before leaving London he had begun to transfer the best of his library to his nephew, Frederick Ouvry ('I liked to sell none of them', he recalled long after, 'but necessity had no law. All my good books went to him.')[2] These were private sales, kept secret to save face, but even these acts of near desperation could not satisfy his continuing needs. From 1847 to 1850, Collier had written or edited over half a dozen major works, at least as many privately printed pamphlets, and a score of papers for inclusion in *The Shakespeare Society Papers* (which he had begun in 1845 and continued to edit) and *Archeologia*, the publication of the Society of Antiquaries (of which he became executive Vice-president in 1848). He received no payment for any of these labours and it is a sad commentary on the rewards of scholarship in mid-nineteenth-century England that at the end of this remarkably productive period Collier should have been reduced to genteel beggary.

There were only three men who might aid him. His 'most serviceable friend', the man from whom he might have taken aid with the least expense of pride, was Thomas Amyot, but Amyot, long suffering from severe ill-health, died suddenly before Collier could approach him, and this left only Devonshire and Ellesmere, men to whom he was already much indebted and for whom he felt some distaste. After so many years of well publicized patronage it was excessively painful to have to beg again for mere subsistence. The frustrated expectations of the past returned to trouble him – those hopes which had been fed and then starved by his noble patrons while the sinecures that rank could bestow had gone to other and sometimes lesser men. The road to Holyport had been strewn with patrons' promises: the abortive term as play licenser! Devonshire's refusal to secure him a magistrate's appointment! Ellesmere's failure to establish him at the Museum! He had not asked for charity, only the position his accomplishments deserved; had he been licenser, magistrate or librarian, his talents would have brought their own rewards. He had been too proud, of course; he had pretended sufficiency when he had none; he had allowed these very rich men, who could have supplied his needs ten times over without noticing the expenditure, to ignore his poverty; he had lived on lies because he could not admit his poverty even to himself. Now he could pretend no longer and his need was revealed for what it was and always had been. Nevertheless, he could not bring himself to ask Devonshire for aid; the 'librarian stipend', though he now thought it niggardly recompense for past service, precluded asking more assistance from that quarter and this left only Ellesmere – the man whom only a few weeks before he had promised himself he would never again petition for any favour.

Within a month of settling at Holyport, Collier wrote to Ellesmere. He was desperately afraid the Earl, in poor health and preoccupied with other affairs, might not respond in time, but Ellesmere was genuinely moved and embarrassed by Collier's distress and immediately secured the old man a civil list pension of £100 from the sum the government awarded each year to needy men of letters, declaring 'I could neither do more nor less.' He could have done more but it was to his credit that he refused to do less.

Collier was grateful, but he was also ashamed. A civil list pension was public charity, and it wounded his self-esteem to know he would be publicly identified as indigent. To Robinson, surely as sympathetic as anyone to Collier's worth and need, the pension was the mark not of success but of failure, and, as he wrote to his brother, he was 'only half and half pleased and sorry' that Collier had accepted the money. 'I dare say', Robinson concluded, 'he will feel something like shame, when it will be made public as it must in a few months.'[3] What Payne would admit to no one, not even Robinson, was that he had begged for the pension. How much greater his humiliation had that been known!

Nevertheless, the stipend gave him financial security to continue the work he loved. During the three years preceding Collier's move to the country, the Shakespeare Society had issued some of its most valuable books but its membership was declining. Even before he left London, Collier was being pressed by printers with overdue bills, and by early 1851 the auditors reported that only 126 of 451 'members' had paid their £1 dues.[4] Once established in the country, Collier was determined to save the organization he had almost single-handedly created ten years before. To encourage subscribers, he immediately announced his intention to complete the edition of Thomas Heywood's plays which Barron Field had begun for the Society eight years before. Fourteen plays had been attributed to Heywood, but Field had published only four before his death,[5] and Collier undertook to edit the remainder. In the six months after he left London, he completed *The Fair Maid of the West, Parts I and II, The Royal King and Loyal Subject* and *A Woman Killed with Kindness*. In early 1851 he followed these with *If You Know Not Me, You*

Know Nobody, Parts I and II and, in May of that year, *The Golden Age* and *The Silver Age.* Editing Heywood was far more difficult than editing Shakespeare (the early quartos were a patchwork of textual confusion compounded by haphazard provenance and careless printing), and Collier's edition was marred by the faults of nineteenth-century editorial practice (he regularized spelling and silently 'corrected' syntax, for example). But his intention was nonetheless 'modern': to produce not the text that the reader might prefer the author to have written but rather the text that the author actually wrote, however incomplete or disjointed that text might be. As Collier stated in his preface to *The Fair Maid of the West,* his guiding purpose was 'to leave the whole drama as we may suppose Heywood would have left it' and to avoid 'the vanity of displaying extensive reading, and of citing recondite authorities' which would merely add 'surplusage'.[6] The principle is a commonplace of modern editing, but Collier was among the first to articulate it and to discipline himself to its demands. Whatever the faults of his Heywood edition, they did not derive from the unnecessary display of irrelevant knowledge of the sort which cluttered the work of many of his contemporaries or from the unhappy 'second guessing' which marred the work of many of his successors. (His notes and comment have been particularly useful to the editors who followed him, at least one of whom savagely condemned Collier's work while shamelessly plagiarizing his notes.[7])

Collier devoted the first year at Holyport to editing Heywood's plays, planning to complete the edition in 1852. By July 1851 he had nearly completed the texts of *The Brazen Age* and *The Iron Age,* and had begun work on *The Four Prentices.* But the cool reception of the first volumes of the new edition discouraged him and he dropped Heywood permanently in favour of a new project which he thought more likely to revitalize the Shakespeare Society: a hitherto unknown manuscript copy of Anthony Munday's *John a Kent and John a Cumber.* It was apparently written in the author's own hand, and had been discovered by Frederick Madden in the family papers of a Welsh M.P. named E.M. Mostyn. Madden, then a member of the Shakespeare Society's board of directors, secured Mostyn's permission to print the play, and Collier quickly put aside Heywood to take up Munday. The project was particularly attractive because he had found many references to Munday in the Dulwich papers and in the Stationers' *Registers,* and he was eager to put that information into print. His long introduction to the play was the first critical examination of Munday; it contained a well-documented memoir of the dramatist and an annotated bibliography of his works along with a careful analysis of the analogues of the play. *John a Kent and John a Cumber* was distributed to the Shakespeare Society's membership in late 1851, but it was no more successful than the Heywood edition in regenerating the organization. In the last months of 1851, the Society showed unmistakable signs of dissolution and all plans for future publication were suspended.

The Society of Antiquaries, too, was beset with internal conflict. Under Collier's direction, it had broadened its activities, and by reducing its dues by half it had tried to bring in new members. But the Society continued to decline. Collier realized that the vitality of these organizations was waning, that the force behind their growth in recent years had been largely of his own creation, and that the interest of the dilettantes who supported them was no longer there. The demise of the Shakespeare Society in particular seemed symbolic of the fate of his own reputation: his work as editor, author and organizer had been prodigious – none of his contemporaries had contributed more to the study of early English drama – and yet he was only grudgingly accepted by many of his peers; he had never lost the demi-monde status of his newspaper past, and his supercilious manner, socially pretentious and prideful, was offensive. Recognized by many, he was appreciated by very few.

While the two organizations through which Collier had achieved professional recognition were declining, his position as the pre-eminent editor of Shakespeare was being challenged. Samuel Weller Singer, whose 1826 Shakespeare had been superseded by Collier's of 1844, had prepared a second edition. Dyce had continued to collect notes for his edition, and it was rumoured that he had a contract with Moxon to publish. But the most formidable challenger was James Orchard Halliwell. Thirty years younger than Collier,

Halliwell was his near-equal in knowledge, and more than his match in energy and competitive spirit. Halliwell, the son of a prosperous London merchant, had revealed his talent early. At fifteen he was writing articles for the London *Parthenon*; at seventeen, when he entered Trinity College, Cambridge, he had published several books demonstrating his knowledge of mathematics and his skill at assembling disparate facts into readable biographies. University life bored him and he left Cambridge without taking a degree, but before he was twenty-one he had accomplished more than many of his associates would attempt in their entire careers: he had prepared and published a catalogue of the Royal Society Library, amassed a large and valuable collection of rare manuscripts, become a Fellow of the Society of Antiquaries, and had been elected while only eighteen to membership of the Royal Society, sponsored by Sir Henry Ellis among others. By the time he reached his majority Halliwell had helped to found the Camden and Percy Societies and had been one of the small group who joined Collier to establish the Shakespeare Society. He served the latter energetically and continuously as board member and editor.

Halliwell was a youth of charm and audacity. He early became a close friend of Thomas Wright, who introduced him to the manuscript treasures of the Trinity College library and he became an intimate friend of both William Jerdan, editor of the *Literary Gazette,* and Joseph Hunter. He was a close associate of Howard Staunton, the international chess champion turned Shakespeare enthusiast and, after he dedicated a volume called *Scraps from Ancient MSS* to Sir Thomas Phillipps, he was a protégé of that wealthy antiquary who happened to possess what was thought to be one of the greatest private manuscript collections in England. But along with his brilliance, Halliwell had a reckless spirit and a perverse taste for the unexpected and outrageous. In 1840 he betrayed his friendship with Wright by stealing manuscripts from Trinity College library which he then surreptitiously sold to the British Museum, to the embarrassment of Sir Henry Ellis. The affair would have ended the career of any other man, but it hardly stained his reputation. Although the crime was well known, Halliwell avoided prosecution. He even managed to maintain his friendship with Wright and Ellis, and although the manuscripts were never returned to Trinity, to carry on much as he had before. At twenty-two, having secured Phillipps's esteem to say nothing of open access to the baronet's house and collection, Halliwell defied his new patron and eloped with Phillipps's eldest daughter, Henrietta. Phillipps broke off all communication with the couple and became Halliwell's greatest enemy, but that didn't trouble Halliwell: the Phillipps estate was entailed to Henrietta by her grandfather's will, and fume though he might Thomas Phillipps could not disinherit the rebellious couple; they would get his millions in the end.

Despite his scandalous private life, Halliwell's dedication to scholarship was never seriously questioned. In his twentieth year he published ten works; in the next, thirteen more. This was to be the pattern of his life. His learning was remarkable, he had an immense knowledge of arcane facts, and although, like many of his contemporaries, his literary taste was questionable, his appetite for scholarship was voracious. No one of his time was more tireless in searching out details of literary history and, with the possible exception of Collier, none was more successful in discovering and publishing them.

Halliwell's interest in Shakespeare was cultivated rather than profound. His concern was not commentary but text, and he set about becoming a Shakespeare authority with characteristic calculation. In 1841, shortly after he helped to found the Shakespeare Society, he bought heavily at the sale of the library of George Chalmers, and this was the beginning of his noteworthy Shakespeare collection. For the next decade Halliwell immersed himself in the study of Shakespeare and his times. He edited three works for the Shakespeare Society on the sources of Shakespeare's plays and five others on Elizabethan drama. In 1848 he published *The Life of Shakespeare,* a valuable book which, although largely derived from data Collier and others had published earlier, revealed fresh information that Halliwell himself had unearthed among the municipal records at Stratford-upon-Avon. These publications were the obvious first steps toward a new edition of Shakespeare's plays, and at the end of 1851 Halliwell had announced plans for a *Folio Shakespeare*.

With such a resourceful competitor at work, Collier's professional position was in jeopardy. The conventional response to this challenge was a second edition of the 1844 Shakespeare, and Collier had made copious notes in preparation for one. But George Whittaker had died in 1847, and his successors in the company were not interested in a new edition only superficially different from the first of which they still had unsold copies. Moreover, a mere revision would not be so profitable for Collier as a significantly new text demonstrating an advance on its predecessor, a text with new authority or fresh critical insights to justify its purchase. Collier had little that was new to add to his earlier effort except minor corrections and incidental information to corroborate his earlier decisions. His notes indicate that in 1851 he had no pressing *literary* considerations for starting afresh. He was still committed to the critical assumption which had directed his first edition: the essential validity of the First Folio text as qualified by various quarto readings and the rejection of unnecessary conjectural emendation.

Collier was thus caught between professional honesty and commercial necessity. His critical bias was conservative; commercial publication, on the other hand, was concerned with producing what would sell at a profit. In his first edition the two had come together fortuitously: the text of the early copies had been both editorially preferable and commercially desirable. But the whirligig of taste had turned. To those who knew how to read them, there were signs that the public's interest in a rigorous text had waned in the six years since Collier's first edition and that any successful new edition of Shakeseare would have to accommodate this change. To his great discredit – and ultimately to his ruin – Collier was prepared to make accommodation.

It is easy to see his decision as a sacrifice of talent and taste to the necessities of commerce, a proud man near the end of his career forced by circumstances to deny the professional standards of a lifetime. But that would be an unduly romantic reading of the case. The fact is, Collier was a professional author; he saw his work not solely or even primarily as the expression of an imaginative necessity but as a commodity produced to meet the demands of others. For all of his professional life Collier had lived by writing to order, for newspapers, for periodicals, or for patrons. This had always been the source of his livelihood, and although he chafed at the physical discomfort it imposed on him, the endless hours in the cramped and airless gallery of Parliament, the night after day drudgery of hackwork journalism, he never seriously questioned its *intellectual* constraints. So far as journalism was concerned, his pen was for sale and he understood and accepted that bargain. His work as editor, critic and historiographer might appear to be of a different kind, in it he had a far wider range of subject to pursue after his own fashion, but this difference was essentially one of degree rather than of kind. Its reward was repute rather than money, but it too demanded conformity to public demand in order to achieve success.

All the professional experience of his life had conditioned Collier to give the readers what they wanted, to search among his own interests for those that most closely matched the taste of the public. If the public now seemed to want a Shakespeare text based on conjecture rather than historical sources, Collier had a corresponding desire to supply it. To our age this complaisance smacks of dishonesty; to his, it was practical necessity.

However one judges it, Collier was ready to disavow the professional commitment he had made twenty years before, to violate the sound critical dicta he had faithfully and at times brilliantly demonstrated in his edition of 1841–44. It was a fateful decision, one he would later call 'the most foolish act of my life'.

14

On 17 January, 1852, Collier addressed the following letter to the London *Athenaeum*:

A short time before the death of the late Mr. Rodd, of Newport Street, I happened to be in his shop when a considerable parcel of books arrived from the country. He told me that they had been bought for him at an auction – I think, in Bedfordshire; but I did not look on it as a matter of any importance to observe from whence they came. He unpacked them in my presence; and I cast my eyes on several that did not appear to me very inviting, – as they were entirely out of my line of reading. There were two, however, that attracted my attention: – one being a fine copy of Florio's Italian Dictionary, of the edition of 1611, – and the other a much thumbed, abused, and imperfect copy of the second folio of Shakespeare 1632. The first I did not possess, – and the last I was willing to buy, inasmuch as I apprehended it would add some missing leaves to a copy of the same impression which I had had for some time on my shelves. As was his usual course, Mr. Rodd required a very reasonable price for both: – for the first, I remember, I gave 12s., – and for the last, only 1l. 10s.

Your readers are no doubt aware that the second folio of Shakespeare, of 1632, is never, even when in good condition, a very dear book; but this copy was without the title-page (consequently without the portrait), – wanted several sheets at the end, – and was imperfect in the middle of the volume. With this last circumstance I was not acquainted at the time, – for I saw only the commencement and the conclusion; but I observed that some of the leaves were blotted and dirty, – and that although the rough calf binding was evidently the original, it was greasy and shabby. On the outside of one of the covers was inscribed, – 'Tho. Perkins, his booke.'

When the volume reached my house, I employed a person to ascertain whether any of the leaves in it would supply the deficiency in my other copy. Finding that I was disappointed in this respect (excepting as far as regarded two torn and stained pages), I put the book away in a closet, – somewhat vexed that I had mis-spent my money. I did not look at it again until shortly before I removed to this place [Maidenhead]; when I selected such books as I chose to take with me from those which I meant to leave behind in the Pantechnicon. Then it was that I for the first time remarked that the folio of 1632 which I had bought from Mr. Rodd contained manuscript alterations of the text as it stood printed in that early edition. These alterations were in an old hand-writing – probably not of a later date than the Protectorate, – and applied (as I afterwards found, on going through the volume here) to every play. There was hardly a page without emendations of more or less importance and interest, – and some of them appeared to me highly valuable. The punctuation, on which of course so much of the author's meaning depends, was corrected in, I may say, thousands of places.

I did not come into possession of this volume – much less examine it minutely – until some years after I had completed the Shakespeare which I superintended through the press, – otherwise I should unquestionably have made great use of it in the notes; – and in particular instances the changes appear to me not merely so plausible, but so self-evident, that, in spite of the principle I adopted of a close adherence to the old printed copies, I cannot help thinking that I should have availed myself of a few of these manuscript alterations in the text. Some of them may have been purely arbitrary or conjectural; but others seem to have been justified either by occasional resort to better manuscripts than those employed by the old player-editors, or, as is not improbable, by the recital of the text at one of our old theatres when the correcter of my folio of 1632 was present, and of which recital he afterwards availed himself.

Having said thus much – which, in fact, is all I can say – of the history of the volume, – I shall now proceed to select a few specimens of the improvements which it contains of the old and ordinary readings of Shakespeare.

Collier concluded his announcement by quoting eleven emendations ('only a few out of hundreds, and by no means the most striking') and stated his intention

to place this relic before, and at the disposal of, the Council of the Shakespeare Society at its next meeting. The members will then be better able to judge of the date and of the peculiarity and importance of the alterations suggested on nearly every page; and if they agree with me, they will, in due time and as their funds allow, print such a selection of the manuscript notes as may best serve to explain, illustrate, or amend the acknowledged defects of the text of the plays of our greatest dramatic Poet.

J. Payne Collier[8]

The letter was an act of exploration. Collier was testing to determine if there were a market for a conjectural text and, if there proved to be one, to establish his claim to supply it. It was therefore a very tentative statement, one easily forgotten if the public were cool to the idea. The point was simply put: he had found a unique and remarkable source of new readings for Shakespeare that encouraged him to reconsider his previous textual assumptions. The emendations were not all good and the best only 'seemed' justified by 'occasional' use of manuscripts, but if others agreed with his interest, he would publish them. Could anything be less assertive, less polemical?

In fact, the letter was a *tour de force* which claimed all and conceded nothing. Collier's deprecatory tone enhanced the presumed value of his discovery. He presented himself as a sceptic persuaded to accept, almost against his will, the possibility of authoritative evidence. It was certainly the most disarming way possible to announce a remarkable editorial about face, for even Collier could not have denied that a renunciation was implicit in what he wrote. Overnight the most restrictive editor of Shakespeare had become – at least potentially – the most permissive, for his assertion that the Perkins Folio emendations might be authoritative was, in the light of his own knowledge, practice and experience, hypothetical to the point of fantasy.

The announcement caused a sensation. That Collier of all editors should thus so completely renounce his former dicta stunned his readers and created, at least initially, an aura of uncritical acceptance around the Perkins emendations. The *Athenaeum* was flooded with letters of comment and inquiry. 'All these communications treat the event as one of the most important and interesting that has for a long time arisen in the history of Shakespeare comment', it reported.[9] 'If the specimens furnished of the corrections are a fair sample', declared a typical correspondent, 'I cannot entertain a doubt that they are founded on an authentic text, more pure than any extant, – and are in no wise conjectural emendations.'[10] Many demanded that the emendations be published immediately. 'If the folio be consigned to the Shakespeare Society, only a limited number will be printed, and a year's subscription must be paid by those who may wish to obtain this one book', wrote one complainant. 'Now, I apprehend, an edition could be published in the usual way, at a much less price than $1l$.'[15] 'Mr. Collier may be assured that his announcement has caused a great sensation throughout Shakespeare-dom', wrote another, 'and that no light responsibility as to the future now rests upon his shoulders. A very early result will, I trust, be, the appearance of a carefully printed volume, adapted for *wide* circulation, containing every minute alteration, in either the text or the punctuation, which has been made in the folio . . .'[11]

Had Collier foreseen the public interest in the emendations, he might have been less generous about offering them to the Shakespeare Society, but he honoured his promise. The publication might give the organization badly needed support, replenish its treasure, subsidize other publications and re-establish the Society in the public esteem – all prime objectives for Collier, and, of course, the Society edition would not preclude a second edition for his own profit.

Despite his gratification, Collier was a bit apprehensive about the excitement he had generated. He felt, perhaps, a niggling sense of guilt for his editorial apostasy and even some alarm at the expectations he had raised. Two weeks after his first announcement, he wrote a second letter to the *Athenaeum* which suggested a caveat of sorts: 'It is to me yet quite uncertain', he wrote, 'what character they [the corrections] really observe, – that is to say, on what authority they were made: – whether they were adopted from purer manuscripts – whether they were introduced by a person who had heard a better text recited on the stage than was given in the folios, – or whether they were merely conjectural. Perhaps all three methods were followed, as opportunity presented itself.' This was a more qualified report than he had given earlier. Moreover, he announced that further consideration had convinced him that one of the emendations he had printed in his first letter was merely 'an instance of speculative alteration, such as would occur to a person on reading the play' and that one of the words proposed in an emendation in *Othello* seemed 'on further reflection clearly wrong'.[12] Collier was attempting to dampen somewhat the enthusiasm he had engendered, but his note of caution went unheeded.

The most important information contained in Collier's second letter was an announcement that, as he had promised, the Perkins Folio would be available to the Council of the Shakespeare Society on the following Tuesday (February 10) and open to the examination of any member of the Society of Antiquaries on the Thursday thereafter in order, he said, 'that any gentleman will have an opportunity of inspecting it, and forming his own judgment.'[13] Later, when some Antiquarians complained they had been unable to attend the meeting, Collier announced that the folio would again be available in the library of the Society at Somerset House. In all, Collier made the folio available for general examination on at least four occasions, and he showed it privately as well. He lent it to Ellesmere for several days and he subsequently placed it in the hands of his publisher for a week, probably to encourage Whittaker & Company's interest in a new edition based on the emendations.[14] 'My desire is, that all who are interested should be gratified as far as possible, and enjoy the means of judging for themselves the value and curiosity of the book', he wrote. All evidence supports the assumption that he was sincere in this statement; anyone who wanted to see the folio had a chance to do so – with only one proviso: 'It must also be distinctly understood', Collier warned, 'that no gentleman is at liberty to make memoranda, or in any way to give publicity to the notes or changes which he may inspect.'[15] These restrictions seemed reasonable; surely Collier had the right to reserve their first publication to himself? Moreover, those who examined the book discovered it contained, in a conservative estimate, over 20,000 emendations. Collier could hardly have studied them all; even a cursory examination would take weeks.

It is necessary to pause in this account of the events initiated by Collier's announcement to suggest what neither friend nor competitor suspected at the time: that Collier's account of the acquisition of the Perkins Folio was not entirely true. The degree of misrepresentation is slight perhaps and it had little direct bearing on the intrinsic value of the book, but it was nonetheless calculated and deceitful. In particular, he almost certainly lied about Rodd's failure to examine the book as well as about his own failure to do so at the time of purchase, and he falsely suggested that the date of sale was at least two years later than it was. Moreover, his manner of repeating the story was suspicious. For example, in his introduction to *Notes and Emendations,* the selection of the Perkins Folio corrections which he published some months after his letter to the *Athenaeum,* Collier recounted the circumstances of the discovery and purchase in greater detail but with subtle modification: he had been in Rodd's shop 'in the Spring of

1849' he declared (his memory of the date was *now* quite precise) when the package of books arrived from the country (the suggestion of an auction had been silently dropped). Rodd opened the package in his presence, and most of the contents were of little interest to Collier, but his attention was caught by 'an excellent copy of Florio's "New World of Words", 1611' – here a rush of unrelated details – 'with the name of Henry Osborn (whom I mistook at the moment for his celebrated namesake, Francis) upon the first leaf, as well as a copy of the second folio of Shakespeare's Plays, much cropped, the covers old and greasy, and, as I saw at a glance on opening them, imperfect at the beginning and end.' He bought both, he again relates, 'the latter to complete another poor copy of the second folio' in his possession.

As it turned out [he continued], I at first repented my bargain as regards the Shakespeare [it is now, inexplicably, a 'bargain' – earlier it had had a 'reasonable price'], because, when I took it home, it appeared that two leaves which I wanted were unfit for my purpose, not merely by being too short, but damaged and defaced [His reasons for rejection were now more precise and contained no reference to another 'person' who examined the book for him.]; thus disappointed, I threw it by, and did not see it again, until I made a selection of books I would take with me on quitting London. In the mean time, finding that I could not readily remedy the deficiencies in my other copy of the folio, 1632, I had parted with it; and when I removed into the country, with my family, in the spring of 1850, in order that I might not be without some copy of the second folio for the purpose of reference, I took with me that which is the foundation of the present work.

It was while putting my books together for removal, that I first observed some marks in the margin of this folio; but it was subsequently placed upon an upper shelf, and I did not take it down until I had occasion to consult it. [Here is a subtle change from his *Athenaeum* announcement: the 'manuscript alterations' he had earlier described as having been discovered before his departure from London had now become merely 'some marks'; this lengthened the period of time before his full realization of their importance.] It then struck me that Thomas Perkins, whose name, with the addition of 'his Booke', was upon the cover, might be the old actor who had performed in Marlowe's 'Jew of Malta', on its revival shortly before 1633. At this time I fancied that the binding was of about that date, and that the volume might have been his; but in the first place, I found that his name was Richard Perkins, and in the next I became satisfied that the rough calf was not the original binding. [Another change from the first announcement in which he declared the binding 'evidentally original'.] Still, Thomas Perkins might have been a descendant of Richard; and this circumstance and others induced me to examine the volume more particularly: I then discovered, to my surprise, that there was hardly a page which did not present, in a handwriting of the time, some emendations in the pointing or in the text, while on most of them they were frequent, and on many numerous.[16]

The studied carelessness of this second account – the interpolation of extraneous detail, for example – suggests that Collier was careful in composing it and that the changes in his story are not inadvertent.

Collier's story is, at the very least, disingenuous. It is inconsistent with the known character and practice of both himself and Thomas Rodd. For example, anyone who knew Rodd would find it hard to believe that he sold the folio as Collier said: if it had only just arrived from the country, if Rodd presumably had never seen it before, would he have sold it on the spot without examination? How could he determine the price? Since the copy was without title page, it would have taken *some* examination merely to determine which folio it was (obviously a First Folio would have been worth more than a Second), and in determining this, how could he have not seen the manuscript notes on almost every page? If he saw some of them, would Rodd not have scrutinized the volume to discover all? And having done so, would he not have determined their potential value before fixing the minimal price of 30s. on the book? It is very difficult to believe that Rodd, surely one of the most astute bookdealers of his time, would allow a treasure to slip through his fingers in the careless manner Collier describes.

But even if we grant that Rodd was guilty of this uncharacteristic lapse of professional caution, what of Collier? What possessed *him* to buy a battered, stained copy of the Second Folio for thirty shillings when, as any buyer of the time knew (and he indirectly admits), copies of the book in *good* condition were readily available from Rodd or another at no greater price? And why should be accept a poor copy if his real purpose was to correct a defective one at home? If one grants that Collier was somehow willing to pay this price merely to acquire a few missing pages for another copy, would he not, at the very least, have examined the book to the extent of making sure that it *had* the pages he sought? Anyone who knew Collier could be certain he would have! It is beyond belief that he inspected the folio closely enough to notice it was missing leaves at the beginning and end but not closely enough to determine if it would serve the only purpose for which he declares he bought it.

If it is difficult to credit Collier's description of the transaction, it is impossible to believe his account of the subsequent treatment of the book: finding the folio lacked the pages he had bought it for, he 'threw it by' and, apparently giving up the plan on which he had already spent the considerable sum of a pound and a half, 'parted' with the presumably *better* copy and kept the battered and defaced one 'for the purpose of reference'! And most surprising of all, we are asked to believe that at no point in this quixotic series of events did he notice the manuscript notes, although later he saw that 'hardly a page [was] without emendations of more or less importance and interest'. This was an astonishing case of selective myopia!

Moreover, it is hard to believe that any editor of Shakespeare, even one busy with other pressing work, would have been guilty of failing to examine the 'marks' in the margins of the folio. Any emended folio, particularly a Second Folio, had an intrinsic interest; corrected folios had been valuable editorial resources since Theobald. Steevens used an annotated copy of the Second Folio which had once belonged to Charles I; Malone consulted another which had been emended by John Frater; Singer had used an annotated copy of the Third Folio in preparing his 1826 edition – and would use it again; Halliwell, too, cited an emended folio in his text for the Folio Shakespeare; and Collier himself had used the Bridgewater Folio emendations in the notes of his 1841–44 edition of Shakespeare. He was, therefore, mindful of the potential editorial value of an emended folio and the notes in the Perkins Folio would certainly have interested him more than he here suggests they did.

But *why* should he thus misrepresent the facts? If the Perkins Folio emendations were on their face as important as virtually every expert who saw them claimed they were, why should Collier lie about the circumstances of its purchase? What possible purpose could be served by an account that any knowledgeable person not mesmerized by the excitement of discovery ought to have found incredible?

Collier was attempting to hide the fact that he and Rodd on first examination had both believed that the folio emendations were not those of a seventeenth-century man of the theatre but a compendium of eighteenth-century conjecture. Later, under the pressure of personal vanity and commercial expediency Collier had convinced himself that the book was more valuable than he had at first believed, but he could not allow others to know how long he himself had been in reversing his judgement, or that Rodd had *never* altered his low opinion of the book and its connections. The elaborate charade that Collier described was fabricated to keep Rodd's opinion from the public as well as Collier's own slow change of heart. As we shall see, Collier probably bought the book from Rodd some time in 1847, not 'in the Spring of 1849' as he said; he shortened the span to make his story more plausible. To have admitted Rodd's low opinion of the book and that his own initial interest in the emendations had been so slight that he had left the book undisturbed on his shelves for nearly four years *after* their discovery, would have damned his announcement at the start. It would have raised unanswerable arguments against the sincerity of his change of opinion; it would have suggested that his enthusiasm for the corrections was based not on his real but minimal belief in their intrinsic worth but on his desire to justify a new edition of Shakespeare.

Collier's initial announcement was therefore founded on falsehood. The lie had no real bearing on the value of the Perkins emendations themselves, but it reveals Collier's ambivalence about them. To assuage his vanity, to justify his hopes, to 'protect' the book from adverse criticism, he falsified a significant part of the story of his acquisition, and for these advantages he committed a dishonourable act and made himself ultimately vulnerable to accusations of far more serious crimes. It was indeed the most 'foolish act' of his life.

15

If the uncritical public acceptance of the notes delighted Collier, the consternation of his competitors gave him an even deeper satisfaction. Dyce, Singer, and Halliwell (as their later editions would demonstrate) intended to reintroduce some of the emendations Collier had expunged from his edition of 1844. This was to be, in fact, their justification for producing new editions of their own. Now Collier's announcement of the Perkins Folio preempted this intention. None had expected this development, and it threw them temporarily into confusion; since Collier's new rationale was their own, they found it difficult to dispute. Moreover, when they scrutinized the Perkins Folio they were – to a man – impressed with its value. They had doubts about some of the corrections (Collier had admitted to some himself), but they endorsed many, and the book had become so famous and so widely credited by the public that any new edition of Shakespeare that hoped to sell would have to take the new readings into account. But – and here was the crux of their anger – Collier's control of the emendation blocked their way. They had been frustrated by Collier's timing, and there was nothing to do but to postpone their editions until Collier published the promised compendium.

Halliwell was perhaps the most non-plussed. He was convinced the Perkins Folio emendations were valuable and likely to make significant changes in the text of Shakespeare. Yet his own *Folio Shakespeare* was virtually complete and the first volume slated to appear in a matter of weeks. He had decided to finance his edition by issuing it in a limited subscription of 150 copies (at £56 per set!), a plan which, if successful, would have made the work 'rare' upon publication (a 'popularly priced' version could come later). But when Collier's announcement appeared his subscription was no-where near filled and now prospective subscribers hesitated to purchase an expensive edition that might soon be made obsolete by newly discovered 'manuscript' evidence. The *Folio Shakespeare* was to be issued serially and Halliwell's only hope was that the Perkins emendations would be published soon, in time, that is, to be inserted into subsequent volumes of his edition.

Halliwell therefore tried to link his *Folio Shakespeare* to the excitement of Collier's announcement. In March, only days after he examined the book at the meeting of the Shakespeare Society Council, he published a pamphlet announcing the imminent publication of his edition and at the same time affirming his high opinion of the Perkins corrections. The emendations, he declared, 'cannot but be regarded as a truly important addition to the sources of information already accessible. . . . We have at last something tangible – some early authority to which to refer when a passage in the text is inexplicable. . . . We may safely accept these corrections as nearly contemporary with the work itself. . . . That the corrector of the folio of 1632 made his emendations conjecturally can scarcely admit of a doubt', Halliwell went on, but this did not limit their worth, for in perusing the Perkins Folio he himself had 'observed more than one of very great value'. However, the bulk of them needed a more judicious editor, someone with 'a somewhat severer canon of judging' than Collier.[17]

By tradition, published textual emendations could be used by other editors without restriction, and once the Perkins corrections were in print, Collier's exclusive control of them would be gone. Collier must have been pleased by Halliwell's endorsement, but he could not have been happy with the promise to use the emendations in his forthcoming edition. This constituted a threat to usurp the commercial advantage of being first to incorporate them into the text itself, and this, of course, was Collier's objective in bringing them forward in the first place. Novelty was everything, and it seemed that Halliwell, poised to print, would publish before Collier could.

But Halliwell could not use the emendations until Collier made them public and if Collier's list of corrections was slow to appear, the *Folio Shakespeare* would be seriously compromised. Halliwell's subscription could not remain open indefinitely, neither could his paid subscribers be kept waiting. Delay would undo him, and, as it happened, there was delay. Although the Council of the Shakespeare Society (Halliwell among them) quickly agreed to Collier's offer, and although

Collier's declared intention and the public's appetite both called for an early issue, he did not publish the emendations until January, 1853 – a year after his first announcement in the *Athenaeum*. In the interim, Collier worked his own field, and Halliwell, somewhat lamely, tried to work *his*. In May, when it was increasingly apparent what Collier's plan was to be, Halliwell wrote in *Notes and Queries* that he had a corrected folio of his own. 'Mr. Collier's discovery was, perhaps, of even greater interest to myself than to others not merely on account of its being an important evidence for the state of the text, *but because I had long since had the opportunity of using a volume of precisely similar character* [Halliwell's emphasis], namely, [a] copy of the third folio with numerous MS. emendations in a coeval hand.'[18] However, the public was interested only in the Perkins Folio, and Halliwell's attempt to claim unique evidence of his own was unsuccessful.

Collier's delay was only part strategic. Whittaker and Company still possessed many copies of the earlier eight-volume *Shakespeare* of 1844 which they had good reason to believe would soon be superseded by other editions. Impressed by the public interest in the Perkins Folio, they offered Collier £120 to edit the emendations as a supplement keyed to the older text, thereby (they hoped) creating a new market for the unsold copies. This offer, however, precluded any prior publication by the Shakespeare Society.

Collier badly needed the £120; his daughters had only a few months to live, and the cost of nursing them at Torquay was forcing him deeply into debt, but he also wanted to assist the Shakespeare Society in what seemed to him was its last chance for survival. He had an honest conflict of intentions which encouraged a fortuitous deferment of decision. When the Shakespeare Society Council learned of Whittaker's offer, it quickly agreed to release Collier from his promise, but Collier declared he would honour it. After several months he worked out an agreement with Whittaker in which the publisher agreed to supply Shakespeare Society members with copies at cost. The Society's edition would contain a special title page in deference to Collier's promise, but the two 'editions' would appear simultaneously.

These negotiations justified some of the long delay, but only some of it. Collier was in no hurry to issue the corrections, knowing that, at least up to a point, delay increased public interest and potential sales. Meanwhile he was hard at work incorporating the best of the readings into his earlier edition of Shakespeare. If the delay were long enough, he should have his new edition ready for publication soon after the list of corrections appeared, thereby maintaining the advantage of being the first to present the changes in the text of the plays themselves.

Notes and Emendations[19] was published in mid-January 1853 and was quickly sold out. Whittaker thereupon agreed to pay Collier another £100 for a 'revised and enlarged' version which appeared in March. Having been too modest in judging the potential sale of the first edition, the publishers were too optimistic for the second. Against Collier's emphatic warning that they risked 'overloading the market', Whittaker printed 30,000, a large second run for such a book, of which only a few over 2,000 copies were sold.[20] Nevertheless, the two editions together sold nearly 4,000 copies in six months. This was an astonishing commercial success, but a professional catastrophe, for Collier printed hundreds of emendations that ought not to have been seriously considered at all, and by publishing so much dross and appearing to accept it as interesting or valuable, he allowed editors who were his inferiors to preach textual method to him. He knew as well or better than Knight, Halliwell, Dyce, *et al.* that an emendation could not be mere substitution – it was one of the tenets in *Reasons for a New Edition of Shakespeare* in 1842 which had made his edition a critical advance. He claimed he wanted the public to have all the 'significant' Perkins changes whether he agreed with them or not and would be more discriminating later in his definitive text, but he must have foreseen the effect of his indiscriminate publication. *Fraser's Magazine,* for example, declared its satisfaction that Collier's book would 'embolden men to produce conjectures which they had before confined to the modest privacy of their own margins. Shakespeare, we may now be sure, never wrote bad metre or non-sense; *ergo,* every passage in which either occurs, is corrupt, and a fair subject for conjecture.'[21] This was anathema to Collier's critical principles.

Ultimately, of course, Collier secured neither the 'authority' of the book nor the credit for his selections. In the beginning, he was afraid to appear to discount any part of the Perkins Folio; later, roundly attacked for his lack of discrimination, he was too proud to admit that he rejected most of them. Thus he allowed his opponents to tar him with the bad emendations (which he rejected) without granting him the credit for revealing the good ones (which they accepted). In the ensuing controversy, Collier lost critical perspective; he moved from the reasonable conjectural emendation of 'nonsense' passages, to alternative readings for unambiguous lines, to declaring the 'possibility' of a suppositious 'performance authority' or 'actors' recollection' in altering passages that required no change. It was a downward path and ultimately a disgraceful one.

But these were later developments. By accident or design, Collier's piecemeal revelations had stimulated public interest. In each succeeding announcement he produced a few more emendations, all pointing toward his new edition of Shakespeare. His first announcement in the *Athenaeum* printed eleven corrections; his next, four. In the six months following, in letters to *Notes and Queries* (recently established by his friend William Thoms), he added another half dozen. After several more months, the first edition of *Notes and Emendations* appeared with eleven hundred corrections (only a twentieth of the estimated total), and the second edition added another hundred. This publication by instalment tantalized the public into a continuing interest and popular sale of each item as it appeared, and it whetted an appetite for a single volume Shakespeare incorporating all the changes into the text itself.

A close examination of the details of this series of announcements reveals that even early on Collier changed his mind about some of the emendations.[22] Although the second edition of *Notes and Emendations* did not differ radically from the first (virtually nothing was cut), Collier subtly altered his initial opinion. Even in the first edition he had frequently announced that he did *not* accept all of the emendations he had printed,[23] but in the second edition he went still further, changing his earlier assertions of value to mere 'suggestions'.[24] In the first edition, Collier had silently ignored the close

similarities which the Perkins corrections had to the conjectures of eighteenth-century editors.[25] (To have done otherwise
would have been to admit they were of a much later date than
he claimed.) But in revising his text for the second edition,
Collier noted many parallels of this kind and even admitted
that some of the emendations he had published without
comment in the first edition had been previously made by
Pope, Tyrwhitt, Warburton and others. Once or twice he even
admitted to doubts about the validity of a Perkins emendation he had previously accepted without question.[26] These
changes were individually insignificant, but collectively they
reveal a lessening of Collier's confidence in the unique
authority of the Perkins Folio.

This newly admitted uncertainty may have reawakened
Collier's interest in the provenance of the book. As its *prima
facie* 'authority' seemed to lessen, he sought an historical
justification for what he wanted and needed to believe. The
impending competition with Halliwell made his search
urgent.

As it happened, Collier received unexpected help in his
search. In April 1853 while he was completing his revision of
Notes and Emendations, John Carrick Moore, a reputable
gentleman and a stranger to Collier, wrote to him to say that
he had discovered a previous owner of the Perkins Folio:

A friend of mine, Mr. Parry, with whom I was lately conversing on
your extraordinary and interesting discovery, told me he many years
ago possessed a copy of the folio 1632 which had marginal notes in
manuscript, and which, being in bad order, he never consulted. This
copy he lost, he did not know how, and gave himself no concern
about it.

When I shewed him the fac-simile of the page out of *Henry VI,*
which forms the frontispiece to your works, Mr. Parry told me he
had no doubt that the copy was the same as that which he lost, as he
remembered very well the hand-writing, and the state of preservation. . . . I urged Mr. Parry to inform you of these circumstances,
thinking that they might interest you greatly, and hoping that if you
could once trace the copy into the hands of one of the name of
Perkins upwards, it might be a clue to further discovery. Whether
from indolence or from modesty, Mr. Parry, I find, has not
communicated with you; and I therefore told him that I assuredly

would, as every fragment of information on such a subject has its value.[27]

The letter could not have come at a better time. Collier had regularly expressed his hope that the previous owners of the folio might be traced, and now on the eve of the second edition, Moore's letter seemed to lead him directly to the source. But even so, he was cautious; in spite of his own desire to secure such corroboration – perhaps because of it – he wanted to be sure. He immediately wrote to Parry, pressing him for specific details to make the identification certain:

> Mr. Moore says that the book was once in your possession – or at all events that you had a copy of the folio, 1632, with manuscript annotations, which you more than suspect to be the identical book now in my hands. Can you at all describe the book to me? How was it bound, and was it shabby and defective? Had it title-page or conclusion? Had it the name of Tho. Perkins on the cover? If so, can you be good enough to inform me who were the Perkins family mentioned by Mr. Moore, and when and where were their books sold? Can you at all bear in mind the character and nature of the MS. notes and were they almost entirely written in the cropped margins of the book?[28]

To Collier's disappointment and annoyance, Parry did not reply. After ten days without an answer, he was exasperated and wrote to Moore, who suggested that Parry might be ill and that Collier should call on Parry in St. John's Wood. Collier did so and, as he was to recount in his 'Preface' to the second edition of *Notes and Emendations,* had 'the pleasure of an interview with Mr. Parry, who, without the slightest reserve, gave me such an account of the book as made it certain that it was the same which, some fifty years ago, had been presented to him by a connexion of his family, Mr. George Gray. Mr. Parry described both the exterior and interior of the volume, with its innumerable corrections and its missing leaves, with so much minuteness that no room was left for doubt.'[29]

However, Parry's first corroboration was conjecture only: the Perkins Folio was a large and heavy volume and, uncertain whether he would actually be able to see Parry, Collier did not carry it with him on his first visit, and as a result Parry could not make a positive identification of the book then and there. When Collier brought the book on a subsequent visit, however, Parry declared that it was indeed the book he had once owned.

Collier immediately composed a short account of these events for insertion into the second edition and, as he reported in the *Athenaeum* within the week, he

took the liberty of forwarding them to Mr. Moore, – and he returned the manuscript with his full approbation as regarded what had originally passed between himself and Mr. Parry. After it was in type, I again waited upon Mr. Parry, only three days ago, in order that I might read the proof to him and introduce such addition and corrections as he wished to be made.[30]

These extraordinary efforts at verification suggest, perhaps, Collier's determination to make his report unimpeachable. At the least, it was a precaution against any criticism from Halliwell, *et al.,* against the provenance. In any case, Collier's claims were modest if significant. In his new 'Preface' he reported that Parry was not definite concerning where the folio had come from but thought the name on its cover suggested Ufton Court, Berkshire, the residence for at least two hundred years of a family named Perkins. Collier conjectured this might have been the family of Richard Perkins, a prominent actor during the Protectorate. But, Collier concluded, 'as has been mentioned elsewhere, the present rough calf binding was not the original coat of the volume; and, as far as my imperfect researches have yet gone, I do not find any Thomas Perkins recorded as of Ufton Court.' Nevertheless, this circumstances did not rule out other possibilities. 'Other points, dependent chiefly upon dates, remain to be investigated, and upon any of them I shall be most thankful for information.'[31] This was an exercise in wish fulfilment.

If his intention was to 'prove' the legitimacy of the folio, Collier failed. Virtually every reviewer accepted the authority of the corrections, but not because of Collier's suppositions about its provenance. 'Intrinsic worth' and 'common sense', they declared, supported the corrections. Collier's suppositions about Perkins and Ufton Court therefore were more useful in satisfying his own uncertainty than in convincing others.

The reception of *Notes and Emendations* was almost unanimously favourable. The popular press treated its publication as an event of unprecedented importance, and the critical consensus was stated in *Fraser's Magazine* which concluded a long review by saying that the book would 'make an epoch in the annals of Shakespearian criticism'.[32] The *Athenaeum,* as might have been expected, declared the book contained 'in all probability' a genuine restoration of Shakespeare's language in at least a thousand places in which he has hitherto been misunderstood,[33] and the *Illustrated London News* noting the 'unparalleled sensation among Shakespearian students' which the book had excited, was of the opinion that the emendations had authority on their face.

In the present state of the case, it is evident that these emendations however good, have little evidence in their favour beyond their internal value [it stated]. We are ignorant of the writer's authority for his corrections. Mr. Collier allows that they might in some instances, be conjectural. Should this turn out to be the fact, this nameless emendator must have been the most extraordinary guesser in the world. . . . On the whole, we think that Mr. Collier has rather under-stated than over-stated the claims of the manuscript emendations in question. . . .[34]

But perhaps the most gratifying comment came from the *Dublin University Magazine* which declared that Collier's *Notes* would 'form henceforth an inseparable pendant to the received editions, and must undoubtedly take the lead over every other compilation of "Notes and Emendations". It is not going too far to pronounce, that in intrinsic value, it is fairly "worth all the rest".'[35]

16

Collier's claim of copyright over his discovery was generally discounted even before the second edition of *Notes and Emendations* appeared. In February, Edward Moxon, Dyce's publisher, obtained a legal opinion that the emendations were not copyrighted and, sensing a popular market, declared his intention to delay Dyce's edition to publish a cheap Shake-speare (six five-shilling volumes) based on the new readings. Collier, forced to act quickly or lose the commercial value of his discovery, put aside his revision of the eight-volume text and contracted with Whittaker to produce a cheap one-volume edition based on the Perkins Folio. The base text (if this edition could be said to have one!) was therefore the Second Folio that Collier and everyone else had previously discarded as having no textual authority, and on to this corrupted body he grafted what he judged to be the 'best' of the manuscript changes in the Perkins Folio as well as 'old readings which, during the last century and a half, have recommended themselves for adoption.'[36] This impropriety was compounded by a total absence of annotation. The only editorial accoutrement was a two-page preface Collier dashed off that read – as it should have – more like an apology than a preface: 'It is not to be understood that the Editor approves of all the changes in the text of the plays contained in the ensuing volume', he wrote. 'But while he is doubtful regarding some and opposed to others, it is his deliberate opinion, that the great majority of them assert a well-founded claim to a place in every future reprint of Shakespeare's Dramatic works.'[37] He hoped, perhaps, to counter the effect of his corruption by labelling it. He advised his readers that he did not intend this to be a pure text of Shakespeare but a conjectural version founded on a unique discovery, the Perkins Folio. It was to be taken as a different *kind* of edition from his library edition, to which he referred all readers who wanted a conventional text based on the old copies.

This rather too nice distinction may have had some validity in his own mind, but his readers ignored it completely. In the public mind, Collier's new text superseded his earlier one. For a purely monetary advantage he prostituted his long-term reputation. Even more serious, the edition would ultimately corrupt Collier's view of himself as a critic. Given his inordinate pride and his refusal to admit any failure of judgement or taste, he would, in the years that followed, feel obliged to justify this publication. He thus shackled himself to the defence of a textual pastiche that, under other circum-stances, he would have been the first to denounce.

The eventual outcome of Collier's decision was disaster, but its immediate result was success. The book was produced quickly, and, at a guinea, sold for nine shillings less than Moxon's. Collier's more formidable competitors were non-plussed. Their editions were annotated and 'critical', but they had counted on a wider sale than scholarship alone would support and now it appeared that the popular appetite for a text based on the emendations would be satisfied by a cheap edition backed by Collier's reputation. To meet his competition they would have to publish immediately. Some could not, others would not. Dyce's ten-volume variorum edition had already been put in limbo by Moxon's cheap edition. Charles Knight, the enterprising publisher-editor who had printed an elaborately illustrated 'Pictorial Shakespeare' several years earlier (in a losing competition against Collier), now pressed forward with a cheap revision ('The Stratford Shakespeare') hastily incorporating some of the Perkins emendations (it was to lose again). Singer decided to announce his ten-volume text and, should the announcement create the interest he hoped, to publish. (It didn't and he didn't – for another two years.) Halliwell's *Folio Shakespeare* appeared, but with an unfilled subscription.

Although all of Collier's competitors had endorsed some of the Perkins emendations, the success of his one-volume edition led them to belittle the value of the Perkins Folio as a whole. Collier had anticipated this reaction. 'There are five – or, as some say, six – gentlemen (including editors and would-be editors) who are vehemently whetting their knives to cut me up for a carbonado,' he declared in a letter to the *Athenaeum*, '. . . and I shall soon have so much ink spilt upon me, that I expect to be blacker than my own name.'[38] As he predicted, each of his rivals entered the lists against him with books and pamphlets attacking the Perkins Folio and its discoverer and touting their own critical perspicacity. These broadsides did not decrease the popularity of Collier's *Notes and Emendations* and the ensuing controversy probably increased the sales of his one-volume Shakespeare, but they were severe irritants, and they laid the foundation for a far more serious confrontation several years later.

Charles Knight, the first to produce an edition of his own,

was also the first to attack Collier's. In early April, he published *Old Lamps, or New? A Plea for the Original Editions of the Text of Shakspere*,[39] a generally temperate if negative critique of *Notes and Emendations*. Knight's chief purpose was to announce the publication of his Stratford Shakespeare, and his harshest words were directed at Collier's declaration of copyright over the Perkins Folio emendations. He demanded that the Perkins Folio be placed in a public institution for examination. A month later Samuel Weller Singer published a vituperative pamphlet, *The Text of Shakespeare Vindicated from the Interpolations and Corruptions Advocated by John Payne Collier, Esq. in His Notes and Emendations*. As with Knight, Singer's purpose was to announce his own new edition, but the imputations he made against Collier were just short of libel. He declared he 'could not bring himself to believe' that Collier 'would indulge a hoax which might lead to mischievous results' and he claimed to be puzzled by several places in which the 'Corrector' of the Perkins Folio had displayed 'remarkable sympathy' and 'remarkable coincidence' to Collier's notes in his 1844 edition of Shakespeare, a comment tantamount to accusing Collier of forgery. About Collier's new one-volume Shakespeare (the 'Pseudo-Shakespeare', Singer called it), he pretended surprise:

What can have converted Mr. Collier to such an entirely opposite extreme of revolutionary rashness? Is it that he has found the adherence to long-exploded typographical errors and evidently erroneous readings had been urged against his edition, and had prevented it from becoming extensively popular, and that the discovery of his pseudo-antique commentary afforded him an apt excuse for furnishing a more readable text?[40]

There was enough truth in the accusation to sting Collier, but Singer's critique was largely vitiated by malice and inconsistency. Having excoriated Collier for using an annotated folio, he himself announced the discovery of not one but two – a Second and a Third – both having emendations which, Singer declared, often agreed with Collier's, 'sometimes for the better'.[41] Singer was to use both these works in his subsequent edition, not so extensively as Collier had in his, but with the same assumption of authority. Moreover, Singer eventually adopted a number of the Perkins corrections, including, as Collier gleefully pointed out some years later, one or two that he had treated with special contempt in 1853.[42]

Singer's book was not well received. 'We cannot but regret that Mr. Singer should have thought it necesssary to convert a public question into what bids fair to become a more private quarrel', noted the *Athenaeum*.[43] The book was too patently a vendetta against the man whose editions had twice supplanted Singer's own.

Alexander Dyce's critique, *A Few Notes on Shakespeare*, appeared soon after Singer's diatribe.[44] When Moxon cancelled his variorum edition, Dyce substituted this book, a compilation of parallel passages and emendations, which attempted to illuminate his own conjectures in the reflected light of Collier's discovery. The book included a sharp critique of Joseph Hunter, who, Dyce implied, was a fool, but his real target was John Payne Collier whose success had rekindled Dyce's old animosity. He could not attack the validity of the Perkins Folio itself because his perusal of it had convinced him that it had some authority and he planned eventually to use it himself if he could. His method, therefore, was to damn with faint praise. 'My opinion', he wrote, 'is that while [the Perkins Folio] abounds with alterations ignorant, tasteless, and wanton, it also occasionally presents corrections which require no authority to recommend them, because common sense declares them to be right.'[45] Like Halliwell, Dyce charged Collier with misusing the corrections. In particular, he criticized *Notes and Emendations* for announcing standard alterations as 'new readings' based on the Perkins Folio. 'Mr. Collier will excuse me when I say that this is not the only part of his book which is calculated [sic] to mislead the reader. Who would not suppose, from the language used [in a correction in *As You Like It* (V,iv)] that the lection '*them*' was now for the first time brought forward? The fact is, that, Mr. Collier alone excepted, every recent editor has printed "them", without even thinking it necessary to notice the obvious misprint of the old copies.'[46] The comment suggests Dyce's weakness as much as Collier's. Collier was unmindful or secretive about the number of corrections in the folio that were standard eighteenth-century emendations, but Dyce was wrong to assume that changes from the early text should be made without comment. In the line he cites here, for example, far from showing Collier to be dishonest, Dyce actually proves him to be candid, for as Dyce suggests, Collier here printed a 'correction' from the Perkins Folio although it was an emendation he alone among modern editors had rejected in his 1844 edition. Dyce's comments were small-minded and niggardly. If he avoided Singer's personal animus, his *Few Notes* nevertheless suggested more heat than illumination. Significantly, it was Hunter rather than Collier who responded to Dyce, in *A Few Words of Reply*,[47] and ironically it was Collier, almost as much as Dyce, who bore the brunt of Hunter's 'defence'. Hunter's pamphlet in fact, was a resumption of the quarrel he had picked with Collier in 1839. It demonstrated how easily old animosities could be refreshed by new controversy and gave still more proof of the appetite for dispute among Shakespeare scholars in the mid-nineteenth century. ('How little charity they have for one another's failings', the *Athenaeum* declared, 'how full they are of unreasonable suspicion – how ungenerous in the praise of what is really good, . . . how quick-sighted in the discovery of defects.'[48])

James Orchard Halliwell differed from Singer, Dyce and Hunter in having no initial personal dislike for Collier. His objective was merely to establish his own critical reputation by diminishing another's, and to do that he was prepared to use any means. Collier had long before sensed Halliwell's ambition and feared it, perhaps because he saw in Halliwell traits – both good and bad – which matched his own. 'Mr. Halliwell would have made many more friends, if he had been a little more straight-forward in his dealings', Collier had written some years before, a comment that might have been made about Collier himself. 'He is too fond of doing things underhandedly, and then congratulating himself on the success of his cunning.'[49] Halliwell had delayed his *Folio Shakespeare* for nearly a year in order to incorporate the new emendations into his text, and when *Notes and Emendations* at last appeared in January 1853, Halliwell was confounded by Collier's declaration of copyright. When Collier subsequently announced his one-volume edition, Halliwell's opinion of the

Perkins emendations changed abruptly. Since he was not to have the commercial advantage of the corrections, they were *ipso facto* worthless, and when the first volume of his edition was published in May 1853, its notes bristled with attacks on the Perkins Folio emendations. Now Halliwell declared that the corrections were not worth serious consideration, that all were patently bad or unnecessary. When Collier's one-volume edition appeared in June and was more successful with reviewers than Halliwell's *Folio,* he was embittered. He may have been appalled by the quality and effect of Collier's edition, and his new opinion of the Perkins emendations may have been the result of honest doubt, but it is hard to separate his *volte face* – and the asperity with which he declared it – from the fact that Collier's discovery had given him a professional advantage that Halliwell could not match.

Halliwell's pique was intensified by the reviews of the first volume of his *Folio Shakespeare* which dismissed it as an expensive recapitulation of previously published material. His *Prospectus* had promised that the edition would increase in value, but the first volume did not support that promise and to many the initial price £40 (raised to £60 when the subscription remained unfilled at publication) was exorbitant. One of the most negative notices of the book appeared in the *Athenaeum,* which declared that Halliwell lacked the 'competent learning, painstaking carefulness, unimpassioned calmness, and . . . sound discriminating judgment' necessary for a textual critic. It cited his numerous errors in transcription, damned his failure to cite the authorities he used, criticized his silent emendation of the text, and condemned his presumed failure to comment on the major difficulties of the play ('not one of them – so far as we have noticed – is got rid of, or even lightened'). It concluded that if Halliwell 'really possesses powers adequate to such a task as he has assumed, he must rouse himself, – shake off his drowsy antiquarian fondness for heaping illustration upon illustration, [and] emancipate himself from the commentator-like propensity to pick holes in the labours of other men.'[50]

The review enraged Halliwell and he leaped to the conclusion that Collier had written it. His assumption was ludicrous. Although the *Athenaeum* had been the venue for

Collier's announcements, it did not support his claims for the
Perkins Folio without reservation, and its editorial integrity
on the subject was demonstrable: it had fairly and fully
noticed all the books and pamphlets criticizing Collier and the
emendations; its letters columns had remained open to all.
There is no evidence to support Halliwell's charge that the
journal committed the impropriety of allowing Collier to
condemn – anonymously – a work critical of himself or, for
that matter, that Collier would have done so. The charge was
nonsense on the face of it as Halliwell, less buffeted by
circumstances, would have had the good sense to realize. But
Halliwell did not pause. Within a matter of days he published
not one but three pamphlets condemning Collier, the Perkins
Folio, and the *Athenaeum* with varying degrees of vehemence.

It is impossible to determine which of the pamphlets came
first (all were privately published and widely distributed
among Halliwell's friends and the press) but they had a
cumulative effect. *Observations on Some of the Manuscript Emendations of the Text of Shakespeare* attacked the Perkins Folio. 'I have
not at present discovered a single *new* reading in Mr. Collier's
volume that will bear the test of examination', declared the
man who,[51] only a few months before – after close examination – had called the book 'truly important', 'authoritative',
and 'safely acceptable'.

The second pamphlet, *Observations on the Shaksperian Forgeries
at Bridgewater House,* was to have much more serious results for
Collier. It concerned the Bridgewater manuscripts that Collier
had discovered among the Ellesmere papers and published in
New Facts Concerning the Life of Shakespeare nearly twenty years
before, the same documents that were the subject of Hunter's
renewed attack. As the title suggests, Halliwell solemnly
declared that these manuscripts were not authentic, that they
were not merely 'fabrications' but 'forgeries' and (a subtle
qualification) '*modern* forgeries' at that. The pamphlet was
intended as an indirect puff for his own Folio edition, but it
had other purposes as well. Although Halliwell seemed to
absolve Collier of any wrong-doing ('it is possible', he wrote
'that ... Mr. Collier has been deceived'[52]) he nonetheless
implicitly accused him. If these were 'modern forgeries',
someone had composed them *recently* and suspicion must

inevitably fall on the man who had discovered and published them. Moreover, Halliwell encouraged that view by challenging Collier to a defence:

Only one record-reader, as far as I know, viz. the Rev. Joseph Hunter, has made a personal examination of these MSS [Halliwell declared]. He has not yet expressed any opinion publicly, but I have reason to think that his views on the subject coincide with my own. It is clearly Mr. Collier's duty, as a lover of truth, to have the originals carefully scrutinized by the best judges of the day.[53]

This statement is a pastiche of misinformation and innuendo. Nearly eight years before Hunter had published his doubts about the Bridgewater manuscripts in *New Illustrations of . . . Shakespeare* (1845), but, he had privately admitted to the Earl, these doubts had been satisfied when he saw the manuscripts themselves, and he gave no explanation for his subsequent return to his original opinion. Only the owner of the manuscripts, the Earl himself and not Collier, had control over who could or could not see them, and in the years since Hunter's book, they had been easily available to interested scholars. Moreover, subsequent to Hunter's comments, Halliwell himself had seen the documents, called them genuine, and used them in his *Life of Shakespeare* (1848). Halliwell's arguments for believing the documents false in 1853 were no more compelling than those he had advanced for their authenticity in 1848. His statement was, to put it kindly, inexact: it was *his* opinion which now 'coincided' with Hunter's rather than the other way round, and the significant question was not the authenticity of the Bridgewater manuscripts (Collier himself came to doubt them) but Halliwell's motive for making the charge when he did. By demanding that Collier 'prove' the Bridgewater manuscripts were not 'modern forgeries' he established an insidious pattern of guilt by assumption that would recur again and again in the years ahead.

But Halliwell's most extended response to the *Athenaeum* review was a third pamphlet called *Curiosities of Modern Shaksperian Criticism*, in which he declared that the *Athenaeum* was prejudiced in Collier's favour:

If I am correct in thinking that the whole of the Shaksperian MSS.

in the possession of the Earl of Ellesmere are modern forgeries, – that an important letter, discovered at Dulwich College, has been misinterpreted, – or, that some remarkable ballads are compositions of comparatively recent date – it is unnecessary to say that the chief of the far-famed Shaksperian discoveries of Mr. Collier are of small value indeed; and Mr. Collier is generally understood to be one of the *Athenaeum* reviewers![54]

The comment suggests that Halliwell did not remember the details of the review: it did not support Collier's contention concerning the Bridgewater manuscripts, and had actually *agreed* with Halliwell's suggestion that they be examined anew by experts. The new charge of 'misinterpreting' the Dulwich letter from Mrs. Alleyn to her husband (dated 20 October, 1603 and published in Collier's *Memoirs of Edward Alleyn*) was more complicated. Halliwell printed a facsimile of the letter to 'prove' that Collier had added words concerning Shakespeare which could not have been a part of the original. The letter was badly decayed, but Halliwell claimed that what remained could not support Collier's transcript. Significantly, in this, the first mention of possible forged insertions into the Dulwich manuscripts, Halliwell failed to mention that he himself had seen the original letter and Collier's transcript before Collier published the letter in 1841, and that he had not then noticed any significant discrepancy between the two – not until 1853, that is, after the Perkins emendations had enhanced Collier's reputation and the *Athenaeum* review had hurt his own did Halliwell charge Collier with misfeasance.

The pamphlets criticizing Collier's use of the Perkins Folio did not convince the reading public. The most popular of them was not a serious attack but an anonymous burlesque entitled *The Grimaldi Shakspere, Notes and Emendations on the Plays of Shakespeare From a Recently-Discovered Annotated Copy by the Late Joseph Grimaldi, Esq. Comedian,* which lampooned the pretensions of both Collier's book and its critics. As its title suggests, the sixteen-page pamphlet pretended to be the compilation of 'early manuscript corrections' made by the great English clown Grimaldi and it parodies Collier's text, which suggests how widely known *Notes and Emendations* must have been. 'No future edition of Shakspere [sic] can ever dare to appear without all these additions and corrections,' it declared, 'and as they are all copyright, and may not be used by any one but me, it follows that the Bard is in future my private property, and all other editors are hereby "warned off".'

The story of the discovery of *The Grimaldi Shakspere* parodies Collier's: it was found in a book-stall in Islington: 'a mere bundle of dirty leaves, without a beginning or end', its discoverer writes. 'I took it up – could it be? – my heart leaped at the hope! – yes, *it was* – the players' edition of Shakspere. I asked the price. "Two and sixpence," replied the bookseller, "as it's a biggish book." It was plain he could not read, and knew not its value.'[55] *The Grimaldi Shakspere* prints many funny emendations and concludes by declaring they 'are as good as any given in the Perkins Shakspere', which it calls another 'humorous work'.[56]

This light hearted burlesque apparently angered no one, not even the *Athenaeum* although it received its share of jibes in the *Grimaldi Shakspere* which called it the 'Fourpenny Exterminator' which is 'rabid in defence of my rival, and regularly burkes opponents'.[57] The journal publicized the pamphlet in a long and generally complimentary review, reprinting many of its best parodies.

Aside from the pamphlets, there was only one negative comment concerning *Notes and Emendations*. In July, *Blackwood's Edinburgh Magazine* scorned the 'Old Corrector' of the Perkins Folio and extolled the virtues of Halliwell's *Folio Shakespeare*. The review seemed to be as much irritated by other reviewers as by Collier's book, and it condemned English periodicals in general and *Notes and Queries* (which it called *Gnats and Queries*) in particular. However, *Blackwood's* support of Halliwell does not seem to have helped fill his subscription.[58]

Although *Notes and Emendations* was generally applauded, it did not revive the Shakespeare Society which died soon after the book appeared. The popular mythology of the next generation would have it that the Society disbanded because of scandal and charges of forgery against Collier,[59] but facts as well as good sense disprove this. The Society failed because it was not able to attract enough members to pay for the cost of printing and distributing its publications: few members were willing or able to edit texts and so fewer titles were distributed, which made membership less attractive, which led to fewer members. In ten years, the Society had produced a uniquely valuable series of reprints, but this was a monument to the interest and dedication of a handful of its founding members who used up their initial reservoir of energy and interest without finding a new source to replace it. For its two last years it had barely eked out an existence, relying more and more heavily on the labours of Halliwell and Collier, who between them had produced much of its distinction and most of its publications. When the Perkins Folio widened the schism between these two stalwarts, the last remaining support for the organization gave way. The publication of *Notes and Emendations,* which had initially been endorsed with enthusiasm by all the Shakespeare Society council (including both Halliwell and Knight), did not encourage new members – in fact, it discouraged them: members paid *more* for the book with its special title page than did the non-subscribers who bought the Whittaker trade edition.

In July 1853, the Society issued what was to be its last publication, David Laing's edition of Thomas Lodge's *Defence of Poetry, Music and Stage Plays, et al,*[60] and it advertised, but did not carry out, plans for reprinting some of its earlier publications in large paper limited editions for sale to the general public;[61] it also tried to sell its back catalogue to non-subscribers in a uniformly bound set,[62] but this had few buyers. The final blow to the Society was the sudden death of Collier's old friend, Frederick Shoberl, who had printed all the Society publications. He had generously extended credit for long periods. The Society's debt to him was always large and months in arrears, but when Shoberl died in debt, his executors, less generous than he, demanded immediate settlement.[63] As a result the Society's remaining stock of books was sold, first in piecemeal fashion and then, a few months later, at auction. The proceeds were sufficient to pay all outstanding debts for printing and distribution. At Christmas-time 1853, the Society held its last meeting and voted to dissolve. Thus, the Shakespeare Society died of natural – or at least predictable – causes. It was not an ignominious or dishonourable end, and although it was a loss to Collier it liberated him from what had become thankless and enervating chores.

In April his eldest daughter, Mary, died of tuberculosis, and in September his second daughter, Jenny, succumbed to the same disease. Their suffering had been severe, their convalescence was increasingly expensive and it is hard not to agree with Robinson that the end of their suffering was a 'release' for everyone. Collier was not demonstrably affectionate, he was always a bit austere with his family, but he was a fond parent and these deaths grieved him deeply.

Ironically, Collier was released from this financial burden just as he was better able to bear it. The success of the Perkins Folio emendations, together with an increase in Mary Louisa's annuity (her brother and two sisters were to die within the next three years), assured him of greater financial and professional security than he had ever had before. It was a remarkable change from only three years before when, poverty-stricken and wounded by the results of the British Museum investigation, he had desperately sought refuge in the country.

In early December 1853, Collier moved out of his brother-in-law's villa and into a house of his own nearby. His family numbered only five now – Collier, his wife, his sister-in-law, and his two remaining daughters. The older daughter, Emma, was a somewhat reserved woman in her late twenties with a vigorous, practical mind and the ability to run the day-to-day affairs of the family; the younger, Henrietta Robinson, was betrothed and would soon marry. Mary Louisa's sister, Emma Pycroft, was now invalid, suffering intermittent and sometimes violent fits of depression, followed by amnesia, and these incidents of madness made the seclusion of a single-family home especially desirable.

The new house was a handsome cottage close to Maidenhead railway station with a garden extending to the river's edge (its name was 'Riverside') and it suited Collier exactly. 'Being now in his *own* house', Robinson reported after his first visit, 'he receives attentions, as a man of letters, from the gentry of the neighbourhood, which he had not when he was the inmate of Robert Proctor. This flatters him as it ought, for he feels he is justly appreciated.'[64] He was now a 'resident

celebrity' of the town, a personage of reputation who
occasionally lectured on English drama at the Guildhall. After
years of uncertain position, he was at last eminent and
financially secure. His health was uncertain; he still had
attacks of quinsy and his lumbago and arthritis occasionally
made walking difficult, but even when ill, he could work in his
garden and, on sunny days, receive friends there in magisterial
audience. He was professionally busy, too. He had agreed to
edit the works of Michael Drayton for the Roxburghe Club[65]
and he worked intermittently on the 'second edition' of his
multi-volume Shakespeare which, after a suitable passage of
time, he intended to put on the market. More immediately, he
was about to publish the shorthand notes he had made at the
time of the 1811 Coleridge lectures on Shakespeare, lectures
that had never been printed and that many believed lost.
Thus he lived and worked – leisured, comfortable, and respected.

With this new security, Collier's relationship with his
patrons Devonshire and Ellesmere changed. Although he was
still nominally Devonshire's 'librarian', his 'duties' were few.[66]
Collier had a position of his own now, and the difference
between patron and protégé was reduced, at least in Collier's
mind. Moved by gratitude and, perhaps, wanting to establish
a higher position for himself in his patron's eyes, Collier made
two remarkable gifts. In June 1853, he presented the Perkins
Folio to Devonshire,[67] and a few weeks later he offered the
Larpent manuscript plays, which he and Thomas Amyot had
purchased nearly a quarter of a century before, to Ellesmere.[68]

In later years, gossip and malice encouraged the belief that
Collier sold the Perkins Folio to Devonshire for several
thousand pounds, and some suggested that his motive was to
sequester the volume from the eyes of his competitors. Neither
story was true. Devonshire wanted the Folio very much.
(Shortly after Collier announced its discovery, the Duke had
journeyed to London with the sole purpose of seeing the
prize.)[69] No doubt he would have been willing to pay Collier
well for the Folio but it was a gift. Moreover, although Collier
still had proprietary interest in the volume and would until his
second edition appeared (in 1858) he did not retain control
over who could see the volume. It was put in Devonshire's

library, first in London (while Collier needed it for his new edition) and later at Chatsworth. Although it was less accessible than it might have been, say, in the British Museum, it was nevertheless available. Since Collier's debt to Devonshire was greater than that to Ellesmere, the fact that he gave the Duke the Perkins Folio suggests the high value he placed on the book.

The transfer of the Larpent manuscripts was more complicated but no less generous. For a long time after Collier and Amyot purchased the manuscripts from Larpent's widow in 1830, the whole of the collection was stored in Collier's various residences. Eventually it was divided between the two owners, and when Amyot died in 1850, there was a rumour that his widow planned to sell his share at auction. Collier believed that the collection should be kept together, and having no space to house all of it himself, he proposed to reassemble the collection and to offer it for sale to a suitable repository. Amyot's widow agreed, and Collier offered the whole collection to the trustees of the British Museum.[70] The Museum refused (an unfortunate decision which permanently separated these plays from the rest of the licence copies now among the Museum's manuscripts), whereupon Amyot's widow made plans to sell her half of the collection separately. Collier therefore offered the collection to Ellesmere for the amount he had paid in 1830 (£180) plus an undisclosed amount to Mrs. Amyot.[71] It was a virtual gift: individually auctioned, the hundreds of manuscripts in Collier's portion alone would have brought many times £180. (Ellesmere would pay more to have the manuscripts bound.) The Earl accepted immediately and the manuscripts were placed among the treasures in the library he was then completing at Bridgewater House. As a result the collection was kept intact, Collier was released from the burden of housing the manuscripts, Mrs. Amyot was endowed, and a benefactor handsomely rewarded. Although this transaction was to be of great importance to scholars a century later, it was not made public at the time. In fact, the matter was so private that Ellesmere's son, who inherited the Bridgewater Library a few years later, did not know how the Larpent manuscripts came to be in it and had to ask Collier.[72]

Discretion characterized all of Collier's dealings with Ellesmere, even in trivial matters. Outsiders often assumed he had influence with the Earl, and since this reputation flattered him, Collier encouraged it. However, the fate of the go-between is that he carries the onus of power with few of its advantages and none of its protection. Shortly after he transferred the Larpent manuscripts to Ellesmere, Collier performed a service for the Earl which was to provoke the hatred of Sir Frederic Madden, Keeper of the Manuscripts of the British Museum. The circumstances of this affair were initially so inconsequential that Collier himself left no record of it. It would, however, bring on the catastrophe of his life.

VI

THE ELLESMERE THEFTS AND
LITERARY COOKERY
'I declare war to the knife . . .'

17

Collier had not been the only loser in the British Museum Controversy. Panizzi's victory also blocked the previously auspicious career of Frederic Madden. As the seventh son of a marine officer in Portsmouth, Madden had been born with few social advantages, and his eminence was the result of intelligence and discipline rather than luck or the favours of others. He had been a brilliant student and a prodigy: in school he learned Latin, Greek and Hebrew, and he subsequently taught himself Anglo-Saxon; at twenty he was master of a dozen ancient and modern languages. He learned to read and classify a wide spectrum of ancient Greek, Latin, and Coptic scripts, and by the time he joined the Museum at twenty-five he was an accomplished paleographer. Like Panizzi (who came five years later) he was initially hired to assist in cataloguing the printed books, but in a year or two his real talent was recognized, and in 1828 he became Assistant Keeper of Manuscripts. Shortly thereafter he edited *Havelok the Dane* for the Roxburghe Club, the first of a half dozen early texts he was to publish in the course of the next decade. He became a Fellow of the Royal Society in 1830, a Knight of the Guelphic Order two years later, and when his immediate superior, Forshall, became Secretary to the Museum in 1837, Madden was his obvious successor as Keeper of Manuscripts. Before the controversy it was generally assumed that, if precedence meant anything at all, Madden, like his illustrious predecessors through the hierarchy of the Museum, would eventually become Principal Librarian.

The tragedy of Madden's career was his initial failure to see and, later, to accept the fact that this ambition was never to be realized. Madden assumed that his five-year seniority to Panizzi would outbalance the latter's political connections, that, in short, precedence would override the forces of change. He entered the controversy of 1847 comfortable in the expectation that Panizzi would be put down once and for all and that his own star would rise and shine. The commission's endorsement of his competitor therefore astounded him, but it did not encourage him to find professional accommodation with Panizzi. He swore revenge against the 'Italian upstart' and remained as determined as ever to become Principal Librarian when Sir Henry Ellis retired from the post.

Madden was prodigious in pursuing this goal. He produced works of great scholarship (his edition of Wycliffe's Bible in 1850, the culmination of twenty-two years' labour collating sixty-five manuscripts, was monumental) and he assumed the social pretensions he thought concomitant to his aspiration (he inveigled a place in Victoria's household and expended more money than he could afford in sustaining it). His every act was weighed to determine its effect on his ambition; when a son dared to marry an 'unsuitable' woman, Madden disowned him. He became an engine of opportunism; all of his considerable talent was directed to reaching his 'rightful place'. He never made it.

Thomas Amyot had introduced Madden to Collier in the late 1820s when Collier was working at the Museum collecting material for the *History of English Dramatic Poetry,* and often in the years that followed Collier sought Madden's help in reading manuscripts. They shared many interests: both were intense and sophisticated anitiquarians; both were committed to scholarship; both were active in the Society of Antiquaries and in the Camden Society, and they regularly exchanged information and privately printed pamphlets. As Collier was purchasing agent for Devonshire, so Madden was for Lord Clive, and they therefore attended the same sales and frequented the same booksellers. They were wary of one another, of course – it would have been hard to choose between them for shrewd self-interest and competitiveness – but over a span of twenty years they developed mutual respect. Madden admired Collier's wider historical knowledge, and Collier acknowledged Madden's greater paleographic skill; when Collier completed his life of Shakespeare for the 1844 edition, for example, he asked Madden to scrutinize it in the light of Madden's study of Shakespeare's will and orthography. And, of course, they were allied, each for reasons of his own, in the catalogue controversy. When Collier was named Secretary to the Royal Commission they were co-conspirators against Panizzi, and when Panizzi emerged triumphant from that confrontation, they were equally outraged. In the years that followed, each sought to salve his injured pride, to reaffirm a social position worthy of his large self-esteem and to seek professional compensation for the loss he had suffered.

Shortly after Collier moved to Riverside, Madden and Collier had a serious falling out, and, although the circumstances were kept more or less secret at the time, the confrontation embittered them and eventually provoked calamity. The cause of this disagreement seemed innocuous. Madden was as prodigal in the acquisition of manuscripts as Panizzi in the pursuit of books, and he was not too scrupulous about how he got them. Indeed, a manuscript librarian bent on enlarging his collection in the mid-nineteenth century could not afford to be. There were hundreds of muniment rooms through the British Isles with valuable documents and indigent peers frequently disposed of family records, sometimes publicly and wholesale, sometimes privately piece by piece, to scores of dealers and collectors eager to lay hands on them. When manuscripts appeared on the market, therefore, tracing their provenance was often difficult or impossible, and a zeal for determining ownership might on occasion be indiscreet. This *modus operandi* has never been wholly absent from the sale of antiquities, and Madden was no more fastidious than he needed to be. (It was he who purchased Halliwell's cache from Trinity College, albeit through Thomas Rodd, although he must have known its source.)

Among the readers in the British Museum manuscripts in 1852 was George Hillier, a paleographer with special interest in geographical manuscripts and a reputation as one of the best among a dozen manuscript readers who could be hired to trace family lines or legal claims in the charters, rolls and seals of public and private manuscript collections. Hillier, employed by the Duchess of Norfolk on such a commission, was a frequent visitor at the Museum where he struck up acquaintance with Madden and became a close friend of Madden's assistant, a man named Sims. In December 1852, Hillier told Madden he had manuscripts for sale, and although Hillier was not a regular dealer in manuscripts, Madden bought several concerning the Mostyn family in Flintshire, Wales. In the middle of May 1853, Hillier brought Madden a second bundle which contained, as Madden recorded in his diary, 'some papers from Ld. Ellesmere's Muniments'. Hillier's story was that he had acquired the manuscripts from a 'country dealer', and Madden apparently did not question him further. His failure to do so created the ensuing dispute. It was well known that the Ellesmere papers had been kept intact in the Bridgewater Collection for well over two hundred years, and it is inconceivable that Madden should not have had some doubts about the source of Hillier's documents. Nevertheless, he kept these doubts to himself, and on 16 July 1853 he bought the manuscripts. On 6 September he purchased twenty-seven more and on 19 September, another 116 from the same source.[1]

The matter might have ended there; most manuscript collections were so carelessly maintained and so incompletely catalogued that any shady dealings in them would remain concealed, but an unusual event precipitated a sequence of disaster. A month or two after Madden's purchase, a Mr. Wigmore of Penarth, Wales, was reading manuscripts at the Museum and came across rolls which he concluded must once have belonged to his good friend Lord Mostyn. Wigmore wrote to Mostyn, and in January 1854 Mostyn inspected the rolls and declared they almost certainly came from his library. The rolls, of course, were those supplied by Hillier. This confrontation was inconclusive. It was obvious that the manuscripts had once belonged to his family, but Mostyn could not prove they had been stolen and as a result his solicitors saw no legal means to force their return. Madden and Hillier were safe enough from Mostyn, but Madden was alarmed by the other papers he had had of Hillier. The Ellesmere documents were so distinctive they might be

recognized at once as belonging to the Bridgewater Collection.
Moreover, Madden recalled that Collier had published a
collection from the Ellesmere papers for the Camden Society
and when he consulted his copy of the *Egerton Papers* he
discovered that it indeed contained not one but *two* of the
Hillier documents! Madden realized his danger. Ellesmere
was no Mostyn; he would never have sold the documents, and
he would be relentless in pursuing their theft if it were
suspected. Moreover, Collier often consulted the Museum
manuscripts and it seemed only a matter of time before he
discovered Madden's misdeed.

It is difficult to know when Madden first became aware of
his peril; his diary entries give unreliable evidence. His entry
for Friday, 17 March 1854, for example, contains an artful
admission of doubt concerning Hillier and the Ellesmere
manuscripts: 'I begin in my own mind to think Mr. Hillier is a
great scoundrel, and quite in the Halliwell line', he wrote,
immediately listing the page numbers of earlier entries that
recorded the purchases from Hillier. 'It is said that Mr. H. has
also been employed by Lord Ellesmere, to arrange papers, etc.
and it is singular that last year Mr. H. offered me for sale a
document signed by the Members of Lincoln's Inn, headed by
Chancellor Ellesmere, which might well have come out of
Lord E's muniment room.' This is a disingenuous passage.
Madden here implies that Hillier's guilt had only just
occurred to him, whereas, in fact, his confrontation with
Mostyn nearly two months before had given him ample
evidence of Hillier's dishonesty. Moreover, the passage implies
that the Bridgewater charter had only been *offered* to him
(whereas he had bought it) and that only one document was
involved (whereas he had purchased at least 165).[2] Madden
knew Hillier had never been 'employed by Lord Ellesmere, to
arrange papers, etc.' Hillier was not a bibliographer or a
cataloguer, and it was well known that in recent years only
Collier had 'arranged' the Bridgewater papers. Moreover, of
all the Ellesmere documents he purchased from Hillier,
Madden here singles out the one for which theft could be
proved, a manuscript Collier had published. Madden's
uncertainty (that the documents 'might well have' been
stolen) is feigned. The means for satisfying his doubt were too

readily at hand – in a well known book which Madden himself owned – to believe his disclaimer. The conclusion that Madden is here preparing a contingency defence is inescapable. 'I feel much annoyed at the whole affair', the entry continues, 'for if Hillier is a rascal, he has been allowed the most liberal access to our volumes of State Papers and Autographs, under the belief that he was working for the Duchess of Norfolk. Further than this, my attendant Sims, has contracted an unusual intimacy with Hillier, which gives me much uneasiness. I intend to keep a very strict watch henceforth upon all that Mr. H. does or says.'[3]

A *watch* only? Would it not have been wiser to consult with Collier immediately if his fears were as he described them? Clearly, Madden's intention was not to investigate the crime but to cover it up. He had questioned Hillier about the source of his manuscripts. In a diary entry for 22 March, that is, five days after the entry just quoted, he wrote that Hillier replied 'in very unsatisfactory terms, which confirm my belief that there is unfair play somewhere' and that Hillier may have 'pillaged' Mostyn's muniment room. Obviously, there was sufficient reason to suspect that he had done the same to Ellesmere's.

Madden now had cause to believe that he was the receiver of stolen goods, but two days later, on Friday, 24 March, he sent *all* of the Ellesmere manuscripts to be bound. This was an attempt to hide the contraband: the binding would take some weeks during which the manuscripts would be protected from any chance discovery by Collier, and once bound they would be less readily identifiable. Mostyn seemed unwilling or unable to bring criminal charges and it was possible, therefore, that bound and catalogued in the Museum collection, the Ellesmere manuscripts would go undetected.

The events that followed cannot be determined exactly – the Madden diary and correspondence became abruptly silent about the business, but a few facts can be adduced. Hillier had left still more 'Mostyn manuscripts' with Madden for possible sale, and on 17 April, almost immediately after making the diary entries just quoted, Madden returned all of them to Hillier. Thereafter, the 'unusual intimacy' that had developed between Sims and Hillier bore strange fruit: at some time in the next month or two *Sims* sold several of the Mostyn manuscripts to Thomas Phillipps (Halliwell's father-in-law). This sale was fateful. Phillipps was a good friend of Lord Mostyn, and when he learned of Mostyn's visit to the Museum and of his suspicions that the manuscripts had been stolen from Mostyn's muniments, he restored the documents he had purchased to his friend in a widely publicized act of generosity.

Madden now realized that *his* purchases from Hillier were very likely to be revealed, and he attempted a preemptive defence. At least eight months had elapsed since he had reason to know that the Ellesmere manuscripts he had purchased were contraband. Any defence of this delay now would be a weak one, but he had to make the best of it. On Friday, 6 October, Madden wrote to Collier: Did he, by any chance, know anything about a document concerning an association of Lincoln's Inn signed by Thomas Egerton? Collier was puzzled by a query whose answer could be so easily found, but he replied immediately that if Madden would look in the *Egerton Papers* he would find the document in question. He went on to say that he had made the copy himself, 'to the best of my recollection, from the original, which was then in the house occupied by Lord F. Egerton (now Earl of Ellesmere) in Cleveland Square'.[4] A day or two later, Madden replied that the

document to which I referred, and which, it appears, was printed by you in the Egerton Papers, p.108. in 1840, I purchased for the B.M. in July 1853, of a person named *George Hillier,* who had access about that time, I believe to Lord Ellesmere's Muniment Room. If I am not giving you too much trouble, I should be glad to see you as soon as possible to identify the document, as well as to shew you some other Papers, which appear to have come from the same Depository.

If this proves to be the case, I should be glad of your advice how to communicate with Lord Ellesmere, and what steps should be taken, before the matter is laid before the Trustees.[5]

On the same day Madden wrote to Hillier asking where he got the Lincoln's Inn charter. At first, Hillier refused to answer the question, but he immediately thought better of it. 'I plainly say there are three or four MSS. you had of me which I am doubtful about – and that the document in question is one',[6] he replied, declaring that he didn't have these doubts until after the sale. He would like, he said, to 'state' his information in person. Madden's 'reply' was to deny Hillier access to the Museum manuscripts (on the authority, he declared, of Sir Henry Ellis), and when Hillier wrote again asking to talk with Madden, Madden refused, despite the fact that he had unanswered questions concerning the other manuscripts. Madden's intention was to limit the investigation to the Lincoln's Inn document and to one or two less readily identified manuscripts and to avoid an investigation that would uncover the many other Ellesmere manuscripts from the same source. If that could be done, he had a good defence: he had apprised Ellesmere (through Collier) of the possibility of fraud and thus had demonstrated good faith: he would immediately suggest restoring the document to the Bridge-water Collection 'where it belonged' and that might be the end of it. But if all of the Ellesmere papers were to be uncovered, Madden would be revealed as a knowing accessory to theft. How could anyone believe he had acted in good faith when he purchased so many documents obviously derived from a well known collection without tracing their provenance? One might be honestly – if incompetently – careless about a single charter, but not about 140 manuscripts! And how could he explain having had the papers bound while suspecting they had been stolen? or the lapse of time between his first 'suspicions' of Hillier and his letter to Collier?

On 12 October, Collier visited the Museum and inspected the Lincoln's Inn charter, identifying it by his mark, a faintly pencilled 'C' in the margin which the binder had almost but not quite obliterated. He agreed to inform Ellesmere and Madden was relieved. He said nothing to Collier about the many other manuscripts he had acquired at the same time and from the same source. Madden then agreed to see Hillier. As he wrote in his diary, he 'stated what had passed' and wrote a short report to the Museum trustees on what he called 'Mr. H's case'. A visit to Lord Mostyn's solicitor satisfied him that Mostyn did not intend to claim 'any right or title to the MSS. I have purchased'.[7]

Several days later, Collier wrote to Madden enclosing

Ellesmere's reply. Ellesmere was, he said, 'much obliged' to both Madden and Collier for their efforts to apprehend the culprit. He had, however, never authorized Hillier to use his manuscripts, and (as Collier would have known) Hillier could not have seen them in the muniment room because there was none during the extensive renovation of the library at Bridgewater House. Perhaps the manuscript had been stolen during the move to the new building? Madden replied on 23 October, enclosing Hillier's letter admitting that the manuscript was not his at the time of the sale. Collier, Madden declared, 'might take such steps as Lord E. thinks requisite to prove or disprove [Hillier's] statement, the result of which I shall be very anxious to learn'.[8]

Thus far, all had gone according to Madden's plan: the case was limited to the Lincoln's Inn document, Ellesmere would undertake such legal proceedings against Hillier as seemed necessary, the trustees would give up the manuscript to Ellesmere, and Madden's 'misjudgment' in buying a stolen manuscript would be mitigated by his bringing the business out into the open. But Madden had not taken account of Collier. The fact that a document had been stolen from a collection that Collier had responsibility for impugned his reliability, and he therefore pressed Ellesmere not to settle the case without first determining how the manuscript had been taken from the collection and to find out if others were missing. Ellesmere followed this advice and after several weeks succeeded in tracing the patterns of the theft. The results were all that Madden could have feared. On 10 November, Ellesmere's private secretary reported to Collier that the Ellesmere papers had indeed been removed from Bridgewater House during the renovation and stored at Worsley Hall in Manchester, the residence of Ellesmere's son, Lord Brackley. There a man named Dandy had asked permission to use some of them in connection with work he was doing for the Duchess of Norfolk. Lord Brackley gave it without consulting his father, and the papers Dandy requested had been sent in two boxes to Norfolk Hall, where Dandy read about half of them before turning them over to George Hillier. Dandy made a list of the papers he gave Hillier, and later when the documents Hillier returned did not correspond to Dandy's list, Hillier convinced Dandy that his list was in error. The papers were returned to Worsley Hall and eventually went to the new library at Bridgewater House. But the difference between Dandy's list and Hillier's concerned not one document but many. Collier wondered – and Ellesmere wanted to know – whether the British Museum had purchased other documents from Hillier.

Collier wrote to Madden on 13 November, noting that Ellesmere wanted a complete accounting of the 'real or supposed 2 boxes of papers', but even then Collier did not suspect the papers were in the Museum. 'I do not see', he wrote, 'that it makes much difference in the case.' Nevertheless, Ellesmere wanted 'some account of what was determined by your Trustees... if you can properly supply me with the particulars.'[9] The trustees, of course, knew nothing about the other manuscripts and they merely declared their purchase of the Lincoln's Inn roll to be lawful. When this was reported to Collier the disparity between his request and the trustees' reply caused him to sense the truth. On 15 November, he wrote to Madden again and suggested as much.

Lord Ellesmere is evidently surprised (as I am) at the course taken by the Trustees... Were the case my own, I should not hesitate in applying at Bow Street for a search warrant. The B. Museum may have many other MSS. belonging to Lord Ellesmere, of which the Trustees have said nothing, and regarding which, perhaps, they entertain no suspicion. It would be an odd exhibition to see Mr. Hillier at the bar of the Old Bailey as the thief, and the Trustees, at his side, as the receivers of stolen goods. It strikes me, but I do not presume to give any opinion, that when the Trustees know (as they must) that they are in possession of stolen goods, they ought at once to do all in their power to set themselves right with Lord Ellesmere and the public. If I am not mistaken, they will next hear from Lord Ellesmere's Solicitor.[10]

Collier's letter must have staggered Madden but still he did not make a clean breast of the affair to the Museum trustees. He continued to deny the possibility of other stolen manuscripts in the collection, and apparently they did not press him for proof. Ellesmere, for his part, consulted his lawyer. His interest was to have the manuscripts returned, not to enter into litigation. Sir David Dundas, the Judge Advocate

General, called on Madden and read him an extract of a letter from Ellesmere suggesting the seriousness with which the Earl viewed the affair. As Madden later recorded the conversation in his diary, it was a letter 'in which an insinuation is made that *subsequent* to the discovery I had caused the MSS. to be bound, in order that the *marks* might be obliterated, by which the Papers could be identified! I feel extremely surprised and indignant at such an insinuation, which whether it comes from Mr. J. P. Collier or from Lord Ellesmere himself, I utterly repel and deny. If either of them has really said I had any such intention, I say *He lies!*'[11] This, of course, is precisely what he intended; a comparison of his own dates reveals that he had, in fact, sent the manuscripts to the bindery *after* he had good reason to know they were stolen. This attack on Collier was remarkable, for Collier, quite sincerely, had professed sympathy for Madden whom he initially believed was being victimized by the trustees' intransigence. Of course in doing so he had assumed the trustees knew what he knew; it was only later than he realized that Madden had carefully kept the trustees from knowing the whole story.

It was all to come to an inevitable and shameful conclusion. Ellesmere's solicitor demanded a complete accounting of the manuscripts purchased from Hillier. By 13 December, Ellesmere had apprised the trustees of the extent of the theft and Madden was ordered to deliver all the Ellesmere papers he had purchased from Hillier to a solicitor for transmission to Lord Ellesmere. The manner in which the order was given reveals that Madden was being ostracized, and he desperately tried to qualify the meaning of this action in his diary entry: 'I felt very much surprised that I had myself received no written instructions from the Trustees on the subject and stated my opinion to Sir H. Ellis. He put on the tone of *Principal Librarian,* and told me that *he* was the organ of communication from the Trustees to myself . . . Although I felt and still feel that this is a very improper course, and that I ought to have received written instructions from the Trustees, I made no difficulties in the matter.'[12] It is hard to know what 'difficulties' Madden could have made for anyone at that point. On 6 January, the trustees were informed by the Attorney General and Solicitor General that they must give up the manuscripts which Madden now admitted he had purchased. On 16 January, Madden identified 165 manuscripts which were then given to Ellis for transmission to Ellesmere. 'My part of this business is now at an end', Madden wrote in his diary.[13] So too, he might have added, any chance of advancement in the Museum. He had embarrassed the trustees and condemned himself.

It is unlikely that Madden knew that Hillier's manuscripts had been stolen *directly* from the Ellesmere papers; he was avaricious, but he was not stupid, and he would never have purchased manuscripts that could so easily have been traced back to such a powerful owner. But although he was not an accomplice in the crime, he was certainly a wilfully ignorant partner. Had he been forthright, he would have admitted his initial error, informed Ellesmere of the extent of the purchase, and, certainly, would not have bound the manuscripts to hide the evidence. Rather than admit a lesser fault, he committed a crime.

A public scandal would have redounded against them all, and the business was therefore kept quiet; it went unreported in the press. Neither Ellesmere nor the Museum sued Hillier. (Had either done so, Madden would have been publicly implicated.) Silence protected them all: the trustees' decorum, Madden's reputation, and Hillier's freedom. In fact, Hillier not only went unindicted, he *kept* the money he received for the manuscripts! He solemnly vowed he would exclude himself from reading in the British Museum (he was, in any case, barred at the time) and that he would forever give up reading manuscripts, but this was no deathbed promise; within a year or two he regained access to the Museum and was busy once again among the manuscripts of the country-side, even – astonishingly – the Mostyn manuscripts. Neither was Sims fired. The only casualty was Madden's amour-propre and the small standing he had with the Museum trustees. This loss, however, increased his hatred, not of himself (he continued to think he had been cruelly abused by everyone), but of the trustees, of Ellesmere, and of Collier. Most of all, Collier! Collier who had printed the damning document which revealed the crime! Collier whose marks had positively identified it! Collier who, Madden claimed, had 'prejudiced Lord Ellesmere's mind against me', and had urged a 'full accounting'![14]

When, a little over a year later, Sir Henry Ellis at last stepped down as Principal Librarian, Madden was excluded from serious consideration as his successor. In ludicrous self-delusion, Madden continued to think himself the likely choice. His diary of the period is replete with recrimination and foolish hope. He formally declared his candidacy to the trustees, 'simply', he wrote, 'to point out my own claim, but without any begging or petitioning. If they are *honest* men (which I doubt) the mere facts stated are sufficient . . . to include my name as *one* of the *two*, which by Act of Parliament, must be submitted to the Queen.'[15] When Panizzi's appointment loomed, Madden lashed out: 'It is hard to think that if this cursed fellow had never come to England with a rope round his neck, and entered the Museum as a subordinate in 1831, I should now have had the fairest chance of a good house and 1000 £ per annum. And [what] has *he* done for the Museum and the Public that *I* have not done, ay, and ten times more?'[16]   It was precisely what Madden had 'done' for the Museum which made his appointment impossible. With his part in the Hillier affair still fresh in the trustees' minds, Madden was the last man they would have chosen to succeed Ellis. Madden's bitterness against those he thought had brought him to this pass was unbounded. He was a man who could nurture revenge; he could keep it alive for years if need be. With Collier he wouldn't have to wait that long.

18

'We are about to be inundated with new editions of Shakespeare', the *Athenaeum* reported in late March, 1853. Some of these, it declared, were 'rendered necessary by the usual demands of purchasers, – others by the corrections introduced into the text through Mr. Collier's very important volume.' It would all end, the journal concluded in mock dismay, with 'every intelligent man turning editor for himself.'[17] There had probably never before been so many editors with so large a public wanting to read their work. Speculation about Shakespeare's text became more widespread than it had been before or would be again, and Collier had shrewdly manipulated his presentation of the Perkins Folio to create and ultimately to satisfy that appetite.

Much of this speculation was published in *Notes and Queries,* a weekly periodical devoted to brief correspondence on literary subjects. The paper was founded in 1849 by William Thoms, a good friend of Collier, his associate at the Society of Antiquaries and in the Camden Society, and his supporter against Panizzi during the Museum controversy. Collier was a frequent contributor to the paper, Singer was another, and Halliwell and Dyce occasionally submitted comments or asked questions in its pages. Largely as a result of their interest, *Notes and Queries* was often glutted with notes on Shakespeare. It was Thoms's policy not to exclude any pertinent communication, but he more than once complained that Shakespeare seemed to be distracting attention from other important topics.

Among the more prolific contributors to *Notes and Queries* was Andrew Edmund Brae, a man of many interests and arcane knowledge. Little was known about him other than that he lived in Leeds and the fact that every two or three weeks he dispatched a note or query to the journal (signed merely 'A.E.B.') on a wide variety of subjects – Oliver Goldsmith or pendulums or ancient inscriptions or English etymology or a dozen other topics. He was a pugnacious correspondent who issued his notes as 'challenges' which, to Brae's apparent irritation, no one accepted.

About two weeks before Collier announced his discovery of the Perkins Folio, Brae began a series of ten letters suggesting various emendations or restorations of the text of the Shakespeare plays. Brae was not very original, his taste was poor, his imagination humdrum, and his 'readings' wrong or pedestrian. Nevertheless, Thoms printed all of them, and all were ignored by the better-known editors who contributed to *Notes and Queries*. This infuriated Brae. In particular he was angry that while most of the country was applauding Collier's 'old corrector', his criticism of the Perkins emendations went unnoticed. His most significant objection concerned one of the Perkins corrections that Collier had singled out in his first announcement, a word in *Measure for Measure* (II,ii). According to the folio, Isabella, pleading with Angelo for her brother's life, says she will bribe him 'Not with fond *sickles* of the tested gold . . . but with true prayers.' 'Sickles' seemed to make no sense and early eighteenth-century editors had changed it to 'shekels', but that emendation had not been universally accepted. (In 1842, Collier himself had printed 'shekels' but suggested 'cycles' might actually be the right word.)[18] It was therefore of some interest that the old corrector of the Perkins Folio had made a change in the line by altering *sickles* to *sirkles* (i.e., 'circles'). 'The word of the poet was, . . . I have no doubt, *circles*', Collier declared in his first *Athenaeum* announcement of this emendation, 'in reference to the shape which "tested gold" bore as money.'[19] Two months later Brae attacked this reading by arguing that 'sickle' was a Latin equivalent for the Hebrew 'shekel', that Shakespeare was merely Anglicizing it in the passage, and that 'sickles' should be allowed to stand as it was in the folio. 'The real corruption has been that of Shakespeare's commentators, not his printer's; and I hope that some future editor of his plays will have the courage to permit him to spell this, and other proper names, in his own way.'[20] Brae did not mention either Collier or the Perkins Folio in his note, but he expected Collier to reply. Collier didn't.

Brae tried again with another Perkins emendation from *Measure for Measure* (I,i) which, by changing only one word, made sense of the Duke's first speech, otherwise unintelligible in the folio version. In a note published 1 May, Brae argued for the unemended folio reading and stated his opinion that any alteration of the speech was 'sheer perverseness'.[21] Once again Brae did not mention Collier or the Perkins Folio by name, and once again Collier did not reply. However, shortly thereafter Halliwell used *Notes and Queries* to announce his own emendation (which was in fact identical to the Old Corrector's) that he claimed to have found in an emended copy of the *Third* Folio. Halliwell's note did not mention Collier, the Perkins Folio or Brae's note, and Brae was once again stung by what seemed to be deliberate neglect. He immediately responded, determined to get the recognition he thought he deserved, demanding to know the evidence on which Halliwell based his opinion, but Halliwell did not reply.

Brae tried a fourth time. One of Collier's announcements in

the *Athenaeum* (27 March 1852) contained a newly discovered Perkins emendation correcting a line in *Coriolanus* (III,i) which had puzzled all Shakespeare's commentators. In it, Coriolanus opposes distributing corn from the public store-houses to a hungry populace, arguing that the public would take it as a sign of weakness. According to the First Folio, Coriolanus asks 'How shall this *bosom multiplied* digest/The Senate's courtesy?' For this, Collier announced, the 'old corrector' had substituted *bisson* (i.e., 'blind') *multitude*. It was one of the better Perkins corrections (widely accepted by subsequent editors) and both Singer and Halliwell announced their approval of the substitution in *Notes and Queries*. Halliwell (still in the period of his support for the book) was particularly enthusiastic. He declared it 'a ray of light.... The correction *"bisson multitude"* seems to me to be clearly one of those alterations that no conjectural ingenuity could have sug-gested.'[22] Here at last was an ideal circumstance for Brae: the giants stood together and he took aim at all of them, 'dissenting from the general acclaim with which the proposed substitution of this latter phrase has been received'. He wrote, 'it is due to the notoriety of the emendations, as well as to the distinguished names by which it is advocated, to explain the grounds upon which I declare my adhesion to *the old reading*.' He then listed five elaborate reasons, none compelling, for his preference, and sat back waiting for the defensive replies. Again, none came.

Brae's frustration was made the more painful because Singer and Collier were carrying on an exchange in the pages of *Notes and Queries*[23] and would not deign to notice him. Even his attempts to enter *their* controversy were passed over in what seemed to him 'studied rebuke'. In spite of repeated attempts over a period of eight months, Brae failed to be recognized as an opponent worth noticing.

The publication of Collier's *Notes and Emendations* in January 1853 galvanized Brae into more direct action. In commenting on the '*sirkles* for *sickles*' emendation noted above, Collier revealed a change of opinion. In his enthusiastic announce-ment in the *Athenaeum* twelve months before, he had written that he had 'no doubt' about the correction and that it 'put an end to all difficulty'; but in *Notes and Emendations* he now admitted to being ambivalent. The 'true word may be circles', he wrote. 'Nevertheless, "sheckels" may be right, and it is used, exactly with the same spelling, by Lodge in his "Catharos," 1591.'[24] Collier probably had not seen Brae's comment on the emendation; it was the newly discovered analogue in Lodge which convinced him that his earlier judgement was wrong, but Brae was furious that Collier had not cited him as the authority who changed his mind.[25]

The cause of Brae's anger was picayune, but its effect was to be significant. Brae's oblique criticism of the Perkins Folio before the appearance of *Notes and Emendations* now became a direct assault on the book and a personal attack on its author. For some time, he had been developing a theory about a stage direction ('writing') that eighteenth-century editors had inserted near the conclusion of the first ghost scene in *Hamlet*. The insertion derived from Hamlet's lines in Act I about 'setting down' his impressions after his confrontation with the ghost, and Brae argued, rather obscurely, that where Hamlet began to write determined whether his subsequent madness were real or feigned. Since the stage direction did not appear in any of the early printed texts, his theory had no textual source, but he pursued the point in a note in March 1852, and when that too got no reply, he wrote again in September, asking whose edition had first inserted the stage direction. The issue, he declared, was a 'subject of challenge'. It wasn't clear what or whom Brae was challenging, and there were, therefore, no replies. Five months later, in February 1853, after the publication of *Notes and Emendations* (with what Brae took to be a 'slighting' omission of any reference to him), he renewed the question of the stage direction in a direct attack on Collier. Although none of his earlier notes had suggested even indirectly that Collier had a special interest in the subject, Brae now accused him of a 'failure to respond'.[26]

Collier was then in Torquay with his daughters (Mary was dying) and he was astonished by Brae's implication that he had ignored a query directed to him. He replied immediately that he did not have back issues of *Notes and Queries* with him in Torquay, but he would be happy to try to answer the question if 'A.E.B.' would ask it once more. 'To whomever these initials belong', Collier wrote, in an unfortunately patronizing manner, 'he is a man of so much acuteness and learning, that, although I may deem his conjectures rather subtle and ingenious than solid and expedient, I consider him entitled to all the information in my power. I do not, of course, feel bound to notice all anonymous speculators (literary or pecuniary) . . .'[27]

Brae did not repeat the question, neither did he write Collier directly for the information. It is hard to avoid the impression that his real interest was not to receive an answer but to create a controversy, and, perhaps, to entrap. He could easily have learned and may already have known that the stage direction was first put into the text by Rowe in 1709. He may have thought that, if Collier declared the Perkins Folio had the stage direction, he would have to admit that the Old Corrector wrote after that date, i.e., that the emendations were eighteenth-century conjectures rather than authentic seventeenth-century corrections. Brae's note implied that Collier had deliberately avoided answering a question which would damn the folio.

Two months later, in April 1853, Brae sent a letter to *Notes and Queries* containing an *ad hominem* attack on the Perkins Folio and suggesting that the annotations were 'pseudo-antique' and could be accepted only by 'blind and superstitious faith'.[28]

His private opinions were even more rash, embittered by what he took to be a personal affront:

As for me I declare *war to the knife* against Mr. Collier's folio [he wrote in May 1853]. From its first announcement in 1852 I have continued to be more and more convinced of its being an enormous *manufactured* humbug – at present wrapped in mystery but sure of being brought to light some day or other. I do not however think that Mr. Collier has any part in the deceit – but I do look upon it as a marvellous and instructive example of the decadence of human judgement that he should suffer himself to be so wholly blinded by the *vanity of discovery*. The prestige of Mr. Collier's name carries with it all the influence of the public press – the public at large, who will not, or cannot, judge for themselves, go with the tide – and all we, poor mice, can do will be to knaw at the meshes one by one which have been cast over Shakespeare's text and so assist in freeing it from the coil. . . . Hitherto I have only attacked indirectly by a side wind – hence my papers on 'bosom multipled' – . . . I shall now attack more openly providing that no objection on the part of the Editor intervene.[29]

Brae's own 'vanity of discovery' had been injured, and his capacity for retaliation was enormous. He began an unrelenting and envenomed attack on the Perkins readings. Other correspondents to *Notes and Queries* disagreed with some of the emendations Collier had published, the publication did not discourage such critics, but no other correspondence on the subject had the animus of Brae's 'notes'. 'Shall we – misled by the prestige of a few drops of rusty ink fashioned into letters of formal cut – place implicit credence in emendations whose only claim to faith, like that of the Mormon scriptures, is that nobody knows whence they came?' he asked.[30]

Brae's motivation was obscure. It was not personal – he did not know Collier and they would never meet. Collier didn't even know Brae's name. Yet Brae had leaped to a 'war to the knife' and his knife was sharp. When a friend suggested that Collier might be prepared to 'retract' some of his support for the Perkins emendations (which had never been total in any case), Brae was not appeased. Even if Collier should qualify his opinion, Brae wrote, 'he can never wash out the stain from his name of having, to use the mildest phrase, *so foolishly* abetted so very trumpery a deception – I shall not give utterance to all my surmises about this folio. I shall not hazard a guess as to its fabrication but I have strange suspicions – the sign of the beast is very apparent.'[31] It is significant that the terms 'fabrication' and 'pseudo-antique', which suggested that Collier was a party to deception and possible forgery, were first used by one who had never seen the Perkins Folio and had no reason, other than his own anger, to believe that the issue was forgery rather than mere misjudgement. If, in fact, the Perkins Folio emendations were demonstrably eighteenth-century, as Brae believed, they would not have had to be forged; certainly Collier himself would not have used such 'eighteenth-century' evidence to 'fabricate' a 'seventeenth-century' hoax. Simple logic disproved Brae's accusation, but his attack went beyond logic.

When Collier's one-volume edition appeared, Brae assumed its lack of notes was merely an excuse to deny him recognition[32] and his series of 'Readings' to *Notes and Queries* became so querulous that Thoms found them increasingly difficult to print. In one note Brae condemned an emendation by the 'Old Corrector' who 'whether by anticipation or imitation I shall not take upon me to decide', had made the same mistake as the rest of the commentators. After presenting an *outré* emendation of his own, Brae declared, 'I trust I may be left in the quiet possession of whatever merit is due to this restoration. Some other of my humble *auxilia* have, before now, been coolly appropriated, with the most innocent air possible, without the slightest acknowledgement.'[33] The charge was unjust. Brae's hatred was fired by his *failure* to influence other critics.

Having failed to damn the Perkins emendations on interpretive grounds, Brae attempted to do so on philological ones. Drawing on his considerable linguistic knowledge, he sought a 'test word' which would prove that the corrections were of 'recent' origin. On 20 August, he wrote to Thoms declaring that he had found what he was looking for:

I wish to communicate to you *under this date* that I have succeeded in detecting a *test word*, in Mr. Collier's marginal corrections, which certainly did not exist 100 years ago.... If the employment of this test word cannot be *proved* by the Collier party for more than 100 years back then the very simulation of greater antiquity in other respects (which has deceived so many *good judges*) must convict the whole affair of illicit fabrication!

I almost stood alone in my opposition at first – recently, so many winkers have begun to open their eyes, that I have been induced to fly at higher pitch, and endeavour to attack *the honesty* of the production, which, as you know, I always suspected, but until now despaired of being able to prove.[34]

It was not until ten days later that Brae divulged the word to Thoms:

the alteration of *chair* into *cheer* in *Coriolanus* (IV,iv – cited on page 361 of *Notes & Emendations*) and of *chats him* into *cheers him* (same play, page 352). I shall boldly allege that the word 'cheer', *in the sense used* [i.e. as an acclamation] was not in existence until within the last forty years.

Brae's research had satisfied him that the use had not existed before 1818:

Thus I trace the phrase *'a cheer'* in the singular, to modern *parliamentary conventionality* – used in reporting of debates. . . . I understand that so late as 1812 nothing of the kind existed.[35]

Thoms, of course, realized that by tying the usage to parliamentary *reporting*, Brae was indirectly implicating Collier in a fraud. He had earlier cautioned Brae against personal attacks and Brae had seemed to accept the warning, but this note convinced Thoms that Brae was intent upon personal vilification. In his reply, he wrote

It is one matter to differ with Mr. Collier on questions of literary criticism and another to charge him with being a party to a gross imposture (and how, if such a charge is to be brought forward is he to be separated from it?). He may or may not be a competent editor of Shakespeare – on that question all who know him may hold very different opinions but that he is a man utterly incapable of participating in anything so gross, as the putting forth as genuine N. & E. a series of modern fabrications no one who knows anything about him will for one instant doubt.[36]

This was evidently not the response Brae had expected, and he replied to Thoms's caution with disdain. Because of 'the personal complexion' Thoms was 'pleased to confer upon the matter', he wrote

it is impossible I can trouble you any farther upon a subject which to me is merely one of great literary interest. . . . I utterly repudiate and protest against the doctrine (to me a monstrous one) that any doubt as to the genuineness of matter which happens to be in the possession of, and believed in by Mr. Collier, must necessarily be a reflexion upon that gentleman's personal honour . . . I never doubted Mr. Collier's pure and unsullied honour and I firmly and literally believe every tittle of his account as to his acquisition of this folio in its present state.[37]

A curious comment! If the folio was a 'manufactured humbug', *someone* must have done the 'fabrication', and it would take more naïvety than even Brae seemed to possess to believe that such a charge would not rebound against the man who first brought forth the 'deception'. During the next four months, Brae published four more notes in *Notes and Queries*, none of them concerning Shakespeare, Collier, or the Perkins Folio.

But Brae had by no means given up his attack. His manner with Thoms was friendly, but Brae's correspondence with others reveals that Thoms had become an enemy along with Collier – 'Thoms Collier & Co' he called them. Thoms, Brae declared privately, had 'closed' the pages of *Notes and Queries* to him on the subject of the Perkins Folio, and this was accomplished 'through [Collier's] influence'. Thus, Brae declared, he had been denied the 'only *effective* publication of the day in which the true cause of Shakespeare might have been defended'.[38] As Thoms's letter shows, he had cautioned Brae, but he had not refused him access to *Notes and Queries*. It had printed other notes criticizing the Perkins Folio and other publications would have taken Brae's correspondence if, as he claimed, *Notes and Queries* wouldn't. His failure to publish the accusations along with the results of his research on 'cheer' suggests that he recognized the force of Thoms's advice and didn't want to be publicly exposed as a jealous fool.

But if Brae's confidence in his evidence did not increase, his personal animosity to Collier did. 'However thin-skinned Collier may *pretend* to be about his immaculate folio, he cannot even himself, weak minded as he is, *honestly believe in it'*, he wrote to a friend in February 1854,[39] and the following May he wrote with delight that he had seen a catalogue of a book auction which listed *Notes and Emendations* as 'impostures'. 'Capital!' he declared. 'There is no mincing of the matter.'[40] But as yet he made no public declaration about 'cheer' or about 'fabrications' or 'impostures'. He was waiting his chance.

It was not long before he thought he had found it. In July 1854, Collier began what was to become a sequence of four letters to *Notes and Queries* concerning one of Coleridge's early lecture series.[41] Five years before, Coleridge's daughter-in-law had collected all of the critic's literary pronouncements and published them in two volumes, part of the collected *Literary Remains* that had been appearing off and on since Coleridge's death. From various manuscripts and notes, she had been able to reconstruct many of Coleridge's commentaries and, in particular, his lectures of 1818, but she had found no trace of his notes for the Shakespeare Lectures of 1811–12 (if in fact they had ever existed; Coleridge often lectured extempore), and she had reprinted only the 'Prospectus' Coleridge had produced to advertise the series. Collier had attended these lectures and had taken lengthy shorthand notes, but in the forty-five years that followed he had destroyed some of the notebooks in which the notes were kept and mislaid the rest. While preparing his Shakespeare in the mid-forties he had remembered his transcripts but he could not find them. However, when he moved from Geys to Riverside, he went through all of his papers with the intention of throwing away everything of no value, and in this process he found his old notes. 'Unluckily', he reported to *Notes and Queries,* 'they are not complete, for although each lecture is finished, and, in a manner, perfect in itself, my memoranda (which are generally very full, and in the *ipsissima verba* of the author) only apply to seven out of fifteen lectures, viz. to the first, second, sixth, seventh, eighth, ninth, and twelfth.'[42]

In his first letter, Collier reprinted the 'Prospectus', the first paragraph of which outlined the scope of the series: 'Mr Coleridge will commence on Monday, November 18th (1812)'. Collier's version ran, 'a course of Lectures on Shakespeare and Milton...'. The quotation contained a conjectural error in the date, '(1812)' instead of 1811. Perhaps because the lectures extended from the last months of 1811 into the first of 1812, Collier's memory of the year was wrong, and in his note he regularly referred to the series as having occurred in 1812.[43]

Brae used Collier's announcement of the Coleridge transcripts to discredit the Perkins Folio. In October 1855, he composed a letter declaring that the 1812 date proved Collier had forged the account, and, by an unexplained logic, that this proved he had forged the Perkins Folio too. Brae's rationale was, on the face of it, bizarre. He had no shred of evidence of wrong-doing; there is unimpeachable evidence that Collier had attended the lectures and had taken lengthy shorthand notes.[44] Brae was motivated entirely by frustrated pride and an animus against a man whose reputation he coveted – a man he didn't know. His announced intention was to destroy Collier's character through the Coleridge notes and, once that was done, to push the Perkins Folio after it.

If it can be shown that the producer's hands are not clean from literary fabrications in other matters, [Brae wrote] the downfall of the marginal corrections must follow as a matter of course.... The presumption – the plagiarism – the vulgarity – the imbecility – of those wretched libels on the text of Shakespeare were as nothing to convince of their imposture; but had the prestige of their sponsor been less – had they really been dependent solely on their own merits – they would have been at once cried to scorn.

To dispel that prestige, by laying bare the taint of CONTRIVANCE, is the real object of this exposure; if the scene now opened is effectively followed up, it may, perhaps, at length extort a second confession, similar to Ireland's, of Shakespearean forgeries.... [45]

This was war to the knife indeed! It is difficult to believe that Brae took his 'evidence' seriously, and his use of it suggests that his plan was devious and malicious from the start. He submitted the letter to – of all publications – the *Athenaeum*, and he did so anonymously, calling himself merely 'A Detective'. It must have been apparent even to him that no reputable periodical would print an anonymous, potentially libellous charge, and especially not the *Athenaeum*, in which Collier had announced the Perkins Folio in the first place. Brae seemed intent on making sure the piece would be rejected: his letter to the journal said that it had to be published 'intact and entire, without addition or curtailment', yet apart from taste and law, its length alone would have made this impossible. His true intention was revealed in a threat which accompanied the article: if the *Athenaeum* refused to print the piece 'it is the writer's intention to have the letter immediately printed for diffusion through the post-office' – with an attack on the *Athenaeum* attached! To its credit, the *Athenaeum* refused to be either bullied or blackmailed. The argument from the date 1812 was unimpressive, it declared; Collier had indicated the date was conjectural by printing it between parentheses; Brae's article, in its opinion, was 'a mere waste of words'.[46]

All of which came as no surprise to Brae, and he immediately had the letter printed as a pamphlet adding, on the grotesquely misguided assumption that it supported his case, his exchange with the *Athenaeum*. (The printing was poor and replete with grammatical and typographical errors which showed Brae's haste to broadcast his diatribe.) In early November, through a middleman, he offered the pamphlet to John Russell Smith, a Soho publisher with a modicum of reputation who was often the conduit for shady publications. Although Smith did not know 'the Detective's' identity and never met Brae, he agreed to imprint his own name on the title page and to issue the pamphlet, now called *Literary Cookery with Reference to Matter Attributed to Coleridge and Shakespeare*. Smith sent review copies to various journals and advertised it for sale.

The sequence of what then followed is not clear, but apparently some of those who read the review copies recognized the scurrilous nature of the pamphlet and complained to Smith, who belatedly discerned its libellous nature and feared he might be sued. Within a week or two of agreeing to publish, he withdrew the book from sale and wrote to the periodicals to whom he had sent copies asking them to 'pass it by in silence'.[47]

They did, but Collier didn't. He had ignored Brae's abuse in *Notes and Queries*; throughout 1854 and 1855 he was at work on the Roxburghe edition of Drayton's poems and would no doubt have been surprised to learn that this preoccupation had been interpreted by Brae and his cohorts as evading a controversy. But the libel of *Literary Cookery* could not be ignored and Brae at last succeeded in galvanizing Collier's attention. The reaction was severe.

Collier may have heard about *Literary Cookery* from Thoms (to whom Smith had sent the first review copy!).[48] Predictably, he was enraged. His friend may have cautioned him to ignore the pamphlet, but if he did, Collier rejected his counsel and immediately hired two eminent lawyers, Sir Frederick Thesiger and Sir Robert Lush, and went to court, demanding that Smith 'show cause' why he had not committed libel. In preparing his case, Collier made a lengthy affidavit in which he swore to the details he had previously published concerning his acquisiton of the Perkins Folio, declaring that in the spring of the year 1849 he had purchased the Second Folio of Shakespeare's plays from Thomas Rodd –

which copy contained, when I purchased it, a great number of manuscript notes purporting to be corrections, alterations and emendations of the original text, made, as I believe, by the same person, and at a period nearly contemporaneous with the said folio itself.

He also swore to the truth of all the statements in *Notes and Emendations* concerning the discovery, contents, and authenticity of the of the manuscript notes, and further to the details of exhibiting the book, its acquisition by Devonshire, and the circumstance of the publication of *Notes and Emendations*. Finally, he swore to the accuracy of the information he had published concerning the Coleridge lectures in *Notes and Queries*. He admitted the error of date.[49] It was an elaborate, indeed a gratuitous, defence, but the degree of Collier's anger is revealed in the fulness of his statement.

Although Smith had already withdrawn *Literary Cookery* from sale (only a few copies if any had been sold), Collier proceeded with his suit. In mid-January 1856 the case was heard in the Queen's Bench before Collier's old acquaintance, John Campbell. Thesiger argued that Collier had no objection to discussion or to a fair consideration of the genuineness of the notes, but he contended no one had the right to accuse him of forgery. The mere accusation, he declared, 'would be fatal to the character of any man'. It was the more irritating since Collier had given a detailed account of the way in which he acquired the folio. The libel was obvious: *Literary Cookery* charged him with 'having forged the notes himself, or published them knowing them to be forged'. However, Campbell denied Collier's request. The pamphlet 'certainly transgressed the limits of mere literary criticism', but it was not a case in which the court ought to interfere, because Smith had voluntarily withdrawn the pamphlet, few copies had been sold, and Smith had indicated that he did not intend to circulate the rest. Collier's reputation, Campbell declared, was untarnished by the affair. Collier was 'a most honourable man, whose labours had been of infinite benefit to the literature of this country' and since his action 'had been most satisfactorily vindicated; it was, therefore, not necessary to interfere for his protection.'[50] The effect, but not the word of Campbell's ruling, was to enjoin Smith from publishing the pamphlet and to deny Collier redress.

This result must have been disappointing to Collier, but it was not unreasonable; strictly speaking, Collier had no legal case because the action for which he sued had already taken place; if he had wanted damages he would have had to file differently. Still, Campbell did not condemn *Literary Cookery* as strongly as he could have (as things turned out, this would have been useful to Collier), and he avoided a hard decision. His opinion was perhaps more political than judicial, an attempt to please both parties. (A month or two after the case was decided, he wrote a pamphlet suggesting that Shakespeare had been trained as a lawyer and, in a curious gesture, dedicated it to John Payne Collier![51]) The case was not a *cause célèbre*, either to the public or Collier's friends. Although Robinson was in regular correspondence with the Colliers and saw then several times during the period of the trial, he did not mention the suit in his diary or letters.

Literary Cookery was outrageous – transparently malicious, contemptible in its anonymity, and bearing, in its author's own words, 'the sign of the beast'. In the usual course of events, such acts of perverted imagination are discounted, ignored and consigned to oblivion by the good sense of history, and this ought to have been the fate of *Literary Cookery*. But it wasn't, primarily because Collier was not able to forget it. The whole affair might well have been forgotten except that, disreputable though it was adjudged and ineffectual though it seemed at the time, Brae's pamphlet was to stimulate new charges a few years hence, and Collier was to be indirectly responsible for its doing so. One of the flaws in Collier's character was his inability to release himself from controversy, and now the insubstantial charges in an obscure pamphlet swept him on to disaster. In July 1856 Collier published *Seven Lectures on Shakespeare and Milton*, his shorthand transcripts of Coleridge's 1811 lectures. The transcripts were short, comprising only 150 pages of large, heavily leaded type, and Collier had initially planned to 'fill out the book' with a memoir of Coleridge, but after the *Literary Cookery* suit he enlarged the introduction by inserting into it an overlong account of Brae's attack and the whole of his sworn affidavit. Only fifteen copies of *Literary Cookery* had been circulated before it was suppressed[52] and hence few had read it, but hundreds read

Collier's preface to *Seven Lectures* and what had been a little known case of libel became a public scandal, for, without any justification, Collier linked his quarrel with Brae to his disagreement with Singer and Dyce over their three-year-old pamphlets denouncing the Perkins Folio. His rebuttal was temperate, but it should not have been made in the context of *Literary Cookery*: neither Dyce nor Singer was in any way connected with that disreputable work.

Collier's reply to Singer was the more severe. He declared that Singer had 'denounced most, if not all, of the [Perkins] corrections as undeserving a moment's consideration, as vulgar, stupid, imbecile, ignorant and spurious, with a thousand other derogatory epithets', and then had gone on 'to print in the text of his new edition of Shakespeare the very words which, in the inconsiderateness of his animosity, he utterly rejected.'[53] Collier was more heated than necessary, but what he said was essentially true: many of the Perkins emendations which Singer had denounced in 1853 had been silently incorporated into his edition of 1856.

Collier's rejoinder to Dyce was more subtle and more mischievous. Although wholly unrelated to the context of Coleridge's lectures, a good part of Collier's preface was devoted to a description of the most common causes of textual errors (e.g., mishearing, errors in shorthand transcription, mispronunciation, typographical inversions); it was a perceptive examination of the problem of textual transmission and the dangers such errors create for editors. However, virtually all his examples of textual confusion were drawn from Dyce's editions of early dramatists. Beaumont and Fletcher, Tourneur, Peele, Webster, Middleton, and Marlowe – all were culled to demonstrate Dyce's editorial faults, and although Collier interspersed two or three errors from his own works among them, these did little to dull the point of his selection. On the basis of Collier's fifty-page catalogue of errors, Dyce appeared to be a remarkably unimaginative and clumsy editor.

It was a gratuitous addition to Collier's real business in publishing Coleridge's lectures, and it did him great harm. This 'defense' inflamed old animosities as it was intended to do. Dyce and Collier had made a grudging reconciliation to the extent that they corresponded occasionally and talked to one another in the street, but with the appearance of *Seven Lectures* they were once again – and this time would remain – enemies.

The obvious relish with which he settled a score with his two old antagonists obliterated the more important fact that Collier had significantly changed his opinion of the emendations themselves. Although he had never endorsed all of the corrections in the folio, he had implied a general confidence in them. Now, however, he was at pains to declare that his one-volume edition of 1853 had not been intended to be definitive. It was, rather, a slightly edited printed *facsimile* of the Perkins text which included 'the entire body of such emendations as were deemed at all worthy of notice or preservation', a compendium of the folio changes and by no means to be taken as an established text. Collier's new second edition of his multi-volume *Shakespeare* – which, he declared, was in preparation – would be a reaffirmation of the rules 'that the old copies should be implicitly followed wherever possible. . . . I am now for adopting no other course, unless it can be clearly established that the emendation proposed is *required*; and in the new edition I am now in the act of printing, I shall carefully exclude all questionable introductions'.[54] This was an emphatic restatement that he did *not* approve of all the Perkins corrections and that his previous publication of them should not be so construed. Unfortunately, interlaced as it was with his diatribe against Singer and Dyce, this point, essential to Collier's intention, was lost.

Also virtually unremarked was Collier's statement that his claim of copyright was meant only to be a demand that any correction taken from his edition of *Notes and Emendations* should fully credit the Perkins Folio. He was sure he had the legal right to restrict republication if he chose, but, he declared, 'whenever I was appealed to on the question, I never for one moment hesitated to give the fullest licence for the unrestricted employment of any of my materials. The only condition I ever imposed was, that they should state the source of their information.'[55] It was this, he claimed, that Singer had failed to do. Again, it was an important point, and Collier disclaimed copyright thereafter.

Collier's 120-page preface helped to make *Seven Lectures* a big book with a larger commercial appeal. For much the same reason, he appended 120 pages of what the half-title page called 'A List of Every Manuscript Note and Emendation in Mr. Collier's Copy of Shakespeare's Works, Folio, 1632.' This was a gross misstatement that Collier almost certainly did not compose. In the preface he makes it clear that he intends to list only those changes which 'were deemed at all worthy of notice or preservation'. Corrections that he thought obviously poor – and there were thousands of them – he did not reprint, and he also omitted all stage directions. (Later Collier would be accused of surreptitiously omitting some emendations from the list.)

To entitle this collection the 'complete' list of Perkins corrections may have helped the sale of *Seven Lectures,* but it caused consternation at Whittaker and Company. Collier published his new book with Chapman and Hall, and Whittaker was angered because, he declared, he had 'purchased' the corrections from Collier, and he still had over eight hundred copies of the second edition of *Notes and Emendations* on hand.[56] Collier replied that Whittaker had overprinted against his advice and that he had never sold his right to reprint the Perkins emendations.

Collier's text of Coleridge's lectures caused hard feelings, too. The Coleridge family was particularly angry that Collier had not offered his transcripts to Mrs. Coleridge when she was preparing her edition (Collier said that they had been misplaced at the time) and declared that they had a presumptive right to their publication. The *legal* case was uncertain, since the text derived from copies that Collier himself had made rather than from Coleridge's manuscripts, and the copyright law of the time did not make such subtle distinctions. Coleridge's heirs did not take any legal action, but the edition became controversial.

Later scholars would thank Collier for preserving the shards of some of Coleridge's most important lectures, but by using the edition of *Seven Lectures* to settle old and unrelated scores Collier revealed a confusion of intent. Robinson's reaction to the book reveals the general response: 'Collier does not conciliate by his manners', he confided to his diary. The preface, he declared, had more interest than pleasure in it, and the defence of the Perkins Folio 'of which so much has been said' was 'very wearisome indeed'. About the introduction, Robinson was even more emphatic: 'As I presume it is controversial and in self-vindication', he wrote to Collier, 'I wish it unwritten, for even the successful defence implies the having suffered injustice.'[57]

Seven Lectures gave wide circulation to ill-founded anonymous charges of forgery which few would have credited otherwise. In publishing the book Collier awakened dormant distrust and animosity. He would come to regret it.

19

He would come to regret it, but not immediately. Ultimately these petty quarrels would be seen for what they were. None of the participants were free of professional jealousy – not Halliwell or Singer, certainly not Dyce or Collier. Their successors would rightly condemn the selfish interest each took in his 'discoveries' and accomplishments and the animus with which reputations were attacked and pride of place defended. There had been critical disputes before this and there would be others after, but none, perhaps, so bereft of generous feeling, none so quickly envenomed. It did not help that the adversaries were well aware of the perverting effect of their quarrels. Probably all his opponents would have agreed with Collier when, two years hence, in the preface to his new *Shakespeare*, he disparaged such competition:

How strange it must ever appear that, on a subject which excites the interest and admiration of all mankind, and regarding which all mankind ought to unite in one purpose, – that of clearing the language of Shakespeare from undoubted blemishes, – private jealousies and personal enmities should be allowed to interfere with the accomplishment of an object so inestimable. When I consider the utter insignificance of an editor, in comparison with the great master it has been the business of his life to illustrate, I know not how sufficiently to apologize for bringing my own position so prominently before the reader.[58]

But recognizing the disease did not keep Collier from being its victim. The statement was made at the end of a preface condemning the vices of his opponents.

Collier's self-condemnation was sincere, but he was no more able to ignore the lure of controversy than were his antagonists. The only 'sufficient' way for him to 'apologize' would have been to cease making private anguish into public discord, but he couldn't do that – no more than Dyce, Halliwell, or Singer could. Thus, in the fall of 1856 and through 1857, as he continued to edit and to print the second edition of his Shakespeare, there was no let-up in his self-justification and, of course, no let-up in his need for self-defence.

The terms of his agreement with Whittaker for a revised edition are unknown, but Collier worked steadily on the revision for well over two years. The edition of 1844 had been published one volume at a time. This time Whittaker intended to withhold publication till the whole was complete, a commercially astute procedure, for Collier's chief competitors produced their editions in 1856 and 1857, and when his own appeared in 1858 he had the advantage of being able to recapitulate his earlier claims and refute theirs without giving them the same opportunity. The sequence gave Collier 'the last word' – or so he thought. Singer's edition had appeared in the spring of 1856, and in the fall of that year Howard Staunton, a close friend of Frederic Madden, began to issue an illustrated edition (*Routledge's Shakespeare*) in shilling monthly parts. In July 1857 Knight published a new *Student's Edition of Shakespeare*, his earlier text brought up to date with Perkins emendations, and just before the end of the year, Dyce published the multi-volume edition he had been labouring on for many years.[59] All of these editions took sharp issue with Collier's *Notes and Emendations* while adopting many of the 'old corrector's' readings, sometimes with credit, sometimes without. Collier, we may be sure, kept careful track of all of them, and the notes he wrote to accompany his text expressed his continuing animosity.

The eighteen months following the appearance of *Seven Lectures* were also a time of personal anguish for Collier. On Christmas Eve 1856, his sister-in-law, Emma Pycroft, died unexpectedly, possibly by her own hand. Her illness had grown progressively worse after the family moved to Riverside, and for long periods she had been deranged and difficult to control. Nursing her sister through the last months of her life had been a severe strain for Mary Louisa Collier, who was now the sole survivor of her family, and within a month she had a relapse of her chronic heart condition. As the weeks passed and she made little improvement, it was apparent that she suffered from more than a weak heart. Collier's fears were confirmed when it was discovered she had cancer. Collier's own health was poor too. Several months before Emma's death he had suffered yet another onset of arthritis which crippled his hands. Sometimes the disease immobilized him completely.

Nevertheless, he continued to work. He propped himself up in bed, and gripping the pen between his thumb and forefinger, he wrote the notes to his text of Shakespeare. On days when this was too painful, he collated or read galley proofs, dictating his corrections to one of his daughters. In this excruciating fashion he worked throughout 1857 on his Shakespeare edition. In addition, he completed four short articles on Raleigh for the Society of Antiquaries and a selection of papers from the archives of the Trevelyan family for the Camden Society. Sir Charles Trevelyan, a scion of that line, had been particularly helpful to John Pycroft Collier, securing him a post in the Treasury and ensuring his success there, and Collier's volume, the first of three for the Camden Society, was intended to repay this kindness.[60]

In March 1857, his revision of Shakespeare only half completed, he contracted with the publishers Bell and Daldy for an edition of Spenser. It was to give him the opportunity to 'free' Spenser's text from what he believed were the barbarities of Henry Todd's edition of 1805. 'Though far from rich, I am not in want of money', he wrote to the publishers, and for perhaps the first time in his career he made a contract without considering financial return. He asked only 100 guineas for his labour, a low fee for an editor of his reputation, only slightly more than he had received for the almost equivalent work on Shakespeare ten years before. What he wanted in lieu of royalty was greater control over the design of the edition: the number of pages in each volume, the quality of the paper, the kind of type, the placement of notes, etc. 'I will do my best', he wrote to the publishers, 'not for your sake, nor for my own, but for the sake of the author, whom I love above all poets, if I do not admire him as much as I do Shakespeare.'[61]

After lengthy correspondence, the publishers agreed to Collier's stipulations: the edition would print *all* of Spenser's works, prose as well as poetry, complete, and would include the *Shepherd's Calendar,* complete with notes made during Spenser's lifetime, and *A View of the State of Ireland,* two works omitted in past editions. His notes, he declared, would be brief and the text would adhere strictly to Spenser's orthography and maintain the chronological order of publication. His declared objective was to make it 'the standard of "Spenser's Works" – prose and verse'.

Completing this edition was to be more difficult than Collier could have imagined when the contract was signed in 1857. When he began the Spenser edition, Collier's prestige was high and seemed secure; when he finished it, his reputation was in ruins. Not the least of this worries in the next few years would be the knowledge that public controversy was keeping him from what was to have been the culminating achievement of his career, and when the Spenser edition appeared at last in 1862 – much later than expected – it was to be overshadowed by the remnants of controversy.

Collier's season of discontent was presaged by the death of his wife on 10 December 1857. She had been acutely ill for the previous ten months, and her death was a release from great pain, but this did not assuage Collier's grief. Their marriage had developed into one of deep affection. They had married for practical considerations, and for over forty years they had met those considerations: they had endured – themselves and an uncertain life – together. Now Collier was alone. Mary Louisa's death deprived him of a known and trusted part of his existence, and her burial next to their two oldest daughters in Brompton Cemetery reminded Collier that his own death would not be too far off. He knew he would be cared for. (Emma Letitia would remain with him until his death, and Mary Louisa's will made him sole heir to the Pycroft annuity, which would give him financial security for the rest of his life.) But he was more aware of what was past or passing than of what was to come, and this sense of loss was increased by the deaths within a year of his two greatest patrons. Ellesmere died in February 1857, and Devonshire succumbed to a paralytic seizure in January 1858. Despite the affection of his family, Collier felt singularly vulnerable and overwhelmingly alone.[62]

This sense of mortality intensified Collier's determination: 'My first object is to finish the 2[d] edit. of my Shakespeare,' he wrote to his publishers. 'Upon that I have staked my credit, and nothing shall interfere with it so as to make it worse than it would have been otherwise. I would rather do nothing more and die, than neglect it.'[63] This was not hyperbole. Collier was no longer impelled by financial need but by feelings of professional culpability. He had never endorsed all the Old Corrector's emendations and had frequently declared that history alone must judge them, but he was more than merely their 'discoverer'. He had issued three editions of the notes and had incorporated them into an egregious popular edition. His reputation had made the book a literary sensation, and he must have realized that the emendations had obscured the text of Shakespeare more than they had illuminated it. It was not the judgement of posterity but his current reputation as a sagacious editor that he would 'rather die than neglect'. He wanted to complete his new edition of Shakespeare to correct the excesses that the one-volume edition had seemed to condone.

The most important passage in his preface to the new edition was a *mea culpa*:

I was amazed at my own Discovery; I somewhat hastily and eagerly ran over the proposed emendations; and frankly own that from the first I was disposed to attach more value to the whole body of alterations, than not a few of them really merited. That is my unreserved admission, and let my adversaries make the most of it. . . . If I had been prudent, I would (as, indeed, I did afterwards) have merely printed the old text and the new in opposite columns, and have thus left the latter to make its way in the world. I was, however, too anxious to enforce and illustrate the merits of my extraordinary acquisition.[64]

This was a remarkably candid admission. It was not a disavowal of the Perkins Folio – he still firmly believed many of its corrections to be authentic – but something perhaps even

John Payne Collier

Henry Crabb Robinson

William, 6th Duke of Devonshire.   Portrait by Sir Edwin Landseer

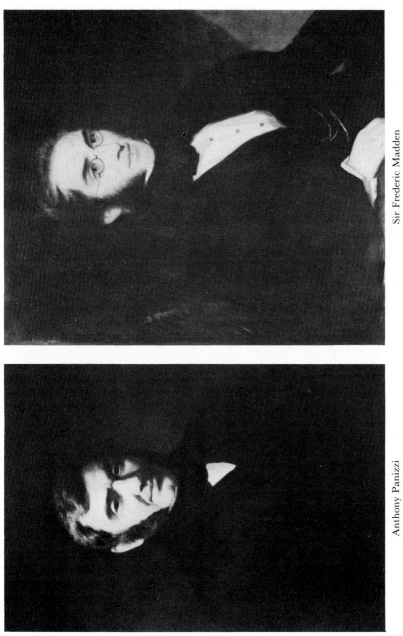

Anthony Panizzi

Sir Frederic Madden

Dr. Henry Wellesley

Alexander Dyce

more difficult, the confession of a failure of discrimination. He also admitted that he had been careless in collating the folio with the emendations of earlier editors, omitting 'in several important instances, to point out where various editors, from Rowe downwards, had guessed at the very same emendations that had made their appearance, as I believed for the first time, in my corrected folio, 1632.'[65]

By March 1858,[66] then, Collier had drastically altered his initial authority, and by discarding many corrections he had earlier espoused, he reaffirmed his dictum that no conjectural emendations should be allowed if the original text were at all intelligible. Moreover – and this is significant in the light of later accusations against him – this change was prompted not by the criticism of his opponents (Collier had won the competition for public approval) but by a personal desire for accuracy and a wish to undo the damage done to Shakespeare's text by the one-volume edition. He wanted, finally, to be 'right' as well as successful.

But if Collier's intention in thus admitting past errors cannot be faulted, the context in which his apologia appeared must be. Had he merely stated his change of perspective, corrected the excesses which the new emendations had produced in the text, and left the judgement of the changes to any subsequent critic who cared to make it, there might have been a small chance that the new edition could have dispelled the animosity which the Perkins Folio had provoked. Unfortunately, Collier was a tenacious adversary. He could not admit his own faults without also excoriating those of Dyce and Singer, and instead of resolving differences, his admission incited new retaliation.

He had, of course, been provoked himself. A fair judgement of his long quarrel with Dyce would suggest that, although both had been intemperate and abusive, Collier was more sinned against than sinning. Dyce had made the first breach in their friendship with little or no provocation, and although Collier was vindictive in turn, Dyce had been the more irascible and devious. Such was his treatment of Collier's first edition of Shakespeare, so too of *Notes and Emendations*. Moreover, Dyce replenished the fires of this quarrel in his edition of Shakespeare which, when it at last appeared, loudly denounced the Perkins Folio while it silently adopted many of its emendations.

Collier could not let this pass and in the preface to his new edition, he assailed Dyce in personal terms, recounting their years of friendship, describing Dyce's 'disloyalty', and condemning his disingenuous use of the Perkins corrections. Collier illustrated his charges with examples carefully selected to damage rather than to clarify differences. He attacked Dyce not only in the preface but in his notes throughout the edition, repeatedly pointing out, in a patronizing and bemused manner, a multitude of 'errors' in Dyce's editions of other Elizabethan playwrights.[67] Collier was angry, his motivation was personal, and his intention was unworthy. He was a skilled polemicist; he knew how to wound without showing obvious malice. The casual reader of the edition might have suspected a grudge in the recurrent references to Dyce – virtually all of them deprecatory – but he probably would not have accused Collier of animus. Nevertheless the public was tired of the quarrel, which was neither new nor amusing. In reviewing Dyce's *Shakespeare* a month or two before, the *Athenaeum* had deplored the continuing controversies over Shakespeare's text: 'New readings required explanations, explanations led to comparisons, and comparisons to discussions and quarrels. Rings were formed, . . . Holborn prize-rings – for rival commentators and rival editors, Singer, Collier, Knight, Dyce, and others, to fight out their quips, and oddities, and follies, – and Puck of the old Folio grinning aside at the mischief he has made.'[68] In such a climate, Collier's attack was a gross error of judgement and of taste. His preface did not sway any uncommitted reader and by continuing the controversy he disfigured his new edition in a way even the *Athenaeum* would condemn. 'These parts of a general allegation will suffice to show the reader what sort of literary polemics he may find in . . . these volumes,' it declared in its review. 'We leave them to his merciful consideration.'[69]

But if Collier's remarks caused public boredom, they recharged private animosity. He had been severe with Dyce, but not, he believed, beyond the range of decorum. He knew they could never again be intimates, but he did not think they were now to be sworn enemies. Dyce, he declared to a friend six months after his Shakespeare appeared, 'was envious (to a degree) and selfish (to an excess), but his manners are extremely agreeable, his scholarship remarkable, and his labours unceasing. I wanted to do him all the justice in my power, in spite of the manner in which he had treated me. I was willing to fancy myself superior to resentment.'[70] The comment demonstrates an astonishing lack of self-awareness and sensibility. Others were less deceived: 'You have hit [Dyce] in the very centre of Aberdeen granite heart', Peter Cunningham gleefully wrote to Collier,[71] and those in the 'ring' with Singer or Dyce were enflamed by Collier's criticism of the old Scot. Dyce himself was rancorous.

Collier was neither physically nor psychologically prepared for the counterattack. Dyce published *Strictures on Mr. Collier's New Edition of Shakespeare, 1858,* in June 1859, and it was venomous. Collier's edition, Dyce declared, was such an 'artful misrepresentation as, I believe, was never before practised, except by the most unprincipled hirelings of the press',[72] and while accusing Collier of intemperate language he himself fulminated against Collier's 'artifice', 'deliberate misrepresentation', 'obstinacy', and 'stupid alterations'. 'I feel myself justified in saying', Dyce wrote, 'that the disingenuousness of Mr. Collier has no parallel in the history of literary controversy, – that, compared to him, the angry and abusive Scioppii of the olden time were "honourable men".'[73] This was only the first thunderclap of a storm which was to break over John Payne Collier, a torrent welcomed by no one more eagerly than the Reverend Alexander Dyce.

VII

THE MUSEUM INQUISITION

'. . . not a natural hand of any period.'

20

About the time Dyce's book appeared, a new adversary joined the attack on the Perkins Folio. His name was Clement Mansfield Ingleby, and, in the end, he would be Collier's chief prosecutor. Ingleby was an unlikely person for the role: initially he had little or no interest in Shakespeare and no personal or professional hostility to Collier – in fact, they were never to meet – but he was nevertheless to pursue Collier with an intellectual tenacity which matched Madden's vengeance and the jealousy of Dyce.

Ingleby was thirty-five years younger than Collier (he finished at Trinity College, Cambridge, the year Collier moved to the country) and the son of a wealthy Birmingham solicitor. He had studied law, but his real love was metaphysics and mathematics, and he left his father's practice to take a chair in logic at the Midland Institute. Although he was to publish several books on Shakespeare,[1] his concern with literature was ratiocinative rather than aesthetic or critical, and his interest in the Perkins Folio had more to do with the puzzle of the book's provenance than with the quality of its emendations.

Through the columns of *Notes and Queries,* Ingleby met Andrew Brae, and they soon made up a kind of two-man vigilance committee. Ingleby was Brae's confidant while the author of *Literary Cookery* tried out his recipes in *Notes and Queries* in 1853 and 1854, and they continued to be regular correspondents for years. It was to Ingleby that Brae declared his 'war to the knife' against Collier, and when the Queen's Bench decision blocked Brae, Ingleby took up the cause.

Ingleby's attack began with friendly correspondence. In

May 1853 he wrote to Collier criticizing the Perkins emendations and condemning Collier's 'refusal' to answer Brae in
Notes and Queries. Collier, who always answered letters, even
hostile ones, replied cordially and with candour, declaring
that, if anybody else had discovered the Perkins Folio he, like
Ingleby, would have been sceptical of it. Collier made no
strong claim to Ingleby (or anyone else for that matter) that
the folio's *provenance* alone could prove the authority of the
corrections; *that* proof could be determined only by their
aptness in correcting obvious errors in the text. 'I feel a sincere and strong regard, even without personal knowledge, for
all intelligent and capable lovers of Shakespeare', Collier
wrote. 'At all times I shall be happy to hear from you on any
question relating to the common object of ours and mankind's
admiration.'[2] It was a generous reply, but it failed to mollify
his antagonist. When Brae thought Collier's one-volume
Shakespeare had unfairly usurped his emendations, Ingleby
used the columns of *Notes and Queries* to accuse Collier of
inconsistency and misfeasance.[3] In doing so, he misquoted
Collier's editorial description, an error which Collier pointed
out in a devastating rebuttal in the next issue. Brae and
Ingleby were undertaking a desperate search for evidence to
inculpate Collier, and their correspondence indicates they
were unable to find it.

During the next two years, Ingleby returned to the study of
logic and apparently forgot about the Perkins Folio, but the
publication of the 'complete' list of emendations in *Seven
Lectures* rekindled his interest. In October 1856 he wrote an
article for the *Birmingham Journal* describing his 'difficulties of
belief' in the Perkins Folio and implying that Collier was
devious; in late November 1856, he gave a lecture at the
Midland Institute in which he declared 'that the Perkins
emendations were fabrications, and in adopting them Mr.
Collier had been a dupe.' Collier, he continued, had 'been
duped in the case of the Bridgewater manuscript [sic]; and
though he was an honourable man, his judgment had been
swamped so that he could not tell genuine matter from
spurious.'[4] Brae approved. 'It is very much to the purpose', he
wrote to Ingleby after reading the newspaper report. 'Indeed, I
quite envy your talent – derived I presume from a study of

Antony's speech over the body of Caesar – of bringing into strong relief the most damning facts and in the same breath declaring your belief that Brutus is an honourable man.' But Brae implied that he himself had given up the attack. 'I fear that little good can be done now to stem the torrent . . . Not but that I acknowledge your hints to be plain enough, but so long as they are directed against an *imaginary culprit* they can serve to little purpose.' Secretly, of course, Brae was even then writing *Literary Cookery,* attempting, perhaps, in his own way to make the 'imaginary' concrete, but unaccountably he did not tell Ingleby he was doing so and Ingleby did not discover the identity of the author of *Literary Cookery* for three years. (Ironically, it was widely believed that Ingleby had written it.)

Ingleby's animadversions about the folio created little stir and he soon stopped commenting on it in public. In early November 1856, Brae reported to Ingleby that since 'this precious volume' (as he sardonically called the Perkins Folio) had 'at length found a purchaser in the Duke of D. . . . speculation respecting it, whether pecuniary or mental may cease.'[5] For his part, Ingleby saw little use in pursuing the question further.

Despite the best efforts of Collier's rivals, the public still thought highly of the Perkins Folio emendations. The only way remaining to discredit them was to damn the book itself, to find in it evidence that the corrections were spurious. Several of Collier's adversaries, Dyce among them, were eager to examine the folio without Collier's knowledge, but so long as the book was in the possession of Devonshire such perusal would be difficult. There is no evidence that Collier placed any restrictions on the book when he gave it to Devonshire. It is unlikely that Devonshire would have been party to a conspiracy to sequester the folio, and in any case had Collier wished to hide it, he would not have let the book out of his hands. It is probable, therefore, that Dyce or anyone else could have seen the folio, but not without Collier's knowledge and, perhaps, not without his presence while it was examined. The book lay undisturbed during the life of the sixth Duke of Devonshire. However, in January 1858 the Duke died, and his cousin, another William Cavendish, took possession of the dukedom and with it Chatsworth, its library, and the Perkins

Folio. Collier had intended to dedicate his revised edition of Shakespeare to his old friend, and now he asked permission to dedicate it to his successor, and the new duke agreed. He admitted that he had less interest in the library than his cousin, but he made it clear that he intended, in his words, 'to respect what I have no doubt were the Duke's wishes in respect to your pension', and to support those projects, notably the facsimiles of the two *Hamlet* quartos, which had been left incomplete when the old duke died.[6] The new relationship was cordial; it reassured Collier that he would not lose the Devonshire patronage, and it probably deterred some of his enemies from requesting an immediate *post mortem* examination of the Perkins Folio.

But it did not destroy their interest. Ingleby, for his part, became more keen than ever to see the book and began an intensive comparison of Collier's published accounts of the folio emendations, hoping to find discrepancies which would condemn Collier. He was convinced that the revisions Collier made in the second edition of *Notes and Emendations* proved culpability of some sort, and this belief sharpened his desire to lay hands on the folio itself. He communicated of his suspicions to Brae, who answered that they 'carried no *new* conviction' to him. Brae's motive had changed markedly and his letter reveals that Collier and not the folio was now his primary target.

I have been from the first entirely convinced [Brae wrote Ingleby] that the compilers of this clever experiment upon the credulity of the age are still living, and if not actually seated at the proprietor's writing table are in easy communication with it!

But why, [he continued to Ingleby] should you 'hope to entreat from the pages of the Folio something "damnatory", damnatory of what? It is the very circumstance that there is nothing to damn – nothing to lay hold of in these corrections that has saved them from conviction long since ... These concoctions *assert* nothing, but assume everything – *forgeries* they cannot be called because they imitate no specific or individual hand-writing. *Anachronisms* they cannot be proved to be because no *specific date* is alleged for them, drive them from one century and they take a refuge in another. Nay, they avoid even the chance of refutation to which they would be exposed if they were to stand or fall together – if they were component parts of an entire whole so that the disproval of one would affect them all! But, no, they are saved by the master stroke of *limited liability*! If you bring overwhelming evidence against one – or against one hundred – what better would you be? Would you not be told that so far from *all* being vouched for, even by their discoverer, he himself has rejected many! Everything about them is vague and eluding, and when you come to do battle with them you find nothing but a shadow to fight with. It is to this they owe their impunity and it is this that has crushed all attempt to disprove them, for the simple reason that there is nothing to disprove.[7]

This is an accurate description of the emendations and of Collier's presentation of them, and to a mind less set on condemnation, it might have suggested that Collier was not guilty of fraud and that he had never pressed the claims for the folio as vehemently as his readers had assumed. But this perspective was not Brae's, and instead of suggesting a resolution to the problem, his statement merely reveals his exasperation with it.

Early in 1859, Ingleby wrote to Devonshire requesting permission to see the Perkins Folio. The Duke immediately replied that he thought the book was at Chatsworth, but that it would be made available to Ingleby at Devonshire House in London a few days hence. Unfortunately for Ingleby, he became ill and missed the appointment,[8] and when he recovered he altered his plans. Instead of writing to Devonshire to explain why he had missed the appointment and to request another, he called on Sir Frederic Madden and suggested that *Madden* ask the Duke to loan the folio to the Department of Manuscripts of the British Museum 'in order to subject it to a paleographic examination'.[9] Just why Ingleby turned to Madden is not clear because they did not know one another well. According to Ingleby, they had met briefly in '1855 or 1856' when Ingleby had sought Madden's opinion of the Perkins Folio and was told that Madden had never expressed a judgement about the notes and, in fact, had never seen the book. According to Ingleby, this was the only time he had called on Madden, let alone talked to him about the folio, and it is therefore very curious that three years later, having at last secured permission to examine the folio, he should have gone to Madden to urge an examination by the Museum before he had set eyes on the book himself. Did he have reason to know that Madden was now interested in examining the Perkins Folio, that he suspected the book, or Collier or both? According to Ingleby's account (given, it should be noted, *after* the Museum examination had created a major literary controversy), Madden immediately agreed to the request. He declared, however, that he could not examine the book at once because 'he was then so fully occupied',[10] but whatever his other occupations were, they do not seem to have delayed him for long.

Madden had wanted to see the folio for years. Several months earlier, Collier had sent him a copy of the newly completed facsimile of the 1604 *Hamlet* quarto, and in acknowledging the gift, Madden had mentioned his interest in looking over the Perkins Folio. Whether this was a 'request to the Duke's librarian' (as Madden later called it) or merely an incidental statement of interest cannot be determined because Madden's letter is lost, but Collier apparently did nothing to put the folio in Madden's hands. Ingleby's news that the book was available and already in London must have excited Madden, and he wrote to Devonshire almost immediately (on Friday, 13 May) asking that the book be placed in the Museum for his examination.

Madden was as keen as anyone to examine the book but he took great pains to disguise his personal interest. For example, in his diary he implied that his interest in writing to Devonshire was not to satisfy Ingleby (whose visit is not even mentioned) or his own heightened curiosity but to accommodate Dr Frederick Bodenstedt, a visiting German scholar who was in England gathering information for a history of dramatic literature. Bodenstedt, according to Madden's account, wanted to see the Perkins Folio but did 'not know how to accomplish it', and, as Madden explained, it was merely to assist a visiting foreign scholar that he promised Bodenstedt to write to the Duke 'and ask him to allow the M.S. to be placed under my care at the Museum for a short time'.[11] This statement is almost certainly false. Bodenstedt may have indicated a desire to see the folio, but he was no stranger to England or to Devonshire. In fact he called on Devonshire shortly after the Duke returned to town, and it is highly unlikely that he would have asked Madden to do what he could easily do himself. In any case, the folio would be *less* accessible to Bodenstedt at the Museum than in the library of Devonshire House.

Madden's account, in fact, demonstrates that his diary is not altogether reliable and that he was not above omitting details or twisting them to ensure that the judgement of a future reader – whom he obviously expected – would coincide with his own. Madden wanted to appear wholly disinterested and to hide the fact that a kind of cabal had formed against the book even before it was sent to the Museum, but his real motives break through in an unguarded statement that he wished 'very much to see this much talked of volume'. In point of fact, the folio was *not* 'much talked of' in the spring of 1859 except among a small group of Collier's antagonists. So far as the public was concerned, the folio deserved neither the high praise Collier had given it in 1852 nor the opprobrium that Singer, Dyce, *et al.* had heaped on it in 1856. That it had lain available but unconsulted among the books of Chatsworth library for two years since the death of Collier's patron suggests there was no general interest in seeing the book.

So keen was Madden's interest, he personally delivered his request to Devonshire House, hoping perhaps to talk with the Duke directly and to carry the book away with him then and there, but Devonshire was out of town. Twelve days later, with no prior communication from the Duke, a messenger delivered the Perkins Folio to Madden at the Museum. Devonshire had ordered it sent as soon as he returned to London (so much for the presumed conspiracy to hide it away!), and Madden immediately put aside all other business to examine the book (so much for his disinterested response to the request of others!). What followed would be called, by those who conducted it, the Museum Inquisition.

21

According to Madden, the first time he saw the Perkins Folio was on the evening of 26 May 1859, when Devonshire's messenger put the volume in his hands. If true, this is a curious circumstance, for Madden had had earlier opportunities to examine the book: he was an active member of both the

Shakespeare Society and the Society of Antiquaries in the spring of 1852 when on at least five occasions over a period of several months Collier showed the folio to those organizations. Since Madden had a keen interest in both Shakespeare and paleography, Collier's discovery ought to have intrigued him, and if he failed to see the book in 1852, he may have deliberately avoided doing so. Some who read Collier's first announcement urged him to deposit his discovery in the British Museum for a 'full' paleographic examination[12] but Collier ignored this suggestion, and it is conceivable that Madden may have been irritated by what he considered a professional slight. It is significant, perhaps, that Madden's interest in the Perkins Folio did not become apparent until after its legitimacy had been publicly questioned and after the Hillier affair and the Panizzi appointment had embittered him against Collier.

Although it took seven years for the Perkins Folio to arrive at the Department of Manuscripts at the British Museum, it took only half as many hours on that May evening to fix Madden's opinion that the writing in the book was not genuine. In his first comment about the folio his condemnation was complete – all that followed during the next few months was to be elaboration. 'I spent the evening in examining this much talked of volume', he wrote in his diary. 'It is bound in rough calf and on the upper cover is written "Tho. Perkins his Booke" in a hand that looks strangely modern.' The writing was not simply 'modern' – vague though that term would be – but *strangely* so, a comment which suggests something false and surreptitious about the book. At first glance Madden was ready to find forgery – writing *intended* to be passed off for what it wasn't. If the cover sharpened his expectations, the writing inside fulfilled them.

The manuscript corrections do not satisfy me, [he wrote] and I observed that the forms of the letters differ very much from each other, and yet evidently all proceed from the same pen. There has also been a great deal of *painting* certain letters and altering forms... apparently for the purpose of making the writing look older than it is. I cannot believe it to be a genuine hand of the 17th century, but I feel fairly puzzled how to account for the *object* of the corrector, who seems partly as if he were altering the plays for the stage, and partly as if he contemplated a new edition.

Whatever his puzzlement, Madden had apparently found the evidence he thought might be there: 'Collier is certainly mistaken in supposing the writing to be nearly as early as the date of the volume (1632)', he wrote, and, he continued ambiguously, 'I am exceedingly pleased, however, to have the volume in my hands, although disappointed at the result of my examination.'[13]

Pleased, yes. Disappointed, no. Whatever reasonable doubt one might have about Madden's motive before he examined the folio, it is surely dispelled by his actions immediately thereafter. If his sole purpose had been to make an objective assessment of the book itself, and if, as he was to declare on several occasions thereafter, Collier was a friend for whom he felt a genuine concern, he surely would have communicated his opinion to Collier at once. He did not. The first person Madden wrote to announcing his verdict was not John Payne Collier, neither was it Dr Frederick Bodenstedt, the man for whom Madden was later to say he secured the book; it was Alexander Dyce. In the next day or two he wrote several more letters – to Ingleby, to Howard Staunton, who was then completing his own edition of Shakespeare, and to others – but he sent no word to Collier who, for the time being, was unaware that the Perkins Folio was undergoing scrutiny. Four days after the book was in the Museum and after it had been closely examined by several of Collier's arch competitors, Madden wrote to Thoms, inviting him to see the Folio and urging him to extend the invitation to Bruce.[14] It was clearly Madden's plan to give the anti-Collierites the first look; the belated invitation to Thoms and Bruce, both Collier supporters, was intended to demonstrate Madden's objectivity in the examination, but his failure to inform Collier directly belies that intention.

Madden's note to Dyce was written on Thursday evening, shortly after the book was delivered to the Museum. It was mailed the next morning, and Dyce appeared at Madden's chambers early Saturday. In the meantime, ignoring all other work, Madden continued his examination, and his condemnation became progressively more sweeping. On Thursday he had immediately determined that the writing was not 'A genuine hand of the 17th century'; on Friday, it was 'not a genuine writing either of the 17th or 18th century',[15] and by the time Dyce arrived on Saturday, Madden had the 'fixed opinion the writing was *not* of the 17th century, nor a genuine handwriting of any period.'[16] The implication was obvious: Madden in effect declared the corrections to be forgeries. Not unexpectedly, this news delighted Dyce, whose only regret was that he had not been able to include it in *Strictures,* which had just been published.

Dyce urged Madden to declare publicly that the writing was factitious, but Madden, in the first of several uncharacteristic attempts to avoid public statements of his own, refused, and instead gave Dyce permission to *report* that this was Madden's opinion. Dyce was happy to do so, and the news spread very quickly. On Monday and Tuesday many came to see the notorious folio, *none* of them were supporters of the book or of John Payne Collier. Thomas Watts, Superintendent of the Reading Room, and John Winter Jones, Keeper of the Printed Books, both close associates of Panizzi with vivid memories of Collier's part in the Museum controversy of a decade before, came and condemned. John Forster, the editor of the *Examiner* and Dyce's confidant, arrived with William Charles Macready, the actor. Macready had earlier declared the Perkins Folio a great boon but now he denounced it. Howard Staunton openly decried the book, while his friend Madden stood by declaring that his own 'unbiased opinion of the writing' supported Staunton's views.[17] Of course, Ingleby (a shadowy figure in Madden's account) came repeatedly, gleeful at the outcome, and laying plans to publish an exposé. At last, Bodenstedt saw the folio along with Hunter and Panizzi himself. Madden was soon to complain that the popularity of the book was forcing him to spend all his time 'showing' it.

And 'show' it he did: the folio was kept locked in Madden's office and could be seen only with his permission and under his watchful eyes or those of his assistant Nicholas Hamilton. The control Collier had imposed on the book while it was in his charge could not have been greater than the surveillance it now received. Thoms, one of the few of Collier's supporters invited to visit Madden's chambers, had earlier expressed a very qualified approval of the folio. Madden hoped Thoms could now be persuaded to renounce his former judgement by a guided examination of the book itself. But Thoms refused to have any part in what seemed to be an intrigue. He wrote to say that if Madden had any doubts 'as to the genuineness of the Shakespeare' he did not wish to see it because, as Madden later told the story, 'it would kill Collier if it should turn out that he has been deceived.' The reply provoked scorn from Madden. Thoms' 'nerves' were 'strangely influenced by his friendship for Mr. Collier', he wrote,[18] dismissing Thoms as a potential collaborator – and as a friend. (A year later Madden still bore a heavy grudge against Thoms for this refusal.) Meanwhile, the notoriety of the folio grew, and Bodenstedt reported that Devonshire had told him the book could remain at the Museum indefinitely.

For the first week Madden's judgement was echoed by every visitor, and the book began to be the subject of rather wild speculation, but on Wednesday, 1 June, the folio was inspected by John Bruce, an antiquary of considerable reputation (he had served on the council of the Camden Society with both Collier and Madden), who declared he could 'see nothing in the writing which would excite suspicion'. Unlike Ingleby, Staunton, Dyce and the rest, Bruce had no personal stake in the outcome of the investigation and his judgement was therefore likely to represent the 'general public opinion', which, Madden knew, would make the ultimate decision for or against the Perkins Folio emendations – and John Payne Collier. Madden's reaction was swift and sharp: 'I confess I am much surprised at this, since Mr. B. has had much experience in examining papers of the 17th century', he wrote in his diary. 'I am *convinced* only of one thing, that the writing of the MS. notes in the Perkins folio is *not of the 17th century* and not a *natural hand of any period.*'[19] Bruce returned the next day and continued his examination with Edward Bond. Bond, the curator of the Egerton manuscripts at the Museum, had earlier made a cursory examination of the book and had agreed with Madden, but now he began to doubt his initial judgement. Bruce confirmed his opinion that the writing was genuine, and, to Madden's consternation,

Bond now agreed that the Perkins Folio was probably not a forgery. ('Even Mr. Bond seems to waver', Madden reported.) Bond's defection from the ranks of the committed was very serious, for his reputation as a paleographer was as good as Madden's, and if he now credited the folio, Madden would have to reconsider his own judgement or prepare to do battle. He chose the latter. 'My assistant, Mr. Hamilton completely coincides with myself', he wrote, 'and even does more, by declaring that some of the writing is *very recent.*'[20] Neither Hamilton nor Madden tried to define what they meant by 'recent' (let alone how such dating was determined), but the implications of the term were clear to anyone who heard them on the subject: 'very recent' meant within the lifetime of, say, the seventy-year-old discoverer of the Perkins Folio.

When Bruce disagreed, Madden replied that the writing was not only forged but *recently* forged. This was Madden's characteristic tactic: when his charges against the folio or Collier were questioned, he produced not new evidence but new charges. However, despite his emphatic assertions, Madden was unsure of his evidence. He continued to declare that the handwriting alone disproved any claim to a seventeenth-century origin, but he now sought non-paleographic evidence to prove the writing to be recent. He thought he found it in the volume's binding which he believed was eighteenth century and, he declared, the writing 'certainly' *post*dated the cover.[21] Everyone agreed that the book had been re-bound (although Collier had initially thought the book was still in its original binding, he had long since come to the conclusion that the present cover was 'the second or third coat' that the book had worn). There was no dispute about this fact, but Madden nevertheless diligently went about verifying it. He lifted the end papers to reveal a watermark which along with the exposed millboard of the cover, proved that the book had been last bound in the reign of George I. However, this evidence had little to do with the point at issue, that is, whether the emendations had been made after the book was bound. Madden gave no evidence for his opinion that they had been and, in fact, a note he made during his initial examination of the folio indicated he then thought the ink writing *pre*dated the binding.[22] He apparently changed his mind only after his judgement of the age of the writing was questioned.

Ingleby meanwhile pursued another course. His chief interest in seeing the folio had been to verify the presence of the stage direction 'writing' in the first ghost scene of *Hamlet,* a subject which Brae had first espoused in the pages of *Notes and Queries* six years before. The value of this evidence is very uncertain, and its connection with the Perkins Folio tenuous. It will be recalled that Brae believed that the stage direction was significant in determining Hamlet's character, and he had tried to promote his theory through the columns of *Notes and Queries* without success. In particular, when Collier failed to declare whether the direction was among the Old Corrector's emendations, Brae concluded that Collier was hiding something, and when Brae subsequently discovered that the stage direction had first appeared in Rowe's edition of 1709, he concluded that the Perkins Folio *had* the stage direction among its emendations and that Collier was attempting to hide that fact because it would 'prove' the corrections had been made after Rowe. Of course, since Rowe's source for the emendation might have been a *seventeenth*-century gloss that the Old Corrector might have discovered before him, Brae's assumption was unsound, but when Brae was driven from the field by Collier's court action, Ingleby took up the issue and pursued it. His initial examination in the Museum satisfied him that the direction had indeed been written in the folio and subsequently erased, and this convinced him that Collier had erased it to cover up its source in Rowe. This was a puzzling conclusion since dozens of other Rowe emendations – to say nothing of many published by Rowe's successors – were left unaltered in the book and the 'writing' addition was no more damning than many of those which remained unexpunged. Ingleby's desire to implicate Collier was apparently stronger than his logic.

Both Ingleby and Madden sincerely believed the marginal comments to be forged, and Madden, at least, was determined to prove Collier the forger. But their case rested solely on Madden's professional judgement that the ink writing 'was not a genuine handwriting of any period', and their evidence, as distinguished from their opinion, was virtually nonexistent. Hence, when a reputable scholar like Bruce disagreed, there was very little that Madden could put forward to reinforce his conclusion. And when Bond began 'wavering' in his opinion that the emendations were forged, it became obvious that something else was needed, something concrete, dramatic and irrefutable. Fortuitously – perhaps too fortuitously – something else was found.

According to his account in *An Inquiry*, it was Hamilton, Madden's assistant, who discovered the pencil marks. About the beginning of the third week of June (the date in this version is uncertain) Hamilton noticed, for the first time, a number of half-obliterated pencil marks in its margins. There were not very many of them, probably not more than thirty or so in the whole volume, and they were very faint. Some seemed to have been 'rubbed', perhaps in an attempt to erase them, and all were very difficult to see, but those that were still legible seemed to form words and phrases and these, unaccountably, appeared to be in a modern cursive script. Closer examination revealed that many of these words and phrases were identical to the ink emendations that purported to be in a seventeenth-century gothic hand and appeared in close proximity to their ink counterparts in the margins of the folio.

The connection between the two sets of annotations was at first obscure, Hamilton reported, and he puzzled over them for some time before, suddenly, he found a curious connection: some of the modern cursive pencil writing lay *under* the 'gothic' ink emendations. The implication was obvious – the 'modern' writing was made *before* its 'antique' counterpart. As Hamilton was later to recount the story, he immediately carried his discovery to Madden.

This account, later publicly attested to by Hamilton, Ingleby, and Madden himself,[23] was almost certainly false in one essential detail: it was not Hamilton but *Madden* who discovered the 'pencil counterparts' to the ink emendations, and the event was recorded by Madden in his diary several days after it occurred.

I noticed today for the first time, [he wrote under Friday, 17 June 1859], a great number of pencil marks in the margins of the Shakespere, and in some instances, I think I can perceive traces of pencil *under* the *ink,* which, in that case, must have been subsequently written. The importance of this discovery is such that I shall subject the volume to a very searching examination leaf by leaf, to satisfy myself on the subject.[24]

Two days later, on Sunday, 19 June, he noted that, in spite of feeling ill, he scrutinized the book and

to my very great surprise I ascertained beyond doubt that a perfectly modern hand has made many hundreds, perhaps thousands of corrections in pencil in the margin, partly for the correction of the punctuation, partly for new readings, and partly to draw attention to passages to be altered. These corrections are *most certainly* in a modern hand, and from the extraordinary resemblance of the writing to Mr. Collier's own hand (which I am well acquainted with) I am really fearful that we must come to the astounding conclusion that Mr. C. is himself the fabricator of the notes! It is *most certain* that the pencil marks are *anterior* to the corrections in ink, and served, indeed as the guides to them, and it is no less *certain* in my opinion that the same hand wrote both the *pencil* and *ink* corrections.... But what a position does this place Mr. C. in! I really see no escape from the proofs afforded.

On the day following, Madden recorded that he 'communicated to my assistant Mr. Hamilton the discovery I had made as to the recent pencil notation in the Perkins Folio'.

There can be no doubt which account – Hamilton's or Madden's – is the truth. Madden wrote within days of the event; Hamilton several months later; Madden's details are specific; Hamilton's general and derivative. However, the fact that Hamilton – and Madden – should lie about who made the discovery is less puzzling than the circumstance of the discovery. If the dating in Madden's diary is correct, the Perkins Folio had been in the British Museum for over three weeks when the 'pencil counterparts' were seen for the first time. Literally dozens of interested people had examined the book – Ingleby, Bodenstedt, and Dyce had each scrutinized it for hours; a facsimilist employed by Ingleby had traced at least one whole page from the book; Hamilton had spent every minute he could spare from regular duties studying its pages; and Madden himself had studied the folio, by his own account, for the equivalent of four or five days – and yet, we are to believe, *no* one had seen the damning pencil marks before that memorable afternoon, when Madden chanced to find them – 'hundreds, perhaps thousands of corrections' in a 'perfectly modern hand'! Of course, Madden's diary account grossly overstates the case. He had himself earlier noted the many pencilled editorial marks – unsuspicious in themselves – which Collier has made in his own 'undisguised' hand throughout the volume, and these comprise all but a handful of the 'thousands' of marks at which he now professed astonishment. Anyone who examined the folio even cursorily during the first weeks it was at the Museum would have seen these pencil notes and would have assumed, rightly, that they were marks Collier made when he edited the emendations for publication and when he prepared the folio as copy for the compositor who set the one-volume 1853 edition. There were also a number of marks that Collier made to direct the work of *his* facsimilist who reproduced a page for the frontispiece of *Notes and Emendations* and several dozen additional facsimiles that he subsequently distributed as gifts to friends. In addition there were many other pencil notes for cross-reference which were undoubtedly Collier's own as well as the ticks, crosses and checks that any reader might have made at any time since the folio was published. All of these innocuous pencil marks were apparently included among the 'hundreds, perhaps thousands of corrections' Madden 'discovered', and although he implies that he never saw any of them before that fateful June day, other readers of the book must surely have done so without attaching any importance to them. Obviously Collier made them and just as obviously they were not suspicious.

However, this was not true of the thirty or so 'pencil counterparts' to the ink emendations. The purpose of *these* notes is obscure and highly suspicious, and of these perhaps six or seven (no one – not Madden, Hamilton or Ingleby – ever made a complete census of the number they found) appeared to be *under* the ink. Of the fifteen most damning examples that Hamilton was later to produce in facsimile in *An Inquiry*, the most important were those which Madden found and recorded in his diary that afternoon. It is remarkable that, although Madden had apparently overlooked these marks throughout his three weeks' scrutiny, he nonetheless found all the most critical examples, widely dispersed in the Perkins

Folio though they were, within an hour or two.[25] It is significant, also, that although the pencil marks were extremely faint – some of them can be reconstructed into words only through fanciful extrapolation – Madden was able immediately to identify the pencil marks as being in Collier's handwriting.

Perhaps the most damning example which Madden found that day was an emendation in *Richard III* where the printed stage direction 'exit' (which indicates the departure of the murderers with Clarence) is given an ink addendum, 'with the dead bodie', under which, in barely discernible strokes, one can reconstruct 'with the body' in pencil.[26] Although any determination of the style of the pencil script could here be hypothetical at best, in his first diary comment Madden declared he was 'confident' that the pencil phrase was 'in Mr. Collier's writing' and he followed this declaration with a fulsome condemnation of Collier.

I really feel so astounded at the fact, that I know not how to describe it [Madden wrote]. I never could have suspected Mr. C. of fraud, and in fact have always defended him, but *now* the evidence seems overpowering against him. And *if* he is the forger, what terms can be too harsh to apply to his conduct in this affair! It is really too monstrous! I regret much that I had not made this discovery about the pencil marks when I shewed the volume to Mr. Dyce & Dr. Bodenstedt, but I shall feel it my duty to let them know the fact, and then they can draw their own conclusions. I made a series of *eye facsimiles* of the various forms given to the same letters by this *pretended old annotator,* and the evidence is complete, that the whole is a gross fabrication. The hand that wrote THO. PERKINS HIS BOOKE on the cover of the folio, certainly wrote the whole of the marginal annotations. q.e.d.[27]

Madden protests too much. As his own diary testifies, he *had,* in fact, suspected Collier of fraud almost from the beginning. Certainly he had never seriously defended him – as his list of preferred viewers of the folio proves. Moreover, the 'evidence' which he discovered so belatedly was damning only by supposition. As the syntax suggests, Madden had been looking for a 'forger' all the while, and he could not have been astonished to have found guilt in the only place he had looked for it. But whatever his motives – and the note seems disingenuous on the face of it – Madden was quick to broadcast his 'evidence'.

I communicated to my assistant Mr. Hamilton the discovery I had made as to the recent pencil notation in the Perkins folio and went over a portion of the volume with him, in which we discovered many more examples of the *very recent* handywork [sic]. Mr Hamilton afterwards showed them to Mr. Bond who is now convinced of the fraud that has been committed.

The 'wavering' Bond now firmly recommitted, everyone urged Madden to publish his conclusion.

They wish me to put myself forward to make it public, but I shrink from this. After my long acquaintance with Mr. C. and many of his friends, 1 *cannot* undertake to pull off the mask he has worn hitherto so successfully. He deserves reprobation, but let another do it. I suggested to Mr. Hamilton that he should draw up an article on the subject, and he said he would do so, and send it to the Saturday [Review] Magazine.[28]

No reader of Madden's diary can take his claim of delicacy born of 'long acquaintance' very seriously. His feelings toward Collier were emphatically hostile, and as his private comments demonstrate he was very eager to be given credit for exposing the Perkins Folio and its discoverer – particularly its discoverer. But he was also cautious; his own reputation was vulnerable to Collier's private knowledge, and it was therefore useful to Madden to be able to mount his attack behind the façade of Hamilton's apparently unprejudiced announcement. Of course, no one reading Hamilton's account would be likely to disassociate him from his immediate superior in the Museum; the masquerade was unlikely to deceive anyone, but it was useful to Madden in so far as it denied Collier a justification to answer him directly. Madden's motives were not disinterested, and Collier had the means to prove it, but if Madden remained publicly neutral, Collier could not reply without appearing guilty of an unprovoked personal attack.

Meanwhile Madden was able to press his case against Collier through others: the first person he wrote to conveying the news of his discovery was Staunton, whose Shakespeare had just been published. Staunton, Madden knew, could make the best and quickest use of the new evidence against Collier. 'I wrote Mr. Staunton, to inform him of my discovery of the pencil notation in the Shakespere folio, and my opinion of its recent character', Madden wrote in his diary. 'Employed still in making memoranda from this volume. The fraud here so successfully practised puts Chatterton and Ireland completely in the shade. Who would have supposed that the name of Collier was to be added to the list of literary impositors?'[29]

Madden wrote to Staunton on 20 June, and five days later the two most recent parts of Staunton's edition of Shakespeare were very favourably reviewed in the *Supplement to the Birmingham Journal* (in an article that Madden noted was written by Staunton himself!). The review ended with the suggestion that a great exposé was about to be made:

Before laying down our pen, [Staunton wrote] let us add here that if any reader thinks Mr. Staunton has spoken too severely of Mr. Collier's annotated folio . . . he will do well to suspend his judgment. The Perkins' folio was bought by the Duke of Devonshire for a very large sum, and its authenticity has been questioned by several eminent Shakespeareans – the late Mr. Singer especially. The Duke has allowed it to be placed in the British Museum, in the care of Sir F. Madden. For some time a minute examination has been made, and one of the ablest palaeographists of the age asserts that there is not one of the 'annotations' older than the time of Rowe; and we hear that several of the 'emendations' can be shown to have been made during the present century! At present our information is confidential [!] but Shakespeareans must not be surprised if they find that a literary forgery has been perpetrated which throws those of the Ireland family and the later issues of Byron and Shelley letters completely into the shade. None but those who have been engaged in the enquiry can at present decide; but we hear the whole case will soon be submitted to the judgment of the literary world.[30]

The repetition of the analogy and the metaphor suggests that Staunton may have been echoing the opinions Madden had confided to him, but even if the association went the other way (Madden may have written his diary note after reading the *Supplement* review) its effect is the same – they were of a single mind as to the effect and use of the discovery. Staunton enclosed the review in a letter he sent to Madden on 29 June and suggested a threat: 'I should have much preferred', he wrote, 'that the first step towards the exposure of the unparalleled forgery of the Perkins folio be made by the Museum authorities, and I have waited impatiently therefore for the appearance of Mr. H's letter. . . . I have no doubt if the results of your examination is not immediately published in London it will be printed first in the country Journals.'[31]

The threat was real and not from Staunton alone. Ingleby had resurrected Brae's test-word thesis concerning the emendation of 'chair' to 'cheer' (arguing that 'to cheer' in the sense of a 'hurrahing or shouting approval' was not in use before the first decade of the nineteenth century and hence that the emendations were all modern), and about a week before Staunton published Madden's opinion in Birmingham, Ingleby had managed to have his case against 'cheer' inserted in the London *Bulletin* from which, by means of anonymous correspondents, it was soon copied into other newspapers both in London and the provinces. 'It is evident that the "old corrector's" alteration is a modern deception', the *Bulletin* declared. 'It is unnecessary to dilate on this point; the mere statement of the fact must satisfy every one who sees it that the corrections to which Mr. Collier has attached so much value are the work of some ingenious person, who is, perhaps, alive now, and amusing himself with the success which has attended his stratagem.'[32] What was developing was a competition as to who should be credited with first exposing the 'forgery' of the folio, and although Hamilton did not need much prodding, Ingleby's offensive encouraged him to complete his account with dispatch. The piece did not appear in the *Saturday Review*, according to Madden, because it was written as a letter to the editor which that journal would not accept. *The Times*, however, did, and on 2 July 1859, it appeared.

22

Hamilton's letter precipitated what was to become the most prolonged, complex, and intensely pursued literary controversy of the nineteenth century, and to make the case against Collier clear, it must be quoted at length:

To the Editor of *The Times.*

Sir,

Perhaps amid the press and distraction of politics which are now agitating the great world you can find room for the account of a most extraordinary deception which has been practised in the republic of letters, some details of which I now beg to lay before you. . . .

Thus Hamilton began, and after briefly describing the publication of *Notes and Emendations* in 1852, the one-volume Shakespeare of 1853, and the 'complete list' of emendations in 1856, he continued:

These publications were accompanied by what professed to be a minute account of the appearance and history of the recently-discovered folio. It is, however, notorious that by a considerable number of persons interested in the subject the descriptions thus given were never deemed sufficient or satisfactory in a matter of such deep literary importance.

In common with others, I had often desired to see the volume, which meanwhile had become the property of the Duke of Devonshire. This wish has at length been gratified. Some two months ago his Grace, the present Duke, liberally placed the folio in the hands of Sir Frederick [sic] Madden, Keeper of the MSS. in the British Museum, with the understanding that, while it should be kept by Sir Frederick Madden in the strictest custody, it might yet be examined, under proper restrictions, by any and all literary persons who were anxious to do so. I at once seized the opportunity, and determined, avoiding all Shakespearian criticism, to attempt an accurate and unbiased description of the volume from the literary point of view alone. Discoveries soon occurred, to which it seems advisable immediate publicity should be given, and which I now send you in as clear a manner as the narrow scope of a letter will permit.

It was not accidental that in this introduction Hamilton had twice mentioned the name of Sir Frederic Madden. The intended impression was that the information that Hamilton was about to give came largely from Madden's own explorations. Hamilton's account reads like an extract from Madden's diary. Certainly the first 'discovery' to be described was his;

the 'rough calf' binding was made, Hamilton declared, 'probably about the middle of George II.'s reign' and emendations 'could not have been written on the margins of the volume until after it was bound'. They were made, not in the seventeenth century, but 'round the middle of the 18th'.

As to the writing itself, it was, Hamilton wrote,

of two kinds, – those, namely, which have been allowed to remain, and those which have been obliterated with more or less success.... The corrections thus variously obliterated are probably almost as numerous as those suffered to remain and an importance equal to them....

Of the corrections allowed to stand, some, on a hasty glance, might, so far as the handwriting is concerned, pass as genuine, while others have been strangely tampered with, touched up, or painted over, a modern character being dexterously altered by touches of the pen into a more antique form. There is, moreover, a kind of exaggeration in the shape of the letters throughout, difficult, if not impossible, to reconcile with a belief in the genuineness of the hand; not to mention the frequent and strange juxtaposition of stiff Chancery capital letters of the form in use two centuries ago with others of quite a modern appearance, and it is well here to state that all the corrections are evidently by one hand; and that, consequently, whatever invalidates or destroys the credit of a part must be considered equally damaging and fatal to the whole.

At times the correction first put in the margin has been obliterated, and a second emendation substituted in its stead, of which I will mention two examples which occur in *Cymbeline* (fol. 1632, p. 400, col. 1):

'With Oakes unshakeable and roaring Waters,' where *Oakes* has first been made into *Cliffes*, and subsequently into *Rockes*. Again (p. 401, col. 2),

'Whose Roof's as low as ours: Sleepe Boyes, this gate,' on the margin (a pencil cross having been made in the first instance) *Sleepe* is corrected into *Sweete*, afterwards *Sweete* has been crossed out, and *Stoope* written above.

There is scarcely a single page throughout the volume in which these obliterations do not occur. At the time they were effected it is possible the obliterations may have appeared complete; but the action of the atmosphere in the course of some years seems in the majority of instances to have so far negatived the chymical agency as to enable the corrections to be readily deciphered. Examples of these accompany this letter, and I shall be surprised if in the hands of

Shakspearian critics they do not furnish a clue to the real history of the corrector and his corrections.

I now come to the most astounding result of these investigations, in comparison with which all other facts concerning the corrected folio become insignificant. On a close examination of the margins they are found to be covered with an infinite number of faint pencil marks and corrections, in obedience to which the supposed old corrector has made his emendations. These pencil corrections have not even the pretence of antiquity in character or spelling, but are written in a bold hand of the present century. A remarkable instance occurs in *Richard III.* (fol. 1632, p. 181, col. 2), where the stage direction, 'with the body,' is written in pencil in a clear modern hand, while over this the ink corrector writes in the antique and smaller character, 'with the dead bodie,' the word 'dead' being seemingly inserted to cover over the entire space occupied by the larger pencil writing, and 'bodie' instead of 'body' to give the requisite appearance of antiquity. Further on, in the tragedy of *Hamlet* (fol. 1632, p. 187, col. 1)

'And crooke the pregnant Hindges of the knee,'

'begging' occurs in pencil in the opposite margin in the same modern hand, evidently with the intention of superseding 'pregnant' in the text. The entire passage from, 'Why should the poore be flatter'd?' to 'As I doe thee. Something too much of this' was afterwards struck out. The ink corrector, probably thrown off his guard by this, neglected to copy over and afterwards rub out the pencil alteration, according to his usual plan, and by this oversight we seem to obtain as clear a view of the *modus operandi* as if we have looked over the corrector's shoulder and seen the entire work in process of fabrication.

Thereafter Hamilton listed three examples of ink emendations which overlay 'a modern pencil' equivalent, two of which had been published by Collier in *Seven Lectures*,[33] and he followed this with examples of three ink corrections with pencil equivalents that did *not* underlie the ink, only one of which Collier had noted earlier.[34]

Hamilton concluded the letter by declaring:

I conceive it positively established that the emendations, as they are called, of this folio copy of *Shakespeare* have been made in the margins within the present century...

While I am personally responsible for the conclusions I have been driven to by the discovery of the above-mentioned facts, the accuracy of the facts themselves and the fidelity of my statement of them have been carefully and scrupulously examined by men having greater ability and experience in such matters than I can lay claim to. Moreover, these are points which may be tested by any persons interested in the subject, and who will be at the pains of verifying for themselves the truth of what I have here advanced. I have only to add that I hope shortly to lay before the public, in another form and in fuller detail, other particulars relating to this remarkable volume.

I am, &c.

N. E. S. A. Hamilton

Department of MSS, British Museum, June 22.[35]

The charge contained in the letter – however veiled – was devastating. An officer of the National Library had accused the country's leading Shakespeare critic of dishonesty for, if the pencil marks were what Hamilton declared they were, Collier could not have overlooked them, and if he had seen them, why had he kept them secret except to perpetrate a fraud?

The charge was invidious. Collier was well enough known to make the charge noteworthy, but not distinguished enough to be able to refute it from a position of authority. Attack such a man and his reputation is bound to suffer, if only because he loses immunity from scandal. The devastating effect was most clearly indicated by the reaction of Crabb Robinson, surely as sympathetic to Collier as anyone could be, who declared that the letter would 'sadly detract from J. P. Collier's character as a critic'; the accusation, coming as it did from such a source and through the medium of *The Times,* was itself enough to create suspicion. Robinson apparently credited Hamilton's claims against the Perkins Folio, but he was not yet ready to believe Collier guilty of fraud. ('His enemies', Robinson wrote, 'will, of course, ascribe to him *privity,* though that seems absurd.'[36]) Nevertheless, even Robinson believed that the burden of proof rested upon Collier. His friends would be willing to withhold final judgement until his answer appeared, but he had to defend himself or be judged guilty.[37]

At seventy, isolated and in painful ill health, Collier faced the greatest crisis of his life. At a time when he might have expected the rewards of a distinguished career, he had received instead the accusation of fraud. Disappointment alone might have sapped his energy and embittered his defence, but Collier's reaction was immediate and forceful. Within three days he addressed his own letter to *The Times*:

As I live entirely in the country, and take only a weekly publication, I did not see your paper containing [Hamilton's] letter until an hour ago. I shall reply to it briefly and positively.

First, as to the pencillings in the corrected folio, 1632, which I accidentally discovered. I never made a single pencil mark on the pages of the book, except crosses, ticks, or lines, to direct my attention to particular emendations. I have not seen it for four or five years, but I remember that on the board at the end (there was no fly-leaf there) I wrote various words, and made several notes, which I never attempted to erase:... and by that writing I may be convicted, unless somebody, which I do not believe, have taken the pains to imitate my hand. What is clearly meant, though somewhat darkly expressed, is that I am the author both of the pencillings and of the notes in ink.

Collier described the affidavit which he had sworn and filed in the Queen's Bench attesting to the truth of his accounts of his discovery of the Perkins Folio and he affirmed yet again that 'since it came into my hands, in 1849, I have not made the slightest addition to the notes in pencil or in ink.' Hamilton's description of the folio's binding was not new. Collier declared that he had 'all along admitted, privately and in print, that the rough calf binding of the corrected folio, 1632, was the second or third coat the book had worn.' The 'imperfect erasures and alterations of emendations, denoting changes of mind or better information on the part of the maker of the old marginal notes' he had himself described. 'Mr. Hamilton can, I think, point out nothing that I have not anticipated.' As to the pencil marks, he had never seen them. The book, Collier declared, had been inspected in 1852 by both the Society of Antiquaries and the Shakespeare Society and he had, in fact, publicly advertised its availability for examination by anyone interested and 'no one who inspected it discovered, or at least pointed out, any of the pencil-marks which it seems are now visible.'

The emendations themselves had been widely accepted. 'The Rev. Mr. Dyce' had 'declared in his own handwriting, that "some of them are so admirable that they can hardly be conjectural"', and he had adopted many of them in his recent edition. Since the value of the emendations was at best intrinsic why, Collier asked, would he have forged them in the folio? 'I might have appropriated [them] to myself and, having burnt the corrected folio, 1632, I might have established for myself a brighter Shakesperian reputation than all the commentators put together. If, therefore, I have committed a fraud, it has been merely gratuitous.'

Finally, he added a word about 'certain paragraphs stating that the late Duke of Devonshire gave me a large sum for my corrected folio, 1632' – an obvious reference to Staunton's comment in the *Birmingham Supplement*.

It was a free gift on my part, frankly accepted by his Grace, . . . a poor return for the many essential and substantial favours I had received at his hands during a period of 30 years. . . . It is clear, therefore, that if without motive I imposed upon the public, I did not without conscience victimize the man to whom I was so deeply indebted.[38]

Collier's letter, while cogent, did not satisfy his readers or mollify his accusers. To most it was a 'reply' rather than an 'answer', and even Robinson showed no great enthusiasm for it. It was satisfactory, he wrote, an 'absolute denial of all privity in the fraud, if any'[39] (a rather ominous way for Robinson to have put it!). In effect, Collier had waived any defence of the genuineness of the folio emendations in favour of absolving himself of wrong doing and this may have looked suspicious. Moreover, he did not offer any explanation for the pencil marks other than the suggestion that they might have been made since he had seen it, 'four or five years' before. The public wanted more.

The response of his accusers was gleeful: 'To my mind any thing more pitifully impotent in reply . . . it is hardly possible to conceive', Staunton wrote to Madden after reading Collier's letter. 'His refusal to write any more upon the subject will be taken, I fear, like his refusal to read Mr. Singer's "Vindication" as a convenient mode of escaping an encounter in which he feels assured of defeat.'[40]

Collier's defence could have been stronger, for Hamilton's accusation was inconsistent and founded on unjustified assumptions and deliberately misleading descriptions, particularly regarding the erasures. To divide the emendations into those 'which have been allowed to remain, and those which have been obliterated with more or less success' suggests an editorial judgement *subsequent* to that which 'fabricated' the original emendations – and yet the new substitutes are, he declared, in the same hand as the old. To prove dishonesty here Hamilton would have to demonstrate that the changes supported his contention of modernity. This he didn't, and probably couldn't, do. In fact, the whole argument he presents is disingenuous, for he must have known that Collier himself had described both the way the 'old corrector' had made his erasures and the fact that emendations were written over them. What Hamilton announced as a new revelation had actually been described by Collier himself in the first edition of *Notes and Emendations,* and, moreover, the *very examples* that Hamilton produced with such an air of discovery had been described in exactly the same detail by Collier himself over seven years before.[41]

Collier might have exposed this obvious prejudice to good effect, but he didn't. Age, infirmity, anxiety and excessive haste all added to the weakness of his reply. He was particularly handicapped by being unable to consult the Perkins Folio. He had not seen the book since preparing *Seven Lectures* at least three years before, and until the results of the Museum's 'inquisition' were fully published he could not defend himself with particularity. It is clear that he was unprepared for the announcement of pencil *under* the ink emendations and he appears to have been puzzled by it. This could have been a display of pretended innocence, of course, but surely Collier would have had some sort of explanation ready had he known that pencil marks *might* be found under the ink. His answer (that he had not seen them) seemed evasive, and as a result his explicit denial of the *implied* accusation (that he had written all the emendations in the folio) appeared inculpatory. It seemed somehow guilty to protest an innocence which no one had directly questioned.

Collier's letter delighted Madden: 'A weaker and more shuffling composition never was read! [he wrote in his diary]'. He does not venture to deny that the notes are a modern fabrication, but merely says he did not write them, and tells the old story of Rodd and Mr. Parry, as having possessed the volume previous to himself. I think his friends even must now give up the case. Henceforth the authority of the famous *Perkins folio* is gone, and its notes must be taken as the gleaning and conjectures of Mr. Collier. This is an atrocious imposture!'[42] If Madden's initial motive was, as he declared it to be, merely to prove or disprove the validity of the handwriting in the folio – without jeopardy to Collier's reputation – he could now claim to have satisfied it, for although Collier apparently still believed the writing to be of the seventeenth century, he was no longer willing to defend that belief in print. But Madden wanted nothing less than Collier's confession or his 'exposure' as a forger and a fraud – and his reaction reveals that the motives he had declared six weeks before were not honest. If they had been, Collier's letter would have satisfied his purpose and there would have been an end of it. Madden wanted more, and he became increasingly vengeful.

Collier's best defence came unsolicited and unexpected from Hepworth Dixon, the editor of the *Athenaeum*: Collier had written incidental reviews for that periodical and Dixon was therefore an acquaintance but not a personal friend. The *Athenaeum*'s editorial comments were always anonymous, but Dixon was almost certainly the author of any which, over the previous six years, had concerned the folio, first announced, it will be remembered, in that journal. Dixon had consistently supported Collier, but his support was not unqualified. For example, he had never granted the folio the authority of age or provenance (which Collier claimed) and he accepted only the inherent 'excellence' of the emendations themselves. Dixon, that is, had never thought the identity of the 'old corrector' to be much more than an interesting conjecture, and Hamilton's charges therefore struck him as both unwarranted and beside the point. Moreover, he had seen the folio while it was in the Museum and he had not found Madden's conclusions convincing. This enraged Madden who reported in his diary that Dixon was 'a little conceited coxcomb perfectly ignorant and self sufficient, and determined to see nothing that he did not choose to see'.[43]

In his defence of Collier, Dixon granted the possibility that the emendations were not old, but he was very severe on those who called them forgeries. He commended Devonshire for making the book available for public scrutiny but suggested that the Museum investigation was prejudiced and hinted that a cabal might be working aganst Collier, that 'more responsible persons than Mr. Hamilton are understood to concur in the statement put forth though not approving, we should hope, of the bold, hasty, and indecent manner of the statement'.

Hamilton, Dixon asserted, offered opinions rather than facts, conjectures rather than proofs. There was no evidence, Dixon claimed, for the view that the emendations are newer than the book's binding or that the pencil-writing is more modern than the ink.

But this gentleman appears to be able to see anything he wishes to see. For instance, he makes much of the insertion of [the] stage direction 'with the dead bodie': asserting the word 'dead' is put in to fill the space and cover larger pencil marks. What will the reader say, who turning to the folio finds the ink insertion on two lines, the word dead within the margin, and absolutely separated by a printer's rule from the pencilling which Mr. Hamilton insinuates that it is fraudulently put in to cover?

In short, Dixon declared, the evidence which Hamilton presented was conjectural and erroneously described. But even more important, it was irrelevant.

Supposing the case proved – supposing it allowed that the underlying pencil writing is in a free modern hand, that the marginal notes of punctuation are only such as are used at this day in a printer's office – what would the investigation have done? Taken away the external authority of the corrections. Just so much; no more. But the folio never had any ascertained external authority. All the warrant it has ever brought to reasonable critics is internal.... [The emendations] stand or fall by their own strength....[44]

By suggesting that the paleographic evidence was of little importance in contrast to the intrinsic literary value of the corrections, Dixon undermined Madden's case against Collier, for if the age of the writing were no longer in contention, if, that is, Collier and his friends were now willing to accept the possibility that the emendations were composed much later than he had originally conjectured, the charge of forgery would be unreasonable; if there were no forgery, there could be no forger, and Collier could be accused of nothing more serious than poor critical judgement. Despite Madden's fevered assertions, the writing alone could not convict Collier, and Madden therefore had to find some other incriminating evidence or give up the attack. Nevertheless, Madden's belief in the damning evidence of the pencil marks was as strong as ever. He urged Nevil Maskelyne, Keeper of the Mineral Department of the Museum, to examine the book with a microscope, and Maskelyne found what he thought was evidence of Hamilton's earlier charge that the pencil lay beneath the ink. But Madden knew that this evidence would be useful against Collier only if it were supported by non-paleographic evidence, something apart from the writing which would prove Collier to have been deceitful in order to hide his part in its manufacture.

Madden therefore turned to Collier's earlier accounts of the Perkins Folio, and scrutinized them for some sign of falsehood which would impugn Collier's word and suggest his complicity in the greater crime. For example, if it could be shown that contrary to his story, the book had come into his hands *without* notes, he must have put them there and their 'intrinsic value' would certainly not absolve him of fraud. By extension, if it could be proved that Collier had falsified any *part* of his account, doubt would be cast on the whole of it. Thus Madden's best hope lay in contravening Collier's story.

Just when Madden remembered Parry is not clear. His diary accounts suggest that it was not until 11 July that he learned that the old man was 'still living, and in full possession of his faculties'. Two days later, on 13 July, to Madden's 'surprise and gratification', Parry himself unexpectedly arrived at the Museum to examine the book.[45] Madden implies that Parry came of his own volition, but it is far more likely that Madden sought him out. In any case, four days after Dixon's article appeared, Parry was ushered into Madden's sanctum and shown the Perkins Folio by Madden and Hamilton.

In the second edition of *Notes and Emendations,* Collier had declared that Parry had positively identified the book in the fall of 1852 and, 'without the slightest reserve' had given him 'such an account of the book as made it certain that it was the same which, some fifty years ago, had been presented to him by ... Mr George Gray.' Collier declared in this account that Parry had 'described both the exterior and interior of the volume, with its innumerable corrections and its missing leaves, with so much minuteness that no room was left for doubt.'[46] This verification was the keystone of Collier's account of the provenance of the book. Now, nearly seven years later, Parry looked at the book as it lay on Madden's table and declared that he had never seen it before. As Hamilton was to write in another letter to *The Times* composed on the very day Parry examined the book, Parry's 'surprise was hardly less than our own' that the Perkins Folio was *not* his, 'that it differed in edition, in binding, in corrections – in fact, in every particular in which a book can differ – from the folio Shakespeare formerly in his possession, and which he expected to have placed before him.'

In Parry's denial, Madden had found the wedge he sought, and Hamilton's subsequent letter drove it home: 'Thus has the last testimony to the authenticity of this volume failed as completely and more remarkably than any of the preceding.... I forbear to comment on facts which I cannot elucidate, but the world will no doubt anxiously wish for explanations which the interests of literature seem imperiously to demand.'[47]

Parry's denial was even more incriminating, at least in the popular mind, than the paleographic discoveries had been. If Parry was to be believed, Collier had deliberately attempted to falsify the provenance of the book, and why would he have done so if he had not known that the true story would have revealed fraud? Parry's testimony, in effect, said Collier lied to cover the truth that either he himself or someone known to him had fabricated the corrections that now filled the Perkins Folio margins.

The same issue of *The Times* that carried Hamilton's letter printed Maskelyne's report of his 'scientific' examination of the book that provided new evidence that pencil marks underlay some of the ink:

In several cases...the ink word and the pencil word occupy the same ground in the margin, and are one over the other....

I have nowhere been able to detect the pencil-mark clearly overlying the ink, though in several places the pencil stops abruptly at the ink, and in some seems to be just traceable through its translucent substance, while lacking there the generally metallic lustre of the plumbago. But the question is set at rest by the removal by water of the ink in instances where the ink and pencil intersected each other. The first case I chose for this was a *u* in *Richard II.*, p. 36. A pencil tick crossed the *u*, intersecting each limb of that letter. The pencil was barely visible through the first stroke, and not at all visible under the second stroke of the *u*. On damping off the ink in the first stroke, however, the pencil-mark became much plainer than before, and even when as much of the inkstain as possible was removed the pencil still runs through the ink line in unbroken even continuity. . . .[48]

These letters were a powerful reply both to Collier's defence and the *Athenaeum*'s rebuttal, and the public judgement seemed to turn against Collier. 'Mr. Collier's best friends must regret to see his name [attached] to these unsatisfactory notes', the *Bulletin* declared. 'He has unfortunately got mixed up with what has been proved to be a literary imposture, and the sooner he disconnects himself from it the better.'[49] Ingleby was overjoyed. His book (begun shortly after he had first seen the folio at the Museum) was almost finished and would now be published in the midst of the public controversy. In his excitement, Ingleby was emboldened to ask Madden for permission to announce that he, Madden, had been the first to uncover Collier's forgery. 'Have you any objection to my publicly giving you the credit of first detecting by external evidence the fabrication of the Perkins notes? Of course I wish in my book to give honour to whom it is due', he wrote. 'May I do so in *your* case?'[50] Madden had sedulously avoided any public declaration that it was he who had directed the inquisition against the folio. It was a politic stance, for if the charges against Collier were discounted, he would have nothing to answer for; if, on the other hand, they were believed, he could in time reveal himself as the authority behind the exposure. His reply to Ingleby's request indicates that he thought that time had come; he immediately consented. 'In consequence of the publicity given to the case of the folio Shakespeare of 1632 previously belonging to Mr. Collier, I feel no hesitation in acceding to your request', he wrote. 'It is certainly true that the credit of first detecting the fraud by the external indices [i.e., the pencil marks] belongs to myself.'[51] When Ingleby's book came out, the conflict would be in the open, but Madden now thought his case was secure.

Collier had hoped that his letter to *The Times* would indeed be his 'last word' on the subject, but in the face of Parry's denial his silence would seem to corroborate Parry's story and to imply his own guilt, and he therefore wrote a second letter to *The Times*.

I saw Mr. Parry twice upon the subject in the year 1853 [he wrote] – first at his house in St. John's-wood, when he told me (as he had previously told a common friend) that he had recognized the corrections instantly, from the facsimile which accompanied the earliest edition of my *Notes and Emendations*, 8vo. 1852. Very soon afterwards, for greater satisfaction, I brought the corrected folio of 1632 from Maidenhead to London, and took it to St. John's-wood, but I failed to meet with Mr. Parry at home. I therefore paid a third visit to that gentleman, again carrying the book with me. I met him coming from his house, and I informed him that I had the corrected folio of 1632 under my arm, and that I was sorry he could not then examine it, as I wished. He replied – 'If you will let me see it now, I shall be able to state at once whether it was ever my book.' I therefore showed it to him on the spot, and, after looking at it in several places, he gave it back to me with these words: – 'That was my book, it is the same, but it has been much ill-used since it was in my possession.'

I took Mr. Parry's word without hesitation; and it certainly gave me increased faith in the emendations, to which I never applied a microscope or magnifying glass beyond my own spectacles.[52]

Collier professed to be at a loss to understand Parry's comments. 'Mr. Parry *may* now be unwilling to stand by what he said in 1853', Collier wrote to a friend shortly after his letter appeared. 'Then the book was in high repute, and he might be glad to claim kindred with it. I only know what I showed him and what he said of it. Perhaps, now the fact is recalled to his mind he may remember it.'[53]

This, however, was not Parry's reaction. He apparently felt threatened by Collier's renewed assertion that he had been shown the book and positively identified it, and on the day that Collier's letter was printed in *The Times*, Parry returned to the Museum to consult with Madden. Once again, Madden's diary account suggests that he came of his own accord, but Madden may have sent for him. 'Mr. Parry called again on me today', he wrote under the date of 19 July, 'for the express purpose of denying Mr. Collier's statements, and placed in my hands to read, a draft of a letter to the *Times* to that effect.' Madden thus implied that Parry on his own initiative had written a reply to Collier's mis-statements in his *Times* letter. This is almost certainly untrue. Parry did write a letter, but he did so in consultation and, as the letter itself said, at the behest of Hamilton. It was addressed not to the newspaper but to Hamilton. Moreover, Madden himself inadvertently reveals that he had made a suggestion on its substance. 'Mr. P . . . is unwilling to do, what any other man would', he wrote in his diary, 'i.e., boldly accuse Mr. C. of falsehood. Thus Mr. C. in his Preface to 2d. ed. of "Notes and Emendations", says that Mr. P. described the *exterior* of his Shakspere to him. This is a *lie*, for Mr. Parry never described it, and *if he had*, Mr. C. *must at once have known that it could not be the same as his own.* There is no excuse for this. A copy in smooth calf, lettered, of the edition 1623 could never be mistaken for the rough sheep unlettered copy of 1632 belonging to Mr. C.'[54]   Whether Madden had been misled by Parry's description and poor memory or whether he, in fact, projected these differences himself isn't clear. Certainly it is suspicious that Madden now said the folio was bound in *sheep* whereas earlier he had repeatedly described it in his own notes as being in rough calf, and since he had read Collier's account of his conversation with Parry in 1852, he should have known that Parry made his initial positive identification not to Collier but to Moore. The diary entry, therefore, is erroneous and suspect. It raises questions as to why Madden felt it necessary to cover his tracks in this fashion.

Hamilton's answer to Collier's reassertion of Parry's identification took nearly two weeks to prepare and print. It consisted of a short letter to *The Times*, which appeared on 1 August, enclosing Parry's 'letter' to him. Since Parry's note was, in fact, produced by their joint effort, Hamilton's covering letter was disingenuous:

Sir, –

I beg to forward you the following communication, which I have just received from Mr. Parry in reference to Mr. Collier's letter of the 7th inst.

I may add that Mr. Parry states, in conversation, that his *Shakespeare* was bound in smooth dark leather, with a new back, which was lettered; that there was no name of any former possessor written on the cover; and that part of the margins containing the emendations had been ploughed off by the carelessness of the binder.

On the other hand, Mr. Collier's folio is of the edition of 1632; it is bound in rough light-coloured sheep, not rebacked nor lettered at all; has on the upper cover, written in a bold recent hand, 'Tho. Perkins his booke'; and the corrections have not been injured by the binding. I am, Sir, your obedient servant,

N. E. S. A. Hamilton

Parry's letter, addressed to Hamilton and dated 28 July (fully ten days after Madden reported it to have been written), followed:

My dear Sir,

In reply to your application I have only to make the following statement, in which you will see that Mr. Collier's memory and mine are in question.

In Mr. Collier's letter to *The Times*, printed July 19, 1859, he states that he was coming to call on me in 1853 with 'the corrected folio of 1632 under his arm,' and that he showed it to me in the road, and that I gave it back to him with these words, 'That it was my book – it is the same; but it has been much ill-used since it was in my possession.'

Now, I believe Mr. Collier to be utterly incapable of making any statement which is not strictly in accordance with his belief. I remember well meeting him, as he says, in the road, and as I was then very lame from having hurt my knee by a fall, and was using sticks to assist me in walking, he kindly did not allow me to turn back, but walked with me in the direction I was going. I well remember some of the conversation we had during our walk; but I have not the slightest recollection that the volume of *Shakespeare* was then under his arm, or of my having asserted that 'it was my book.'

Previously to this interview with Mr. Collier he had shown me the facsimile which he mentions in his letter, when I immediately said, on seeing it, that it was from my book. I now believe that I was mistaken, and that I was too hasty in so identifying *the volume* from a facsimile of a part of a page of it. At that time Mr. Collier knew that there were several corrected folios of *Shakespeare* in existence, but he did not tell me that there were. At that time I did not know that there was any other corrected folio in existence, and I therefore supposed that Mr. Collier's facsimile could only have been taken from my book. It was not till the 14th of this month that I learnt from Sir Frederick Madden that there are five or six corrected folios now in being, but he (Sir Frederick) did not tell me so till he had laid on the table Mr. Collier's corrected folio, and then he seemed surprised that I did not recognize it.

Again, I repeat that, having frequently since the 14th of this month, when I saw Sir Frederick Madden, tried to recollect everything about the book, I cannot remember that Mr. Collier ever showed me the book, but I well remember his showing me the facsimile. I may be wrong, and Mr. Collier may be right.

I have a very strong impression that *my* book was a copy of the edition of 1623, and was rather surprised when I saw Mr. Collier's 'Supplemental volume' (1853) to find that *his* book was of the edition of 1632.

I may also add that I certainly did not tell, and could not have told Mr. Collier, that Mr. Gray 'was partial to the collection of old books,' for I believe he set no value at all on them.

Believe me to be, my dear Sir, yours very truly,

F. C. Parry.[55]

Madden was not entirely happy with Parry's letter. 'I pointed out that one or two paragraphs destroyed the effect of the rest of the letter', he wrote in his diary of 28 July. He particularly disliked Parry's comments that he might be wrong and Collier right. 'I wished this sentence to be withdrawn, as it will certainly be caught hold of by Mr. C's friends, but Mr. P. said it was only meant as an expression of courtesy to Mr. C. and it is to remain.'[56]

Courtesy or not, the disclaimer was necessary, for as Parry knew, and as Madden and Hamilton must have deduced, the letter and Hamilton's introduction were shot through with misstatements. The fact that Hamilton's note ascribed information to Parry 'in conversation' which Parry was apparently unwilling to put down over his own signature, indicates that they were both aware of the discrepancies. The case against Collier's story was that he had kept information from Parry and had shown him only the facsimile, that only later did Parry discover the difference between his book and the Perkins Folio. This version is flatly disproved by Moore's letter to Collier, which Parry knew about, and by Collier's letter to

Parry (see pp. 157–8). Moore made it clear that it was *he* – not Collier – who first showed the facsimile to Parry and heard Parry's unsolicited positive identification. Moreover, Collier's subsequent letter to Parry described those very characteristics of the folio which Parry later said surprised him at the Museum: it identified the Perkins Folio as the 1632 edition and declared his understanding that Parry's book was of the same date. Parry's declaration that he had not been informed of the discrepancy (if any) is untrue. Finally, Collier's letter specifically described the book as 'shabby and defective' and without a title page or conclusion, that it had 'the name of Tho. Perkins on the cover', and that the emendations were in its 'cropped margins'. Collier's description of the Perkins Folio could hardly have been more complete. He had described his meetings with Parry, including Parry's identification of the folio, in his preface to the second edition of *Notes and Emendations* which he had shown to Parry before it was printed. Parry had made one or two small corrections in the text, agreed to its publication, and, until the Museum inquisition began, had never disputed the facts it contained. Parry's disclaimer therefore came too late, and his implication that Collier had tricked him is inexcusable, for he still had Collier's letter and therefore could not have 'forgotten' the true facts. His comment that he 'may be wrong and Mr. Collier may be right' was no 'expression of courtesy' but rather an attempt to cover a blatant falsehood.

The most logical explanation of Parry's behaviour is that he felt himself under suspicion of having had a hand in forging the emendations himself – a ludicrous fear since he was almost totally ignorant of Shakespeare textual emendation. It is very probable that Madden sought him out, impressed him with what Madden believed was irrefutable evidence of the folio's fabrication, and suggested that he, Parry, as the source of the book ought to have an explanation ready. Parry, a man in his seventies, whose original attachment to the folio was at best tenuous (not to say questionable) feared scandal and attempted to extricate himself. It seems unlikely that Hamilton and Madden believed his explanation, but it was useful to them and they shaped it to their own ends.

The Parry incident is significant because it reveals the

nature of the case being made by Madden and Hamilton, and because it was very influential in directing public opinion against Collier. Largely as a result of this 'external' evidence of supposed malfeasance with the book, Collier's defence lost public sympathy. The 'general public voice is against Collier', Henry Crabb Robinson wrote in his diary. '. . . I can't believe in his being a party to the fraud.'[57] This is a significant comment not only as evidence that a consensus had formed against his old friend but that Robinson himself now believed fraud had been committed. This was the central issue: not whether the emendations were old or new but whether they had been put there to *deceive* others. Robinson's comment reveals that the book was now generally believed to be not a mere curiosity which Collier might have misread, but a deliberate forgery.

However, Madden's part in all this had not gone unremarked by at least some of those who saw him at close hand. Bond in particular was suspicious. When Thomas Duffus Hardy, a good friend of Madden and Assistant Keeper of the Public Records, suggested that a list be published of all those who thought the Perkins Folio a forgery, Madden declared it a capital idea and offered to head the list. But Bond would have no part of the scheme. Collier, he declared, had not disputed the judgement that the emendations were more recent than the seventeenth century and hence there was no issue between them.[58] Certainly there was no reason to call the book a forgery. Madden's real motive must have been clear to Bond, and when he refused to sign, the scheme collapsed, irritating Madden and giving him pause.

Hamilton, too, seemed briefly to veer away from the course he and Madden had begun together. He wrote an anonymous article for the *Saturday Review* that thoroughly denounced the folio but unexpectedly suggested that Collier himself 'had been taken in by one as competent, to say the least of it, to commentate as himself.'[59] The conclusion of the article was that Collier was not guilty of fraud, and coming from Hamilton this was a startling observation that greatly troubled Madden. 'I do not like its tone', he wrote in his diary.[60]

These reactions may have accounted for Madden's sudden

change of heart concerning Ingleby's request for attribution. In late July, Ingleby wrote thanking Madden for permission to declare him the 'true discoverer' of the forgery, and Madden immediately wrote Ingleby declaring that he no longer consented to his name being used. Ingleby, no doubt somewhat startled by Madden's *volte face,* nevertheless dropped all reference to him in the manuscript.[61] In the face of the general public outcry against the book, Madden's reaction was cautious, but he sought yet more external evidence to inculpate Collier. He began to go beyond the folio and to examine other Collier publications for evidence of fraud. There were, for example, Hunter's old charges against the Bridgewater manuscripts that Collier had discovered and published nearly twenty-five years before. (A probably related comment in the *Critic* for 9 July suggested they might be looked at more closely.) In addition, there were Halliwell's old suspicions of the letter of Mrs. Alleyn that Collier had found in Dulwich and printed as part of the *Alleyn Papers.* (There is no indication that Halliwell had a part in this recollection; in fact, he remained remarkably quiet throughout the whole of the Museum inquisition.) Madden would ultimately follow these 'leads' to dramatic ends.

The Perkins Folio had now been sequestered in the British Museum for two months under the close surveillance of Madden and Hamilton, and there were public complaints of this procedure. A correspondent in the *Athenaeum* who signed himself 'An Antiquary' declared on 29 July that he had been allowed to see the book for only 'five minutes, during which time I was obligingly assisted to form a *correct* notion of the genuineness of the writing by the dogmatic assertions of the official who superintended my inspection.' When he tried to see it again he was told that the book 'was no longer visible to the public. The official who brought the answer was good enough to add, that I was very fortunate to have seen the book for five minutes, as many applications had been refused altogether.'[62]

Another correspondent complained 'that there has been evinced a strange disinclination to exhibit the Shakespeare Folio to any but those of the anti-Collier clique or such as will be content to view the tome through the spectacles of Mr. Nicholas Hamilton.'[63] The evidence is strong that even though very serious charges were being made against him, Collier and his supporters had been virtually denied access to the book – unable to substantiate his defence from its pages or to determine whether the book was in the same state as when he gave it to Devonshire five or six years before.

In late July, Collier therefore asked Devonshire to place the folio where he and his friends could see it without interference from Madden. Devonshire at once agreed and asked Madden to return the book to his solicitor, Mr. William Currey. The unreliable nature of Madden's diary is revealed in the way he recorded this incident in its pages. There he quoted the Duke as saying, 'very properly, that he thought Mr. C. and his friends might very well have come to look at it while it was under my care at the Museum and allowed of his own accord, that he thought he ought not to let Mr. Collier have the volume at his own disposal. I said that I perfectly agreed with his Grace and I suggested that when the volume was returned to Mr. Currey . . . he should make arrangements for Mr. Collier and his friends to see it at his house or office. The Duke assented to this, and said he would act accordingly.' This conversation was fabricated. The letter which Madden wrote to accompany the return of the folio suggests that Devonshire had no suspicions of Collier and that it was *Madden* who pressed the Duke to restrict Collier's use of the book. 'Although it is right Mr. Collier and his friends should have free permission to inspect the volume', Madden wrote to Devonshire, 'yet that under the peculiar circumstances in which Mr. Collier now stands (a position rendered still more questionable by the discovery of some forgeries at Dulwich College since I last had the honour of seeing your Grace) such arrangements should be made by Mr. Currey as should secure the volume from any possibility of being tampered with. Several gentlemen have expressed this opinion to me, and I cannot but agree with them, even for the sake of Mr. Collier himself.'[64]

There is no evidence that Devonshire supported Madden's opinion, nor that he restricted Collier's use of it at Currey's. But there *is* evidence that Devonshire was not satisfied with Madden's inspection of the folio at the Museum and that he asked four members of the Society of Antiquaries to examine it (a proposal which incensed Madden) and that the judgement of these men, although never made public, did not support Madden.[65]

23

A few days after the folio was returned to Devonshire, Ingleby's book was published. Although it had been virtually finished before Hamilton's letter of 2 July, Ingleby had shrewdly withheld publication to take full advantage of the developing controversy. Its format (a small octavo of only 116 pages nearly half of them filled with reprints from *The Times* correspondence) hardly suggested its audacity, but it was boldly titled *The Shakespeare Fabrications, Or, The Ms. Notes of the Perkins Folio Shown to be of Recent Origin.* Much of the book was a rehash of Hamilton's argument, but it had a new twist: the Museum 'case' was based on internal paleographic evidence of forgery whereas Ingleby's was derived from what he called 'external' evidence, e.g., test words and the like. *The Shakespeare Fabrications* was, in fact, a kind of sequel to *Literary Cookery,* from which its tone and most of its substance derived; it was a logical extension of Brae's diatribe, buttressed by previously uncollected data, some of which had been suggested by Brae himself. Significantly, Ingleby did not show Brae his book until it was in print, and Brae later complained that it subverted his own intention to revise and reissue *Literary Cookery.*[66] It was, therefore, more than a little ironic that Ingleby dedicated his book 'to Andrew Edmund Brae, Esq., who first . . . by a philological process, discovered and proved that [the Perkins emendations] were modern fabrication.'[67] Perhaps something more than dedication was due to Brae, whom, as the *Athenaeum* was later to put it, Ingleby 'lauds on the fly-leaf and robs on every other.'[68]

Ingleby put much of Brae's published and unpublished arguments into his text with almost no change in substance and only a little improvement in style. For example, Brae's chief 'proof' against the folio had been the 'chair' into 'cheer' emendation which he had first introduced some years before as evidence that the emendations were 'modern' (see p. 195–6) and it was around this 'evidence' that Ingleby built *his* case.

Moreover, Brae's earlier accusation that Collier had altered his book after his announcement was echoed in *The Shakespeare Fabrications* without reference to Brae: 'I have stated certain facts,' Ingleby declared in his preface, 'which raise a strong suspicion that the Perkins folio received two MS. emendations, and that it lost a MS. stage-direction, in the year 1852: *i.e.,* while the folio was in Mr. Collier's possession.'[69]

The 'lost stage direction' was the 'writing' emendation in *Hamlet* of which Brae had made so much in the columns of *Notes and Queries* six years before (see p. 192), and Ingleby now repeated the charge (with no new evidence or argument) that the ink insertion had been erased after Brae had made it a public issue. The assertion that the folio had recently 'received' new emendations, presumably by Collier's hand, was a more important charge, but it too had been suggested by Brae.[70] What Ingleby declared, in effect, was that Collier had inserted two 'remarkable' emendations – one by the late Sidney Walker and the other by Dyce – into the folio *after* its discovery was first announced in January 1852. Walker's emendation concerned a line in the folio text of *All's Well That Ends Well* (V, iii) in which Bertram declares he had been entrapped by his wife: 'Her *insuit comming* with her modern grace,/Subdued me to her rate;'. The italicized words are obscure and frequently had been emended by early editors, but in his 1844 edition Collier had argued for the folio text (with the somewhat tortured interpretation: 'Her *solicitation* joining with her *common* beauty...' etc.)[71] and seemed to accept it without difficulty. In April 1852, in the midst of the excitement over the discovery of the Perkins Folio, W. N. Lettsom wrote a letter to the *Athenaeum* remarking that among the Shakespeare notes of Sidney Walker, which Lettsom was then editing for publication, he had found the suggested emendation 'infinite cunning' for 'insuit comming'. It was an excellent correction (it has since become standard) and several weeks later Singer referred to it in a letter to *Notes and Queries*. Collier, who had apparently missed Lettsom's original letter to the *Athenaeum,* immediately addressed a query to Singer asking where the emendation had appeared, but he received no answer, and six months later, when the first edition of *Notes and Emendations* was published, Collier announced that the emendation was among those in the Perkins Folio. He noted Walker's suggestion, but implied that the Old Corrector had preceded him.[72] Following Brae, Ingleby found Collier's failure to print the emendation in his first announcement of the Perkins Folio inconceivable since it was 'the best, or, at least, one of the *few* good ones to be found on its margins.'[73] He therefore was sure that Lettsom's announcement had suggested the emendation and that Collier had subsequently written it into the Perkins copy.

Even more damning, in the view of Brae and Ingleby, was an emendation in *King John* (III, i). In the folio text of that play, Constance warns the Dauphin that 'the devil tempts thee here,/ In likeness of a new *untrimmed* bride.' Six months after Collier had announced his discovery of the Perkins Folio (and six months before his first edition of *Notes and Emendations*), Singer used the columns of *Notes and Queries* to announce Dyce's emendation of 'uptrimmed' for 'untrimmed'.[74] Just why Singer rather than Dyce made the announcement isn't clear. The emendation was not in either edition of *Notes and Emendations,* but three years later, Collier included the correction in *Seven Lectures,* indicating that it had been in the Perkins Folio all along. Brae and Ingleby were certain that, once again, Collier had expropriated a new emendation for his Folio. 'It is ... instructive that so remarkable an emendation was omitted from Mr. Collier's *Notes and Emendations*', Ingleby declared. 'The fact is, it was not invented when the first edition of that work was published.'[75]

Much of the argument of *The Shakespeare Fabrications* derived from Brae, but the book contained two new charges of Ingleby's own devising: the first he claimed to have discovered when the Perkins Folio was examined in the Museum. There were, Ingleby declared, 'remarkable discrepancies' between the folio text and 'Mr. Collier's account of it'. Collier, Ingleby alleged, had pretended to give a 'complete list' of the emendations in his supplement to *Seven Lectures* but had, in fact, printed 'much less than half', and that even a casual perusal of the folio revealed that there were several thousand corrections that Collier had not mentioned at all. There were, as well, 'discrepancies' in Collier's description of the corrections he *did* print: some were written on erasures, for example, without his having so indicated. And Collier's reading of some of them actually changed in the course of his various published accounts. For example, in the folio text of *Much Ado About Nothing* (II, i) Benedick speaks of Beatrice as 'huddling jest upon jest, with ... impossible conveyance'. The 'Old Corrector' has changed 'impossible' to 'unportable' by altering the 'im' to 'un', deleting 'possible' and substituting 'portable' in the margin. Collier had transcribed this in two different ways: in *Notes and Emendations* (1853)[76] he printed the correction as 'importable', but in *Seven Lectures* (1856)[77] he printed it as 'unportable' and still later in his new edition of *Shakespeare* (1858) he printed 'importable' which, he stated in a note (II, 27), was the Perkins reading. 'Mr. Collier must have forgotten', Ingleby sardonically commented, 'that the "Old Corrector" had altered this word, between 1853 and 1856.'[78]

Finally, *The Shakespeare Fabrications* made a second new charge that Brae had nothing to do with. Ingleby strongly implied that Collier fabricated the folio emendations to provide 'authoritative' evidence for his own earlier conjectures. The suggestion had been first made in 1853 by Singer (who had died only a few months before Ingleby's book appeared). The Old Corrector, according to Singer, had a 'most wonderful sympathy with Collier's suggestions in his edition of 1844.'

'Were these coincidences only occasional', Ingleby wrote, quoting Singer, 'we might think them possible, but when they occur on all occasions, we cannot conceive them altogether fortuitous'.[79]

Ingleby set about proving the point by printing what he called 'a tolerably complete list' of these 'coincidences' in several pages of tables. In each case, a 'suggestion' which Collier had made in notes to his 1844 edition was, indeed, matched by a corresponding change in the folio. This new evidence suggested a unique connection between Collier's preferences and those of the 'Old Corrector', and as such it was far more incriminating than the earlier circumstantial evidence that Brae had investigated. Here, for the first time, was a motive beyond mere cupidity, which only Collier could have had.

It is curious that Collier allowed this evidence – and its damning implication – to stand without refutation. In fact, the correlation Singer and Ingleby announced has never, heretofore, been examined to see if it were valid. It isn't. A close examination of Ingleby's lists in *The Shakespeare Fabrications* shows that he misstated the facts and that his judgement was in gross error. Contrary to his assertions, his illustrations prove not a 'wonderful sympathy' but a clear lack of correlation between Collier's textual preferences in his *Shakespeare* (1844) and the Perkins emendations. Ingleby's tables cite thirty-one instances in which Perkins's emendations are identical to 'suggestions' Collier had made in 1844, but this presentation is very misleading and tantamount to falsification. A check of his references reveals that only eleven of these thirty-one 'suggestions' were emendations which Collier actually adopted in his text, and of these nine were commonplace corrections of typographical misprints in the Second Folio. Of the remaining twenty, eleven were 'suggested' in Collier's notes but *not* adopted in his text and hence, in effect, *discounted* by him; of the remaining nine, two were instances in which, contrary to Ingleby's implication, Collier actually made suggestions *differing* from the corrections which later appeared in the Perkins Folio. But most remarkable of all, in the remaining seven instances, Collier had indeed printed alternative 'suggestions' which the 'Old Corrector' later put in the folio, but only to *reject* them out of hand as unacceptable emendations by earlier editors. In short, nearly twenty-five per cent of the Perkins emendations which Ingleby cites are *direct contradictions* of Collier's judgements in his earlier edition. Ingleby deliberately misconstrued his evidence by using the word 'suggestion' to mean both 'preference' and 'mention' without regard to the contextual purpose. He implied that the Perkins Folio contained thirty-one emendations which Collier had introduced into his 1844 text without 'authority' whereas, in fact, there were only *two* which support Collier's earlier conjectures – and these not unique to Collier – and *seven* which support readings which Collier was at particular pains to disavow in his earlier work.

Ingleby, of course, worked from the Perkins Folio text (as it was given in *Seven Lectures*) back to Collier's 1844 text. Since there were fewer corrections in *Seven Lectures* than in Collier's *Shakespeare*, going from the folio to the Shakespeare was more likely to produce the positive correlation Ingleby was seeking. However, the reverse procedure – comparing Collier's textual emendation in 1844 to the Perkins Folio corrections – reveals an even more dramatic negative contrast. For example, in discussing *A Midsummer Night's Dream*, Ingleby cites two 'suggestions' which Collier made in his edition which were subsequently found in the margins of the Perkins Folio, but he fails to note that both these 'suggestions' had been made by earlier editors and that *neither* had been accepted by Collier, although one ('princess' to 'impress' in II,ii)[80] had been adopted by several earlier editors. Even more significantly, Ingleby fails to point out that seven other 'suggestions' in the 1844 text do *not* appear in the Perkins Folio at all, and of these, Collier felt strongly enough about six to incorporate them into his text. Conversely, seven other 'suggestions' which Collier mentioned in his 1844 edition of this play in order to *reject* them, appear as corrections in the Perkins Folio. (Five of these were by previous editors, e.g., Rowe and Theobald, and two were emendations which Collier had specifically rejected in 1844 in favour of alternatives of his own.) Far from suggesting a positive correlation – and hence a motive for forgery – a comparison of Collier's emendation in his *Shakespeare* (1844) with those in the Perkins Folio shows a striking dissimilarity between them. Of course, one might argue that in forging the Perkins notes Collier deliberately contradicted his earlier preferences in order to 'cover his tracks' and provide a 'defence' in case his fraud were detected. But if that were his intention, it is unclear why he did not then 'use' this defence when Ingleby declared a 'sympathetic' correlation between the two works. Moreover, Collier's close control of the Perkins Folio forestalled the chance that others would *find* the exonerating evidence he had thus 'planted'. One must conclude that Ingleby's tables actually argue *against* his accusations. They are strong evidence that Collier would not have written the emendations in the folio.

The Shakespeare Fabrications was as close to libel as Ingleby dared to make it, and he feared Collier might sue[81] – Collier had, after all, gone to court once before and he had declared his willingness to do so again. But despite his bold rejoinder, Collier was very hesitant. 'My enemies are still actively at work,' he wrote to a friend in mid-September. 'I have set my lawyer upon Mr. Ingleby's book, for I hear that some parts of it are actionable. Is it so? I only want to know the fact; for even if it be actionable I am not sure that I should not be playing the author's game by proceeding against him.'[82] The *Literary Cookery* suit had not given him satisfaction, and he had no reason to think another attempt at legal vindication would be more successful. Collier was sick, and he was tired. 'He wants vigour to defend himself as he ought', Robinson declared.[83] Moreover, he knew that Ingleby was not his chief antagonist. The promised Museum pamphlet was yet to come and that surely would have to be answered. He decided to hold his fire for that encounter.

But although Collier held back from replying to Ingleby, Hepworth Dixon, the intrepid editor of the *Athenaeum*, did not. What incited Dixon was Ingleby's reiteration of Brae's old claim that the *Athenaeum* had refused to publish *Literary Cookery* because of a bias in Collier's favour. Dixon, who had assumed that the legal restraint against the pamphlet had quieted that slander for good, was furious that it should be dredged up again. In addition, he had a genuine sense of outrage at what he considered an attack against Collier by accusers who hid behind the massive pillars of the British Museum. Although Madden had kept his own name out of Ingleby's dedication, Dixon knew how closely the two had collaborated on the book. Dixon had inspected the folio at the Museum and had seen the manner of its presentation there, and he was convinced that the case against Collier was trumped up and unbecoming to a department of the national library. He was, in short, determined to give Hamilton and Brae a thorough drubbing and to strip Madden of his pretended disinterest, forcing him to own up to his part in the controversy.

Dixon's review, which appeared on 20 August, evoked the reaction he sought. He dismissed Ingleby as 'a mere child in literary fence ... [with] a very weak case and a very warm spleen' who declared a blatant prejudice on every page.

'In the long story of literary quarrels,' he wrote, 'we remember no case in which the premises were so frail and the assumptions so gross.' There was little in Ingleby's 'new' facts, 'beyond this bitterness of spirit'. He scorned Ingleby's retelling of the discredited story of *Literary Cookery* and the *Athenaeum*, declaring that 'a gentleman of more taste' would have known that it was the tone and style of the letter which alone had kept it from publication in the journal. The test word 'cheer' was unconvincing and the 'writing' erasure, meaningless. 'A controversialist who can draw such conclusions from such premises is capable of any feat in logic.' Collier, Dixon wrote, was sorely mistreated. 'We will not waste a word in defending a veteran man of letters, – a gentleman, we grieve to say, bowed by age, infirmity of health, and domestic afflictions – from this reckless and wicked charge.'

So far as the date of the Perkins emendations was concerned, Dixon reiterated his conviction that it was a point of no importance whatever – that not age but the intrinsic value of the emendations was their justification.

No evidence is yet before us against their being considered of the latter part of the seventeenth century [he wrote]. . . . but the 'proofs' laid open to us in a brief inspection of the tome by those who were themselves convinced of their modern character, only served to impress us with the necessity of extreme caution in drawing conclusions from lines and dots which are invisible to many eyes.

Ingleby's 'case', Dixon concluded, was therefore little more than rehashed gossip, trumpery 'evidence' and personal attack; it would not warrant attention except for the aegis under whose authority it was issued. It would not even be worth reviewing except that

the mysterious and vindictive inquisition into the nature of the Collier Folio going on in the department of Sir Frederick Madden [has] drawn public attention to the topic of which it treats. . . . The tribunal is objectionable on every ground save one: the judges are competent. . . . In all other respects it fails. We need not insist on the impropriety of turning the British Museum into a literary bear-garden, and the officers of that institution into fierce literary partizans and polemics. . . . Their services belong to the nation and not to the newspapers. Their responsibilities are to the public, and neither to the bookseller nor the book collector. They have no public commission to pronounce on the validity of texts and the date of handwriting. It would be absurd for them to ask the world of letters to accept a sentence at their hands of which the grounds are locked up in the presses of an inaccessible room of the British Museum and the interpretations are scattered on the wings of the newspapers .... An inquiry taking place under these circumstances even if conducted with a calmness and impartiality of which the articles in the newspapers show no trace, would fail to carry weight.

Dixon concluded that the Perkins Folio should be placed before another tribunal – a truly impartial one this time – to arrive at an unprejudiced judgement.[84]

It may be significant that although Madden's diary is regular in reporting the developing details of the controversy, especially those which came from 'the Collier faction' as he called it, there is not a word in it referring to Dixon's review or the charge that Madden had turned his department into a 'literary bear-garden' with 'fierce literary partizans and polemics'. In fact, for nearly a month after Dixon's review appeared, Madden recorded nothing whatever about the controversy. It was as though Dixon's attack, by openly accusing Madden, had stunned him into silence. When he finally wrote again on the subject in his diary, however, his fury against Dixon ('this dirty editor')[85] could hardly be contained.

Staunton and Ingleby leaped to Madden's defence. Articles denying Dixon's charge immediately appeared in the *Critic*, the *Literary Gazette*, the *Illustrated London News*, and elsewhere. A reply in the *Birmingham Gazette* sparked by Staunton (if not actually written by him) was typical of these:

Whatever Sir Federick's opinion may have been he has very slowly allowed it expression [the article declared], and we believe it was not till the prying eyes of the other officers, Mr. Bond, Mr. Hamilton, and others, had led them to similar conclusions, that Sir Frederick admitted what opinion he had formed of the famous notes. As some hints have been given that the officers of the Museum may have formed part of an anti-Collier conspiracy, common justice requires the statement of the fact that the volume fell into friendly hands, and that the recent discoveries have been put forth by very unwilling pens.[86]

Even Madden's friends must have smiled when they read this 'vindication'.

The effect of Dixon's review was to redouble Madden's efforts to seek out *new* evidence of Collier's crimes. The 'pamphlet' that Hamilton in his letter of 2 July had promised 'shortly' was put off (it would not appear for another five months) while Hamilton and Madden ransacked Collier's published works for evidence of forgery. Madden's rage was directed at anyone who denied Collier's guilt. 'I am sick of the whole affair', he wrote. 'If an angel came from Heaven and said that Mr. Collier was the forger in the notes in the Perkins folio, there would be persons found to declare it false!'[87] His anger easily spread to society as a whole, which more and more he thought universally corrupt. The world was evil and against him. ('Villainy everywhere, high or low', he wrote. 'From the prince to the pauper, where is there a grain of honesty?'[88]) As might be expected, his declarations became most extreme when others seemed to come to Collier's defence. When Madden heard that the American critic Richard Grant White had argued that the pencilling might be of the seventeenth century, he was thrown into a fury. 'I really am tired and disgusted with the whole business!' he declared. 'I believe Mr. C. to be, in a literary point of view, the greatest swindler and imposter the world has ever yet witnessed, and posterity, I am certain, will confirm my verdict.'[89]

Posterity might, but not all his contemporaries would. Madden's bitterness, in fact, deterred some who shared his dislike for Collier but distrusted his obvious vindictiveness. In October, Dyce coolly announced that he had come to the opinion that Collier had *not* forged the Perkins emendations. Some were 'too good', he said, for Collier to have invented them.[90] This turnabout outraged Madden. Dyce, after all, had written a book against the folio; he had declared publicly that the emendations were fabrications, and privately that Collier had made them. Dyce was the first person Madden had notified when he received the folio from Devonshire; he had been privy to Madden's inquisition from the very beginning, and as much as anyone outside the Museum had urged an official exposé of Collier's pretensions. Now he was stepping back, withdrawing from the enlarging controversy, disavowing Collier's guilt and seeming to leave Madden, now virtually committed, on his own.

The reasons for Dyce's reversal can only be guessed. His vanity may have been bruised by Ingleby's slighting references to himself *vis-à-vis* praise for Madden in *The Shakespeare Fabrications,* or, despite his previously emphatic declarations to the contrary, he may always have thought Collier innocent of forging the Perkins emendations and wanted now to protect himself from being publicly identified in the accusation. From the first he had been discreet, not to say secretive, in abetting the attack, and if Collier's reputation was to be destroyed, as now seemed probable, Dyce may have had qualms about being known as one of his prosecutors.

But even Dyce's disavowal could not deter Madden. It seemed rather to steel his determination to convict Collier with new 'evidence' of dishonesty. Any accusation against Collier, no matter how old, incidental or unsupported, was pursued. For example, sometime in the past, Dyce had told Madden that Collier had 'confessed' to forging a letter of Izaac Walton in the *Freebooter,* a newspaper Collier was said to have edited forty years before. The story was the merest hearsay, and Dyce's only motive for passing it on was malice, but Madden had remembered it and used it now. Shortly after Dixon's review, Thomas Arnold, a police magistrate, was sent by his close friend Anthony Panizzi to search the Perkins Folio for evidence justifying criminal prosecution of Collier. Arnold found none admissible in court but nevertheless thought there was enough to make an article in *Fraser's Magazine.* Madden helped him along with the story of the Walton letter. Arnold said he would use it with a 'rough hand' against Collier ('so much the better', Madden wrote in his diary).[91] Arnold's piece, which appeared in December 1859, included the Walton accusation and suggested there were similar crimes in Collier's past about to be brought to light. It also identified Madden as the source of the information.[92]

The search for incriminating evidence occupied both Hamilton and Madden virtually full time during the last two months of 1859. Hamilton sought evidence of forgery in Collier's accounts of early ballads, and Madden pursued a similar course in the Devonshire collections. He sought among

other things a sketchbook of Inigo Jones from which Collier
had quoted. Madden was sure the reference was fabricated,
and now the manuscript was missing! When his search failed
to turn up the book, Madden declared that Collier had
concealed it to hide his fraud. Another search at Dulwich
College was more successful. In early autumn, Hamilton had
been despatched to follow up the accusation made some years
earlier by Halliwell that Collier had misquoted the letter of
Mrs. Alleyn to her husband (see p. 169). To Madden's great
satisfaction, Hamilton not only confirmed Halliwell's charge
but also found several other documents in the collection, all
initially discovered by Collier, all printed by him in the Alleyn
Memoirs (1841), and all 'forged'. The Ellesmere manuscripts
were re-examined too. In November, Madden went with
Hamilton to Bridgewater House to look at the documents that
Hunter had questioned long before and, to his 'astonishment',
he found that these, too, were 'forged' by the *same* hand that
had fabricated the Perkins Folio emendations and the
Dulwich documents – that is to say, by John Payne Collier,
whom Madden now called 'the greatest literary knave that
ever lived'.[93] Finally, Madden's search took him to the State
Paper Office, where Duffus Hardy, a zealous supporter of
Madden's inquisition, declared he had uncovered another
unsuspected forgery – a document first printed by Collier in
The History of English Dramatic Poetry nearly thirty years before.
Yes, Madden declared, it *was* forged, and in the handwriting
of the Perkins Folio. Thus, as the months passed and Collier's
friends grew restive ('Where is the Museum pamphlet?' the
Athenaeum wanted to know),[94] Madden and Hamilton col-
lected their evidence.

Collier was waiting too, with exasperation and increasing
tension. The public did not spring to his defence. Except for
Hepworth Dixon, most of his defenders spoke privately. While
many believed the charges against him false and malicious,
they thought that he had shown a want of critical judgement
in the way he had used the Perkins emendations. His was a
difficult case to defend: his opponents were multiform, there
was a barrage of calumny in the papers, much of it
anonymous and, of course, the promised 'bill of particulars',
the British Museum pamphlet, did not appear. July passed,

and August. Soon it was October, still no pamphlet. Christmas passed. Nothing. How could one counter 'the facts' if none were forthcoming? Robinson tried to be optimistic: 'The friends of Collier wait until the enemy has spent his fire.'[95] But in fact Collier's support was dissipating.

Madden and Hamilton collected their evidence for the 'Museum pamphlet' together, but Madden rewrote much of the preface, selected its lithographic illustrations, and made the final revision of its text. Initially Hamilton – not Madden – was to be its nominal author, but Madden became dissatisfied with this plan. For one thing, he had been identified as the source of evidence against Collier not only by Dixon, Collier's defender, but also by Arnold, one of his assailants. More important, Madden had not fully appreciated that in trying to avoid culpability he might altogether lose the credit for his detection. With growing displeasure he watched his assistant Hamilton receive most of the public recognition, leaving Madden the private satisfaction of settling with Collier but little else. When an Edinburgh lawyer wrote to Hamilton (in care of Madden) asking him to serve as an expert witness because he had 'traced most unmistakably the frauds connected with the folio Shakespeare', Madden was furious. Apparently without consulting Hamilton, he wrote back declining the offer on Hamilton's behalf![96] And when Hamilton struck a bargain with Bentley, the publisher, to receive £100 for his book, Madden's anger burned deeper still. Hamilton to get £100 for doing so little! It added to Madden's conviction that his own achievement would never receive its due. 'What humbug is editing and printing', he complained, 'but it can hardly be otherwise, for if a man really knows what he is about, and takes the utmost pains for years, he gets no thanks for his labours and his work is unnoticed.'[97]

If reputation and money were to be made in the exposure of Collier, Madden wanted his share. He was ready to drop the mask of the disinterested observer:

I feel that the time is come to disguise no longer from the public my real sentiments on this scandalous affair [he wrote in his diary on New Year's Day 1860]. Had I even wished to remain silent the article in Fraser's Magazine . . . in which my name is prominently introduced, would be sufficient to cause my taking decisive steps at once to let the world know, as well as Mr. Collier and his friends, my opinion of this unparalleled forgery.[98]

He needed only the proper time and place to speak out.

VIII

AN INQUIRY AND A REPLY

'In all probability Mr. Rodd named you to me . . .'

24

In January 1860, nearly seven months after he had promised that 'fuller details' of his charges would appear 'shortly', Hamilton published the 'Museum pamphlet', *An Inquiry into the Genuineness of the Manuscript Corrections in Mr. J. Payne Collier's Annotated Shakspere, Folio, 1632.* Hamilton's obvious objective, like Ingleby's *The Shakespeare Fabrications,* was to arraign Collier, but he differed from the learned doctor in basing his attack not on the lack of intrinsic merit in the corrections which, he declared in his *Preface,* 'could hardly be conclusive' (p. ii), but on *'external* grounds, the authenticity of the handwriting' (p. v). This, he believed, damned not only the Perkins Folio, but also other manuscripts that Collier had discovered and published. This assertion was coupled with an announcement and a lie. Hamilton's *Preface* declared, for the first time publicly, that it was Frederic Madden's judgement that the emendations were forged, not an unexpected piece of news, but a somewhat awkward one coming from Hamilton whose purpose was apparent in the statement which followed. 'The correspondence between certain pencil-marks in the margins with corrections in ink, *first noticed by myself'*, Hamilton wrote, 'led him to a closer examination of the volume . . .' (emphasis added).[1] This statement, approved by Madden, is false. It is flatly contradicted by Madden's diary entries and by his correspondence which, as we have seen, proves it was Madden who discovered the pencil marks. Madden had his own reasons for wanting to set himself at a distance from the discovery of the most dramatic – and damning – evidence against Collier, and Hamilton was therefore encouraged to take credit for it.

Hamilton denied prejudice against Collier. His concern, he declared, was to arrive at the true facts, but his real objective was readily apparent:

I naturally supposed that Mr. Collier ... would have hastened to lend his aid to sift to the bottom the particular evidences against the credibility of the volume, which I had brought so distinctly and prominently to his notice. In this, however, I was mistaken. So far from assisting in an inquiry, in the results of which he, more than any living man, must have been deeply interested, he has only broken silence to give utterance to a desire, rather petulantly expressed, and under circumstances impossible to regard, that he and his Folio might be let alone, and considered privileged from further scrutiny.[2]

This was a grossly distorted interpretation of Collier's letters, as anyone who had read them would know. But there was an even more insidious suggestion in Hamilton's remarks. Collier had not been invited, directly or indirectly, to help 'sift to the bottom' the evidence which Hamilton and Madden were extracting from the volume, and he would certainly have been turned away had he arrived at the Museum to offer his 'assistance'. To imply that he had refused an invitation to participate in the Museum's examination was outrageous. The prejudice in that suggestion permeates the whole of *An Inquiry*.

Hamilton's announced intention in publishing the book was 'to redeem the pledge' given to the public in *The Times* of 2 July, to give 'other particulars relating to this remarkable volume.'[3] The pledge was not redeemed. True, Hamilton repeated the charges in greater detail than the columns of *The Times* had allowed, but he gave no new evidence concerning the folio, no 'other particulars' which might support his earlier contention. In particular, the book produced no new information about the pencil marks, surely the most damning 'evidence' against the Perkins Folio in the first announcement, the justification for Hamilton's first letter, and for Maskelyne's subsequent description. The discussion in *The Times* had been suggestive only, and more information was needed before they could become, as Hamilton and Madden obviously hoped they would, decisive evidence against Collier. In particular, Hamilton's charge could be proved only by a pencil *word* in demonstrably modern script underlying an 'antique' ink equivalent, but if Maskelyne had found such evidence, he had not yet made it public. Although Maskelyne indicated that he tested several suspected emendations, he gave only the example from *Richard II* to support his conclusion, and if one reads his letter with care, it was evident that his illustration did not prove the point, for in that instance the pencil mark was not a word but a 'tick', a mark which might have been made at any time from the seventeenth century to the nineteenth. Moreover, Maskelyne's comment that 'in several places' the pencil stopped 'abruptly at the ink' suggested that some of the pencil writing might have been made *after* the ink corrections were written (else why did it stop 'abruptly'?). The 'scientific evidence' was therefore incomplete, and it was a reasonable expectation that *An Inquiry* would produce the results of all of Maskelyne's experiments on the book along with a more complete statement of his conclusions.

It didn't. The first third of Hamilton's book (fifty pages) was merely a rehash of Collier's account of the folio's acquisition, Parry's involvement, the Museum investigation and its results – all of which had been described more succinctly in *The Times*. This recapitulation was particularly redundant since, like Ingleby, Hamilton reprinted the *whole* of *The Times* correspondence in a 25-page appendix to the book. There was no new information concerning Maskelyne's investigation. In fact, the only previously unpublished information in Hamilton's discussion of the book was a 20-page summary of his collation, undertaken at Madden's request, of the folio emendations in *Hamlet* as they contrasted with Collier's list of them in *Seven Lectures*. The comparison did indeed demonstrate his contention that Collier had included fewer than a third of these corrections in his so-called 'complete list' in *Seven Lectures,* but the damning conclusions which Hamilton tried to force from this fact were obscure. In fact, the collation might more easily have been construed to support Collier's innocence than to condemn him. Why would he have inserted several hundred corrections into the folio text of this play only to omit two-thirds of them when he published what purported to be the full list? As Hamilton suggested, some of the omitted corrections were so demonstrably bad that they might well have embarrassed Collier and decreased the apparent value of the whole, but if Collier recognized this by omitting them in his printed text, why would he have written them into the folio in the first place? Moreover, Hamilton showed that Collier appeared to have misread, to no substantive effect, a number of the folio insertions.[4] If, as Hamilton and Madden believed, Collier had himself fabricated the ink emendations, why should he have misread his own writing? Or, if he had deliberately misread to remove suspicion, why had he not made the book available earlier to reveal the discrepancy? Hamilton's list of *Hamlet* corrections was therefore not germane to his contention, and since it was the only 'new evidence' he provided against the Perkins Folio, one wonders why, except to pad out a thin volume, it was included at all.

Hamilton's discussion of the Perkins Folio was essentially a repetition of already published information, and if he had printed only the two-thirds of the book which its title announced, it would not have attracted the interest it did. What made the book significant was not the old claims against the folio but new 'evidence' of forgery that Madden and Hamilton had been sedulously collecting since the first accusation was made months before. Instead of supporting his original accusation as he had promised, Hamilton made new ones of a much more serious kind against other, superficially unrelated manuscripts that Collier had discovered and published in the previous quarter century. The effect was to widen the scope of the controversy and profoundly deepen the crime of which Collier was implicitly accused.

At first glance, this tactic might seem a bad one, the result of carelessness or frustration, but it was shrewdly consistent with Hamilton's motives. If either he or Madden had been actually concerned with disproving the validity of the Perkins emendations, he would indeed have had to produce new evidence to discount them, but Hamilton's primary intention (which was, of course, Madden's as well) was not to prove that the Perkins emendations were forged but rather that Collier was a forger, a related but separable objective, and since

Madden and Hamilton rejected Ingleby's case for internal evidence, there remained only two possibilities for proving their case, both circumstantial, but each in itself potentially sufficient to convict Collier.

The first and more preferable (because more irrefutable) of the two was to prove that the Perkins Folio had contained no ink writing when it came into Collier's possession (i.e., that it must have been emended thereafter either by his hand or under his guidance). Madden, Hamilton and Ingleby all believed this to have been the case, but short of an unlikely stroke of luck, it couldn't be proved. The best that could be mustered in its behalf was *negative* support of inconsistency in Collier's account of its acquisition or subsequent use (e.g., the Parry testimony); finding *positive* evidence of corrections after Collier bought the book was much less likely.

For this reason, Hamilton followed a second line of argument in *An Inquiry* by declaring that the writing in the Perkins Folio was identical to that used in other documents, which, if genuine, would necessarily have been written at different times by different scribes. It was for this reason that he emphatically and repeatedly declared that 'the whole of the forgeries treated in this volume [the Perkins Folio] *have been executed by one hand.*'[5] If the writing *were* identical in all the doubtful documents, the inescapable conclusion would have to be that Collier had forged it, for he was the sole link among them; he had claimed to discover them in a wide variety of disparate places over a period of many years, and he alone had published them all. If one hand had made them, it must have been his.

Chief among these 'new forgeries' were the five Ellesmere manuscripts which twenty-five years before Collier had published in *New Particulars* (1835), declaring he had found them in a bundle among the Bridgewater papers. In subsequent years the documents had been bound together (although they had no intrinsic connection) and often reexamined. Five were in dispute: I, a list (Collier had dated it 1608) of shareholders of the Blackfriars playhouse which included Shakespeare; II, a letter signed 'S. Danyell' and addressed to Thomas Egerton thanking him for patronage (without reference to Shakespeare); III, a petition which listed Shake-

speare as a player and shareholder in Blackfriars in 1589; IV, a
warrant appointing Robert Daborne and Shakespeare, among
others, to be instructors of the Children of the Revels in 1609;
and V, a letter addressed to Sir Thomas Egerton and signed
'H.S.' (whom Collier suggested was Southampton) recom-
mending Burbage and Shakespeare to the Chancellor. In
1845, Hunter had been the first to declare that three of these
(I, II, V) were 'modern fabrications' and although he later
qualified his condemnation somewhat, they remained suspect.
Eight years later, in 1853, Halliwell had picked up Hunter's
old charge and extended it, declaring that I and V were
'unsatisfactory', II and III 'doubtful', and IV a 'modern
forgery'. Although both Hunter and Halliwell had severely
discounted the genuineness of the manuscripts, neither had
done so absolutely. Now, seven years after Halliwell, Hamilton took up the case once again. He followed Halliwell closely,
in fact his arguments were taken verbatim and *in extenso* from
Halliwell's pamphlet, but whereas Halliwell had limited his
condemnation, Hamilton alleged that all of the Bridgewater
papers were palpable forgeries. Moreover, he declared, 'no
one, I think, who examines them carefully ... can doubt but
they they are all the work of the one pen', a declaration which
ignored Hunter and Halliwell's specific disagreement on this
point.

Although the charge against the Ellesmere manuscripts was
not new, it was nonetheless damning, because it was linked to
another. Hamilton declared that the emendations that Collier
had discovered many years before in the pages of the
Ellesmere First Folio Shakespeare were modern forgeries
written by the same hand that had fabricated the Ellesmere
manuscripts. The folio presumably had been in the family
collection since its publication in 1623, and when Collier
announced, in *Reasons for a New Edition of Shakespeare* (1841),
that he had discovered manuscript corrections in the book,
there had been some surprise at the discovery but no suspicion
of it. Now, however, Hamilton saw the corrections as part of '*a
series* of systematic forgeries which have been perpetrated,
apparently within the last half century ...'. The Ellesmere
folio, according to Hamilton

was supposed to be the finest copy of the first folio in existence, [but] little seems to have been known about it, until the year 1842, when the late Lord Ellesmere, then Lord Francis Egerton, lent the volume to Mr. Collier. How long it remained in that gentleman's custody I am not aware. . . . The alterations in this first folio are not numerous, but they are frequently identical with those afterward discovered by Mr. Collier in the folio of 1632; the identity in one or two instances being strikingly significant. Prior to their discovery by Mr. Collier, it does not seem, so far as I can learn, that any alterations were known to exist in the margins at all. He is certainly wrong in attributing them to the time of the Commonwealth; they are not only modern, but, decidedly, *by the same hand* as those in his more famous copy of the second edition.[6]

The statement was a virtual declaration that Collier had committed forgery: he alone had used both folios and he had discovered the writing in each. Hamilton's argument was internally inconsistent, of course; if 'little seems to have been known' about the Ellesmere folio before Collier used it, it was not particularly suspicious that no 'alterations were known to exist on the margins' before he found them there. Despite its seriousness Hamilton presented no evidence to support his accusation and he suggested it was up to Collier to refute the case against him.

Hamilton did not stop with the Bridgewater Collection. Once again, guided by Halliwell's pamphlet, he had searched the Alleyn Papers at Dulwich for evidence with which he might condemn Collier's use of Mrs. Alleyn's letter to her husband. The letter was still preserved in the Dulwich College library where Collier had found it in 1840, and close examination convinced Hamilton that Halliwell's contention was correct, that the letter, although much decayed, still had enough of its text to disprove the reference to Shakespeare which Collier had claimed to find in it twenty years before. Halliwell had blamed the disparity on Collier's careless transcription, but Hamilton called it an outright fabrication.

Even more important, the search at Dulwich unearthed three other documents that Hamilton denounced as obvious forgeries. The first was a letter of John Marston which Collier had found and published in the *Memoirs of Edward Alleyn* – the first publication of the Shakespeare Society in 1841. 'In its general aspect the writing of this letter certainly resembles Marston's genuine hand', Hamilton wrote, 'and has no doubt been executed by some one to whom that hand was familiar; but I soon noticed the existence of numerous modern pencil-marks underlying the ink, and on looking closely into the document, detected that *the whole of the letter had been first traced out in pensil, after the same fashion as the pencilling in the annotated folio of Shakspere's Plays,* 1632.'[7] This fact satisfied Hamilton that the letter was forged – and by the same person who had forged the Perkins Folio.

The other two documents had also been published in the *Memoirs,* and although there was no pencil beneath the ink, Hamilton denounced them. One was the poem beginning 'Sweet Nedde, nowe wynne an other wager'[8] which mentioned, among other details, 'Will's new play' which Hamilton declared was 'a forgery from beginning to end, although executed with singular dexterity.'[9] The other was a 'list of Players', including Shakespeare's name, which had been attached to a genuine document first published by Malone. Hamilton stated that it was forged, in the same hand that had written the 'H.S.' letter in the Bridgewater library. These three documents had never before been questioned, but Hamilton denounced them without analysis or corroborative details. Unlike the other accusations in *An Inquiry,* this judgement appears to have been Hamilton's own, for Madden had not yet examined the Alleyn papers when the book was written.

The last document that Hamilton condemned was a manuscript from the State Paper Office, purporting to be a petition on behalf of the Lord Chamberlain's Players in 1596 asking the Privy Council for permission to expand their theatre. It was, presumably, a copy of the original and gave the names of the signers, among them Shakespeare. It was easily the most important of the disputed documents, and when Collier had first printed it in his *History of English Dramatic Poetry* nearly thirty years before, he had emphasized its value: 'This remarkable paper', Collier had written, 'has perhaps, never seen the light from the moment it was presented, until it was very recently discovered. It is seven years anterior to the date of any other authentic record, which contains the name of our great dramatist, and it may warrant various conjectures as to the rank he held in the company in 1596, as a poet and as a player.'[10]

Hamilton took credit for being the first to recognize the spuriousness of the petition, but Duffus Hardy, then an Assistant Keeper of the Public Records and a fervent opponent of the Perkins Folio, may have brought it to his attention. In any case, Hamilton asked four experts (Madden and Hardy; Sir Francis Palgrave, Deputy Keeper of Public Records; and John Sherren Brewer, an authority of the State Papers of Henry VIII) to examine the petition, and after a brief examination (Madden's diary suggests it took less than an hour) the group unanimously declared that the document was 'spurious' and demanded that the Master of the Rolls attach their disclaimer to the document. In Hamilton's view, this made the petition a certified forgery, a 'treason against the Majesty of English literature'.[11]

An Inquiry, then, was much more than a rehash of old charges. Its failure to disclose the promised 'details' of the Museum examination of the Perkins Folio was largely overlooked in the welter of new accusations it contained and in light of the magnitude of the fraud that it suggested had been systematically carried out by the most eminent Shakespeare scholar in England. Before *An Inquiry,* Collier had only to exculpate the Perkins Folio; after it, his entire career was condemned and his character stigmatized. He was, in effect, accused of deliberately corrupting the manuscript collections of his patron Ellesmere, of Dulwich College, and of the State Record Office itself by introducing forgeries into them and of compounding this outrage by deluding the public with their subsequent 'discovery'. The crime, if real, was unprecedented in the history of English letters. The earlier impeachment of the Perkins Folio was by comparison almost trivial, and the key to the new accusations was the 'strangely modern' handwriting which Hamilton (through Madden) claimed to find in *all* the disputed documents. It pointed to a single source of infection, a forger of unprecedented knowledge and skill, no longer a mere 'old corrector' of the Perkins Folio but a fabricator of monstrous propensity.

There is a public fascination with enormous crimes which is not evoked by lesser ones. Reasonable and just men who would scorn ill-supported accusations of misdemeanours are sometimes prepared to credit more serious charges with less evidence. The possible 'crime' of the Perkins Folio was discounted by many, even by some most antagonistic to Collier, because rightly or not it seemed a relatively minor offence; but the charge of forgery on the scale Hamilton now described was a different matter. His new 'evidence' was circumstantial and the 'crime' he described hypothetical, but this lack of proof was not a significant deterrent to the public clamour which *An Inquiry* evoked. What Madden and Hamilton had failed to prove with the 'scientific' examination of the folio they ultimately succeeded in establishing by unsupported assertion. Simply put, by raising the level of the indictment, they secured a conviction, at least so far as most of the interested public was concerned.

As might have been expected, the journals which earlier had been most vehement in suggesting foul play in the Perkins Folio now overlooked the absence of the new evidence that Hamilton had promised, and seized on the new charges. The *Critic,* for example, wrote:

That there has been forgery committed – in fact, a whole series of forgeries, and by the same hand – we do not suppose that any reasonable and unprejudiced person, after this lucid and temperate statement of facts, will doubt.... If Mr. Collier values his reputation, he will come forth from the retreat to which he has betaken himself, and will establish his innocence of any complicity in these matters upon something sounder than mere assertion, upon something more dignified than an assumed disdain.[12]

The *Literary Gazette* was more moderate, but no more flattering:'For more than thirty years Mr. Collier has been known in the literary world as the keenest critic living of Shakspere and his times,' it declared, 'but how can that reputation be justified if the vaunted discoveries made by him prove to rest upon no more solid foundation than the MS. emendations of the "Old Corrector"?'[13] Even Robinson was shaken by the Museum book and its reception. He could not, he declared, examine questions like this because on the one hand he lacked the learning and on the other he was unwilling to think Collier a forger. But for the first time he had serious doubts about Collier's story. 'Indeed', he wrote in his diary, 'if he were guilty I could not call him my friend.'[13]

The question was, could Collier answer Hamilton? The new charges were portentous, nothing less than an assault on the reputation of one whom even his attackers called the 'foremost Shakespeare scholar'. That he *would* answer none doubted; to allow Hamilton's charges to remain undisputed would be, in effect, to admit that his career had been based on fraud; even if he were guilty he would have to say something, give some explanation for the remarkable series of fabrications which Hamilton, writing as his preface noted, under the aegis of the 'Department of Manuscripts, British Museum', had published.

There was some question whether he would be physically able to reply. As Robinson noted, Collier 'wanted the vigour to defend himself as he ought'.[14] He had passed his seventy-first birthday almost on the day Hamilton's book appeared. He suffered repeated attacks of quinsy; his rheumatism made it difficult for him to walk; his hands were frequently too swollen to hold a pen. Moreover, he had been waiting for the attack in increasing apprehension for over half a year. Nevertheless, aged, ill and nearly alone, Collier fought back. In less than two weeks he composed a 6,000-word reply to Hamilton and within another month he expanded this article to a 72-page pamphlet. He had not been idle during his long wait. He had 'new evidence' of his own.

25

The name was Wellesley, Dr. Henry Wellesley, Principal of New College, Oxford, a man of reputation and a scholar of importance. Wellesley had never met Collier, but he was troubled by Hamilton's accusations, particularly the implication that Collier had written the emendations in the Perkins Folio after he bought it from Rodd. Wellesley was disturbed, he told friends, because he himself had seen the Perkins Folio in Rodd's shop before Collier owned it, and it had *then* contained a profusion of notes. Among those to whom Wellesley mentioned his concern was S. Leigh Sotheby, an auctioneer and antiquary who knew Collier slightly, and

Sotheby reported the comment to Collier. Collier immediately wrote Wellesley asking for details, and on 13 August 1859, Wellesley replied. Although he did not recollect the precise date, he had been in Rodd's shop 'some years before' when a case of books arrived 'from the country'.

One of those books was an imperfect folio Shakespeare, with an abundance of manuscript notes in the margins [Wellesley wrote]. He [Rodd] observed to me that it was of little value to collectors as a copy, and that the price was thirty shillings. I should have taken it myself; but, as he stated that he had put it by for another customer, I did not continue to examine it, nor did I think more about it, until I heard afterwards that it had been found to possess great literary curiosity and value. In all probability Mr. Rodd named you to me, but whether he or others did so the affair was generally spoken of at the time, and I never heard it doubted that you had become the possessor of the book.[15]

The value of this information was obvious. The charges against Collier were based on the assumption that the folio had had no emendations in it when he purchased the book from Rodd and that he had subsequently assumed the guise of the 'Old Corrector' and written all the marginal notes. Wellesley's testimony seemed to disprove this claim. Since there was general agreement that all the notes were in the same hand, if Collier had not made them all, it followed that he could not have made any. If Wellesley's account were true, then, Collier could not be the 'Old Corrector', and since Madden had declared that the other imputed forgeries were in the 'Old Corrector's' hand, Collier, by extension, could not be guilty of fabricating *those* either.

Collier received Wellesley's letter within a few weeks of Hamilton's dispatch to *The Times* in July 1859, but Collier was canny and did not publish it immediately. He had heard of Madden's excursions into the Alleyn papers and the Ellesmere manuscripts, and good tactics required that he know all the charges the 'Museum pamphlet' was to contain before he answered any one of them. He therefore waited for his opponents to play their cards, sure now that his own hand held the trump he needed. Three weeks after *An Inquiry* appeared, he played it. In the *Athenaeum* of 18 February, 1870, he published his reply:

After a delay of more than seven months, Mr. N. E. S. A. Hamilton, as the mouthpiece of the Manuscript Authorities of the British Museum, has published his pamphlet against me [Collier wrote]. I began to be almost afraid that it would not appear at all, or at least during my life, while I could vindicate my own conduct and character; for, at the age to which I have arrived, no man can calculate upon having much time to spare.... The manner in which I have been pursued, especially since I committed the great offence of discovering the Corrected Folio of Shakespeare's Works, 1832, only shows how small a reputation in an inferior department of literature is sufficient to secure the bitterest hostility.

Collier then quoted Wellesley's letter of the previous August. The letter, he asserted,

will at once put an end to the discreditable insinuations (if they amount to no more) that I am the real author of the MS. notes in the Perkins Folio. They were all in the margins of the volume when it came into my hands in 1849, although from causes I explained, I was not aware of their existence till some time afterwards.[16]

Wellesley's letter was the core of Collier's defence of his use of the Perkins Folio, but since *An Inquiry* had made new charges against him, Collier answered them as well, partly by reassertion of earlier arguments, as in the case of Parry and the disputed Bridgewater documents, partly by introducing new evidence, as in the case of the Dulwich manuscripts and the petition in the State Paper Office. Hamilton had insinuated that Collier had deliberately misled Parry into thinking the folio had once been his. This, Collier declared, was false.

He reminded his readers that when he had announced Parry's identification of the folio seven years before, Parry had verified his account.

Upon these points, I cannot be mistaken, though Mr. Parry seems to have forgotten them ... I impute no blame to Mr. Parry: I have no personal acquaintance with him beyond what I have stated, but I believe him to be a man of honour and probity, and he is known to persons for whom I have the highest respect and esteem. [When] he went to the British Museum and saw Sir F. Madden, Mr. Hamilton, Mr. Maskelyne and others, he may have become confused, and they may have passed and re-passed the different folios of Shakespeare before his eyes until he did not remember which edition had been his own.[17]

The statement which Madden and Hamilton had received from Parry was highly questionable, Collier declared; so too were Hamilton's charges of forgery in the Bridgewater documents. Collier cited yet again the several authorities who, over a period of many years, had seen the manuscripts and had attested to their authenticity and value. The corroborating opinions of Dyce and Halliwell had been published before; both had testified more than once to the genuineness of the papers and neither had ever suggested the documents were made by a single hand. To these authorities Collier now added a third equally eminent: Joseph Netherclift, the facsimilist who had copied the Bridgewater documents for Collier's pamphlet. 'Surely', Collier wrote, 'if I had been conscious that all were forgeries, it was not likely I would have placed them, without the slightest scruple or control, in such skillful and knowing hands.'[18]

Hamilton's implication that Collier had deliberately falsified the transcription of Mrs. Alleyn's letter in the Dulwich collection was illogical on the face of it, he declared. The letter still existed only because Collier *himself* had taken special pains to preserve it. 'If my object had been to commit the imputed fraud, nothing could have been more easy than for me to have rubbed away a little more of the crumbling paper, and who then could have detected the trick?'

Finally, as to the petition from the players at Blackfriars Theatre, the State Paper manuscript which Hamilton, Madden, Hardy, *et al.* had condemned as forged by the 'Perkins hand', Collier declared that it had been found for him nearly thirty years before by Robert Lemon, Sr., then chief curator of the Office and now deceased, who not only unearthed it, but had a copy made for Collier.[19] Lemon was dead, but Collier's account was corroborated by his son, Robert Lemon, Jr., who succeeded his father at the State Paper Office. In response to a query from the *Athenaeum*, Lemon *fils* supported Collier: 'The Petition of the Players of the Blackfriars Theatre . . . was well known to my father and myself, before Mr. Payne Collier began his researches in this office', Lemon declared.[20]

Having thus produced Wellesley's letter, refuted Parry, added Netherclift's support to the earlier judgements of Dyce and Halliwell, and evoked the corroboration of Lemon's letter, Collier rested his defence.

Of Mr. N. E. S. A. Hamilton I knew nothing until I saw his accusatory epistle in the *Times* of the 2nd of July last; but according to the specimen before me, he does not seem very well qualified for the office of a literary detective.

He was surprised, Collier said,

that the Manuscript Department of the British Museum had entrusted such a cause to such obscure hands ... From Sir Frederic Madden, however, with whom I have been acquainted for more than thirty years, with whom I have often corresponded, and with whom I have exchanged books, I looked for rather different treatment.[21]

Collier's defence was a bravura performance, and it had the effect of reassuring his friends. Robinson, for example, declared in his diary that Collier's reply was 'successful beyond my expectation' against Hamilton's 'malignant' charges. Collier's 'tone', Robinson wrote, 'is manly and simple, and will propitiate many, and I see no fault in any part of his reasonings, though some faults may have escaped me.'[22] Nevertheless, Collier's letter did not produce an immediate public reaction in his favour. The public, in fact, was rapidly becoming sated with the controversy. It was prepared to believe the worst of Collier, perhaps, but the controversy was seen as a conflict among titans. The public observed the quarrel as it might a play, not as active participants who must decide but as observers awaiting the dénouement. In the public mind Collier's letter merely changed the positions of the players. Its chief effect was to tear away the veil of Madden's presumed disinterest. Collier clearly implied that his real antagonist was not N. E. S. A. Hamilton, but Frederic Madden.

For his part, Madden had to determine Collier's real intention. How far, he must have wondered, was Collier prepared to go? Was it significant that Collier had voiced only a sense of insult at Madden's behavior? Was he deliberately limiting his response, hoping that Madden would make amends of his own? Or would he now go on to suggest the little-known reasons for their animosity? In particular, would Collier now trumpet the details of the Hillier affair? Madden had good reasons for wanting that business left buried, and the fact that Collier had not dredged it up might have suggested to him that if he were now to retreat from his accusation of forgery, Collier would say no more about Madden's past indiscretions.

Madden seems to have been ready to pull back a bit. At least he was not ready to reply to Collier's comment. Somewhat to his dismay, he realized that he had become pretty much alone in asserting Collier's guilt, that the Shakespeare editors who were the most likely to gain from Collier's demise were strangely absent from the public dispute. Staunton, Dyce, Halliwell, Hunter – where were *they*? Off preparing their next editions, no doubt. They had urged him to the fore while they remained quietly behind the scenes. They had, Madden bitterly noted in his diary, 'been a great deal too silent in the business. *They* surely ought to feel indebted to me for the detection of a series of impostures which disfigures not only the text of Shakespeare's plays, but falsified the new facts known of his life.'[23] But now, when he needed their support, they were absent. Staunton, for example, was eager for Madden to denounce Collier in time to help promote his forthcoming edition of Shakespeare, but Staunton himself had written nothing – at least not over his own name – against Collier or the folio, and he was not prepared to do so now. Why, Madden wondered, should he fight his fight alone? For the time being, then, he held back, as he put it, 'remaining quiet, although burning with indignation'.[24] He was keeping an option open; if Collier by some chance were to say no more, Madden, too, might remain silent and the Hillier affair might remain buried.

But that was only a possibility, and Madden knew he had to prepare for the worst. Wellesley's testimony devastated the attempt to make Collier the forger of the Perkins Folio emendations, and Madden was determined to discredit Wellesley in any way possible. On 20 February, two days after the appearance of Collier's letter to the *Athenaeum,* Madden wrote to Wellesley demanding details:

I shld. feel extremely obliged if you could from memory or memoranda furnish me with more precise information on the subject.

1. Mr. Collier states that he purchased his copy of the 1632 edition of Rodd in the Spring of 1849. May I beg to ask of you were you then in London or whether you could fix with certainty, if at this time you saw the volume in Rodd's shop?

2. Mr. Collier's copy of Shakespeare was bound in rough calf (or sheep) without any letter on the back, and having the name [Madden here reproduced] 'Tho. Perkins his Booke' written in large letters on the outside of the upper cover. Its appearance is so striking as to attract the notice of any one who examined the volume. Do you remember that this was the binding &c. of the copy you saw at Rodd's?

Probably at this distance of time you would not be able to speak as to the number or nature of the manuscript notes – you are probably not aware that Mr. Collier's folio (now the Duke of Devonshire's) is still in the hands of his Grace's solicitor Mr. Currey, 9 Old Burlington St. and it would be very important, should you be in town, to spare time to look at this volume, and judge if it is the same noticed by you in Rodd's hands.[25]

Wellesley replied by return post that he would look at the folio as soon as he had an opportunity, but he couldn't be sure when that would be and he had 'very little hope of furnishing ... any additional information of importance.'[26]

Nevertheless, within three days Wellesley visited Currey's office, examined the book, and wrote to Madden again:

Happening to be called to London upon business yesterday, I obtained a sight of the Shakespeare at No. 9 Old Burlington St. and am of opinion that it is the same which I saw at Rodd's shop. With respect to the name of Perkins on the cover its appearance in my opinion is not such as to attract notice, or strike the eye of an ordinary observer. It is much faded, and become nearly of the same brown as the leather, so that unless you had directed my attention to it, I probably might not have noticed it. When I saw the book at Rodd's the MS. notes in the body of the book engaged my chief attention, and the binding is so manifestly of a later century that such a particular as a modern name upon it, apparently immaterial at that time, would not have dwelt on my mind.

In addition, Wellesley had consulted his bills from Rodd and found that the latest was dated March 1849, but he might have seen the book before then. 'I have not been abroad for more than thirty years past, and cannot say that in the spring of any year I have not been within easy reach of London, or staying there for a short period', he concluded.[27]

Madden's reaction to Wellesley's letter dispels any doubt about his true motives in the affair. If his interest had been merely to determine the origin of the marginal notes, as he maintained it was, he surely would have let it be known that Wellesley had examined the Perkins Folio and positively identified it as the same he had seen in Rodd's shop with the emendations already on its pages. But Madden did *not* make Wellesley's declaration public, and Wellesley, perhaps dismayed at finding himself in the midst of an acrimonious quarrel, was not ready to make the announcement himself. He had responded to the requests of men of presumed probity; he had declared what he believed to be the truth and had got little public thanks for his information; he could only incur the calumny of Collier's enemies by volunteering more. For his part, Madden was silent *because* Wellesley's identification exculpated Collier. His real motive was to indict the man, not to discredit the book. He was motivated not only by personal animosity but by a desire to find a 'simple' answer to the question of the emendations. 'If Mr. Collier's the forger', he wrote in his diary, 'everything in the whole business can easily be accounted for; by supposing Mr. Collier to be guiltless, everything is inexplicable!'[28] This, of course, was not true – only Madden's judgement that all the forgeries were in a single hand would be 'inexplicable' if Collier were innocent, but he blocked out all other possibilities.

Collier's letter to the *Athenaeum* ought to have created a 'reasonable doubt' of his guilt. Moreover, his claims for the book (as opposed to the emendations) had been reduced almost to non-existence: he was obviously no longer able to make any case for its 'authoritative' provenance; the corrections, he now declared, must be judged on their *intrinsic* merit only. He had thus given up some of his reputation for perspicacity to shore up his character as an honest man. But the trade-off came too late: his critical reputation suffered by this latter day admission, but his character was not enhanced. The controversy had already gone beyond reasonable argument and had become, instead, grist for the weeklies. The fact that Collier, once again, had published his answer in the *Athenaeum* guaranteed the continued enmity of that paper's rivals, particularly the *Spectator,* the *Illustrated London News,* and the *Critic,* which had undertaken to be the champions of the 'museum authorities' against the 'Collierites'. Typically, the *Spectator,* within a week of Collier's letter, responded vituperatively. The effect of Collier's answer, it declared, was 'to make his position even worse than before'. His reply was 'weak', 'shifty', and 'irrelevant', and it 'deliberately avoided the evidence'. Why, the *Spectator* asked (in an irrelevancy of its own), had Collier pretended to publish a 'complete' list of the emendations in *Seven Lectures* when he actually printed fewer than half? As for Wellesley's statement, well, there was no supporting evidence that the book he saw was the Perkins Folio.[29]

An article in the *Critic* of the same day was even more vehement. It was by William Vaux, who called himself 'Vindex', but it might have been written by Madden himself, so clearly did it voice what Madden wanted the world to believe. The purpose of Vaux's 'review' was to vindicate the Manuscript Department of the British Museum. It was 'purely accidental' that the examination took place at the Museum, Vaux declared. 'The book was sent there as a convenient place for its examination, out of deference to the wishes of many who have no connection with it or its officers.' Although Collier had declared the book had been kept from him, Vaux wrote, no difficulty had been placed in his way. 'If Mr. Collier did not avail himself of the ... opportunity [he] probably better than any one else – could tell, if he chose, why he did not.' As to the delay of the Museum pamphlet, it was caused by the announcement that the Duke of Devonshire was undertaking a new investigation of the folio. 'Doubtless the *Athenaeum* could tell what secret causes prevented this much-wished meeting taking place.' In any case, Hamilton withheld publication of *An Inquiry* because he did not have 'the slightest wish to prejudge the case'.[30]

These were gross mis-statements of fact, and Vaux was

either lying or he had been deliberately misinformed by Madden. Anyone in the Museum would have known that it was not 'accident' that brought the Perkins Folio there, and Madden at least knew that its presence there had been kept from Collier by design. Moreover, Madden knew there was to be no 'new investigation' of the folio – he had ascertained that from Devonshire himself – and apparently he had not told Vaux of Wellesley's positive identification of the folio, since Vaux declared Wellesley's account to be 'hazy and unsatisfactory'. Lemon's verification of the State Paper had to be discounted, Vaux declared, because Lemon was one of Collier's 'thick-and-thin supporters' – a remarkable argument to be made by a man who was himself a pseudonymous partisan.

Collier's reference to Joseph Netherclift was to have repercussions. Netherclift was the foremost facsimilist in England. He had trained his son, Frederick, to be a copyist and lithographer, and for several years father and son carried on the business jointly until they suffered a falling out and Frederick set up his own shop. One of Frederick's first customers was Hamilton who engaged him to make the lithographs which illustrated *An Inquiry*. Netherclift senior had examined the Perkins Folio with great care on several occasions (he had, for example, made at least nineteen facsimiles from it for private distribution by Collier), and he had seen no pencil marks corresponding to those his son now reproduced in his facsimiles for Hamilton. He determined to disassociate himself from *An Inquiry*, and in a letter to the *Athenaeum* he denied any connection with it:

As the general reader may suppose that I have been engaged by both parties, permit me to state, that not myself, but my son, F. G. Netherclift, who is separated from me and in business alone, was employed by the party at the British Museum on the fac-similes in Mr. Hamilton's pamphlet. I had no knowledge of it or part in it, nor, under the circumstance, would I have attempted to show pencil marks over or under any ink writing by the mode of printing; whilst, from my knowledge of facts, and my high respect for the character of Mr. Collier, for whom I have made very numerous fac-similes in the course of the last thirty years, I could not have joined in any way to aid this causeless and cruel persecution against him.[31]

Netherclift's letter brought the question of the pencil marks to the fore once again. Although the pencil was the basis for declaring the emendations a *modern* forgery and as such constituted a damning piece of evidence against Collier personally, it was not an easy 'proof' to accept. *Why* would any forger let the book out of his hands without first *erasing* the pencil? It seemed beyond belief that someone expert enough to execute the supposed ink forgeries would be dimwitted enough to leave behind tell-tale evidence of their fabrication. The pencil marks seemed almost *too* convenient a proof of forgery, and there was a predisposition to believe Collier when he implied in his *Athenaeum* letter that the pencil marks were made after the book left his possession. 'I never saw them,' he declared, 'and they were never seen by anybody . . . until the Perkins Folio had found its way to the British Museum. There, and there only, they originated, I mean of course the discovery of them . . .'[32] He meant – of course – the *fabrication* of them, and Joseph Netherclift's declaration that his son was involved in a 'causeless and cruel persecution' of Collier left little doubt as to where Netherclift thought the pencil marks had originated and why they had been made.

It was an awkward position for the 'Museum faction'. Once again, an unimpeachable witness had volunteered to support Collier's story. Netherclift's reputation was such that he had nothing to gain and much to lose by publicly allying himself with a man accused, albeit by indirection, of forgery. How could his evidence be discounted?

It couldn't, in fact, at least not directly, but there were attempts at explaining it away, the most ingenious of which was made by yet another anonymous writer in the *Critic*, who suggested the pencil *had* been erased but had reappeared: 'The explanation of this is that, when you think you have rubbed out the marks, what you have really done is . . . removed the looser particles of the plumbago, and you have *roughed up the surface of the paper, so as to hide for a time the indentations and the plumbago, which has entered, as it were into the pore of the paper.* This concealment, however, is only temporary, and when the surface of the paper has been well pressed, and the roughened portions have had time to regain their position, the marks reappear.'[33] This fanciful explanation however did not refute the charges of collusion, and a week later Hamilton felt it necessary to defend the Museum once again.[34] Madden disapproved of the new defence. He was waiting for Collier's next move.

It was not long in coming. From the first Collier had intended to publish his rebuttal in more substantial form than the pages of an ephemeral weekly newspaper. He was sure that a pamphlet version of his defence would have a brisk sale and about such things he was seldom wrong. Within three weeks of the letter, therefore, his expanded *Reply*[35] was in the press, and within a month, in the bookstalls. It was essentially a 72-page recapitulation of his earlier concise answer, but it had a few novelties, and in one of them Madden realized his worst fears.

Collier's *Reply* seemed at first a mere rehash. He once again complained about the delayed appearance of *An Inquiry* and reiterated details of the purchase of the Perkins Folio, neatly inserting into the chronology the new information of Wellesley's corroboration. He repeated the account of Carrick Moore's letter of the phenomenal good luck of Parry's positive identification and of his own subsequent dismay over Parry's recantation. All of this Collier had written before, but in his repetition he was working up to a more subtle and shocking point, the suggestion that the British Museum authorities might deliberately have doctored the book to incriminate him. There was good evidence that the book was misused while it was in the Museum, Collier implied. 'I apprehend, on the showing of my antagonist, that something has been obliterated with or without the consent of the present noble owner of the book', he wrote, and perhaps something had been added, too? Certainly the pencilling was not in the book when he owned it, as Netherclift's recent letter had proved, but, apart from that, why was it there? To what purpose was the pencil notation inserted?

Is it not strange [Collier asked] if pencil-marks can be pointed out, as supposed instructions for such words, and fragments of words, as Mr. Hamilton has given us, that not the smallest trace of pencil is to be found in connexion with the entire lines, sentences, and parts of sentences, which abound in the Perkins folio? ... Supposing for an instant, – I only suppose it – that anybody had maliciously and surreptitiously introduced these specks and spots for the purpose of discrediting the ink emendations, it would have been very easy to have applied them as hints for a lithographer in forming such short words as 'wall,' 'now,' or 'over' (which Mr. Hamilton has relied upon), but impossible to have annexed them to whole lines and sentences without their being observed in an instant, and followed by the naked eye.[36]

The pencil writing was therefore not of a kind to be useful to one fabricating the ink emendations, but only to one wishing – surreptitiously – to *discredit* them. His own pencil marks were clearly of another sort:

I declare most positively, in the face of the whole world, that, while the Perkins folio was in my hands, I never saw a pencil-mark in it that I had not made myself, either as a note of reference to some other book, or as a point of observation connected with the book itself. If I wanted to be sure not to forget to look at a particular passage in *Malone,* or in any other commentator, or if I wished to note something that required again to be examined in the folio, I took the ordinary method with a pencil that I always kept at hand; but that I thus added the slightest hint with reference to any projected alteration of the language of the poet I deny in the strongest form in which it is possible to clothe a denial. If a fancy should ever cross the mind of any one who has ever seen me write, that such and such a word or letter in Mr. Hamilton's lithograph is not unlike my hand, I can only say that for the last fifty years my handwriting must have been familiar to many in the British Museum; and that if the likeness has been more than merely accidental, the fact has an origin not much to the credit of our national establishment.[37]

Now, given the evidence which should argue for his innocence, why should anyone in the Museum have undertaken to prove that forgery had been committed? Collier protested he was at a loss to understand the motives behind the Museum inquiry and then proceeded to suggest a shocking explanation:

I was always upon good terms with Sir F. Madden, whom I have known for more than a quarter of a century, and upon two occasions I was of some service to him. Of one of them I can say no more; but of the other I may remark that it occurred within the last two or three years, and it was when he had involved himself in an awkward scrape by purchasing manuscripts, which he ought to have known had been dishonestly come by.

The manuscripts, Collier confided, had 'in some way escaped' from the Ellesmere collection, and one of them was very well known, having been printed 'in a volume, with which Sir F. Madden ought to have been well acquainted. . . . Really and truly, if Sir F. Madden had then been indicted for receiving stolen goods, knowing them to have been stolen, it might have gone hard with him.' After piously declaring, 'I should willingly have been one of his witnesses to character', Collier continued,

Some men can forget an injury who never can forget an obligation; but I assure Sir F. Madden he was not in the slightest degree indebted to me on the occasion: all along the Earl Ellesmere was convinced that the Keeper of the Manuscripts had only acted carelessly, not criminally.[38]

Thus, by fact and innuendo, Collier suggested fraud by the Museum and a personal vendetta motivating Madden. With studied casualness, Collier exposed Madden's more or less secret transgression to public knowledge and condemnation and hurried on to what he declared was the 'real' question of the Perkins Folio – not the pencil marks but the intrinsic value of the emendations. 'To have only suggested them would have made the fortune of any man', he wrote, 'and, if I were the real author of them, what could have induced me *to foist them into an old folio and to give anybody else the credit of them*? The charge is so ridiculous that it carries its own contradictions.'[39] Misguided by Madden, he implied, the Museum authorities had forgotten the merit of the corrections and been carried away in a rush to meaningless microscopic detail.

If I forged them, the least they can do is to give me credit for them; and I can only say that I would fain accept them upon any other terms than that of having been their fabricator. Only make out for me a legal and legitimate paternity, and I will adopt the numerous and well-looking family with joy and gratitude.[40]

Having answered the case against the folio, Collier directed his *Reply* to the other charges against him, those concerning the Bridgewater papers, the Dulwich manuscripts, and the petition in the State Paper Office. For the Bridgewater 'forgeries', his defence was yet another re-telling of their discovery, their examination by Joseph Netherclift, and their enthusiastic acceptance by Dyce and Halliwell. His argument was what it had always been: if these were forgeries, surely many others besides himself had been misled by them! As for the Dulwich manuscripts, Collier declared they had been 'most unfairly thrown into the scales, in order that they may weigh against me with the rest of Mr. N. E. S. A. Hamilton's accumulation of trash and trumpery'.[41] Chief among the Dulwich documents which Hamilton had declared 'modern' forgeries 'in the same hand as the Perkins emendations', was the 'list of players' which included Shakespeare's name. Collier had published the list in his *Memoirs of Edward Alleyn* in 1841 and until *An Inquiry* appeared, no one had disputed its authenticity, but now, almost twenty years later, Collier was forced to defend the scrap. Fortunately he could do so with a hitherto unknown bit of evidence. In 1796, Edmond Malone, the great Shakespeare scholar, had published another *Inquiry*[42] that decisively proved, partly on the basis of documents Malone had found at Dulwich, that reputed 'Shakespeare manuscripts', 'unearthed' and published by William Henry Ireland, were, in fact, forgeries. The book was highly successful, and according to Collier, Malone planned a second revised edition and carefully corrected a copy of the book to that end, filling it with marginalia and interleaved insertions. The second edition never appeared but, Collier declared, 'some years' after *Memoirs of Edward Alleyn* had been published, he had purchased the copy of *Inquiry* that Malone had annotated, and among the scraps pasted in the volume was one in Malone's handwriting which clearly alluded to the imputed list of players. In addition, Malone's book supported Collier's version of Mrs. Alleyn's letter. In Collier's view, a sentence in the text indicated that, at least as early as 1796, Malone had seen the reference to 'Mr. Shakespeare of the Globe'. Thus, whatever the authenticity of these documents, their existence had been confirmed by Malone when Collier was a mere boy. If they were forgeries, Collier could not have been their forger.

Hamilton's aspersions were as small-minded as they were

maladroit. Why, Collier wanted to know, did he seek out such paltry, unimportant details in minor documents and ignore significant, undisputed discoveries that Collier had made among the Dulwich manuscripts? What of the unique actor's 'part' of *Orlando Furioso*? What of the dozens of letters and other Alleyn documents Collier had discovered and published? 'All these receive no comment', he noted with disdain, 'and with very good reason I can well believe.'[43]

Finally, as for the supposed 'forgery' in the State Paper Office, Collier declared that Lemon's letter had settled the question once and for all. That it was genuine Collier had no doubt, but genuine or forged, its existence had been known before Collier had ever visited the Office or used its collection. As Collier summed up his case,

beyond all cavil or dispute, are, 1. That the manuscript notes were in the Perkins folio when I bought it in 1849, if not fifty years before that date; – 2. That I discovered the Bridgewater House manuscripts precisely under the circumstances stated, and that the authenticity of some of them was maintained by the best judges of our day, both literary and artistic; – 3. That the Dulwich manuscripts were in the condition I have described them at least as far back as the year 1796, as is evidenced, among other proofs, by Malone's *Inquiry* of that date; – and 4. That with regard to the Player's Petition of 1596, if it be a forgery at all, it was a forgery before I set foot inside the State Paper Office, before I commenced my researches there, and before I even knew where the Office was situated.[44]

It was to be his last public statement on the controversy, his last defence. '*Hic arma repono*', he wrote at its conclusion – and he meant it.

26

Whatever hope Madden had had of avoiding a direct confrontation was swept away by Collier's public accusation. The pamphlet was published on 16 March 1860, and Madden, according to his diary, read it promptly. 'I am perfectly astonished at the man's audacity and villainy', he wrote the next day. 'He is a *blackguard* to all intents and purposes. Of course, the infamous charges made by him against me and my Department must be answered, and however unwilling hitherto I may have felt to appear in print, I am now compelled to come forward.'[45] Others urged him on. Hamilton argued that Collier had 'relied' on Madden's 'previous silence' and had ventured 'daring insinuations' against the whole department that Madden must answer.[46] Staunton, too, redoubled his efforts to have Madden write something he could use in the final volume of his Shakespeare, then about to go to press ('Bring that weak impostor, Perkins, to a moral gibbet', he wrote to Madden. 'Pray don't hold back'.)[47]; and James Lowe, editor of the *Critic* and author of that journal's most brazen criticism of Collier, suggested Madden write something for his columns (for pay, of course), in answer to Collier's 'extraordinary statement'.[48]

These entreaties were reassuring but unnecessary; Madden's rage was motivation enough. Immediately after reading the *Reply* he dispatched a letter to *The Times* hotly denying Collier's charges against the Museum:

Mr. J. P. Collier.... has insinuated, on no obscure terms, that the recent 'pencillings' on the margins of this folio were inserted at the British Museum, and further, that if these pencillings should be thought to resemble his own handwriting, it is only to be ascribed to the fact that his hand must have been familiar to many in the Museum. I feel it, therefore, due to the Duke of Devonshire and to the Museum to declare that during the time the folio Shakespeare was committed to my charge, it was kept strictly under my own custody and responsibility, and I deny most positively that any note, either in pencil or ink, was made in the volume.... As to the offensive personalities of Mr. Collier towards myself, they appear to be designed only to divert attention from the real points at issue, and I shall not notice them here, further than to declare that Mr. Collier has knowingly misrepresented the facts.[49]

Madden's letter attempted to avoid the central issue of the Hillier affair. It also seemed to suggest that only Hamilton had been accused of deception and that Madden's assertion that the Perkins Folio had been under his 'own custody and responsibility' was sufficient proof that it had not been tampered with. Madden's declaration – like Collier's own – was merely an assertion of personal honesty and his airy dismissal of 'offensive personalities' was an unconvincing attempt to deflect the charge against himself.

The letter to *The Times*, which was quickly reprinted by other papers, was the first of two replies that Madden wrote; the second was a longer letter written in response to Lowe's request for the *Critic*. In his first draft Madden ignored the Hillier affair and confined himself to his account of the 'circumstance' which led to the 'Collier Folio' (as he now called it) having been 'placed in his hands' by the Duke of Devonshire. Madden had asked for the book, he wrote, because Ingleby and Staunton 'more than once' had expressed their opinion that the emendations were 'of recent origin' and had sought his opinion on the subject. Madden declared that he had 'expressed great surprise at their statement' and manifested 'the utmost unwillingness to believe that so large a body of notes could have been fabricated, or, if fabricated, could escape detection.' Nevertheless, Madden's story went on, he wrote to Collier on 6 September 1858, asking that he might 'procure' a 'sight of the Folio'. To this request, Madden declared, he received no answer. In May 1859, Mr. Watts, Superintendent of the Reading Room, introduced Professor Bodenstedt who 'expressed his great desire to see the Collier Folio' and Madden 'promised them to gratify, if possible, their and my own wishes on the subject, as well as to give several of my Shakesperian friends an opportunity of examining the volume.' Accordingly he wrote to the Duke and received the Perkins Folio on 26 May. On the evening of that date, he declared, he

wrote letters to Professor Bodenstedt, the Rev. A. Dyce, Mr. W. J. Thoms (a friend of Mr. Collier) and, I believe, Mr. Staunton, inviting them to see the volume.

Having thus succeeded in obtaining the volume my next step was to examine it critically on paleographic grounds, and this I did on the following morning very carefully, together with Mr. Bond, the Assistant Keeper of my Department, and we were both struck with the very suspicious character of the writing – certainly the work of one hand, but presenting varieties of forms assignable to different periods – the evident painting over of many of the letters, and the artificial look of the ink. The day had not passed before I had quite made up my mind, that the 'Old Corrector' never lived in the seventeenth century, but that the notes were fabricated at a recent period. On the 28th Mr. Dyce came to see the volume in my study, on the 30th Mr. Forster; on the 31st Professor Bodenstedt, and on the 1st and 2nd of June, Mr. Bruce (another friend of Mr. Collier). On the latter day, also, Mr. Hamilton first examined the volume, and called my attention to the numerous words expunged in the margin, either with an acid or rubbed out, apparently with the finger, and many more half effaced. The motives of the 'Old Corrector' in this proceeding began to appear most enigmatical.

... From the commencement of June not a day passed without the volume having been inspected constantly in my study by literary and other persons, and almost always in my presence. There was no preference given, nor am I aware that any special 'invitations' were sent out (as Mr. Collier says) to any one to come and examine the book. It was on the 6th of June, when Dr. Mansfield Ingleby was examining certain passages of the volume very closely, that he first directed my attention to a pencil-mark which appeared to him to be under the ink; but I did not then pursue the inquiry. Within a week, however, afterwards, Mr. Hamilton again spoke to me on the subject of the pencillings he had discovered some of which seemed to be underneath the writing. On this being pointed out to me, I again looked through the volume page by page, and was inexpressibly astonished to discover hundreds of marks of punctuation and corrigenda in pencil, more or less distinct in an apparently modern hand which were evidently intended as a guide to the 'Old Corrector,' and in all cases followed by a corresponding alteration of the text in ink. Entire words were also found written in pencil by the same hand, followed by a similar correction in ink; and to my eyes, as well as those of Mr. Bond and Mr. Hamilton, it seemed undeniable that several of these pencillings *did underlie the ink*. The scientific assistance of Professor Maskelyne (who now saw the book for the first time) was then requested, and the result of his examination by the microscope was to prove the fact, which to a practised eye had previously appeared all but certain. Now then I would ask, by whom and at what time could these recent pencillings have been made? Certainly not at the Museum. It is a simple impossibility; but if any further denial is required, I declare positively that the whole of these pencillings, together with the ink notes, must have been in the volume when it was first sent to me, and that during the time it was in my care, it was kept in the strictest custody. The charges so boldly advanced by Mr. Collier, that 'thousands of specks and atoms' might have been made in the volume in the Department of Manuscripts, and then construed into letters, as well as his insinuation that the fac-simile published by Mr. Hamilton (so faithfully executed by the lithographer, Mr. F. Netherclift, Junr.) is unfair or imaginary, are absolutely and wholly void of foundation. But writes Mr. Collier, he expected different treatment from Sir F. Madden. And wherefore? It is true that for nearly thirty years I have been on terms of literary friendship with Mr. Collier, but is it on that account I am not to be allowed to give an opinion on a forged document, because he happens to have printed it? Other editors and lovers of Shakespere have been and are still my friends, besides Mr. Collier, and from my official position, I felt bound to examine the volume and give a conscientious opinion of it. The most absurd reasons have been assigned by Mr. Collier and his party for my conduct – in one place, that I was hostile to him, because he had been proposed to be head of the Museum; and in another, because he had given his folio Shakspere to the Duke of Devonshire, instead of depositing it in the Museum! As to the former, I can only say I never heard of such an intention until I read it in the *Athenaeum* of the 18th February; and as to the latter, I assert that I knew not that the folio had been given to the Duke, until so informed by Dr. Ingleby, in 1858.

Madden declared that Collier's description of 'what may have happened' when Parry came to the Museum was false:

Mr. Parry came of his own accord to see me, and I received him in my study. On his entry there was no one else present, and I placed the Collier folio on the table before him, and requested him to tell me if it was the copy formerly in his possession. Mr. Parry looked at it externally and internally, and then, without the slightest hesitation, declared that *it was not his book, and that it has never been shown to him* by Mr. Collier. I was astonished at this declaration, and sent for Mr. Hamilton, to whom Mr. Parry repeated his statement, and, at my request, wrote [it] down....

The letter concluded with Parry's (or rather, Madden's) statement, already quoted, and the vague disclaimer Madden had written to *The Times*, adding that Collier might have proposed 'the nomination of a tribunal of competent persons' to examine the whole of these Shakespere forgeries.[50]

As soon as Lowe read the piece he knew it would not do because there was no explanation of the purchase of the Bridgewater MSS from Hillier. This was the 'extraordinary statement' that had prompted Lowe to solicit Madden's reply in the first place. Lowe immediately wrote to Madden that he must answer concerning the Ellesmere papers.[51] This, of course, was the very subject that Madden wished not to mention.

Nevertheless, at Lowe's demand, he tried to defend his position. In the letter finally published in the *Critic* he wrote:

For the sake, apparently, of diverting the attention of the public from the real points at issue, he has not scrupled to bring a charge against me which he must have known to be false . . . he refers to the purchase by me of certain documents which 'had escaped from Lord Ellesmere's collection,' and his charge is that I bought manuscripts which 'I ought to have known had been dishonestly come by.' . . . Never was any transaction so wilfully misrepresented! The facts are these: In October 1854 (not two or three years ago, as Mr. Collier states) some circumstances occurred which induced me to doubt whether a number of loose papers and an original document on parchment in a very damaged state, which had been purchased some time previously from a person of great apparent respectability (and who stated he had bought them at Shrewsbury), were fairly come by, and whether the parchment document might not have 'escaped' from Lord Ellesmere's library. As soon as this doubt arose I wrote to Mr. Collier, and requested him to come as soon as possible to examine these manuscripts, as I wished to communicate the result to Lord Ellesmere before I brought it to the notice of the Trustees. Mr. Collier came a day or two afterwards, and was shown the whole of the documents purchased. Mr. Collier then wrote to Lord Ellesmere, who knew nothing of the matter but expressed his obligation to myself; and it was only by means of a letter from the individual of whom I had bought the papers (communicated by me to Mr. Collier) that it was ascertained how they had been lost. It was at my suggestion that Lord Ellesmere applied to the Trustees for the restoration of the manuscripts; and it was not till after the meeting of the committee, on the 11th November, that Lord Ellesmere thought of referring the matter to his solicitor, and, after some legal discussion, the whole of the manuscripts were finally restored to Bridgewater House. What 'service' was rendered to me by Mr. Collier in this affair, I am at a loss to understand. On the contrary, I have good reason to believe that Mr. Collier prejudiced Lord Ellesmere's mind against me. I had acted throughout openly and without reserve. I had bought the manuscripts of a respectable individual; I was quite unconscious of the real ownership; I was the first to assist in the restoration of the manuscript to the owner.

As to Collier's statement that Madden had been 'ignorant' in not recognizing the documents because they had been published by the Camden Society, Madden was scornful: the book had been published thirteen years before. 'Is it not requiring rather too much, even of the most accurate memory, to recall to mind two papers in the middle of a thick quarto volume, after such a lapse of time?' he asked. 'When I received Mr. Collier's volume from the Camden Society, I did what I doubt not some other members might have done, that is to say, place it on a shelf of my library unopened. . . . So much for the "obligation" which Mr. Collier says some men (meaning myself) can never forgive!'

Madden declared that, far from having any prejudices against Collier, he was actually his friend and supporter and he called upon two men who knew his opinions at the time – Mansfield Ingleby and Howard Staunton, no less – to attest to the fact that he was loath to believe Collier guilty of any crime until the evidence forced him to it.[52]

Subsequent issues of the *Critic* carried the letters from Ingleby and Staunton supporting Madden's claim. Ingleby wrote that he had called on Madden

in order to learn his opinion of the notes from his own mouth. He told me that he had never expressed any opinion whatever about the notes, and had never so much as seen the Folio. . . . I cannot fix the date of this visit. In the spring of 1859 I again called on Sir F. Madden. I told him that I had been unsuccessful in seeing the Perkins Folio at Devonshire House, in consequence of my being ill in bed at the time the Duke had (as I had been informed in a letter from the Duke) left out the book for my inspection. I said . . . I was convinced that the MS. notes were spurious. Sir F. Madden's reply was, that he could not believe that so large a number of corrections could have been fabricated in modern times; and added, with some warmth, that he was a friend of Mr. Collier's, and was satisfied that Mr. C.'s good faith was above suspicion.

At his request, Ingleby declared, Madden had agreed to write to the Duke to have the folio loaned to the Museum so that it could be given a 'paleographic examination'. Madden, Ingleby continued,

said that he had no objection to do so, but that he was then so fully occupied that he must postpone for the present making the application. . . . On the 6th June . . . Sir Frederic Madden told me that, after a very cursory examination, he had come to the conclusion that *the MS. notes were not in the handwriting of any given period, but were exceedingly clumsy imitations of some handwriting prevalent in the 17th century*. Sir Frederic, however, very earnestly expressed his belief in Mr. Collier's *bona fides*. If that belief has since been shaken, I should think the change must be due to those *damning* pencillings.[53]

On 7 April, the *Critic* printed Staunton's letter of support.

> I can testify [he wrote] that Sir Frederic undertook the investigation of the disputed folio with a marked reluctance, arising out of his long literary acquaintance with the gentleman. . . . So careful was Sir Frederic not to express a decision upon the writing until he had subjected it to the most searching examination, that it was not before the 20th June he communicated to me his opinion. He then told me, not without emotion, that, after a laborious and minute inspection, he had arrived at the painful conclusion – a conclusion altogether opposed to his feelings, and to his convictions before he had the volume entrusted to him – *that the whole of the annotations, from beginning to end, were the work of one hand, and that hand a very recent one*, in a word, that Thos. Perkins His Booke, was an elaborate and scandalous imposition.[54]

Madden's method and intention in his diaries is nowhere better illustrated than in his reference to this letter: 'There is a letter from Mr. Staunton in the *Critic* of today', he wrote in the entry for 7 April, 'entirely acquitting me of any feeling of hostility to Mr. Collier, which is but justice, as my Journal of last year will prove.' The Journal does not, in fact, 'prove' anything of the kind. Actually, the earlier entries show that Madden informed Staunton of his opinion not on 20 June but three weeks *earlier*, on 1 June – before the incriminating pencil marks were found. The later date nicely supports the story of Madden's *slow* acceptance of Collier's guilt. This comment once again reveals Madden's *intent* in the diary: he is writing not for himself – he presumably would not need 'proof' – but for a later reader. The average reader of the *Critic* would not know that Madden's defence and the corroboration of his friends was shot through with mis-statements of fact and interpretation, that, in aggregate, suggest Madden's story was written to mislead. For example, Madden's professed 'unwillingness to believe' that the Perkins Folio emendations had been fabricated is not evident in his diary; his great desire to 'procure' a sight of the book was motivated by his *own* curiosity and distrust of Collier; his 'request' to Collier for a look at the folio was not a direct solicitation but merely a statement of interest appended to a note thanking Collier for the gift of the facsimile of the *Hamlet* quarto and as such demanded no reply. Madden's statement that he had requested the folio from Devonshire at the behest of Professor Bodenstedt and Mr. Watts was, as already indicated, misleading and devious; Madden first informed *Dyce,* not Bodenstedt or Watts, that the folio was in the Museum. And Ingleby's letter proves (unwittingly) that the folio was available to interested scholars at Devonshire House before it went to the Museum. In his published defence, Madden declares that Bond was, from the first morning, a co-examiner of the folio, although the diary reveals that the initial examinations were made by Madden alone, that Bond was only very indirectly concerned with its examination, and that, in fact, Bond expressed serious reservations about Madden's conclusions and thought the writing might be genuine until the pencilling was pointed out to him. In this latter day, Madden obviously was eager to have others appear as involved as ... he in the exposé. In his diary, Madden correctly says that *he* was the first to discover the pencil writing[55] and that he showed it to Hamilton;[56] now, he wrote, Hamilton called them to *his* attention. In any case, Madden was clearly committed to believing the notes forged long before the pencilling came to light, and changing the date of Staunton's *éclaircissement* from 1 June to 20 June was an attempt to obscure this fact. Madden's *Critic* statement itself presents contradictions. He declared that no preference was given in showing the folio nor 'special invitations' sent out to examine the book, forgetting that a paragraph or two earlier he listed the names of those whom he had 'invited' to see it. The facts also belie Madden's assertion of the openness of the folio investigation. Numerous visitors to the Manuscript Department had complained, some in the press, about restricted access.

Neither did Madden's description of Parry's visit coincide with the facts. Parry did not come to the Museum 'of his own accord' and Madden's declaration that Parry had said the book 'had never been shown to him by Mr. Collier' was, at the very least, an incomplete statement of the facts. What Parry had said was that he didn't *recollect* Collier's showing it to him and he immediately qualified that declaration by adding 'I may be wrong and Mr. Collier may be right' – a disclaimer which both Hamilton and Madden had tried, unsuccessfully, to get him to retract. And it was, to use the kindest word, inconsistent of Madden to suggest that the folio might be viewed by new authorities when earlier he had been adamantly opposed to having his opinion second-guessed.

But it was in his addendum concerning the Hillier affair, about which Madden had so much to hide, that his defence was most blatantly in conflict with the truth. He was correct, of course, in pointing out that Collier had misstated the date; it *was* October 1854, six years rather than 'two or three years' before as Collier had said. (This, perhaps, points out how little *public* knowledge there was about the business. Obviously, until the Museum attack brought his retaliation, Collier had been very discreet in keeping the story to himself.) But the rest of Madden's account is largely incorrect or fuzzy. The stolen manuscripts are described as 'a number of loose papers and an original document on parchment in a very damaged state' – when there were, in fact, well over 160 documents, a number of them parchment rolls. Madden knew when he bought the manuscripts that Hillier was not a 'person of great apparent respectability'; from the first (and to his credit) he had been suspicious of Hillier. Hillier had *not* stated that he bought the stolen documents 'at Shrewsbury' and the whole affair came to light, not at Madden's instigation, but because the stolen Mostyn manuscripts, also purchased from Hillier, had been accidentally discovered by a casual reader. Madden did not show Collier 'the whole of the documents purchased' when Collier first came to inspect them; in fact, he tried very hard to hide the knowledge that there were other manuscripts involved. The matter of their theft (not 'loss' as Madden was wont to call it) was detected without any assistance from Madden by Ellesmere himself, who applied to the Museum trustees for their restitution, not at Madden's suggestion but at Collier's. Madden, in fact, tried to thwart that action. Ellesmere consulted his solicitor before, not 'after' the trustees' meeting, and what Madden called the 'legal discussion' that ended the affair was a written *order* from the Museum trustees to *Madden* to give up all the documents he had acquired – the number and variety of which he had tried to keep secret by having some of them bound after suspicions about their provenance had surfaced. On almost every point, Madden misstated the facts. But the most remarkable comment in his article was the declaration that he had 'good reason to believe that Mr. Collier prejudiced Lord Ellesmere's mind against' him, because in making it he unwittingly revealed a *motive* for his malice, contradicting his assertion that he was nonplussed by his good friend Collier's accusation.

Only two other persons had known the whole story of the Hillier affair – Ellesmere and John Payne Collier. The Earl had been dead for over two years, and Collier had determined to write nothing more on the controversy no matter what ensued. 'I would not in my Reply have said so much about Sir F. Madden', Collier wrote to S. Leigh Sotheby shortly after Madden's article appeared, 'if he had not shewn for some reason or another, extraordinary spite against me. . . . Sir F. Madden is in a fury, and can contain himself so little that he condescends to vulgar abuse, to which I shall never condescend, on my part, to make an answer. My answer is in my "Reply," and I mean that, as far as I can, to be *final*.'[57]

Collier often quoted Samuel Johnson's *mot* that no man is convicted except by his own defence, and he was now determined to remain silent. This may not have been a wise course for him. By refusing to correct Madden's misstatements, he allowed them to be taken for truth, and by not pointing out the contradictions, he failed to demonstrate Madden's animosity. On the other hand, Collier was at a singular disadvantage: the charges against him were hydra-headed; each time he refuted one accusation, two seemed to appear in its place. Moreover, his defence was not always consistent or coherent, and his somewhat cavalier style allowed his words to be twisted to work against his meaning.

In any case, he had other defenders, two of whom printed reviews of his *Reply* on the same day that Madden's expanded answer appeared in the *Critic*. The first was Thoms, who as editor of *Notes and Queries* had from the first scrupulously kept the columns of the periodical open to all sides in the controversy and avoided revealing his own confidence in the folio. His review of the *Reply*, however, was clearly sympathetic to Collier although characteristically well-tempered. 'The great fundamental error', he wrote, was Madden's failure to invite Collier to join the investigation when Madden first began to suspect the folio emendations were forged. As a result, 'what might have been a literary inquiry has been converted into a bitter and envenomed personal dispute, which, pursued as it has been, can never lead to the discovery of truth.'[58] Madden's reaction to this criticism was to fire off a letter to Thoms asking 'whether the pages of N. & Q. are open to the replies of himself and friends, or whether it is to be merely a one-sided apology for Mr. Collier?'[59] Although Thoms assured him that *Notes and Queries* was available to everyone, Madden instituted a kind of boycott against the journal and even went so far as to encourage (unsuccessfully) a competitive *memorabilia* section in the *Illustrated London News* in an attempt to damage *Notes and Queries*.[60]

A more emphatic defence came from an unlikely quarter. The *Literary Gazette,* which had heaped scorn on Collier in its review of Hamilton's *Inquiry* a few months earlier, now suddenly appeared as his partisan. Editorial consistency was not a virtue of mid-nineteenth-century English journalism, but this reversal must have astonished even Collier; it certainly enflamed Madden. Collier, the *Gazette* declared, was guilty of two minor faults: he defended himself too vigorously against charges no one had made, and he seemed to blame his adversaries for the fact that his material witnesses were dead. Collier, it declared, was

an odd man, a crotchety man, a man who on numerous, if not numberless occasions, has proved to the entire satisfaction of friend and foe, that he is his own enemy, but at the same time he is a man whose whole literary life has been devoted to the elucidation of the writing and the works of our greatest national dramatist. . . . It is on this gentleman that Mr. N.E.S.A. Hamilton of the MSS. department of the British Museum, has been let loose. . . . If we are right in our conjecture, and if Mr. Hamilton has been merely put forward as a sort of cat's-paw to do the dirty work for men ashamed to own to it, we can only say the attack is the most cowardly ever conceived: if, on the other hand, it is the young gentleman's own bantling, we can only designate it as the most insufferable piece of coxcombry the century has produced.[61]

Because it was a turnabout for the *Literary Gazette*, the review had a notoriety which its arguments would not have had alone. 'I am disgusted with the whole affair', Madden wrote to Staunton immediately after reading the article. 'The Literary Gazette out-Herods Herod!'[62] Staunton was more vehement still in his reply. The *Literary Gazette* was 'a scandalous paper', he wrote. 'Our press is fast sinking to the disgraceful level of the American papers. When it reaches that, there will be nothing for us but revolvers and bowey knives.'[63] Nevertheless Staunton did not come to Madden's defence. In his diary, Madden complained that Staunton 'is very fiery and violent, but really does little or nothing in this Collier inquiry, whereas he might do a great deal, if he thought proper. I feel the silence of the Shaksperian editors, Dyce, Hunter, Halliwell and Staunton is considered by the Collier party as an argument in their favour.'[64] He was later to make similar references in his diary to the 'sneak' Halliwell, the reluctant Dyce, and the excessively silent Hunter. He had hoped and even expected that Collier's editorial competitors would be in the forefront and that he, more or less unobserved, would direct the attack from behind the scenes. Instead, it was Frederic Madden, very much by himself, who was the announced – and denounced – opponent of John Payne Collier.

The tension of the conflict affected him physically. Always a hypochondriac, Madden now began to be afflicted with severe headaches and a hacking cough, and he blamed Collier. 'My cough still troubles me', he wrote. 'Continued notes on C. Damn the fellow! It affects my nerves and my health, to be so basely treated.'[65] His composure was further upset by the rumour that Panizzi would be giving up the position of Principal Librarian to become, of all things, a Sardinian minister to London. It was a ridiculous story which only a man who had never accepted being 'passed over' would have believed; he was confident that if Panizzi left, the position of Principal Librarian would come to him 'as a matter of course',[66] and when inevitably the rumour proved false, he saw it as yet another instance of prejudice against him. Once again he blamed his 'enemies'. Panizzi, whose new reading room, he declared, was a disaster, who had deliberately sacrificed the 'serenity of the library . . . for the sake of obtaining popular approbation';[67] Ellis, whom he declared 'a very pitiful fellow', who 'to gratify a feeling of spite completely gave himself up to the crafty foreigner . . . and secured his own pension of £1200 per annum';[68] the trustees, who ignored his department and denied him his proper salary and position[69] – everyone, in fact, whom he confronted in his miserable and unrewarded existence. In his mind, the world was either a conspiracy and Frederic Madden its victim or it was pandemonium and Frederic Madden its exorcist. Cast low by its malice, he thought himself forced to accept any instrument that would expose and subdue the world's oppressive spirits.

27

Dr Wellesley's letter, Ingleby confided to Madden, 'has done incalculable mischief for he is a man of the highest character and of very high attainments.'[70] His corroboration 'proved' that Rodd had had an emended folio Shakespeare for sale at thirty shillings, and if Rodd had sold such a book, why could Collier not have bought it as he claimed? Wellesley's story encouraged others. Madden reported, in some alarm, that even Maskelyne – he whose microscope had produced the 'scientific proof' of forgery – now declared that he had 'a faint idea, like a dream, of having been shown a copy of Shakspere in Rodd's shop, with MS. notes . . .!'[71] If Wellesley's testimony were not repudiated soon, Madden feared the unresolved controversy would lose its interest. 'The Public will get tired of the whole case, if too much protracted', he wrote in his diary.[72] To allow the affair to become stalemated after Wellesley's testimony would be disastrous to Madden's prime objective of establishing Collier's guilt. He therefore set about discounting Wellesley's story, but it wasn't easy. Since Wellesley had no personal attachment to Collier and his reputation was unassailable, he could be charged with neither prejudice nor incompetence, but only with simple error. Madden had to prove that Wellesley was mistaken, that the book he saw was not the Perkins Folio but another, and that the book Collier bought from Rodd was without marginal notation.

In this project Madden was greatly helped by Wellesley's

adamant refusal to be drawn further into the quarrel. Since his letter to Madden, Wellesley had made no public statement of his opinion, and Madden was very careful to obscure the fact that Wellesley had made a positive identification of the Perkins Folio in Currey's office. Madden confided this information to only one or two close friends and qualified it with his own strong disclaimers. He told Thomas Wright, for example, that Wellesley believed the Perkins Folio to be 'the same he saw at Rodds', but that Wellesley could 'give no proof of this opinion either from the character of the quotes or external appearance of the folio.'[73] (Wright's remarkable suggestion was that Collier may have bought the book that Wellesley saw and afterward used acid to remove the notes so that he would write in his own emendations! Even Madden found that a bit too bizarre to believe.)

Madden realized that the way to convict Collier would be to trace the path of the Perkins Folio to Rodd's shop, turning up a former owner who could testify that the book was sold to Rodd *without* marginal notes – to prove, in other words, that Wellesley was mistaken in his identification and that the book *he* saw (if ever it existed) was sold to someone other than Collier 'The great question', Madden declared in his diary, was 'how Rodd obtained the volume.'[74]

What seemed a possible answer to that question was presented by a Mr. Foss who about this time appeared at the Museum with a manuscript he hoped Madden would buy. During their negotiations they spoke of the Perkins Folio controversy ('As who does not?' Madden commented). Foss, it turned out, was a good friend of Wellesley, and Wellesley had told him that he now believed he had seen the emended folio at Rodd's 'long before the time' that Collier said he bought the book. Excited by this information, Madden declared, 'if this is so, Dr. Wellesley's evidence is worth nothing in Mr. C's favour, but on the contrary is directly against him.'[75] Madden's assumption was wrong, of course. When Collier first announced his discovery he said the purchase was 'some years after' he had completed his first edition of Shakespeare (April 1844) and 'a short time before the death of the late Mr. Rodd'[76] (March 1849). Later, in *Notes and Emendations* he narrowed the time to 'the spring of 1849'[77] and he kept to that

story in his subsequent accounts. The actual time of purchase
was probably earlier – as noted above – to minimize the time
the book had presumably 'lain on his shelves' before he
'discovered' the 'treasure' it contained, but the date was only a
concomitant detail. Certainly it had no bearing on the
significant point of Wellesley's story – that Rodd had mentioned the circumstances to another customer; the date of
Wellesley's conversation, whether it was 1849 or 1847 or 1846,
could not discredit Collier's account.

But Madden thought otherwise. What Foss's story gave him
was a suggestion that Collier had lied about the date of
acquisition, and for Madden that possibility alone was enough
to convict Collier of making up the rest of the story too. He
therefore began an intensive search for evidence to prove
when, prior to 1849, Rodd had sold a Second Folio
Shakespeare for thirty shillings. He immediately sought
Rodd's sale catalogues for the 1840s, and as he noted in his
diary, he 'was not a little surprised but also rejoiced', to find
an entry in Rodd's 'List of Books' for 1 January, 1847, which
corresponded to the book he sought:

'Shakespeare (W.) Comedies, Histories, and Tragedies, *wanting the title
and four leaves at the end, cut,* and in soiled condition, £1.10.0. fol.
1632.'
I firmly believe that this is the identical volume purchased by Mr.
Collier, [Madden declared] and on which he wrote the name of Tho.
Perkins his Booke. Of course at that time the fabricated MS. notes
could not have been in it, or else Rodd would not have failed to notice
them. The means to prove that this *is* the Collier volume are
two – first, to prove that Collier bought his book from Rodd in 1847,
and next to trace the party from whom Rodd obtained himself the
book. Could this be done, I am satisfied that the truth would come
to light.[78]

Madden had curiously shifted his hypothesis: believing
Wellesley had seen *his* folio earlier than 1849 (when Collier
had said he bought *his*) Madden initially had searched the
catalogues for the Wellesley book, hoping to find it had been
sold to someone else before Collier could have bought it.
However, when Madden found not an emended folio but a
clean copy, he immediately reversed his argument and set
about proving that this was the book Collier bought (and

subsequently emended), that the new item was in fact the 'Perkins Folio'. Wellesley's statement that the folio he had seen in Rodd's shop was *emended* was now forgotten and Madden started down a new path, apparently taking no notice that the direction of his inquiry had changed significantly. Madden noted that he immediately showed his discovery to Hamilton[79] and Bond, who relayed the news to Hardy, who told it to the Master of the Rolls. Clearly, the 'Museum authorities' thought this was very important evidence indeed!

Now all that was needed was the information in Rodd's sales account books indicating *who* purchased the folio listed in the January 1847 catalogue. Madden asked James Lowe to see Wilkinson, a partner of Sotheby's, the firm which had taken over Rodd's business at his death, and to have a look at Rodd's books. However, although Rodd had been meticulous in keeping his accounts, Wilkinson reported that the books covering March 1845, until Rodd's death, had been borrowed some years before by a barrister named George Henry Money who had mislaid them. The relevant accounts were considered lost beyond recovery, and the purchase of the 30s. clean folio could not be traced.

Characteristically, Madden's first thought was that Collier had somehow got hold of the account books and destroyed them. The fact that the books had disappeared long before the controversy erupted argued against this supposition, of course, and if the accounts might have made it possible for Madden to 'prove' Collier's guilt, they might, by the same token, have allowed Collier to 'prove' his innocence; that is, they might have shown that he had *not* bought the folio Rodd advertised or that he had bought an emended folio at another time. But this possibility did not occur to Madden. Lacking the evidence he sought, he twisted his hypothesis yet again. In his search through Rodd's catalogues, he had found only the one Second Folio listed in January 1847. Since it was omitted in Rodd's subsequent catalogue for June 1847, he deduced that it had been sold in the intervening months and, moreover (since it was the *only* Second Folio copy Rodd had advertised), that it must have been both the copy Wellesley had seen *and* the copy Collier had bought.

The catalogue description had noted that the copy 'wanted the title and four leaves at the end', and Madden quickly ascertained that the Perkins Folio likewise lacked these pages. 'This precisely corresponds with the deficiency of . . . the copy entered in Rodd's Catalogue, 1 Jan. 1847 and confirms beyond all doubt, that this was the copy bought by Mr. Collier', he wrote in his diary, making no attempt to conceal his sense of triumph. 'The only difficulty remaining is the manuscript notes which Dr. Wellesley says he saw, but which there *must* be some mistake about', he disclosed in a remarkable bit of self-deception. 'If there had been numerous MS. notes at that time, Rodd *must* have mentioned them in his catalogue. Every bookseller could bear out this assertion.' Madden was so secure in his argument that he even let his arch enemy Panizzi into his confidence, hoping, rightly, that Panizzi might for his own reasons fan the fire that Madden had set to Collier's story. Yes, Panizzi declared, it was information of great importance and, he added darkly, Wellesley ought to be confronted with the evidence and asked 'for explanation'.[80]

Apparently it never occurred to Madden that Rodd might have sold the Perkins Folio without listing it in his catalogues. Like most successful booksellers, he had a rapid turnover; most books were in his possession too short a time to be advertised. Moreover, by Wellesley's testimony, Rodd already had a customer for the folio when it 'arrived from the country'. But Madden's frantic attempt to 'prove' that the item in the January 1847 catalogue was the Perkins Folio *sans* notes was beyond reason, an indication of his blind resolve to prove Collier's guilt, and when a thorough search through the sales catalogues of other London booksellers also turned up no emended folios, Madden assumed he had decisive proof that the item in Rodd's catalogue was the Perkins Folio!

In early April, Madden's determination was reinforced by an article in the *Edinburgh Review*. Thus far, that staid quarterly had not pronounced on the controversy, but now it did so in an unsigned article by Herman Merivale purporting to be a review of Ingleby's *Fabrications*, Hamilton's *An Inquiry*, and Collier's *Reply*. It was a careful and comprehensive analysis of the case which concluded in favour of Collier. Alone among the commentaries on the case, it dared to state the primary questions directly: 'Have these corrections been forged at a recent date, and have they been forged by Mr. Collier?'[81] After a careful review of the history of the controversy, the article emphatically answered, 'no', to both questions.

Merivale criticized Collier for carelessness in his defence which inevitably created a hostile suspicion of his story. 'He scarcely ever gives a detailed account of anything without a blunder', Merivale declared. 'He scarcely ever tells the same story twice without variations of more or less importance. He obviously quotes from memory on occasions where the exact wording is of importance and his memory is constantly wrong.'[82] But, Merivale argued, if Collier presented his case badly, he was not thereby a forger, and his accusers were guilty of malice.[83] The compelling evidence in Collier's favour was the intrinsic worth of a few – a very few – of the Perkins emendations which were gradually being incorporated into the received text of Shakespeare, and the way these were scattered among thousands of nearly worthless 'corrections'. 'If this be forgery, we have to suppose . . . the patience and accuracy required to execute an enormous mass of *unnecessary* work. . . . For what purpose? Only to pass off a very few favourite corrections, under the cover of thousands, at which no one would care to look?'[84] Moreover, the character of the corrections argued for their 'legitimacy' – if *not* for their cogency, Merivale continued. The text had obviously been shortened, sometimes grotesquely, either for performance or publication. Time and again the Old Corrector had changed otherwise acceptable lines and made them unintelligible, and some of Shakespeare's greatest lines were cut, a result no scholar would allow. 'We are to suppose', Merivale wrote sardonically, 'that Mr. Collier, intending to palm on the world a set of conjectural emendations as ancient, resolved to back their credit by forging, also, a whole mass of stage alterations of no value or interest whatever.'[85]

Most compelling of all, to Merivale, was Wellesley's corroboration of Collier's account. 'The circumstances, the place, the price, the notoriety of the volume', he declared, 'all serve strongly to show that the book mentioned by Dr. Wellesley is no other than Mr. Collier's folio', and even if

Wellesley were unable to identify the actual book when he saw it, this would 'affect but little his remembrance of a transaction of ten years ago. It is the fact of such a book at such a price having been thus disposed of by Mr. Rodd, which is of consequence – not its outward appearance.'[86]

It was likely, Merivale concluded, that the questions raised by the folio would never be answered, but any theory 'which would dispose of the whole question by a charge of wholesale forgery against any individual, requires a far greater amount of evidence before it can be accepted by fair and reasonable men.'[87]

This article, appearing as it did in an influential periodical, worried Madden more than any other in the controversy. It was a reasonable statement that neither accepted Collier's pretensions about himself nor excoriated the Museum, but as one might expect, Madden thought it 'very one-sided and unfair'. It was, he wrote to Staunton, 'written to support a crotchet, and after all, so little complimentary to Collier that I am not sure whether he will not feel more injured than assisted by it.' But it emphasized for Madden the influence of Wellesley's testimony, which for all his bluster, Madden knew that he had to counter. He had to find some evidence that the book Wellesley saw was *not* the Perkins Folio, something that would 'prove' that the book had no notes when Collier acquired it. His only lead was the difference between the two Rodd catalogue lists and for the time being he wanted this disparity to be kept secret. 'In one of Rodd's Catalogues I have found an entry corresponding to Collier's volume', he wrote Staunton, 'except that it has *no MS. notes* mentioned, and I do not wish this important discovery to be publicly known until it appears in the Quarterly Review which will be out in about a week.'[88]

The *Quarterly* article was being written by Joseph Parkes who had called on Madden several days before to inform him, in confidence, that he was writing an article to answer the Edinburgh reviewer and wanted Madden's assistance in securing particularly damaging evidence against Collier. Madden was happy to oblige. He described the 'palpable' forgeries he had found among the Dulwich papers. He secured a facsimile of Mrs. Alleyn's letter for Parkes and furnished him with several other suggestions, chief among them the items in Rodd's catalogues. This, he promised Parkes, would be an exclusive new bit of evidence which Madden himself was still tracing to its source.

Madden's hopes were dashed when the *Quarterly* article was 'burked' at the last minute to make room for a political essay, and the version that Parkes subsequently printed in the *Critic* on 21 April, 1860 was too truncated to be effective. 'The article is not well written', Madden wrote in his diary, 'and in such haste, that the *date* of the Catalogue has been omitted.'[89] Madden therefore urged Ingleby and Staunton to 'use' the information he had given to Parkes in their own ways. In particular, he told them to press hard to find the previous owner who had sold the advertised folio to Rodd, believing this could disprove Wellesley's identification. Madden urged Staunton and Ingleby to advertise for the person who sold Rodd the Second Folio. 'If the owner could be found, a person of known integrity, whose word could be depended on', he wrote Ingleby in Birmingham, 'the whole case would be cleared up, either *for* or *against* Mr. Collier.'[90] Staunton demurred, but within forty-eight hours of receiving Madden's letter, Ingleby inserted the following advertisement in the *Birmingham Daily Post*:

Who sold, either by public auction, in London or elsewhere, or by private contract, in or about the month of December, 1846, an imperfect copy of Shakespeare, edition 1632, bound in rough calf, which was purchased by Thomas Rodd, of Great Newport Street, London?[91]

Of the many strange turns in the controversy, none was to have a more unexpected effect than this notice.

28

The diligent search which Madden initiated was based on two hunches: he was sure that the folio Collier bought from Rodd could be traced to its previous owner and he was equally sure that, once found, the former owner could identify the folio and prove beyond question what Collier had been up to. As it turned out, he was right on both counts. The previous owner of the Perkins Folio was found and the book *was* positively identified, but the outcome was so contrary to Madden's hopes, that, had he imagined the result, he would never have begun the search at all.

Three days after inserting his advertisement, Ingleby received the following reply:

To the Editor of the Daily Post
Sir,
On the 14th instant I saw an enquiry from a correspondent of the Journal asking who sold Thomas Rodd, of Newport Street, in the year 1846, an old copy of Shakspeare? Would you please allow me, through the medium of your *Daily Post,* to inform Mr. Ingleby, and all whom it may interest, that I sold Thomas Rodd an old copy of Shakspeare, and it came from Clopton House, near to Stratford-on-Avon. When I left Stratford-on-Avon Mr. Rodd visited my house in the Borough, and was one of my kindest patrons with my cast of Shakspeare; and there he saw the old but imperfect copy of Shakspeare. It contained notes which much interested him. As regards the binding, I could not answer whether it was sheep or calf, but that it was in good state of preservation, and I could own it immediately if I saw it.

Your obedient servant,
Mill Warner, late of Stratford-on-Avon[92]

Had Ingleby perceived the implications of this account, he might not have written so triumphantly to Madden on 18 April:

My dear Sir Frederic,
I am happy to say I have found the man who sold Rodd the Perkins Folio in 1846. He is a resident at Stratford on Avon. I am to meet him tonight. Will you inform me what the next step is. Shall I kidnap him and bring him to London [?] – & shall I get him to make an affadavit [?] His name is Mill Warner.[93]

Madden, however, immediately recognized the danger, and he replied at once, trying to cool Ingleby's enthusiasm:

It is satisfactory to find that your inquiry has already produced some result but I do not feel so sanguine as yourself that this Mill Warner was the owner of the 'Perkins folio.' In the first place he does not say he sold his copy to Rodd in *1846* nor can he speak as to its binding, *rough* or *smooth*, which is strange, but he says it was in 'a good state of preservation' (which the Perkins folio was not) and lastly that it contained *notes* which interested Rodd, whereas in the Catalogue of 1st January 1847 Rodd describes the imperfect copy of Shakspeare, *but says not a word about the notes.* Mr. Warner also says nothing as to the date of his copy.

Madden's fear – and his true motive – is revealed most baldly in his conclusion:

It would be very advisable undoubtedly to get a more particular description of this Warner copy, or let him see the folio in Mr. Curr[e]y's hands, but great care must be taken to obtain a distinct and unbiased testimony, or else we shall be vindicating Mr. Collier against our own verdict.[94]

Madden's fear was justified. If this *were* the Perkins copy, Warner's evidence would vindicate Collier: if the folio had notes when Rodd acquired it, Collier could have written none of them, for by Madden's own judgment *all* the emendations in the book were written in the same hand.

Within a day of receiving Madden's instructions, Ingleby met Warner and obtained 'a distinct and unbiased testimony' which he immediately relayed to Madden:

I have had a long and I can inform you very cautious conversation with Mr. Will: Warner (not Mill Warner as the Post had it). It is odd that he knew (so I found out in the sequel) nothing about the Collier Controversy. His Memory *is very loose*: but these statements he committed himself to

1. It was early in 1847 (not in 1846) that he sold his fo. to Rodd.
2. Rodd gave him £5 for it.
3. The fo. was one of the early edn. Date unknown.
4. It was bound in rough calf or sheep – *very sound.*
5. It was deficient in a few leaves.
6. It was stained very badly at the end.
7. On the fly leave or title-page was the name of *** Perkins.
8. It contained many MS notes written at the top, bottom and side of the page.
9. It was on account of the notes that Rodd bought it; and he did so because he knew a customer who wanted such a copy.
10. The fo: belonged to Warner's wife before her marriage with him: and Mrs. W. says her former husband had it from Clopton.

He is sure about the name Perkins because there was a family of that

name at Stratford – and he speculated on the probability of the fo.
having belonged to that family.

Warner is known to Collier, also C. Knight, Halliwell, etc.
etc. – and Wilkie Collins in whose book – 'Mr. Gray's Cash Box'
Warner figures as the hero!

I have addressed a short note to the *Critic* on the Warner folio.[95]

The letter confirmed Madden's worst premonitions: it revealed support – perhaps unimpeachable support – from two
apparently reliable sources (Warner and his wife) that Rodd
had purchased a folio with the name 'Perkins' on it,
containing notes in precisely the manner of the Collier book,
and that Rodd had acquired the book for a customer who
wanted an emended copy. This was almost conclusive 'proof'
of Collier's assertion that the book he had obtained from
Rodd contained the disputed notes when he bought it.
Coupled with Wellesley's story, the chain of evidence was
complete, despite several discrepancies from Collier's account.
Collier had said that he bought the book in the spring of 1849,
while this version suggested 1847. Collier had said that Rodd
had not seen the notes, while Warner said he had; and there
was a remarkable difference between the £5 Rodd paid for
Warner's book and the thirty shillings for which Collier said
he sold it. But these differences, though puzzling, were
essentially minor. The key point was the 'Perkins' identification; it was highly unlikely that *two* folios with the Perkins
name would have passed through Rodd's hands within two
years. Almost equally important was the fact that Rodd had
purchased the book *for a customer*. This would explain its not
being listed in any of Rodd's catalogues. What Ingleby had
turned up seemed to be the proof of Collier's innocence.

And Madden knew it. When he copied the details of
Warner's affidavit into his diary, he omitted both the
'Perkins' identification and Rodd's statement that he was
buying the book for a particular customer, desperately
attempting to ignore the facts that seemed to exonerate his
enemy. 'I confess', Madden wrote disingenuously, in his diary,
'I do not like the evidence, but one thing is certain, that
Warner's copy cannot be the one inserted in Rodd's January
Catalogue 1847. . . . It cannot be the "annotated Collier folio,"

for Rodd sold that for 30s. and it is not in a sound condition,
nor is it badly stained at the end, nor has it any flyleaf of title.
It is a strange mystery!'[96] Not so strange, perhaps, as Madden's
account would try to make it. Whether this was the folio Rodd
advertised in 1847 was no longer important. In all significant
details, the Perkins folio matched the copy Warner had sold:
contrary to Madden's comment, it *is* stained at the end and
very sound; moreover, the missing leaves in the Warner folio
matched an identical characteristic in the Perkins copy. The
absence of the signed fly-leaf was unimportant in the light of
the positive identification which the 'Perkins' name supplied.

Madden must have realized the conclusiveness of Warner's
evidence, but to 'accept' it would be to disprove his case and
to admit that he had been wrong. Such an outcome was
unthinkable. If Warner's evidence could not be disproved, it
had to be discounted – quickly, emphatically, permanently. 'It
is evident if Warner speaks truth, that his copy *cannot* be the
one purchased by Collier of Rodd, nor can it be the one in the
Catalogue of 1. Jany. 1847', Madden wrote to Ingleby. 'My
opinion is that the real owner of the Collier folio, before it
came into Rodd's hands, is still to be sought for.' And yet,
despite his firm intention, a suggestion of the truth slipped
out: 'At the same time', he wrote, 'it is very strange that
[Warner] should say the name of Perkins was on the flyleaf or
title page neither of which are in the Collier folio. Query, did
Rodd really buy an imperfect Shakespere with *Notes,* of
Warner, and sell it to C. *after* the sale of the copy from the
Catalogue of 1 Jany 1847? If so, we may perhaps account for
the name of Tho. Perkins on the cover.'[97] The comment
reveals that Madden knew he had evidence exonerating
Collier. If, as he claimed, his intention had been only to find
the truth, the obvious course would have been to publish
Warner's identification. Instead, he kept it quiet and urged
Ingleby to do the same.

The few anti-Collierites who got wind of Warner's statement were shocked. Staunton roundly scolded Ingleby for his
'indiscretion'. Was he trying to make a case for Collier? He
should have hushed up the whole thing! Did he want Collier
to get off? 'I consider his remarks very ill-judged', Ingleby
wrote to Madden.

Ingleby, in the flush of discovery, sent a letter to the *Critic* describing his meeting with Warner. (He said nothing about his advertisement and implied that Warner had sought *him* out.) He briefly recounted the details of the meeting, adding one new bit of information: that the book had not been 'sold' in the conventional sense but had been a kind of gift. 'On Mr. Warner pressing Mr. Rodd to accept it [the folio] as a present', Ingleby wrote, 'the latter objected to do so, and gave Mr. Warner a 5 *l.* note, as a present for his little daughter.'[98]

Warner himself remained silent. After his letter to the *Birmingham Daily Post* he made no further comment about his folio. Ingleby declared to Madden that Warner appeared to him to be a 'weak and impressible man, and probably eager for notoriety', a judgement which suggests that Warner, unrestrained, might have penned a few words of his own for the pamphlet trade, but he wrote nothing, 'impressed', perhaps, by those who feared the dissemination of his story. Ingleby, for his part, privately told Madden that he was 'satisfied that [Warner] is not deficient in conscientiousness', and that he, Ingleby, was 'strongly disposed to accept his statements'.[99]

Warner's testimony was obviously very damaging to their case and Madden and Ingleby therefore ignored it. For reasons impossible to comprehend, so did Collier's defenders. Of course, the details of Warner's 'affidavit' were kept secret and his identity and whereabouts were known only to Ingleby and Madden, but others probably could have found him and satisfied their curiosity about his folio. The fact that no one did so is odd. They may have feared a trap of some kind, but it is more likely they did not see the importance of Warner's testimony. The fact was, both sides of the controversy had long since become implacable. *No* new evidence, no matter how decisive, would have led to a reasoned conclusion. Madden, Hamilton, Ingleby *et al.* sought only evidence to prove their predisposition, and Collier's defenders – if they could, in fact, be identified at all – were nearly exhausted.

Only one more formidable defence was raised, in the *Saturday Review*. That journal had maintained a decorous silence during the months the controversy had raged, but in April 1860, it published an article which was unexpectedly on

Collier's side. The piece was unsigned but, as Madden quickly ascertained, it was written by John Douglas Cook, the editor. Cook wrote without knowledge of Warner's affidavit, but even without that powerful corroboration of Collier's innocence, his defence was a good one. Only Merivale's article in the *Edinburgh Review* caused greater consternation among the anti-Collierite faction. Cook argued, briefly, that the case against the writing in the Perkins Folio was not conclusive; that the presence of pencil marks – even if they were under the ink – did not prove forgery. There were in existence other manuscripts, entirely genuine, 'of a date as early as the supposed date of the emendations with ink-writing over pencil tracings', he declared. Moreover, the so-called verbal anachronisms, particularly Ingleby's pet 'cheer', could be easily discounted by contemporary analogues. In any case, Cook declared, the emendations 'may be totally destitute of authority without being a forgery', and since the book was 'showered' with many worthless emendations, forgery seemed improbable. 'Is it likely', he asked, 'that an impostor would so prodigally multiply the chances of detection?'[100] Cook was most emphatic about the need to find its former owners and to determine where the emendations came from, a demand that particularly irritated Madden *et al.* They were troubled no doubt because they did, in fact, know its probable provenance through William Warner and much of their anger at Cook's article came from harbouring a guilty secret. Ingleby was particularly incensed, declaring the article 'the most disgraceful that I have seen on the subject'. He was particularly upset by the rough handling he had received in the refutation of his test-word 'cheer'. He had become increasingly strident on the subject. Madden privately rejected it. Ingleby, he wrote in his diary, 'ought to be drawn with the words "Cheer, boys, cheer", coming out of his mouth',[101] and of course, Ingleby could not have been pleased by Cook's reference to him as 'the most virulent, and unmeasured of Mr. Collier's assailants', particularly when he realized that both Madden and Hamilton seemed to be slipping, once again, into a protective anonymity in the battle. But if the *Saturday Review* article tended to support Collier against his accusers, it was not particularly flattering to his talents: Collier, Cook declared, has given his antagonists a handle of which they perhaps were not unwilling to take advantage. He is evidently a man of a loose and inaccurate, which is different from a fraudulent habit of mind . . . his own defence of himself is as weak and unskilful as anything can be. We confess that, to our judgment, it is almost damning proof of his innocence. Could the author of Mr. J. Payne Collier's Reply have forged the most remarkable collection of emendations on a first-rate poet which the literary world has ever seen?[102]

Robinson, who found the article generally reassuring and 'as friendly as any I have heard of', was nonetheless cognizant of the slur to Collier's reputation. 'It would mortify a vain man', he wrote in his diary, knowing better than anyone how vain Collier was and how painful such a 'defence' would be.[103]

The controversy was almost played out in the public mind, but the 'Museum faction' had a few last blasts to sound. Madden's fear that the subject would become *passé* before Collier was fully condemned had almost come to pass, and in a desperate attempt to catch the audience before it was gone, all the anti-Collierites except Madden were preparing to go to press with a pamphlet or book and all of them chose to ignore the implications of Warner's statement. New evidence might raise unanswerable questions and prejudice the success of their books. When after a long delay, the last number of Howard Staunton's *Shakespeare* was published in late April,[104] it was easy to see why he thought Ingleby's discovery of Warner might have been 'indiscreet'; in both his Preface to Volume I and a long appendix ('The Suppositious Shakespeare Documents'), Staunton excoriates the Perkins Folio, implying fraud and virtually declaring Collier a forger. 'A big book had grown up under Mr. Staunton's hand', the *Athenaeum* was later to declare, 'which his passions and violence have converted into a bad partizan [*sic*] tract. Preface, Life, Text, Notes – every main part of the work – is infected with the Collier-morbus.'[105]

In the middle of July, Thomas Duffus Hardy published *A Review of the Present State of the Shakespearian Controversy* – yet another assertion of Collier's guilt in the Perkins Folio. Hardy was a good friend of Madden, but it was not until Lemon questioned his judgement regarding the Players' Petition in the State Paper Office that Hardy became determined to publish an account of his own. Lemon had asserted a position which Hardy thought challenged his. When Merivale implied that it was injudicious for Hardy as an official of the Public Record Office to condemn a document at the State Paper Office without consulting any of the staff of the latter department, Hardy's *amour propre* was injured. He was, he announced in his *Review,* an Assistant Keeper of the *Public Records,* and as such, the *superior* of Lemon, who was only an Assistant Keeper of the *State Paper Office,* which he declared was really more properly called 'the State Paper *Branch* Record Office'. The vehemence of Hardy's declaration suggests that something other than the pursuit of truth and justice may have motivated the original investigation of the Players' Petition. However, aside from his assertion of authority there was little in Hardy's *Review* that was new.

Almost simultaneously with Hardy's book, another old combatant reentered the lists. After a year of uncertainty and frustration, A.E. Brae had finally found a publisher willing to take his expanded version of *Literary Cookery* now entitled *Collier, Coleridge and Shakespeare.* Although Brae told Ingleby that he had diligently studied Coleridge in preparation, the new version was merely a dispirited rehash of the prejudices of the old. The most remarkable part of the new book was Brae's description of Collier's suit in the Queen's Bench. Brae declared neither he nor his publisher (Smith) had known about the suit, implying, in a grand contradiction of the truth, that it had no effect on the distribution of the pamphlet. Brae's new attack was scarcely more successful than his first. It was not suppressed, but it had almost no sale. One of the few papers to review it was the *Athenaeum* which seemed more amused than irritated by Brae's imprecations, calling the book 'a mere waste of passionate words'.[106]

The public quarrel was slipping to an indecisive conclusion. The combatants paused, apparently exhausted, anger spent. The time for attack seemed over, and the time for defence, too. Despite the clearly libellous intent of both Hardy and Brae, Collier kept silent. 'I have made my reply to the charges', he wrote to an American correspondent, 'and upon that I shall rest, without troubling myself, at my advanced age (72) about any revival of what has already been refuted.'[107] His disillusionment with his first attempt at legal redress discouraged him from making a second, but he probably surmised that Hardy and Brae could do him no real harm and that under the circumstances it was better to ignore them. In the fall of 1860 Collier was increasingly convinced that the worst was over and that his own case would ultimately prevail. Influential voices had spoken up on his behalf: the articles in the *Edinburgh Review* and the *Saturday Review*, although they patronized his reputation, had nonetheless argued strongly and effectively that he was innocent of wrong-doing. Thoms's defence in *Notes and Queries* and Dixon's in the *Athenaeum*, although expected, were influential and solid, and Collier believed, with some justification, that his own *Reply* had effectively rebutted the charges Hamilton had set out in *An Inquiry*. As the weeks passed with no new attacks, the diatribes of Hardy and Brae seemed more and more to mark the end of the Museum's attack on him. The case appeared to be forgotten. By October, the *Athenaeum* declared, in a belated review of Staunton's *Shakespeare,* that the issue was *passé.* 'It is useless', it said, 'to attempt the revival of a controversy in which the public interest is dead and gone.'[108] By November, Collier thought the case had been closed in his favour and he could speak of it as a crisis past. 'You mention the late controversy and the different tracts relating to it', he wrote in a letter to Leigh Sotheby. 'That is the subject that has given me more annoyance – I may say distress – than any other occurrence in my life.' Collier was still grateful for Sotheby's help in putting him in touch with Wellesley. 'I do not, and never shall, forget my sincere obligation to you there anent, and the mode in which you enabled me effectually to meet and refute one part of the malicious case against me.'[109] The memory was painful, but, he thought, only a memory. In December he wrote to an American friend that the prevailing public opinion was moving in his favour. 'I am in hopes that, even on this side of the water, a more wholesome feeling is beginning to prevail.'[110]

For the first time in two years, he was content. His family was well and prospering; his sons were established – John Pycroft Collier was, in fact, eminent in his own right; in the late fall his youngest daughter Henrietta married; his life at

Riverside with his daughter Emma was comfortable and secure. 'My health is capital', he wrote to Sotheby, 'and so I trust it will remain.' This was best of all, for it meant he was able to write. When the New Year arrived he was over half way through his life of Spenser. It would be, he was sure, his final labour and, he declared, he was doing his utmost 'to make it not only a last but a lasting work'.[111] Perhaps his was to be, after all, a career of distinction, growing in prestige and capped by his Spenser edition. He would be respected; he would be, perhaps, revered. His many enemies – Halliwell, Hunter, Knight and Dyce, Singer and Staunton, Madden, Hamilton, Hardy and Brae – all seemed to be silent at last. The weeks passed, the papers said nothing. The controversy was over, at least it seemed to be over; or rather, Collier came to believe that it was over and that the result had been in his favour.

It was an illusion. There was another opponent. There would be another book.

IX

A COMPLETE VIEW

'Let him slip down.'

29

The opponent was Clement Mansfield Ingleby and the book, *A Complete View of the Shakespeare Controversy*, was to become the 'final' word on the subject – the primary source for anyone interested in John Payne Collier or the quarrel which branded his life. The controversy was complex but the format of the book was seductively simple: it claimed to be 'a succinct and exact account of the whole question';[1] it discussed all the disputed documents in detail and reproduced most of them in elaborate facsimile. In the century that followed, no one would seriously question the case Ingleby made against Collier. The book, in the words of the *Dictionary of National Biography*, 'practically closed the controversy'.[2]

But Ingleby's work was not what it appeared to be. It was not a 'complete' view but a very skilfully 'ordered' account written not to reveal the truth but to make a case. It was the product of a conspiracy, perhaps the most successful in the history of English letters, for Ingleby had evidence in hand – evidence he himself had uncovered and believed in – which exonerated Collier of forging the Perkins emendations, and yet he published a 350-page book whose sole purpose was to convict Collier of that crime. In Ingleby's own words, the Perkins Folio emendations were the 'hinge' on which all the charges against Collier turned,[3] and Ingleby greased that hinge, knowing the charges were false. The praise bestowed on Ingleby by his uncritical successors is, perhaps, the most outrageous irony of the 'Shakespeare Controversy'.

From the day Collier announced them in 1853, Ingleby thought the Perkins emendations were spurious and that given time and good criticism, Collier himself might disavow the folio.[4] But as the months passed with little change in Collier's manner or in the public's support for the corrections, Ingleby succumbed to Brae's view that the pages of the book showed the 'sign of the beast', that the emendations were not merely bad guesses by some early ignoramus but modern fabrications intended to deceive. Brae convinced Ingleby that 'the prestige of Mr. Collier's name' was the real obstacle to ridding Shakespeare's text of the Old Corrector's barbarisms and that the Perkins Folio could be discredited only if Collier were.

Once convinced, Ingleby set about 'proving' Collier's guilt by any means that came to hand. He had an appetite for controversy, as perhaps fit his ratiocinative mind, and prodded by Brae, he decided that the only way to dislodge the public's romantic attachment to Collier's discovery was to produce an even more romantic discovery of scholarly fraud. He was duplicitous from the start: publicly he called Collier 'an honourable man' whose 'judgment had been swamped', but privately he argued that Collier was guilty. Although he was later to say he 'never doubted' Collier's 'good faith' until 1858, his correspondence from 1856 onward reveals his intention to 'expose' him. By 1859, Ingleby was ready for an open accusation in *The Shakespeare Fabrications,* and as soon as that book was published he began its sequel, the 'complete view' of Collier's outrageous crime.

The crime was to be Ingleby's own. Although Brae's malice had brought him to believing Collier a forger and Madden's vengeance kept him firmly committed to that belief, Ingleby did not share their animosity. He was driven by pride in his own perspicacity; he was determined to demonstrate the superior quality of his critical intelligence by 'exposing' what he conceived to be the malignant imagination of John Payne Collier. He was no paleographer – he admitted as much – and he had little knowledge of either literary historiography or Shakespearian emendation. What he brought to his task was not experience or imagination but an analytical scepticism which was ill-suited to it, and he never questioned the intention of Brae and Madden whose real motives he could not have guessed.

Ingleby's predisposition was for the logically demonstrable, the apparently 'irrefutable' fact, and because there were few of these in the controversy, he belaboured those he found. For example, he continued to support the 'test word' theory of Brae because it seemed to have an historical validity that satisfied his logical turn of mind. For the same reason he had seized upon the pencil marks in the Perkins Folio that Madden had declared were written in Collier's own hand. To Ingleby this was compelling proof corroborating his own powerful belief, and he initially accepted Madden's conclusion without question.

It was, therefore, ludicrous for Ingleby to declare that he had 'no private interest in common with the Department of Manuscripts of the British Museum'.[5] He and Madden had disparate qualifications and motives, but they shared a single objective – to 'prove' Collier a forger. Ingleby irritated Madden, who privately belittled his critical acumen (he was particularly scornful of Ingleby's insistence on the test word 'cheer' because it would not directly implicate Collier), but because Ingleby had no previous public connection with Madden or the Museum, he was a convenience. Through him Madden could direct the attack on Collier while pretending to be a reluctant participant unmoved by petty motives of jealousy or revenge, and it was in this guise that Ingleby presented Madden in the *Complete View*.

To his credit, Ingleby had misgivings. In April 1860, six months after *The Shakespeare Fabrications* was published and only a few weeks before *A Complete View* was scheduled to appear, Ingleby saw 'remarkable discrepancies' between Hamilton's facsimile pencillings and Collier's handwriting.

I must confess to some uneasy feelings lest by overconfidence I may have given currency to a false statement as to the *identity* of the pencillings in the folio with Mr. Collier's handwriting.... If you tell me you have no doubts on the subject [he told Madden],... it will remove from my mind a harmful uncertainty and enable me to proceed in what I am about with a confidence in the fact that I am attacking the real fabricator, and not a dupe or accomplice.[6]

Madden quickly shored up Ingleby's confidence, declaring emphatically that the pencil writing resembled Collier's handwriting 'more than any other person I know, and *this*, if necessary on account of justice, *I shall be willing to testify.*'[7]

Madden's simple assertion was enough. In *A Complete View*, Ingleby would write, '*In my opinion* [the pencilling] indistinguishably resembles Mr. Collier's ordinary handwriting [emphasis added].'[8] Almost immediately Ingleby was assailed by a new doubt concerning one of the 'forged' Bridgewater papers. 'I cannot conceive such a forgery as No. IV, if it be one', he wrote to Madden. 'I cannot believe it a forgery on the word of Mr. Hardy or Professor Brewer. If you condemn it, I shall believe, not till then.'[9] Again Madden replied that he was 'thoroughly satisfied' that all the Bridgewater documents were forgeries,[10] and once again, his mere affirmation was enough to reassure Ingleby.

However, when it came to Will Warner's story, Madden's opinion was no better than Ingleby's own. Ingleby believed Warner, and as a trained lawyer, he knew that Warner's unqualified testimony was significant. It created at the least a 'reasonable doubt' of Collier's guilt and at the most, it exonerated him. In late April and early May 1860, Ingleby had to choose between two courses of action: to keep Warner's account a secret believing it to be true would be grossly dishonest, but to publish it would destroy the case Ingleby had been building for over three years. Collier's guilt was central to Ingleby's thesis: with it, his 'solution' was neat and comprehensive; without it, he had no book at all. In the end, Ingleby sacrificed the truth for personal vanity. In his preface he declared that 'love for the works of Shakespere' may have 'warped his judgment', but it was ambition – not love – which drove him. Like a lawyer representing a client whose interest he places above the law, Ingleby took refuge in a legal quibble: very well, he believed Warner's story; but, he argued to himself, that did not require him to undertake Collier's defence. Ingleby saw himself as prosecutor – not advocate. His purpose was to present the case *against* Collier, let Collier rebut it if he could. Thus was Ingleby reduced to legal sophistry in a case that had no 'court' but public opinion and no 'law' other than what fair play, good sense, and a dedication to the truth – the *whole* truth – might give it. In the end Ingleby denied his responsibility to all of these. The struggle was not brief, his uncertainty coupled with recurrent ill health delayed the book's publication for over six months, but by November 1860 it was in the press and by mid-December it was out.

Thus, even as Collier was perceiving a more 'wholesome feeling', the final attack against him was being prepared. The oblique blows of Hardy and Brae had done little harm; Ingleby's frontal assault would cripple. The ultimate success of *A Complete View* rested on its claim to comprehensiveness. The controversy had become a paper war of charge and countercharge, a welter of publications that few readers, no matter how diligent or interested, could follow. Now came a book promising the 'complete' story, supported by voluminous quotations, many facsimile illustrations, and a comprehensive 'analysis'.

It was attractive and it sold, but it was not new. Most of *A Complete View* was a recapitulation of Hamilton's *An Inquiry* (itself largely a reprint of *The Times* correspondence) and Ingleby's own *Shakespeare Fabrications*. The remainder was an amalgam of long excerpts from Collier's *Reply* (reprinted without permission) and an elaboration of periodical arguments taken for the most part from the *Critic* and the *Athenaeum,* all combined to place Collier's defence in the worst possible light and to compound the charges against him in the most defamatory way. The book showed no vestige of the doubts Ingleby had entertained about Collier's guilt; whatever evidence did not support the Madden–Ingleby thesis was simply omitted.

Ingleby's intention is demonstrated by his treatment of Wellesley. In keeping with his pretence of 'presenting all the evidence', Ingleby printed the whole of Wellesley's previously published letter to Collier, but then, declaring he 'did not intend to insinuate the faintest doubt of Dr. Wellesley's veracity', he proceeded, in effect, to call Wellesley a 'partisan' liar, accusing him of deliberate 'ambiguity' and capping the charge with a false statement: 'My readers must determine these points as best they may', he declared, 'for Dr. Wellesley has unequivocally refused to submit to cross-examination, in a very polite letter which he has addressed to me. This is to play the partisan of Mr. Collier with an amiable candour.'[11] What Ingleby knew and here kept secret was that Wellesley had, in fact, examined the Perkins Folio and had identified it positively and unambiguously as the book he had seen at Rodd's. Ingleby could not discount this irrefutable testimony and therefore he suppressed it. Later in the book in a different context, Ingleby apparently forgot his earlier reference and admitted that Wellesley had seen the Perkins Folio 'and is of opinion, that it is the identical book'.[12] But he claimed there was no 'distinguishing mark' that corroborated the identification.

Another example of Ingleby's shabby method is his description of Collier's dealings with Parry. Again, he reprinted all of Collier's published references to his meetings with Parry, but he did so only to 'prove' that Collier deliberately misrepresented Parry's statement in order to give the folio a 'pedigree' that it did not deserve. In Ingleby's version, Collier tricked the old man:

In reply to Mr. Collier's questions, Mr. Parry gave him, to the best of his memory, an account of the *interior* of his lost folio. He did not speak of this folio as of any particular date. Mr. Collier did not ask him any question as to the exterior of the book, nor did Mr. Parry volunteer any statement about it; but, had allusion been made to it, his memory would have served him to tell Mr. Collier that the binding of his lost folio was *dark, clean,* and *shiny.* Of the inside he could not have spoken with as much precision as he does not recollect ever having read a page of it.[13]

Actually, Ingleby declared, Parry thought *his* book was the folio of 1623 – not that of 1632 – and that Collier *knew* it could not have been the Perkins Folio. The implications of this account are clear: Collier deliberately misled Parry and distorted or falsified his reply.

It is typical of Ingleby's confusion and, perhaps, indicative of a lingering doubt, that he himself provided the evidence that disproves his charge. Among the various facsimiles in *A Complete View* is Collier's first letter to Parry showing that, from the outset, Collier had been very precise with him. In the letter Collier specifically stated that the Perkins Folio was that of 1632 and that he understood Parry's copy was also of that date. 'Can you at all describe the book to me?' Collier had asked. 'How was it bound, and was it shabby and defective?

Had it title-page or conclusion? Had it the name of Tho. Perkins on the cover?' Parry's response is not extant, but it must have corroborated the similarities, or the correspondence would have gone no further. Even more important, Parry never at any time denied Collier's declaration that he, Parry, had approved Collier's presentation of the facts of their conversations *before* they were printed in the Preface to the second edition of *Notes and Emendations*. Moreover, if Parry, as Ingleby now claimed, had never 'read a page' of his folio, how could he have recognized the facsimile that Moore had shown him in the first place?

Significantly, Ingleby's single omission from the voluminous and largely redundant newspaper correspondence reprinted in *A Complete View* is Parry's letter to *The Times*. Instead, Ingleby quoted *indirectly* from a 'manuscript' that he claimed Parry had given him, a procedure that allowed Ingleby to omit Parry's disclaimer. Ingleby's pastiche was intended to 'prove' his contention that Collier manipulated Parry in order 'to obviate the risk of incurring the suspicion of having fabricated the manuscript notes himself',[14] but a comparison of Ingleby's account with the details he left out suggests who the real 'manipulator' was and provides a clue as to why Parry, after seven years, suddenly disavowed his former identification: It was, Ingleby says, 'much to Mr. Parry's credit . . . that, unlike Dr. Wellesley, he does not refuse to be cross-examined'.[15] If the bullying that Parry underwent at Madden's hands in the attempt to get him to change his disclaimer ('I may be wrong and Mr. Collier may be right') and the later manipulation of his story for the advantage of Madden, Hamilton, Ingleby *et al.* suggest what Ingleby meant by 'cross-examination', Wellesley was fortunate to have avoided it!

Some of Ingleby's reshaping of the truth is subtle. For example, he implies that Collier gave the Perkins Folio to the late Duke of Devonshire to keep it sequestered, or, in Ingleby's phrase, 'to maintain great obstacles in the way of a paleographic scrutiny' of the emendations. 'I myself was more than a year, using every means of seeing the book', he declared, 'but the Duke's librarian refused to exhibit it, and the Duke himself did not know where it was; and I never could get a sight of it until it had been deposited in the Department of Manuscripts of the British Museum.'[16] This is a gross misstatement of fact, but one would have to be a careful reader of Ingleby's correspondence and of his earlier published accounts (see p. 299) to know it. A letter from Devonshire to Ingleby in April 1859 proves that the Duke did not hesitate to show the folio to Ingleby and in fact there is no evidence that *anyone* was denied access to the book while it was in the Devonshire collection. 'The Duke's librarian' was, of course, Collier himself, yet there is no indication that Collier refused any request, and there is proof that on at least two occasions after the folio was in the Devonshire collection Collier obtained permission for total strangers to see the book.[17] Moreover, Ingleby's statement in *A Complete View* is a direct contradiction of his own testimony in the *Critic* a little over six months before, when he correctly reported that the Duke had offered to put the book at his disposal.[18] Except for this highly significant deletion, Ingleby's account in *A Complete View* was verbatim from his *Critic* article and the omission was therefore a deliberate falsification.

Another omission is even more serious: *A Complete View* says nothing whatever about Will Warner or his folio. The book reiterates many of the irrelevant details of the case, but ignores the most momentous discovery of all – a discovery made by Ingleby himself. It was not distrust of Warner that caused his omission; had there been any reason to discount him, for example, any suspicion that Warner had lied to defend Collier, we may be sure that Ingleby would have reported it. Moreover, the fact that Madden and Ingleby did not continue the search for the previous owner of the Perkins Folio (begun, it will be recalled, to rebut Wellesley's testimony) indicates that they were satisfied that Warner was, indeed, the man they sought. But once discovered he was never mentioned again, not in Madden's diary or his correspondence, not in Ingleby's correspondence, not in any of their public comments. When they found the evidence they had looked for, they buried it because it unexpectedly vindicated Collier and disproved their preconceived conclusion.

Ingleby's book purports to be independent and impartial, but Madden read it in manuscript, and there is abundant evidence that it was influenced and even directed by the 'Museum faction'. One of the fictions promoted by Madden was his own great reluctance to believe in the possibility of Collier's guilt. In Ingleby's version, on 6 June 1859 Madden told him of his suspicions and asked that they be concealed:

he had come to the conclusion that the manuscript notes were not in the handwriting of any known period, but were exceedingly clumsy imitations of some handwritings prevalent in the 17th century. Sir Frederic, however, still very earnestly expressed his belief in Mr. Collier's *bona fides,* and refused to allow his opinion to be publicly expressed, lest such an expression might be used by Mr. Collier's opponents to prejudice that gentleman's character.[19]

But Madden's diary proves that the first person he wrote to after he got the folio was Collier's chief antagonist, Alexander Dyce, and that Dyce saw the folio in the Museum on 28 May at which time Madden 'gave him leave to state, that it was my [Madden's] fixed opinion the writing was not...a genuine handwriting of any period.'[20] The diary gives further evidence that Madden condemned the writing and Collier's part in it to virtually everyone to whom he showed the book.

There is yet more evidence of collusion between Madden and Ingleby in the way *A Complete View* reports the most curious and suspicious event of the Museum inquisition, that is, the discovery of the pencil marks. Ingleby's account is identical to the one in Madden's article in the *Critic* for 24 March 1860 (which he cites in a footnote). According to this version, Ingleby arrived at the Museum to examine the folio for the first time on the morning of 6 June 1859 and he declared:

During this visit, while I was very closely examining certain passages in the folio, I was surprised by the appearance of a pencil mark or line; and on tracing it by the eye I concluded, perhaps hastily, that it passed under the ink word. I accordingly directed Sir Frederic Madden's attention to it. But Sir Frederic Madden did not appear to attach any importance to the remark, and did not pursue the inquiry I had suggested.

Within a week after this occurred Mr. Hamilton, while poring over the volume, discovered that its margins were covered with minute and half obliterated pencil marks, some of which appeared to underlie the ink, and, what was a new feature, that all of them appeared to correspond with the ink writing. He at once called Sir

Frederic Madden's attention to these circumstances. Sir Frederic accordingly again looked through the volume page by page, and was inexpressibly astonished to discover hundreds of marks of punctuation and corrigenda in pencil, more or less distinct, in an apparently modern hand. . . .[21]

This account, like Madden's from which it derives, is a fabrication. As Madden's diary and correspondence at the time prove, it was *Madden* who first saw the pencil marks in the folio; it was he who pointed them out to Ingleby and Hamilton and not the other way around (see pp. 227-8). As we have seen, Madden had tried to separate himself from Ingleby's attack in *The Shakespeare Fabrications* as well as from Hamilton's report of the discovery of the pencil marks in *An Inquiry,* and when Collier's *Reply* charged him with prejudice because of the Hillier affair, Madden wanted to make that separation wider still. Hence his false account in the *Critic* which put not only Hamilton but also Ingleby between him and the discovery of the prime evidence against Collier. Ingleby's slavish reiteration of Madden's fabrication is evidence of collusion. Why Madden wished the truth to be hidden is less immediately apparent, and as we shall see, more significant.

The passage is typical of the way in which Ingleby manipulated the 'evidence' in *A Complete View,* and it must have created some lingering distaste, for he was neither a fool nor a deliberate villain, and his subsequent use of this evidence is ambivalent: although he pursues the implications of the pencil marks to their incriminating end, he almost immediately discounts their value. After arguing vehemently that they were in themselves damning, he declares they were not really all that important and that '*the primal evidence of forgery lies in the ink-writing, AND IN THAT ALONE*'.[22] This may be evidence of a profound if unexpressed uncertainty in Ingleby's mind, for he was later to state with equal fervour that 'in the correspondence of the pencil and ink – we have the key-stone of the arch. To the pencillings is attached Mr. Collier's "plain round English hand", in which, indeed, those pencillings appear to be invariably written . . .'[23] He cannot have it both ways, but neither could he reconcile his need for the 'pencil evidence' with his doubts about its origin.

The Perkins Folio was the primary subject of *A Complete View,* but Ingleby included chapters detailing the charges against the Bridgewater folio, the Dulwich manuscripts, and the 'forged' State Paper, all of which were mere recapitulations of the evidence that Hamilton had first published in *An Inquiry.* In addition, however, Ingleby appended a list of seven 'suppositions and suspected documents', i.e., 'cases in which documents, cited or quoted by Mr. Collier, have been searched for in the depositories indicated by him, and [not] found'.[24] The range of the list suggests how thoroughly the 'Museum authorities' had been examining Collier's published works, and its brevity suggests how generally fruitless their search had been. Ingleby reprints all these new 'disputed documents' (from Collier's texts), but he makes no attempt to prove their 'spuriousness' from internal evidence. His sole basis for questioning their validity was their apparent absence from the collections Collier cited. Three of the 'suspected documents' were formerly in the Ellesmere collection: two, a 'Certificate of the Justices of the Peace of the County of Middlesex about the Blackfriars' (*c.* 1633), and a 'Letter of Samuel Daniel' (n.d.), had been first mentioned by Collier in *New Facts* (1835); the third, a letter signed by 'W. Ralegh', had been quoted in the *Catalogue of Early English Literature... at Bridgewater House* which Collier had compiled in 1837. Ingleby's clear implication was that Collier had either forged and subsequently destroyed these papers or had lied about their existence in the first place. The charge was outrageous. None of these documents had been considered particularly significant when Collier first described them, none was important enough to warrant forgery; neither had any become so in the twenty-five years which had elapsed since they were first reported. The fact that they were not in the collection in 1860 could hardly be said to impugn Collier's good faith or honesty when he had last used them decades before. As we have seen, there had been at least one large theft (by Hillier) from the collection since Collier had used it, and the enormous collection of manuscripts had been transferred to the new Bridgewater House library in the interim. It was not at all unlikely that individual manuscripts might have been misplaced in the move, but this possibility was ignored by Ingleby.

Another of the 'suspected documents' was a manuscript sketch book of the original designs for several masques of Inigo Jones. Collier had found it in the Devonshire collection and described it a quarter of a century earlier in *New Facts*. Of particular importance was a note accompanying one sketch purporting to describe the traditional early sixteenth-century costume of 'Sir Jon Fallsstaff'. The Jones sketch book had been a particular target for Sir Frederic Madden, who, for reasons he never made clear, was convinced it was a forgery. He carried on an extended correspondence with the Duke of Devonshire and made several trips to the Duke's house at Chiswick searching for the book without success. Unlike the missing Bridgewater manuscripts, there was evidence that the sketch book had been in the collection before Collier saw it, and when Madden's search was unsuccessful he suggested theft to hide forgery.

He was hesitant to make any direct charge himself; instead he turned the 'case' over to Hamilton who was the first to suggest (in *An Inquiry*) that 'the language of the [Falstaff] "description" is, to say the least, suspicious'.[25] Now Ingleby took up the case again and came as close as the laws against libel allowed to saying that Collier had stolen the book from Devonshire's collection. 'Neither of these designs – nor any one of them – nor the "annexed" description can be found at Devonshire House', he wrote.[26] The implication is clear that a manuscript was missing and that Collier knew why. It was a gross insinuation and a false one. (Long after the controversy was over the Inigo Jones sketch book was found in the Devonshire collection – where it had been all along. The Falstaff note is genuine.)[27]

The other three 'suspected documents' that Ingleby lists had all been presumed to be in the State Paper Office. Two of these, 'A Petition from the Inhabitants of the Liberty of Blackfriars to the Privy Council', *c.* 1576 and another petition from the same to the same *c.* 1596, had been published by Collier over thirty years before in *The History of English Dramatic Poetry*; the third, a letter from 'Lord Pembroke' *c.* 1624, had been referred to in a footnote in Collier's *New*

Particulars. Ingleby implies that these documents had either been forged or stolen (he is not clear *which*) and suggests that their absence from the collection was Collier's doing. The charge is unfounded: Collier referred to dozens of manuscripts in his history and none of the three Ingleby cites was so unusual as to warrant suspicion. To suppose that Collier would steal a public document which he had previously discovered and published is foolish on the face of it, and given the chaotic order of the thousands of manuscripts in the State Paper Office, it was not at all unlikely that the documents were merely lost. Certainly there should have been more evidence of wrong-doing before Ingleby made these gross implications.

But, as the summary chapter of his book ('The Vintage') makes clear, Ingleby's interest was not elucidation or proof but calumny. The case, in Ingleby's words, is as follows:

1. One man discovered two folios corrected in manuscript, and (to put the case mildly, say) *three* documents bearing on the life of Shakspere.
2. All the annotations and documents so discovered are forgeries.
3. All the annotations of both folios, and all the documents, appear to be in one handwriting, (or in other words, one man forged them all).
4. Lying underneath or alongside the ink-corrections of one of the folios, are found pencil instructions for those corrections in one man's handwriting.
   Now in the first and fourth sections, two men are spoken of. Add to those,
5. The two men spoken of are *one* man.
6. The man in question occupied the foremost place as editor of Shakspere, and commentator on Shaksperian literature....
7. The editor in question has been already convicted of falsifying a document [Mrs. Alleyn's letter] which so falsified was made to have a curious and interesting bearing on the life and character of Shakspere; but in its pristine integrity had no *such* bearing on Shakspere.

Now this is the case against Mr. Collier.

The declaration is so sweeping – and so unsupported by the facts Ingleby had earlier presented – that it would not need to be rebutted here if its import were not still widely believed.

But only l., which no one disputed, was true. The assertion in
2. was unproven and it does not, in itself, indict Collier. The
statement in 3. is highly unlikely, an assertion by Collier's
antagonists that was essential to their case against him. The
assertion in 4. that the pencillings were 'instructions' was a
matter of conjecture, but not in itself suspicious unless the
writing were proved to be more 'modern' than the ink, a point
which had not been proved; the statements in 5. and 6. are
merely bland assertions or the unproven implications of the
foregoing, and the 'falsification' of 7. was too tenuous an
accusation to hang the rest of the charges on. Nevertheless,
Ingleby continued to a crescendo:

THE MAN WHO LIES UNDER THESE APPALLING SUSPICIONS IS THE RECIPIENT OF A
GOVERNMENT PENSION. Is this scandal to continue? Is no tribunal to be
constituted by the Government for the investigation of the charges
preferred against Mr. Collier? His friends as well as his opponents
have urged him to refer his case to arbitration: . . .

The *complete view* comprized [*sic*] in the foregoing pages will hand
down to posterity the real merits of this case. On these merits it will
sooner or later receive the adjudication of the public. They are not
likely to be far from doing justice in the long run. To them I gladly
commit the task of returning a verdict according to the evidence
adduced.

One word more I will offer in anticipation of a possible charge
against me – viz., that of striking a man who is down. Mr. Collier is
not down. He is not, indeed, upon his legs: but he is bolstered up by
the officious aid of his numerous partisans and friends. When they
'let him slip down' we will not strike another blow.[28]

30

Ultimately, *A Complete View* would be accepted as the final
judgement against Collier, but when it was published in late
December 1860, it seemed an anticlimax. A year before the
press had been eager for any gossip about the controversy;
now it was bored by the subject, and Ingleby's charges, though
scandalous, did not create much interest. The *Athenaeum,* one
of the few journals to notice the book, declared it was 'six
months too late and ten times too big.'[29] Of course, the
Athenaeum was, at least by association, a party to the quarrel,

but the comment is a fair representation of the book's reception. The *London Review* waited nearly three months before bestowing brief praise and, although it had earlier condemned Collier, it now avoided endorsing Ingleby's charges: 'Whether the case is brought home to Mr. Collier as *particeps criminis* we leave to others to decide', it said.[30] There was a general withdrawal from the controversy. The publications that earlier had been eager partisans – the *Illustrated London News,* the *Edinburgh Review, Fraser's Magazine,* and the *Quarterly Review,* for example – said nothing at all. As Vaux was to write in the *Critic* over a year later, 'the combatants themselves, . . . almost with a tacit consent, as it would seem, withdrew from the lists before any absolute decision could be had on the whole case.'[31] Collier withdrew as well. He wanted the controversy behind him: he was busy completing his edition of Spenser and repelled by the thought of continuing to defend himself *ad infinitum* against what he believed were old and malicious insinuations. He therefore renewed his determination not to make the 'poor remainder' of his life 'miserable by further irritating contests', and this time he held to his resolve and ignored Ingleby and his book. Collier apparently did not realize how seriously his reputation had been undermined by the incessant attacks of his accusers, nor did he foresee how well Ingleby's book would satisfy the public's – and posterity's – interest in the case. By leaving the field, he allowed *A Complete View* to become by default what the *London Review* declared it to be – '*the* record of this famous case.'[32] Collier's silence in the face of Ingleby's attack was taken, and still is, as an admission of guilt, and for the next hundred years, not a single voice would be raised in Collier's defence, not a word published to rebut *A Complete View.*

And yet the evidence for rebuttal was there before the publication of *A Complete View* and it would accumulate afterward. Ingleby was able to 'prove' Collier guilty of fabricating the folio emendations only by suppressing the full testimonies of Wellesley and Warner. Their evidence leads one to conclude that Collier could not have forged all the Perkins Folio corrections, and this conclusion is supported by other evidence which for clarity will be presented here although to do so interrupts the narrative sequence. What follows is a presentation of facts and argument, most of which could have been adduced at the time, which, I believe, demonstrate the falsity of Ingleby's charges.

Although Ingleby was clearly an 'interested party' and therefore potentially biased in his presentation, no one heretofore has compared his description of the Perkins Folio with the book itself. Scrutiny of the folio (now at the Henry E. Huntington Library) reveals evidence that at least some of the corrections must have been in the book when it was acquired by Collier. The folio had been rebound at least once in the eighteenth century, before Collier bought it, and it has not been rebound since. In rebinding, its pages were very slightly trimmed, and at several places the binder's knife cut through an ink emendation in the 'Old Corrector's' hand removing part of the correction.[33] There is no evidence of the bleeding or 'blotting' effect which the ink would have made at the end of the paper had the writing been made after the cut. These examples suggest that some of the emendations were in the book when it was rebound, long before it came into Collier's possession.[34]

However, the book's most important evidence can be deduced from the substance of the notes themselves which clearly identify some of the Old Corrector's sources. Throughout the eighteenth century, many readers believed the Third and Fourth Folios to be more 'accurate' than the First and Second, largely because they included plays (except for *Pericles,* apocryphal ones) not found in the first two. It was not uncommon for a zealous reader to 'correct' a Second Folio against one of the two later editions, and collation reveals that many of the Perkins emendations follow – imprecisely but unmistakably – the text of the Third and Fourth Folios. (A somewhat smaller number derive from the First Folio.) The later folios provided the Old Corrector with thousands of possibilities for change, and these seem to have been the primary source of the emendations he wrote into the book. Obviously, these are not corrections which a forger wishing to pass off his handiwork as 'probably not of a later date than the Protectorate' would use. Moreover, the overwhelming number of emendations not derived from the other seventeenth-century folios are derived from eighteenth-century editions.

Even a brief perusal of the Perkins Folio would have revealed to Collier that a large number of the emendations were mere repetitions of the conjectures of fervid eighteenth-century editors. The fact that he lied about the circumstances of his purchase of the folio from Rodd (in order, I have conjectured, to hide Rodd's low opinion of the emendations in the book) reveals his own judgement of most of the corrections as well as knowledge of their probable source. Now, if the book had no emendations in it when Collier purchased it from Rodd, it is inconceivable that he would have forged literally thousands of bad *eighteenth*-century emendations into it in a hand presumably intended to suggest they were made over a century earlier. The *substance* of the corrections so easily traced to earlier editors would on the face of it disprove his contention. It is impossible to believe that Collier would have spent hundreds of hours copying thousands of worthless changes the overwhelming number of which he never reprinted and actually omitted from his 'complete list'.

But if he did not copy all of them, perhaps, it might be conjectured, he added to the many examples he found there. This too is highly unlikely. First, those who have examined the Perkins Folio agree that all of the emendations are in the same handwriting. But even if one assumes that Collier was clever enough to imitate the writing he found in the book, the hypothesis is improbable: since Collier wanted to claim a seventeenth-century provenance for the emendations, it would have been directly contrary to his interest to forge 'seventeenth-century emendations' into a book already replete with corrections first suggested almost a century later. Even assuming he were guilty of such astonishing stupidity, Collier would certainly not have forged his emendations in simulation of a hand which, the emendations prove, must have been written in the eighteenth century. To be creditable as 'seventeenth-century' emendations, the 'forged' additions would have had to be in a hand demonstrably *different* from the Old Corrector's – not one in slavish imitation of it. Finally, many of the emendations in the folio suggest that whoever wrote them had small knowledge of Shakespeare and execrable taste. Ignorance and gaucherie are evidenced in many of the Old Corrector's emendations and it is impossible to believe that Collier – whatever his faults a very knowledgeable scholar – would have forged 'good' emendations merely to ascribe them to demonstrably poor authority.[35]

As it has already been noted, the real Old Corrector collated the book with the other seventeenth century folios. What has not been noticed heretofore is that he also collated it with a number of early quartos, and in doing so he left evidence exonerating John Payne Collier: there are emendations in the Perkins Folio that derive from an *authoritative* source which Collier could not possibly have known. That is, some of the emendations actually correct passages that, before the appearance of the Perkins Folio, no one had reason to believe were corrupt, passages that had never been questioned because they made 'acceptable sense' as they stood in the folio text – but passages that we now know contained printers' errors. In these cases the Old Corrector actually *restored* the original words of Shakespeare's text, not by conjecture but by copying from a unique authoritative source that Collier could not have known.

This may, at first, seem impossible: as we have seen, the only surviving authoritative sources are the early printed copies – the various quartos printed during Shakespeare's lifetime and the First Folio – and Collier's knowledge of these early printed texts was comprehensive; he knew all the extant quartos, and if knowledge of any of them identifies the Old Corrector, he would not be absolved of the crime. However, the key word is 'extant'; Collier's innocence rests on that word.

The evidence in the Perkins Folio proves conclusively, I think, that whoever wrote its emendations must have used, along with other printed texts, the rarest and earliest of all Shakespeare quartos, the 1594 *Titus Andronicus*. Although the *Stationers' Register* recorded an edition of *Titus* in 1593, no copy of that edition was thought to have survived, and by the end of the eighteenth century most editors had concluded that either the *Register* entry was an error or the quarto it announced was never published and that the 1600 quarto of the play – the obvious source for the First Folio text – was the first printed version of *Titus Andronicus*. Like his predecessors, Collier had unsuccessfully sought the earlier edition, but, unlike them, he continued to believe it had been printed. As it turned out, Collier was right, but he did not live to know it.

In 1904, twenty years after his death, a copy of the first quarto of *Titus Andronicus,* 1594, was discovered in Sweden with a provenance that proved it had been in that country for at least a century and a half. No other copy has been found since, and the Swedish copy, now in the Folger Library, remains unique. However, collation of that copy with the Perkins Folio proves that at least one other copy once existed – and was consulted by the Old Corrector.

The evidence for this conclusion is minute but decisive: as Joseph Quincy Adams demonstrates in his facsimile edition of the *Titus* first quarto,[36] the second quarto (1600) was set from a defective copy of the first (1594); thereafter the first quarto was lost or ignored and the First Folio text (and from it all subsequent texts) reproduced the version of the second quarto. Adams records nearly a hundred differences between the texts of the two quartos; most of these are unimportant typographical errors which were later arbitrarily corrected in the folio text. Of the remaining changes, most do not alter the text significantly (e.g., the superscription for several of Aaron the Moor's speeches are printed 'Moore' in Q^1 and 'Aron.' in Q^2). There are also several poetic interpolations in the second quarto apparently intended to compensate for defects in the copy that the Q^2 compositor was using. But more significant to our purpose, there are a dozen or so substantive changes introduced into Q^2 that were carried into the First Folio and from thence into the Second Folio (i.e., into the Perkins edition). When the Old Corrector compared his folio with the 1594 quarto, he discovered these differences and altered the Perkins Folio to conform to the Q^1 text.

He did so very idiosyncratically. He was apparently motivated by personal preference rather than any sense of textual accuracy, and he ignored some useful corrections and made others of his own invention, but in six instances he changed the Perkins text to match Q^1. Four of these changes *might* have been conjectural (i.e., they alter words that seem to need to be changed by substituting logical alternatives)[37] but two could not have been: Adams hypothesizes that signature K4 of the Q^1 used for the copy text in setting Q^2 must have had a hole through the page that obliterated parts of words and that the compositor setting Q^2 inserted letters of his own to fit the space. The substitution of signature K4 verso affected a word in Lucius' speech (V, iii) concerning the disposition of Tamora's body. In Q^1, the line had read 'As for that rauenous [ravenous] tiger, Tamora/No funeral rite . . .' but the hole obliterated the first four letters of the word 'rauenous' ('raue'), and the compositor for Q^2 incorrectly conjectured that the missing word was 'heynous' (heinous) and inserted 'hey' to take the place of the missing letters. The 'corrected' passage thus became 'As for that *heynous* tiger, Tamora . . .' and it appeared thus in Q^2 and so remained in all subsequent folio texts – until the Perkins Folio emendations. There the Old Corrector amended the passage by scratching out the 'hey' of 'heynous' in the printed text and inserting 'raue' in the margin as a substitute, thus restoring the Q^1 reading. (See page 354, Fig. 1.)

To make this alteration, the Old Corrector would have had to know Q^1. 'Heynous', while not so apt a description of a tiger as 'rauenous', is intelligible without emendation; neither sense, spelling nor scansion suggests an error in this line, and before the Old Corrector, no one had altered it or suggested the need to do so. There is no possible explanation for the appearance of this emendation in the Perkins Folio except that the Old Corrector found the word in Q^1, preferred it, and inserted it into his folio.[38]

An equally compelling alteration occurs earlier in the same act. In Marcus's speech before the Roman multitude on behalf of Titus, the Q^1 text contains the phrase 'behold us *pleading*' (signature K3 verso line 33). The compositor of Q^2 changed this to 'behold us *now*', and this substitution was carried into the folio texts without alteration. However, in the Perkins Folio the Old Corrector deleted 'now' and wrote 'pleading' into the margin. (Subsequently he – or someone else – thought differently about the correction, and the deletion was removed and the marginal note partially erased.) Again, the only possible source for this correction is the Q^1 text.

The 'rauenous' and 'pleading' emendations prove beyond question that the Old Corrector knew and used the 1594 Q^1 *Titus Andronicus* and in company with these the other Perkins emendations that follow Q^1 can be assumed to derive from the same source. More to the point, they prove that Collier could not have been the Old Corrector, for if he had found the Q[1] *Titus* he would have trumpeted his find. He had sought the missing quarto for a generation; its discovery would have been an event of great importance, and it is therefore inconceivable that he would have kept his *coup* a secret in order to forge a few inconsequential emendations in a corrupted Second Folio. (And what, in that event, happened to the quarto itself? It would have been one of the most valuable books of its kind; are we to assume Collier disposed of it without trace?) Moreover, his subsequent treatment of the 'rauenous' emendation demonstrates that, far from knowing it was authoritative, Collier did not think very highly of it. He published the emendation without comment in *Notes and Emendations* and in *Seven Lectures*; he adopted the reading in his Shakespeare of 1853 and 1858, both based solely on the Perkins corrections; but when he re-edited the play in 1876 (see below p. 386), he rejected the Perkins reading and printed 'heinous' once again – thus 'restoring' the corrupt folio text. Had he known the emendation was, in fact, based on Q[1], he would certainly have included it among the few Perkins emendations that he admitted into his 'final edition' of Shakespeare's plays.

All the evidence – theoretical, circumstantial, practical, and factual – supports the contention that Collier did not forge the emendations in the Perkins Folio. The marginal cuts prove that the writing was made before the book was rebound in the eighteenth century; the unrefuted testimonies of Warner and Wellesley prove the book contained the emendations before Collier got it from Rodd; and since Collier could not have written the *Titus Andronicus* emendation, the evidence is compelling that he did not insert the other emendations in the book which all who have examined it agree are in the same hand.

But if Collier did not forge the emendations, how does one explain the pencil marks? Of all the 'evidence' brought against him, none was so damning as Hamilton's assertion that there were pencil notes in a modern cursive handwriting under the apparently 'antique' emendations and Madden's later declaration that the handwriting was Collier's. To the public, the pencil notation proved the corrections were forgeries and

Collier a forger. If Collier were innocent, how can the pencil writing be explained? It might be more pertinent to ask how it might be explained if he were *guilty,* for surely it is difficult to believe that any such tell-tale proof of forgery would be left behind when, by analogy, hundreds of other emendations in the book must have been erased. If some, why not all? Nevertheless, the pencil marks are there (although some over the years have become so faint that they cannot be seen without the aid of Ingleby's facsimiles) and their presence demands some kind of explanation.

In the first place, there are two kinds of pencil marks in the book. The preponderance are Collier's unambiguous editorial notes, and such marks are not unusual: many manuscripts that passed through the hands of eighteenth- and nineteenth-century scholars bear abundant evidence of interpolation by over-zealous readers in the form of lengthy comments, single words, lines, crosses, 'ticks', and other forms of notation that no one today would call forgery. Modern day scholarship rightly condemns such marginalia as mutilation, but early editors were not so fastidious, and all of Collier's illustrious predecessors and most of his contemporaries wrote in the manuscripts they consulted whether they owned them or not. (Malone, for example, made marginal notes – in ink – in the manuscript of Henslowe's diary.) After Hamilton's charges in *An Inquiry,* Collier freely admitted to making 'crosses, ticks and lines' in the Perkins Folio, and there are many of his pencilled comments in the margins of the book that announce their purpose without pretence or disguise. Their sole function is to articulate the ink emendations, to cite possible sources, to make cross reference, and to index the peculiarities he found there. These editorial pencil notes are not in question, neither were they under suspicion by Ingleby or Madden (despite the fulminations in his diary) who recognized and understood their innocent function.

The other pencil notes, the 'pencil counterparts' to the ink emendations, are far fewer and of a more suspicious kind. In the view of those taking part in the Museum inquisition, they damned Collier, but their purpose is obscure. One might assume they were intended to serve as a more legible gloss to their gothic equivalents, but the ink emendations they reproduce are no more illegible than hundreds of others not so favoured, and they tend, if anything, to be more legible than most. Neither is there any reason to assume that the pencil notes were for emphasis; no special importance can be ascribed to the emendations thus singled out. In short, the purpose of these pencil marks cannot be guessed, yet there they are, and they appear to be in Collier's handwriting. Why? How?

The answer to these questions leads to the best kept secret of the controversy. These pencillings suggest, indeed, that forgery was committed in the pages of the Perkins Folio – but not by John Payne Collier.

To prove this statement it is necessary to examine the 'apparent' function of the notes and to recapitulate some of the details given earlier. To begin with, neither the form nor the substance of these 'pencil counterpart' notes suggests that they were made *before* the ink emendations. In his attempt to inculpate Collier, Madden declared it 'certain' that they 'served ... as the guides' to the ink 'fabrications', that they were the sole survivors of many other pencil notes, now erased, preceding the ink emendations in the book and serving as patterns for them. Madden argued that the pencil marks that remained proved forgery by their presence and, by their resemblance to Collier's hand, proved him the forger, but there is no paleographic justification for this conclusion, and common sense is against it: why would Collier have needed such a 'guide' for commonplace corrections? And if, as Madden declared, Collier wrote *both* the pencil and the ink insertions, who was 'guiding' *whom*? The ink corrections are not the sort for which a knowledgeable forger would need direction: they are short, seldom more than a single word, unambiguous and easy to remember. Significantly, where a pencil guide *might* have been useful – even necessary – to a forger, none is to be found: at two or three places in the folio the Old Corrector inserted several *lines* of text without any vestige of pencil notation to guide him – or erasure to indicate it was once there. Even more significant, the pencil notes that remain appear only in the margins – there are no pencil marks in the body of the printed text itself; the pencil would, therefore, have been virtually useless as a 'guide' because it fails to indicate the one essential detail any 'forger' would have to know – the *place* in the printed line where the emendation was to the inserted. The simple replication of pencil notes and ink emendations does not, therefore, by itself indicate forgery.

However, according to Ingleby, twelve of the thirty 'pencil counterparts' seem to be *under* ink emendations, that is, they seem to prove that the pencil *preceded* the ink. These twelve were to become the chief 'evidence' of Hamilton and Ingleby, and they were reproduced in elaborate facsimile in *An Inquiry* and *A Complete View*.[39] Now, on the face of it, it is very difficult to imagine a forger – even one who needed a 'guide' – so clumsy as to make his fabrication directly on top of his pencil gloss without first erasing the pencil. (The theory that the pencil was erased and that the 'plumbago' subsequently 'returned' when the book was repressed is nonsense.) Nevertheless, if there is pencil writing under the ink and if that writing can be proved to be in Collier's handwriting, it would seem to be, as Madden, Ingleby, Hamilton, and all their successors have claimed, decisive evidence that Collier forged *some* of the ink emendations, and (since all are in the same hand), by analogy, all of them.

However, none of the examples in the book can be so described. First, the only pencil mark that Ingleby *et al.* demonstrated to be under the ink was that referred to in Maskelyne's letter to *The Times* for 16 July, 1859:

The first case I chose for this was a *u* in *Richard II*, p. 36. A pencil tick crossed the *u*, intersecting each limb of that letter. The pencil was barely visible through the first stroke, and not at all visible under the second stroke of the *u*. On damping off the ink in the first stroke, however, the pencil-mark became much plainer than before, and even when as much of the inkstain as possible was removed the pencil still runs through the ink line in unbroken even continuity....

This is the only evidence published by Collier's accusers to support Hamilton's contention that pencil *writing* underlay the ink, but here the pencil mark is not a *word* but a 'tick' which has no substantive connection to the emendation and to which no date of composition can be assigned. It is entirely possible that someone made pencil 'ticks' in the book in the seventeenth century – there is therefore nothing inherently incriminating in the fact that one of them underlay the ink; certainly the fact does not impugn Collier. Maskelyne states that the example was the 'first case' he tested, and the clear implication is that, having found his 'proof', he made no other tests. Why, given the nature of the critical question and the purpose of the test, did he not examine one of the examples he mentions in which 'the ink word and the pencil *word* occupy the same ground in the margin' [my emphasis]? Why examine a 'tick' that could prove nothing when there were 'words' that might prove all? The question suggests a well kept secret: this was *not* the only 'case' tested. A letter from Ingleby to Madden reveals that Maskelyne tested at least three other 'cases' in the folio. The results of these tests were not made public,[40] but it can be assumed they did not prove forgery or Ingleby would have used them. It is therefore reasonable to assume that the *Richard II* example was the only one that 'successfully proved' what the Museum authorities claimed against *all* twelve of these emendations. If Maskelyne had found a pencilled *word* under an ink emendation, he would certainly have used the more damning example in place of or along with the innocuous one he printed. Close examination of the folio reveals that despite the assertions of Hamilton, Ingleby and Madden, *none* of Maskelyne's remaining examples gives clear and unmistakable evidence that the ink lines overlap the pencil. Madden's extrapolation from Maskelyne's test to other emendations is therefore fallacious.

It is, moreover, significant that Maskelyne's letter declares that some of the pencilling seems to 'stop at the edge of the ink' – an indication that the pencil may have been drawn over the ink in such a way as to *avoid* overlapping it. Close examination of the Perkins Folio itself supports the conclusion that in at least two of the examples cited by Ingleby, the pencil is, in fact, on *top* of the ink and hence must have been written *after* the ink emendation was in the book.[41] In the other examples, the pencil is now too faint to make a clear delineation (in some places it has simply disappeared and can be reconstructed only by reference to the facsimiles Hamilton and Ingleby printed), but in its present state the Perkins Folio does not reveal *any* instance in which the pencil writing can be said to have been made first.

Second, none of the pencilled 'words' that, to use Maskelyne's phrase, 'occupy the same ground' with ink emendations can be identified with Collier's handwriting. They are little more than vague scratches. Even in the facsimiles published by Ingleby and Hamilton they require much imagination to be construed into words and could not, on the basis of comparison, be conclusively ascribed to the hand of Collier or anyone else.

The conclusion one must draw from all of this is that Collier had no possible motive for making pencil marks to 'guide' ink forgeries; that the pencil notes do not demonstrably precede the ink emendations corresponding to them and that in fact some of them clearly were written *after* the ink; that even if the pencil writing were before the ink it could not be ascribed to Collier; and thus that the assertion of Hamilton, Ingleby, Madden *et al.*, that the writing confirms Collier's guilt, is specious. The pencil writing does not and cannot incriminate Collier or prove he forged the other emendations in the Perkins Folio.

Nevertheless, the pen-pencil emendations may reveal forgery – not forgery *by* Collier, but forgery 'against' him. Given what we now know of Madden's motives and the general treatment the folio received after it was delivered into his hands, it is not too far-fetched to believe that the thirty or so 'pencil counterparts' may have been manufactured in the Museum. They could have been of no use to Collier in forgery, but they were essential to Madden and company as 'evidence' of what they believed but could not otherwise 'prove'.

Circumstantial evidence supports this conjecture. First, there are the highly suspicious events surrounding the discovery of the 'pencil counterparts'. Note: the Perkins Folio was under daily scrutiny for three weeks – from 25 May to 25 June – without *any*one seeing the incriminating pencil writing. The book was subjected to chemical analysis for ink erasures; it was taken apart to find evidence of recent tampering; and for the better part of a month it was put through what must have been the most intensive examination ever given a book with the sole purpose of finding incriminating evidence, and yet none was discovered during those three weeks. Madden himself had pored over the volume filling pages of his notebook with a detailed account of his examination (including remarks concerning the many 'pencil memoranda' which Collier made on its covers), but during all that time he apparently found no pencil evidence of forgery. Hamilton and Bond examined the folio at length and saw nothing; Dyce and Forster 'passed all afternoon' with it, and other scholars, no friends to Collier, searched the book for many hours, looking, we may assume, for incriminating evidence; but the careful examination of Dyce, Forester, Staunton, Bodenstedt, Todd and others found no tell-tale pencil marks in the book.

For twenty-two days the search was fruitless, and in this period Madden frequently complained in his diary that proof of Collier's guilt had not been found and that this lack of proof was beginning to shake belief in the forgery. On 2 June, Edward Bond declared his opinion that the ink writing in the folio might be genuine after all. Suddenly and fortuitously in the midst of this widening disagreement Madden discovered the 'pencil counterparts', the evidence he needed to prove the ink emendations were 'modern'.[42] It was an astonishing discovery! There were scarcely a dozen potentially incriminating examples scattered throughout hundreds of pages of the folio, and they had eluded all previous readers, but Madden, by his own account, found *all* of them in one evening. Apparently no one wondered why Madden had been able to find in an hour or two what others had missed in several hundred. But Madden now had 'proof' of Collier's guilt that satisfied even Bond.

Yet more curious was Madden's subsequent desire to hide the fact that it was *he* who had found the damning proof. That it *was* he there can be no doubt; his diary emphatically attests to that fact several times, and his declaration in the letter to Ingleby of 20 July, 1859 (see pp. 245–6) reiterates it. Yet when he showed the 'pencil counterparts' to Hamilton after that night of revelation, he prevailed upon his assistant to say that he, *Hamilton,* had found them. What overweening modesty directed Madden to give his subordinate the undeserved credit for the most important paleographical discovery of the decade? Why was Madden so determined that no one should know that it was *he* who first discovered the evidence that had eluded so many sophisticated readers? The lie served no apparent purpose except to separate Madden from the pencil marks, and he could have had no reason for wanting this unless he knew they were not what they seemed, knew they were, in fact, forgeries themselves. Then, and only then, would he have wanted to be sure that his own involvement was 'safely' secondary to others.

There is circumstantial evidence which supports the conjecture that the 'pencil counterparts' were written into the Perkins Folio at the Museum. At least one of the pencil marks that Madden pointed out to Hamilton appears not to have been in the folio when Collier showed the book in 1852. Collier's only stipulation at the time, it may be remembered, was that viewers were not to make notes of what they found there, but memory alone would serve a knowledgeable editor looking to see how one or two of his favourite textual 'problems' were treated by the Old Corrector, and hence, even without notes, some readings of the folio, as yet unseen or unpublished by Collier, must have been noted by others. When Samuel Weller Singer saw the folio he apparently looked up one of his textual crotchets, the word 'strain'. Shakespeare uses it in at least three plays *(A Winter's Tale, The Merry Wives of Windsor,* and *Love's Labour's Lost)* in passages that previous editors, to Singer's great irritation, called unintelligible and emended in one way or another. Singer, when he first saw the Perkins Folio in 1852, was particularly eager to see what the Old Corrector had done with them. In his view, if 'strain' were emended in any way in the folio, the emendations were *not* authoritative. As his subsequent publication makes clear, the passage Singer sought out was a line of Biron in *Love's Labour's Lost* (V, ii, 833). The folio prints:

> As love is full of Unbefitting straines,
> All wanton as a childe, skipping and vaine...

Sure enough, the Perkins corrector had emended 'straines', as Singer read the emendation, by drawing an ink line through the word in the text ('strai/nes') to delete 'nes' and insert 'ngs' in the margin to make 'strai+ngs' or 'strayings'. This, to Singer's mind, was a gross betrayal of sense. A few months later he published *Shakespeare Vindicated,* and in that diatribe against the folio one of his chief bits of evidence to prove the tasteless impropriety of the Old Corrector was the 'strayings' emendation of *Love's Labour's Lost.* He called it a 'fatal perversion of the language of the poet' that 'could not have been made by any one who could . . . have had old authority for what he or they have done.'[43]

As it happened, Singer had misread the emendation. In *Notes and Emendations* (which appeared several months before Singer's *Vindicated*), Collier had included the reading as one of his examples: there he correctly noted that the slash through the printed word ('strai/nes') was a sign of *division* (not deletion) and that the letters in the margin ('nge' *not* 'ngs') were to be inserted at that point (i.e., 'strai' + 'nes') to produce 'straingenes' ('strangeness').[44] However, despite Collier's published account, Singer persisted in his own reading. When his edition of Shakespeare appeared four years later, he appended a note to the passage ignoring *Notes and Emendations* and giving instead his own recollection: 'Here again', he wrote, 'the corrector of Mr. Collier's folio would change *strains* for *strayings*; but Shakespeare's word was *strains,* i.e., *wanton light, unbecoming behaviour.*'[45]

Three years later, the emendation was one of those Hamilton reproduced in *An Inquiry* as having pencil writing under the ink emendation. The marginal letters 'nge', he declared, were written over a pencil word, 'strangeness', parts of which were clearly visible around the ink and apparently under it. It was, in fact, one of only two examples in the facsimiles which Hamilton declared to have a pencil *word* under an ink emendation. It was, as well, one of the few examples in which the pencil, though light, was readily discernible. In fact, anyone who saw the ink letters in the margin, surrounded as they were – and are – by the pencil letters, could hardly have misread them as Singer did. The intention of the word 'strangeness' is unmistakable. The obvious conclusion is that the pencil was *not* around the ink emendation when Singer saw it. He had, after all, no reason to ignore the pencil – he did not prefer 'strayings' to 'strangeness', *any* alteration of the printed word was ridiculous to him – and he must have examined the page with great care.

Either Singer was uncharacteristically careless and unobservant or someone added the pencil *after* Collier showed the book to him. If this were the case that person obviously would not have been Collier, who would have no cause to incriminate himself in this way. Moreover, if the gloss had been there when Collier used the folio, it is hard to see how *he* could have overlooked the pencil around the emendation, and if he saw it, he would not have been so adamant in asserting there were no such pencil marks in the book. After all, it was a mechanically complicated emendation, and a latter day reader might have written the pencil around the ink as a reminder of the word that the Old Corrector intended.

On the other hand, the pencil addition – if it was an addition – *might* have been put in the folio to discredit the ink note – in the context of the arguments Madden put forward. Close examination of this emendation gives no evidence that the pencil intersects the ink at any point and that a very careful hand might have drawn the pencil in such a way as to make it seem to have been written first. The 'straines' emendation would have been a clever choice for such an interpolation as any would-be forger would have known; it was a point of contention between Collier and Singer and to implant Collier's reading in pencil would, therefore, be very incriminating to him. It was also 'safe' since Singer, who might have attested to the appearance of the text in 1852, was – fortunately or unfortunately depending on one's point of view – dead when Madden 'discovered' the 'pencil counterparts' in 1859.

The circumstantial evidence is very strong, therefore, that the incriminating pencil writing was put in the Perkins Folio while it was in the British Museum – a circumstance which would preclude Collier's having made it. But if not Collier, who? As I have noted, the writing *under* the ink emendations is too fragmentary to be construed into a recognizable hand. Moreover, the 'pencil counterparts' that are *separated* from the ink are so few and so sketchy that positive identification with any other handwriting must be largely conjectural. Indeed, if the origin of the pencilled words had not become so decisive in the case, one would not attempt it at all. However, given the necessity, a fact hitherto ignored becomes significant: the handwriting of Frederic Madden closely resembled that of John Payne Collier. Both men wrote a loose, 'open' cursive script, and they shared superficially similar 'careless' characteristics. If one were looking at isolated examples of a word or two or a single letter only, one might easily take the hand of Collier for that of Madden – or *vice versa* – as Madden, who claimed 'many years' experience' reading Collier's handwriting would have known. If attribution must be made, therefore, it is clear that the damning examples that Hamilton reproduced – under Madden's direction – bear as much resemblance to *Madden*'s hand as they do to Collier's. For example, one of the most legible of the newly found pencil words, 'begging' in the margin of *Hamlet* (p. 187), looks very much like the word as written by Madden in his diary (Figs. 2 and 3). Or again, 'God' on p. 67 of *Measure for Measure* is remarkably similar to its counterpart in the diary (Figs. 4 and 5).[46] Individual letters show other striking similarities, and given time and enough specimens, one could probably match all the 'pencil correlations' with similar examples in Madden's papers. Obviously, if Madden wrote the incriminating pencil words into the margins of the Perkins Folio, he did not mean to do so in his own hand; the point here is that it would have required no studied – and hence no dangerous – *imitation* to create the effect of Collier's writing. It required little skill to pass off his own more or less regular script, carelessly scrawled on to the margins of the book in thirty or so places, for that of the man who, he was convinced, had actually forged the ink emendations but until the pencil was 'discovered' could not be convicted of having done so.

The circumstantial details in aggregate become compelling: there is good reason to believe that at least some of the pencil writing was not in the folio when Collier showed it to Singer in 1852 and that Collier would have had no reason to put it in the book after that date; that the incriminating pencil marks were probably not in the folio when it arrived at the Museum because a score of Collier's adversaries looking for this sort of evidence did not find them; that the pencil notes may have been written into the book by Sir Frederic Madden when he believed the case he had made against Collier was beginning to collapse; and that Madden then covered his work

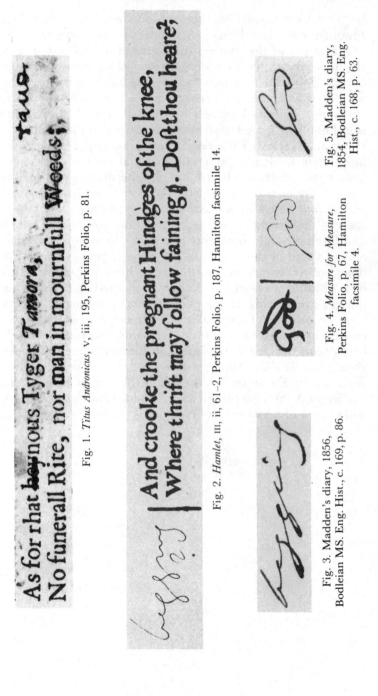

Fig. 1. *Titus Andronicus*, v, iii, 195, Perkins Folio, p. 81.

Fig. 2. *Hamlet*, III, ii, 61–2, Perkins Folio, p. 187, Hamilton facsimile 14.

Fig. 3. Madden's diary, 1856,
Bodleian MS. Eng. Hist., c. 169, p. 86.

Fig. 4. *Measure for Measure*,
Perkins Folio, p. 67, Hamilton
facsimile 4.

Fig. 5. Madden's diary,
1854, Bodleian MS. Eng.
Hist., c. 168, p. 63.

by prevailing upon Hamilton to announce that *he*, and not Madden, had 'found' the pencil marks in the margin.

Madden had the motive, the opportunity, the means and the necessary ability to write the 'pencil counterparts' into the Perkins Folio. He may have believed he was merely providing 'proof' of what he was convinced was the truth, and later, when the Warner–Wellesley testimony proved that Collier could not have forged the corrections, he belied their evidence. If he had fabricated the pencil marks to support a belief he later came to doubt, pride and personal vindictiveness may have kept him from admitting it. By the time he realized his danger, the incriminating details so permeated his diary and papers that he could not with certainty eradicate all of them short of destroying the whole, and this the professional habits of a lifetime would not allow him to do: there was too much else of value in the diaries to destroy any part of them. He therefore chose another way to avoid self-incrimination: at his death Madden left strict instructions that within hours of his funeral every scrap of his personal and professional papers – all the volumes of his diaries, his manuscripts, his correspondence, his professional notes – everything – should be sealed, crated and shipped to the Bodleian Library, there to remain *unopened* until 1920. He must have been convinced that fifty years would obliterate all interest in the case of John Payne Collier and the role Sir Frederic Madden had played in its outcome, and he was right. Well, *almost* right.

X

MEN'S EYES

*'. . . it is my tendency now to think worse of the
world than it really deserves.'*

31

Some of Collier's enemies hoped Ingleby's attack would be a
killing blow. ('He is pinned to the wall', Sir Francis Palgrave
wrote to Ingleby after reading *A Complete View*, 'and let him
writhe and wriggle so much as he may there he must remain
until he has rotted away.'[1]) But Collier lived another twenty-
three years and, judged solely by the quantity of his
publications, these were to be among the most 'productive' of
his life. Despite an occasional attack of arthritis, Collier's
health was good (weather permitting, he would daily walk
three or four miles along the Thames without tiring), and his
mind was as quick and keen as ever. Moreover, Louisa's
inheritance and his pensions enabled his daughter Emma to
maintain a comfortable household, a cook, two maids, and a
gardener. His children were financially independent: Henrietta had married a prosperous wine merchant; William had a
good position at £800 a year with the Legacy Duty Office in
Ireland where he lived with his wife and twelve children; and
John Pycroft was Assistant Paymaster General with £1,300 a
year, quite enough to provide for *his* family of eleven.
Throughout the controversy Collier's children were firm in
their belief that he was cruelly maligned, a belief based on
filial loyalty rather than an understanding of the case, for, as
Collier was often to lament, none of them showed the slightest
interest in literary or antiquarian study.

Neither was Collier suddenly abandoned by his friends. A
few months after Ingleby's book appeared, American supporters presented Collier with a handsome silver inkstand as a
token of esteem, and English admirers commissioned Charles

Baxter to paint his portrait. At home and abroad, his was still a reputation to take notice of; he remained a literary lion – ageing and scarred, perhaps, but a power nonetheless. In the ensuing years he would be appointed to several *ad hoc* commissions (he was, for example, a leader among those who saved the Shakespeare birthplace at Stratford-upon-Avon when American entrepreneurs nearly succeeded in moving the building across the Atlantic) and he was regularly consulted by scholars on a wide range of bibliographical and scholarly topics.

Evidence of Collier's continuing influence can be found in his correspondence with other, generally younger, bibliographers, most notably, William Carew Hazlitt, grandson of the essayist, who was to be the most important among Collier's successors. In 1863, while Hazlitt was compiling his *Handbook to the Popular, Poetical and Dramatic Literature of Great Britain from the Invention of Printing to the Restoration* (1867), he began a correspondence with Collier which was to continue for nearly ten years. It was a 'one-sided' relationship – there was little the seventy-five-year-old Collier could learn from the thirty-five-year-old Hazlitt, and the exchange therefore consisted largely of Hazlitt's questions and Collier's sometimes less than helpful answers. Collier was jealous of his 'unique' knowledge and suspicious of new 'scientific' methods of textual study. ('I really know nothing about signatures in the original impressions of "The Phoenix Nest"', he wrote in response to one of Hazlitt's questions. 'I seldom look at signatures unless to test the perfectness of a copy.'[2]) He was sensitive to the dangers that each generation of scholarship creates for its predecessors – had he not built his own reputation on the ruins of his forebears? – and Hazlitt was a potential competitor, albeit an extremely attractive one, who threatened Collier's past achievement with new improvements.[3] Collier was therefore not always as informative as Hazlitt wanted him to be. 'I am bound to confess', Hazlitt was to write many years later, 'that whenever I applied to Collier for information on literary facts within his presumed knowledge, I always found him anxious to parry inquiry. He usually sent evasive answers to my not unreasonable call for fuller particulars about a book or statement, for which he was perhaps the sole authority.'[4]

It was true that Collier was suspicious and wary, but Hazlitt was insatiable, and he owed Collier much more than he subsequently was willing to admit. When Collier was not blinded by egoism, he could see the talent of the younger man as well as faults which were similar to his own. ('Do not be in too much haste, nor have too many irons in the fire at the same time',[5] he once advised Hazlitt, and he often assumed an intimate – even collaborative – tone with him. 'Your young ardour and my old care may do something',[6] he once wrote in uncharacteristic camaraderie.) Nevertheless, Collier encouraged criticism from Hazlitt that he would never have accepted from others. 'Do not scruple to find fault with me when I am wrong', he wrote on one occasion, 'as I only want to be right'.[7] When his pride clashed with Hazlitt's own large self esteem, it was Collier, as often as not, who made peace. ('Pray keep your temper, and allow for any errors of mine by remembering that I am in my 79th year.')[8] If in later years Hazlitt belittled this interchange, it is clear that he would not have sought Collier's opinions so regularly had he not found them useful at the time.

During the next twenty years Collier produced a prodigious number of books. Most of these were the gleanings of a lifetime of note-taking, but the labour of publication alone would have taxed the energy of a younger man. Between 1861 and 1879 he brought out a five-volume edition of Spenser (1862), published a continuation of the *Stationers' Register* transcript (begun thirteen years before for the Shakespeare Society and now completed piecemeal in *Notes and Queries,* 1861–63),[9] edited a new collection of Trevelyan Papers for the Camden Society (1863), compiled a two-volume *Bibliographical and Critical Account of the Rarest Books in the English Language* (1865) and, during the decade of the 1860s, selected, edited and published over ninety-four rare tracts and collections in nine different subscription series that he produced single-handed (May 1862 – January 1870). In addition he published two ballad collections (1868, 1869), a book of his own occasional poems (1870), a four-part personal memoir (1871–72), and a new defence of the Perkins Folio (1874). In his eighty-seventh year he produced yet another edition of Shakespeare in forty-two parts including the poems and four of the apocryphal plays, which he edited, proof-read, published and sent off to fifty subscribers between January 1875 and January 1878. But even this was not his last work: at the age of ninety he reissued, with slight revision, *The History of English Dramatic Poetry*, first printed half a century before, and when that was finished he complained that he was bored and eager for 'something to do'!

The most important of these 'post-controversy' works was the edition of Spenser which Collier completed and published while Ingleby's catcalls were still echoing. The conclusion of a lifetime's devotion to Spenser, the edition had been planned for fifteen years and laboured over for three. Collier saw it as the crowning achievement of his career. It was not to be his last work, but it was certainly his most elegant, handsomely printed and bound. Its scholarship was good, too,[10] establishing, for the first time, an authoritative text for Spenser. Henry Todd's edition of 1805 had accepted the folio as the base text and only incidentally referred to the quartos, whereas Collier, following the method he had refined in editing Shakespeare, took the extant quartos as his base text, a practice followed by all subsequent editors. It was the first edition to establish the Q^1 of *The Shepherds Calendar* which was thereafter fixed in the Spenser canon. Except for a somewhat lengthy biographical essay, Collier kept his critical apparatus to a minimum, and his footnotes were as brief as those in his first edition of Shakespeare. His editorial tone was chastened too. He corrected Todd's 'inaccuracies', and he condemned his predecessor's 'want of care', but he also praised Todd's learning and dedication. He may have been patronizing a colleague from whom he could expect no rejoinder (Todd had died in 1845), or perhaps he felt secure in his own achievement and thought he should be generous, but for whatever reason, the Spenser edition lacked the pugnacious tone which had marred so much of Collier's earlier criticism.

Despite its quality, the edition was not a success: the public had much less interest in Spenser than in Shakespeare, and although Collier's text was not wholly ignored – it went through two subsequent editions within ten years[11] and was reprinted and plagiarized many times in the next fifty – it received little recognition. The *Athenaeum* was apparently the only journal to notice the work, and most of its review was devoted to a précis of Collier's biography of the poet. Concerning the text itself, the journal was ambiguous, cool, and unknowledgeable. 'Mr. Collier's reputation as an editor of Elizabethan classics is well sustained by the present publication', it said. The verse was in 'as accurate a form as conscientious criticism can procure for it.'[12] Five years later the *Westminster Review* called Collier 'the only worthy successor' to Todd but, characteristically, berated him for his learning: 'The reader of Spenser', it declared, 'does not wish to know . . . how many worthless books Mr. Collier has read.'[13] Although all subsequent editors were to be in Collier's debt for his collation of the early quartos, few would admit their obligation,[14] and the most complete and accurate text of Spenser to appear since the poet's death went virtually unnoticed. Once again Crabb Robinson represented the general opinion: he didn't care for Spenser's poetry, and he was bored by Spenser's life. Collier, he wrote in his diary, 'has laboured to ascertain most insignificant facts which, when proved, mean nothing . . . a more unentertaining piece of biography cannot be well imagined.'[15] What Collier had hoped would be the culminating achievement to his career was a critical anticlimax, and its reception would distress him for the rest of his life. Twenty years later, when death was a daily expectation, he would still feel deep resentment that he would 'never get credit for the great pains' he had taken in the work.[16]

But this disappointment came later, and in the meantime Collier had new projects to undertake, new writing to do. There was something almost demoniac in his need to be 'at work'. All his life, quite literally from his first recollections, he had been a writer – a copyist for his father before he could compose a sentence of his own, and from then on, as court reporter, newspaper hack, secretary, correspondent, editor, he had spent the better part of every day 'putting pen to paper'. He had indeed been 'bred up to authorship', but it was no longer a vocation, it had become a compulsion. He had to have something to do, which is to say, something to write, something to put into print.

Thus, even before he completed reading the proofs of his

edition of Spenser he began what was to be the largest and
most prolonged undertaking of his career: reprinting by
subscription rare early English texts. It was an extension of the
work he had done for the Shakespeare, Camden, and Percy
Societies, and although those organizations (and at least a
dozen others) had issued hundreds of reprints, there were still
many rare works to be rescued from obscurity. It was not, of
course, the first time Collier had undertaken private subscription publication (he had published a half dozen facsimiles
prior to his work with the societies), but what he proposed
now was a programme comparable to that of the Shakespeare
Society itself, a 'reprinting club' of twenty-five members who
would receive, at cost, four to six publications a year in a
uniform small-quarto format. In his announcement in the
Athenaeum he reminded his readers of his past experience as an
editor and promised that these reprints would be produced
more efficiently and cheaply than heretofore. His earlier tracts
had appreciated in value and so would these. 'I have devoted a
long life to pursuits of the kind', he declared, 'and I know the
pecuniary, as well as the intrinsic, value of most of the early
specimens of our literature.'[17]

The response to his announcement surprised even Collier – the first day's mail brought more than his goal of twenty-
five subscribers, and he immediately increased the number to
fifty. He knew the reprints would lose money – but he was
ready to pay for the pleasure of the work. Since his regular
income could not support the expense, he sought help from his
nephew, Frederic Ouvry, a well-to-do lawyer. Alone among
Collier's relatives, Ouvry shared the old man's literary
passions; he had assumed the role of 'heir presumptive' to his
uncle's work. It was Ouvry, rather than his sons, whom Collier
sponsored for membership in the Society of Antiquaries, and
Ouvry followed him through the Society's hierarchy, serving
long in Collier's old office of treasurer and, like Collier,
becoming at last its chief executive officer. Ouvry was a man
of taste and talent, a solicitor whose skill and good luck had
made him wealthy. As his fortune grew, so did his collection of
books and manuscripts, and over the years, with Collier as his
mentor and occasional agent, Ouvry's library became distinguished. It was therefore a foregone conclusion that one way

or another, the best of Collier's books would eventually be acquired by his nephew, and Collier now proposed selling Ouvry the best of his collection, one by one, to pay for his reprints. It was not an easy choice ('I never parted with a book that I did not afterwards, for some reason or other, regret', he once declared)[18] but it was a mutually convenient one; Collier had unlimited use of Ouvry's library, and many of the books he 'sold' remained, in fact, in his own possession. On the other hand, the arrangement was a windfall for Ouvry, because Collier accepted from his nephew far less than the books would have brought at auction. (Collier abhorred the thought of selling his books to anyone else – a public sale, he declared, was 'not to be thought of unless I intended to proclaim my poverty'.[19]) Thus, during the next six or seven years, as money was needed to pay for the new series, Ouvry acquired many of the best of Collier's books.[20]

Six weeks after announcing his subscription plan in April 1862, Collier began issuing his 'red' series, subsequently titled *Illustrations of Early English Popular Literature* and 'divided' into two volumes of twelve issues each. The first number might be taken as typical of the rest: it was *A Pithy Note to Papists All and Some that Joy in Feltons Martirdom* by Thomas Knell (London, 1570), an anti-Catholic ballad in rhyming couplets from a unique copy that Collier had found in the Bridgewater library thirty years before; it was short (twenty pages) and inexpensive (two shillings), and it contained a typographical facsimile of the original title page along with a brief bibliographical introduction. The texts of the 'red' series were to be 'popular literature' in the sense that they were initially printed for public amusement rather than political or social controversy, and the subjects were therefore diverse: Biblical tracts, accounts of murders, lyrics for popular songs, broadsides, etc. The only common element among them was rarity; the originals from which Collier took his transcripts often existed in only one or two copies.

The first series ran for twenty-four months, and as soon as it was completed in April 1864, Collier advertised a second, the 'green' series, which also contained twenty-four monthly issues subsequently collected under the title *Illustrations of Old English Literature* and gathered into three volumes of eight issues each.

The 'red' series had been an unqualified success (Collier had, in fact, refused many would-be subscribers in order to hold to his limit of fifty), and the new series followed an almost identical pattern. This 'green' series, containing longer works, cost more, but the increase in price was apparently no deterrent to attracting fifty members.

This reprinting scheme was not original or unique (Halliwell was publishing his own more modest series at the same time), but it was distinguished by its range of subjects and number of issues, and it remains the largest privately printed collection of early English literary ephemera. By twentieth-century standards, Collier's texts are inferior, illustrating all the faults of careless transcription endemic in nineteenth-century scholarship, but Collier was better than most of his contemporaries and, at least in theory, reluctant to alter his originals. 'I . . . never correct but where it is absolutely necessary for the sense', he wrote to Hazlitt. 'The blunders of old typographers are sometimes valuable and often curious and interesting – I often like an old error better than a modern improvement.'[21] Unfortunately, he was not consistent, and his limitations were exacerbated by age; he often paid others to make his transcriptions, and although Collier was generally an accurate copyist, those he hired were not. 'What I want is the *most extreme accuracy, and fair writing*, which cannot be misread and mistaken', he instructed one of his scribes,[22] but he rarely checked their work, and they, miserably paid (by the sheet), had no real incentive to be more exact than usual. Moreover, it was not standard procedure to correct a reprint against its original; in fact, Collier reprinted many works without seeing the original at all, a circumstance modern editors would condemn out of hand. But in the context of the procedures prevailing at the time, in an age before the typewriter and photography made accuracy relatively easy and therefore to be expected, the texts of Collier's reprints are better than average.

Collier's chief labour in the reprint process was selecting a text, obtaining a transcript (which meant hiring a copier unless a copy were readily available), writing a brief bibliographical introduction, sending the transcript to the printer, correcting printer's proof, and mailing the finished work to his subscribers. The longer the wait, the more time-consuming the process, but at the outset, Collier still had time and energy for other projects. He wrote half a dozen letters to the *Athenaeum* on various topics (Shakespeare's part in *The Yorkshire Tragedy*, a newly discovered poem by Ben Jonson, etc.), and he undertook to revise and enlarge the Bridgewater Catalogue that he had published for Ellesmere nearly thirty years before. The original edition of that work was now rare, and Collier had subsequently collected a wealth of new data, enough, in fact, to double the size of the original text to nearly 2,000 items and to justify a new title. The result, *A Bibliographical and Critical Account of the Rarest Books in the English Language,* appeared in two volumes in April 1865 and was to be one of Collier's most important works. Like its predecessor, the bibliography excluded examples of English drama which Collier had already published in other bibliographies, but it included many tracts related to the theatre that had been previously unknown.

Virtually all the information in the book had been gathered much earlier from the Bridgewater collection, the Bodleian Library, and the British Museum. The new introduction ('probably the last preface I shall ever be able to compose') gave Collier an opportunity to denigrate the British Museum collection in comparison with the Bodleian and, once again, to reiterate his demand – so painfully rejected sixteen years before – for a compendious museum catalogue. In the intervening years Panizzi had become Principal Librarian, and the collection still had no printed catalogue. Collier made a last relatively moderate plea for his alternative: without mentioning Panizzi by name, he approved the librarian's 'energy, ability and acquirements' but condemned his failure to provide 'a concise and intelligible means of reference to the books' which, he thought, 'much counterbalanced the other advantages derived from his position.' At seventy-six, Collier had no energy for polemics and he knew he would not use the national library again. 'I am so near the end of my laborious course', he wrote, 'that the existing stage of the catalogues can make little difference to me.'[23] The reiteration of his old thesis after so many years suggests the depth of his earlier humiliation. He was, in fact, almost paranoid about the subject. 'The authorities of the British Museum . . . owe me a grudge', he wrote to Hazlitt a year or two after his preface appeared, 'and will perhaps pay it off one of these days. They are looking out for an opportunity, as a cat watches a mouse – pretending indifference, and to look another way. Even now, they are *obliged to get my reprints,* as they can, thro' a side channel, because they do not like to appear to encourage me.'[24] This comment is evidence of Collier's state of mind rather than of a continuing Museum conspiracy against him. He evidently preferred the enmity of his old antagonists to their latter day indifference. He would rather have been damned than forgotten.

As soon as *A Bibliographical and Critical Account* was ready for the press in late 1864, Collier announced yet another reprint series. The 'green' series still had another two years to run, but in January 1865, Collier began to issue a 'blue' series that was to be the most ambitious collection of the lot: *Seven English Poetical Miscellanies* originally printed between 1557 and 1602. Unlike its two predecessors, the new series reprinted not pamphlets and tracts but whole books, anthologies of popular poetry running to several hundred pages each. The first was *Tottel's Miscellany* (1557), which Collier called 'the oldest and most interesting in our language, containing as it does the poems of the Earl of Surrey, Sir Thomas Wyatt, and their contemporaries.' The work had never before been reprinted in its entirety, and Collier issued it in three parts, over 300 pages in all, for twenty-five shillings.[25] As this suggests, Collier had transformed an initially modest reprinting scheme into a good-sized publishing project and, for him, a rather risky one, for he now commenced to sell the works individually; one could subscribe to all seven and thereby ensure receiving copies, or one could buy them one at a time, and the loss for unsold copies was Collier's own.

During the next eighteen months, he issued six more miscellanies: *The Paradyse of Daynty Deuises* (1578) in November 1865; *A Gorgious Gallery of Gallant Inventions* (1578) in January 1866; *The Phoenix Nest* (1593) in June 1866; *Englands Helicon* (1600) in two parts in July 1866; Davison's *A Poetical Rapsody* (1602) in three parts in December 1866; and *Englands Parnassus* (1600) in five parts from March to August 1867.

Unlike *Tottel's Miscellany*, these works had been reprinted
before by Collier's notable predecessors Thomas Park, who, in
Heliconia (1815), reproduced *A Gorgeous Gallery, The Phoenix
Nest*, and *England's Parnassus*, and Samuel E. Brydges, who had
republished the other three in privately printed editions from
his Lee Priory Press (1810–14). Collier's texts were better than
those of Parks and Brydges (which Hazlitt and Collier agreed
were mere 'burlesques' of the originals),[26] but the earlier
versions could still be found on used book stalls for less money.
By the time *England's Helicon* appeared, publication costs had
increased, and Collier's price began to deter subscribers who
would pay ten shillings for the reprint of a unique tract but
not thirty for a book available elsewhere. Collier was losing
ten shillings on every copy, and he took to lecturing his
subscribers, somewhat peevishly, in the columns of the
Athenaeum. 'Should my experiment fail here', he wrote, 'I have
had a very handsome offer from the other side of the Atlantic
(where my last bibliographical work has been expensively
reprinted in four handsome volumes) to enable me to carry it
on, not only without risk, but with sure advantage.'[27] There
may have been such an offer, but there is no record of it, and
the American edition of *A Bibliographical and Critical Account*,
which was indeed handsome, was pirated.[28]

In spite of faltering sales, Collier persisted. After *Seven
Poetical Miscellanies*, he continued the 'blue' series with two
more long collections: George Turberville's *Epitaphes, Epi-
grams, Songs and Sonets* (1567), which he announced in August
1867 and published shortly thereafter, and Whetstone's *The
Rocke of Regard* (1576), which he issued in three parts during
the spring and summer of 1868. Although these reprints were
unique, they sold so badly that Collier suspended the series
indefinitely, and in April 1863 began a 'yellow' series of less
expensive reprints of *Miscellaneous Tracts* from the times of
Elizabeth and James I. The 'yellow' series, which continued
off and on until September 1870, was to contain fifteen titles,
two-thirds of them reprinted for the first time in 250 years,
and one, *The Pastorals and Other Workes of William Basse*, was a
previously unpublished manuscript in the possession of F. W.
Cosens. The first issues in the 'yellow' series were of nine
pamphlets comprising the notorious Robert Greene–Thomas

Nashe–Gabriel Harvey quarrel of the 1590s. The quarrel was a well-known event in literary history, but until Collier's publication the whole sequence had never been generally available.[29]

The 'yellow' series flourished for a year, but then it too languished. Collier by now had serious competition from a new generation of specialized printing clubs, notably the Early English Text Society, founded in 1864. Moreover, the 'yellow' series came out erratically, and the public easily forgot the project between issues. In February 1869 Collier complained of the 'slackness on the part of a few of my former encouragers',[30] and to Hazlitt he privately admitted that he had almost exhausted his funds. 'If my friends wish me to continue those reprints', he wrote, 'you and they *must put me in funds.*'[31] His scolding did not help matters. His subscribers dropped from fifty to thirty-five.

The delays in the 'yellow' series were caused by Collier's old failing – doing too many things at once. For a time he had *four* series going simultaneously, the 'blue', the 'yellow', a 'magenta' series (only three were issued) of previously unreprinted works of Samuel Daniel and Michael Drayton (December 1869 to June 1870), and a 'new red' series, three large collections of old ballads and poetry issued as gifts for friends annually on his birthday, between 1868 and 1870.[32] 'I keep myself alive', he wrote to a friend, 'by busying myself about trifles, you may say, hardly worth the trouble. They are worth it, if only because they occupy my time, and keep me from going permanently to sleep.'[33] This multiplicity of publication was, of course, characteristic of Collier throughout his life, but at eighty he could no longer sustain it as he once had, and the 'yellow' series suffered. That it didn't collapse entirely is probably due to his shrewdness in choosing titles intrinsically valuable to a small but solid core of his subscribers.

Thus, for seven years after the controversy that culminated in Ingleby's attack in *A Complete View,* Collier continued editing and publishing, but he had no real hope that he would be left alone to do this work in peace. 'I was once sanguine', he wrote a young correspondent about this time, 'but I have so often been disappointed, that I am now almost misanthropic – at least it is my tendency now to think worse of the world

than it really deserves.'[34] Since no one had contributed to this
state of mind more than Clement Ingleby, Collier was not
surprised when, in 1867, there were new charges from his old
antagonist. He could not, however, have anticipated their
nature, neither could he have foreseen that Ingleby would
enlist a new, redoubtable ally to press them.

32

Ingleby had not been lying in wait; in fact, for a time he had
virtually forgotten Collier, whose silence after *A Complete View*
seemed an admission of guilt. Ingleby had been satisfied that
the old man's career had been destroyed and, the controversy
over, he lost much of his interest in Shakespeare and spent two
years writing *An Introduction to Metaphysics,* the first part of
which appeared in 1864. By the mid-sixties, however, it
became clear to Ingleby and his cohorts that Collier's
reputation, although much tarnished, had not been totally
blackened by the scandal, and, even more vexing, that the
controversy over the Perkins Folio had been pretty much
forgotten. It was not the outcome Ingleby had expected, and it
was not a result he could tolerate. He had not been lying in
wait for Collier, but when he was presented with an
opportunity to renew his condemnation of the old man, he
seized it.

The issue that sparked the new attack was hardly worth
contention: it was whether Thomas Lodge, a minor Elizabethan dramatist and poet, had also been an actor. Collier
thought he had because two early tracts seemed to refer to him
as one. In William Prynne's *Histrio-Mastix* (1633), Lodge was
called a 'player',[35] and in *Playes Confuted in Fiue Actions* (n.d.,
1583?), Stephen Gosson had attacked him for defending
players and had declared that Lodge had 'become little better
than a vagrant'.[36] 'Vagrant' had occasionally been used in
Elizabethan parlance to denote actors, and this, coupled with
Prynne's reference, convinced Collier that Lodge had trod the
boards.

In 1825 Collier had introduced Lodge to modern readers by
including 'The Wounds of Civil War' as one of the new plays
in his edition of *Dodsley's Old Plays* (see pp. 36–7 above), and in

his Introduction to the play Collier wrote that Lodge had 'perhaps been upon the stage', citing Gosson's reference.[37] Six years later, in *The History of English Dramatic Poetry*, this possibility had become more certain: Lodge, Collier now declared, 'was probably himself an actor'.[38] Even so, the detail was of so little importance to Collier that ten years later when he edited Gosson's *School of Abuse* for the Shakespeare Society (1841), he called Lodge merely 'a dramatist'. A few months after the Gosson reprint, however, Collier discovered a document in the Alleyn papers at Dulwich College which, as he later reported in *The Memoirs of Edward Alleyn* (1841), 'for the first time [gave] evidence to prove that, like many of the dramatists of that day, [Lodge] had been an actor as well as an author'. This 'evidence' was a memorial to the Lord Chamberlain from Philip Henslowe in which, according to Collier's account, Henslowe refers to 'one Thos. Lodge' for whom he had been asked to stand bail because Henslowe had 'some knowledge and acquaintance of him as a player'.[39] The memorial was a rough draft which, Collier conjectured, Henslowe had saved after a later copy was sent to the Lord Chamberlain. Collier did not imply that the matter was of great significance (the document was only one of dozens he reprinted in the book and it was given no special prominence), and in the years that followed he finally concluded that the Henslowe memorial was not decisive. One of the last publications of the Shakespeare Society was a reprint of Lodge's *A Defense of Poetry, Music, and Stage-Plays* (his reply to Gosson) edited by David Laing (1853). The reprint included an 'account' of Lodge's life written by Laing in close collaboration with Collier[40] in which the evidence of the Henslowe memorial is specifically discounted: the term 'player', it declared, was 'a name in Lodge's time equally applicable to an actor and a writer for the stage – a playwright'.[41] This admission did not, of course, argue that Lodge was *not* an actor, merely that the Dulwich document did not 'prove' he had been one as Collier had formerly asserted.

For twelve years the issue rested there without further comment, but in 1865 it came up again when Collier included Lodge's *The Life and Death of William Long Beard* in his 'green'

series. In his introduction Collier repeated his earlier opinion
that Lodge 'was a writer for his subsistence; and at one period,
like many others, he coupled the professions of author and
actor...'.[42] A few months later he repeated the comment in *A
Bibliographical and Critical Account*, declaring that Lodge 'driven
to great extremity... joined a company of players, and both
wrote for and acted with them.'[43] In neither of these later
references did Collier mention the discounted Henslowe
memorial as evidence. In fact, he produced no evidence at all
for his statement which was no more and no less valid than it
had been when he first made it nearly forty years before.

No one could have expected what followed. Shortly after
the Lodge reprint appeared, George Kingsley, a good friend of
Ingleby, visited Dulwich College and came across the
Henslowe memorial that Collier had published. To his
surprise – and satisfaction – Kingsley saw that, contrary to
Collier's report, the document did not mention Thomas
Lodge (merely 'one Lodge') and that it did not contain the
phrase concerning Henslowe's knowledge of Lodge 'as a
player'. Kingsley immediately reported his 'find' to Ingleby,
who seized upon the information as an excellent excuse to
revive his attack. In November 1867, Ingleby published a
pamphlet entitled *Was Thomas Lodge an Actor?* containing an
elaborate facsimile of the Henslowe document by which,
Ingleby declared, his readers might 'readily assure themselves
that in no part of the memorial is Lodge called a "player";
indeed he is not called "Thos. Lodge"'. Collier 'professes to
find' these words, Ingleby wrote, but they are not there. 'The
interpolation of the five words needed to corroborate Mr.
Collier's explanation of the misquoted passage from Gosson,
and the omission of two other words inconsistent with that
interpolation, may be thought to exhibit some little ingenuity;
it was, however, a feat which could have cost him no great
pains.'[44]

What Ingleby did *not* tell his readers was that there were *two*
copies of Henslowe's memorial in the Alleyn papers: Henslowe's 'rough draft' which Collier described and which,
indeed, contained the insertions he quoted, and a 'fair copy' in
another hand, which did not.[45] Anyone who consulted the
Dulwich collection in more than cursory fashion would have

seen both – the Alleyn manuscripts were not so numerous or so ill-arranged that either could be overlooked. Yet Ingleby, to his great discredit, omitted any mention of the draft from which Collier's transcript was taken. It was all very reminiscent of the earlier decision to suppress Warner's identification of the Perkins Folio, and since there were others who knew the truth – Kingsley, E. W. Ashbee who made the facsimile, and the Dulwich librarian at the very least – there was, once again, a *de facto* conspiracy of silence to implicate Collier.

Once again, too, Collier refused to answer Ingleby's charge, and at first this seemed a wise decision. Ingleby's accusation was not picked up by the press; it caused no public outcry and no revival of interest in the old quarrel of seven years before. But it didn't fade away either. It became, rather, gossip among those who knew nothing of the evidence and who enjoyed the rumour.

It might never have been more than gossip had it not come finally to a man who had reasons of his own for wanting to see Collier and his work discredited. Two years after Ingleby's pamphlet appeared, the charge against Collier was revived by Frederick James Furnivall, and with it, ultimately, the whole case against Collier. Furnivall, in the end, was to effect what Ingleby unassisted had been unable to bring about – the destruction of the career of John Payne Collier.

The clash between Furnivall and Collier never acquired the notoriety of Collier's dispute with Ingleby and its effects, while ultimately disastrous for Collier's reputation, were insidious rather than overwhelming. Yet a century later theirs seems an inevitable confrontation. Each was an exemplar of the intellectual achievements as well as the petty pretences of his age; each was more dependent than most men on public recognition; and each had unique opportunities to demonstrate his remarkable intelligence and imagination. Furnivall was, perhaps, the more brilliant. An iconoclast, a man of opposites which seldom complemented one another, a radical Christian Socialist passionately concerned with educating the 'working class', he nonetheless devoted most of his energy to indulging his upper-class taste for esoteric subjects or for commonplace ones if he thought (as he often did) they had been obscured by the pigheadedness of others. His interests were many and he founded clubs for them all, some self-serving or sycophantic (he organized the Browning Club during the poet's lifetime), some too specialized and demanding for anything more than an intense half-life among a handful of enthusiasts (the Wyclif Society), and some of great importance and long life (the Early English Text Society and the New Shakspere Society). All of these were lashed into vitality and periodically thrown into disarray by the egoism, wit, whim, jealousy and precocity of one of the greatest critical minds of his generation.

Like Collier, Furnivall saw the life of the mind as an intellectual competition, and he was savage in combat. He was, as Sidney Lee was to declare, 'devoid of tact or discretion in almost every relation of life.'[46] He thrived on disagreement and throughout his long career he cultivated the art of bad manners. Collier was never so flamboyant; he could not afford to be, socially or professionally, and he was in any case more truly conventional than Furnivall. But their real difference was generational. Collier embodied the style of an earlier period which lacked both easy access to literary 'evidence' and clearly established methodology by which to judge and report it. His age confused scholarship with possession and allowed it to become an extension of personality, the product of wit as well as of fact. Furnivall, on the other hand, matured as a scholar in a period that saw the rapid extension of exact standards of reference and evaluation. His career coincided with the advent of 'scientific' taste and method based on a cooperative accumulation of knowledge, the precursor of twentieth-century scholarship. Like many of his peers, then and now, he had a strong prejudice against his predecessors, Collier chief among them, whose objectives he did not share. His own concern was ontogenic, 'the growth, the oneness of Shakspere, the links between his successive plays, the light thrown on each by comparison with its neighbour, the distinctive characteristics of each Period with its contrast with the others, [and] the treatment of the same or like incidents, etc. in the different Periods of Shakspere's life.' The concern of his predecessor, he said, was 'antiquarian illustration, emendation, and verbal criticism – to say nothing of forgery, or at least publication of forg[e]d documents.'[47]

The similarity of their interests made it likely that Furnivall and Collier would cross paths sometime; the similarity of their characters ensured they would cross swords as well. Their confrontation might have happened sooner had Furnivall found his calling earlier. A flirtation with the study of law delayed him, and as a result his first important publication, a reprint of a fifteenth-century epic for the Roxburghe Club, did not appear until he was thirty-six, in 1861 (shortly after Ingleby published *A Complete View*). In 1864, two years after Collier's reprints began to appear, Furnivall founded the Early English Text Society, dedicated to reviving the study of Old and Middle English by publishing rare manuscripts relating to King Arthur. From the outset, the Society's existence was precarious. It had an announced membership of seventy-five (it was actually smaller) composed largely of institutions and a goodly number of Germans (a fact that raised latent chauvinism in many of the Society's critics). Furnivall soon learned as Collier had before him, that subscriptions alone could not repay publication costs, particularly when the texts were manuscripts appealing to only a small number of readers, and within two years the Society was incurring losses that Furnivall could not cover. However, encouraged by Collier's success with his 'red' and 'green' Series, Furnivall decided to increase his membership by broadening the range of the Society's publications in what he called an 'extra series' of reprints of sixteenth-century tracts. This plan, of course, put him in direct competition with Collier in a very small field: probably no more than two hundred persons subscribed to the dozen or so reprinting schemes of the 1860s, and Furnivall's project could succeed only at the expense of Collier's. While it would be wrong to assume that Furnivall deliberately sought such a competition, he could not have been unaware of it. Collier, whose 'blue' and 'yellow' series had already begun to lose subscribers as a result of increasing prices and satiety, quickly felt the effect of his new competitor, and within a few months he began to write those testy letters to the *Athenaeum* complaining of the 'slackness' of his 'former encouragers'. About the same time, the publications of the Early English Text Society began to contain slighting references to Collier that provoked rejoinders.[48]

Appearing in the midst of this competition, Ingleby's tract concerning Lodge acquired an importance it might not otherwise have had. In the fall of 1869, a little less than two years after the pamphlet appeared, Furnivall co-edited the ninth volume in the Early English Text Society 'extra series', John Awdeley's *The Fraternitye of Vacabondes, etc.,* in which he borrowed heavily from Collier's research and, in a remarkable note of 'credit', managed to condemn his source even as he acknowledged his debt:

The extracts from Mr. J. P. Collier must be taken for what they are worth [Furnivall wrote]. I have not had time to verify them; but assume them to be correct, and not ingeniously or unreasonably altered from their originals, like Mr. Collier's print of Henslowe's Memorial, of which Dr. Ingleby complains, and like his notorious Alleyn letter. If some-one only would follow Mr. Collier through all his work – pending his hoped-for Retractations, – and assure us that the two pieces above-named, and the Perkins Folio, are the only things we need reject, such some-one would render a great service to all literary antiquarians, and enable them to do justice to the wonderful diligence, knowledge, and acumen, of the veteran pioneer in their path.[49]

In the next issue of the 'extra series', a collection of three tracts by Andrew Borde, Furnivall again attacked Collier. Collier had written in *A Bibliographical and Critical Account* that Borde was put in Fleet Prison for debt and there died.[50] Furnivall noted that Borde's will suggested he was propertied at his death and proceeded to berate Collier for his 'error' which, Furnivall declared, was yet another example of 'that notorious daringness of invention that has ... rendered him a wonder and warning to the editors of this age.'[51] Whether Borde was in Fleet for poverty was neither proved by Collier's assertion nor disproved by Furnivall's; it was conjecture either way, but the fact that Furnivall took a point of disagreement as a means to accuse Collier of blatant and continuing dishonesty and to imply that this guilt had been proved was very serious indeed. As much as anything that followed, Furnivall's attack on Collier was to create the popular opinion that Collier was guilty of multifarious and *continuing* crimes. As a result of

Furnivall's prejudice and self-interest, Ingleby's old accusations were revived and the controversy renewed in a much
more insidious form. The mutual interest of Ingleby and
Furnivall created what amounted to a sustained attack on
Collier's reputation against which no defence was possible,
because its form was subversive rather than direct, a campaign
of innuendo and imputation repeated so often without
refutation that it acquired the authority of fact. Collier had no
support from those who might have been expected to feel
some indebtedness to him; Halliwell was privately friendly
but publicly noncommittal; William Carew Hazlitt, who had
founded his own reputation on new editions of Collier's early
publications with great assistance from Collier, said nothing
in the old man's defence. In the public mind, the shards of
Collier's reputation, fragile at best, disintegrated.

This is not to say that he was universally condemned. For
example, in 1873, when Furnivall's attack was at its height,
two Scotsmen, James Maidment and W. H. Logan, braved
the onslaught and dedicated an edition of Crowne's plays to
Collier, whom they called 'the distinguished reviver and
exponent of the earlier poets and dramatists of England.' The
gesture touched Collier. 'To have your praise, and that of men
like you, and to deserve it, is the height of my ambition', he
wrote to Maidment.[52] Abandoned by associates who owed him
much, he was particularly grateful to strangers who rose in his
support unasked. Another Scots supporter, who along with
Maidment and Logan comprised the group Collier called his
'Glasgow Friends', was Alexander Smith, the editor and
lexicographer; in 1868 he wrote to Collier praising *A Poet's
Pilgrimage* and thereby initiated an intimate correspondence
that was to continue until Collier's death.[53] But as these
examples suggest, Collier's support was limited to a dedicated
few who had neither the reputations nor the means to counter
Furnivall.

Collier continued writing, but his work now became much
more personal and memorial, a collection of fragmentary bits
and pieces of his career in a quasi-permanent form. In January
1870, he issued a collection of his poems, many of them dating
from the time of *A Poet's Pilgrimage*, which he called *Odds and
Ends for Cheerful Friends,* a gift he prepared to celebrate his

eighty-first birthday. The following year he attempted to revive his flagging publishing programme with a new 'brown' series devoted to unpublished manuscripts. The first was *Nine Historical Letters of the Reign of Henry VIII*,[54] reprinted documents he had acquired many years before and subsequently presented to the Public Records Office. But subscribers were not now interested in his ephemera, and he discontinued the series.

He turned instead to writing *An Old Man's Diary*, a collection of notes from his journals for the years 1832 and 1833, that moment forty years before when *The History of English Dramatic Poetry* had brought him his first success. He subsequently destroyed the original journals and it is therefore impossible to know how much of *An Old Man's Diary* was actually written in the years it covered, but it was certainly not a verbatim transcript of early notebooks; its tone is defensive, less that of the scholar of 1832 building his reputation than that of the defendant of 1871 desperately trying to retrieve it. Collier published the memoir in four parts (from May 1871 to December 1872) and sent them off as gifts (only twenty-five copies were distributed). As a defence of his reputation it was poor because it avoided the accusations which had been levelled against him; as autobiography it was marred by pretension and incompleteness and incipient paranoia.

However, that Collier was paranoic does not mean he had no enemies or that they were not active against him. In the fall of 1873, shortly after *An Old Man's Diary* was finished, Furnivall founded 'The New Shakspere Society', whose announced objective was to determine the order of Shakespeare's plays and hence the development of his art by metrical analysis and 'scientific' examination; its unannounced objective was to destroy the lingering prestige of the *old* Shakespeare Society (the spelling of 'Shakspere' was intended to revive a controversy that the earlier society was thought to have settled thirty years before), and along with it the remaining shreds of Collier's reputation. Furnivall's success with the first objective was only partial; with the second , it was all but complete.

The New Shakspere Society was to produce many excellent

reprints in style and form very similar to those of the 'old' society, but under the direction of the 'Founder', as Furnivall chose to call himself, and with the assistance of Ingleby who served on the 'Committee' controlling the Society, the animus against Collier was pervasive. (Now began the the gossip that the old Shakespeare Society had collapsed because of Collier's 'forgeries'.) As part of his introductory publicity, Furnivall created the position of 'Honorary Vice President' to the Society to which he appointed virtually everyone with even a presumed interest in Shakespeare (including, according to one account, President Ulysses S. Grant), everyone, that is, except John Payne Collier and those of his friends who were still alive and ready to defend him.[55] Thoms, for example, was not dubbed, despite a friendly association with Furnivall, because he continued to defend Collier in print and in private. The slight stung Collier, as, of course, it was intended to do. He probably would not have joined Furnivall and his old enemy Ingleby even if asked, but the public affront was demeaning, and he did not suffer in silence. In a characteristic fashion, he addressed a letter to the *Academy* in which he welcomed the new society, implied he did not deign to join it, and corrected four bibliographical errors in Furnivall's *Prospectus*.[56] Furnivall, as prone to 'letter battles' as Collier himself, replied in the next issue of the journal with a litany of Collier's 'crimes' and copies of the two versions of the Henslowe memorial, one labelled 'original', the other 'Collier'. Significantly, the transcript of the 'original' was not taken from Ingleby but constituted a new, more accurate version of the fair copy; this suggests that Furnivall had himself consulted the Alleyn papers at Dulwich and must, therefore have seen Collier's source about which he said nothing. 'All Shaksperian students distrust every text Mr. Collier has printed or reprinted', he declared.[57]

Collier did not respond, but when an anonymous 'Subscriber' wrote to the *Athenaeum* complaining of the way 'The New Shakspere Society' was excluding Collier and others from membership, Furnivall retorted, this time in the pages of the *Athenaeum*, repeating his condemnation.

When I want to learn how ... to mistake as genuine such plainly

spurious documents as some that Mr. Collier printed from the
Ellesmere Library, and plainly spurious 'corrections' like those in the
Perkins Folio, then I will invite Mr. J. Payne Collier to give me the
'benefit' of his 'experience'. . . . But as to our workers, we are bound,
by the 'experience' of the old Society, to try not to admit into their
number any one who will print in our books such forged documents
and imaginary passages as occur in, at least, two books of the old
'Shakespeare Society'.[58]

This finally provoked Collier to defend his use of the Dulwich
manuscripts in a letter to the *Athenaeum*:

My friends will not require them, but a few words of explanation
may not be thrown away upon my enemies.

Employed as I was, night and day, upon other avocations, it will
not be surprising if I say that I was always most efficiently assisted
by other members of the Council of our *old Shakespeare Society*,
especially by Messrs. Amyot, Cooper, and Cunningham. . . . So of
the documents derived from Dulwich College; Mr Allen copied a
few . . the Rev. Mr. Lindsay (librarian), I think, others; Amyot some;
Cunningham several; and I added the rest. If we made mistakes, I
am sorry for it; but as to the most curious of the papers we could not
well err, because I had lithographs made from them, by permission
of Master Allen.[59]

Furnivall had the last word. He 'replied' to Collier ('Mr.
Alter-Manuscripts' as he now called him) in the next issue of
the *Athenaeum*, declaring his own unblemished intentions in
founding the New Shakspere Society, berating his foes, and
scorning Collier's defenders:

If the notorious Alleyne and Lodge letters are covered by Mr.
Collier's words of last week, 'the documents derived from Dulwich
College,' Mr. Collier now abandons his former position, and makes a
statement which will gladden the heart of my friends, Mr. N.E.S.
Hamilton and Dr. Ingleby, which will no doubt appease Mr. A.E.
Brae. . . . We may doubtless suppose that the above-named 'letters'
were among the 'I added *the rest*,' and then we can accept Mr.
Collier's excuse for them, 'If we made mistakes, I am sorry for it.'
They were certainly funny things to call 'mistakes.' If Mr. Collier
will but give us a list of them, we will enlarge our definition of the
word, and end the matter.[60]

Certainly much of Collier's criticism of Malone was careless
and incorrect, certainly he made errors in transcribing and

interpreting the Alleyn manuscripts, but these faults – serious though they were – did not include the hypocrisy of which Furnivall was guilty. He condemned Collier for 'not taking the trouble' to check his charges before criticizing Malone, precisely the fault he himself committed in imputing forgery to Collier and distorting his defence. 'I am sure I have made many blunders', Collier declared in a letter to the *Athenaeum*. 'All I ask, is to be treated fairly when they are pointed out . . . and not to have it imputed on all occasions that I had some bad motive for misrepresentation.'[61]

The quarrel was not a major controversy of the nineteenth century, but its effects were significant in the twentieth. Furnivall's attack was to be the keynote of the general condemnation of Collier that has continued to the present day. Throughout his long career (he lived until 1910), Furnivall repeated his assertion of Collier's guilt. Brilliant, witty, prideful and essentially unscrupulous in his scramble for reputation and renown, Furnivall shaped the view of Collier as *bête noire* with more energy than Brae, Ingleby, Hamilton or Madden had been able to call up. Without serious rebuttal, Collier's guilt was, at last, generally accepted as 'proved'. Furnivall would have enemies in his turn; his penchant for making disagreements into quarrels and quarrels into controversies would destroy much of his great achievement, including the New Shakspere Society which shortly collapsed in even greater disarray than its longer-lived predecessor. But fortunately for Furnivall's continuing reputation, none of *his* future adversaries were to be so ruthless with him as he with John Payne Collier.

33

Collier was prepared to die in his seventies. His parents' deaths had suggested that three score years and ten were to be his measure, and he several times remarked that the Spenser edition would be his 'last achievement'. He had the romantic expectation that his death would come as a sudden, fitting conclusion to his career, one akin to that of his old rival Staunton who died of a heart seizure, at his desk, pen in hand, writing. This, however, was not to be. He was not sorry for the delay, of course, he was interested in life, but he had expected a climax, possibly a tragic immolation, and he was not prepared for slow attenuation of the mind and body. Above all, he had not expected to see his reputation dissipated, his achievements forgotten, and his character destroyed. Had he died at seventy-four he would have been spared the spectacle of his decline; at eighty-four he was its witness; at ninety-four he would be its victim.

During the last decade of his life, Collier left a notebook, the vestige of a journal he kept off and on for many years. It resembled a diary, but it was not a day to day record and it had no clear sequence. The twelve volumes that survive (at least eleven earlier volumes of an indeterminate period having been destroyed along the way) were composed between November 1872 and some months before his death in 1883.[62] They reflect Collier's thoughts as he moved inexorably and, to his surprise, slowly towards death. Neither Furnivall nor Ingleby are mentioned in the journal, but Alexander Dyce often is. It was as though, beset by age and unanswerable accusations, Collier mixed all the quarrels of a lifetime into one – his first – and poured his frustration into a single vessel. It was a bitter cup, for Dyce was dead. When Dyce was dying, Collier had asked Thoms to arrange a meeting with his old antagonist but it never happened. It is unclear what Collier wanted – some expression of mutual regard or regret, perhaps an apology, perhaps forgiveness. Whatever it was he was not to have it. Dyce's death produced an unexpected grief over the passing of a rivalry as binding as love. Their relationship was left unresolved; it made a loose end with which Collier was to fret for the rest of his life; and his journal was to contain many references to Dyce, notes of spleen and affection, of animosity and regard.

In October and November 1873, four years after Dyce's death, this ambivalence motivated Collier to write *Trilogy*, his last defence of the Perkins Folio, and his last retort to his old opponent. He intended to show 'how every editor since the publication of my Notes and Emendations ... has availed himself of them',[63] but the real subject of the book was, the way Dyce had denigrated the folio while he used it without credit. 'This I yet hope to do and hope also to answer the irritation and vexation I now feel at the gross injustice done me', he wrote in his journal. 'Dyce, *my intimate friend for 30 years* conducted himself throughout in this business most enviously.'[64]

It was not a worthy motive and the result was not a good book. Although Collier tried to be fair to Dyce, 'he being now dead', the tone of his defence was resentful. 'If [Dyce] had esteemed me half as much as I valued him, our intercourse would never have been interrupted', Collier wrote in his preface. Dyce, he declared, was a man of 'refined scholarship', but 'defective' judgement, whose 'varied attainments did not enlarge his mind much beyond the sphere of his own wants and wishes.'[65] This comment was a bitter coda to thirty years of intermittent association.

Trilogy was directed at Dyce, but it contained strikes at all those editors who had publicly charged Collier with forgery while privately adopting many of the corrections. He repeated the defence he had made much earlier in his *Reply*, that those who claimed he had forged the emendations (a charge he vehemently denied) should, for consistency if not for justice, then give him credit for the excellence of those they adopted. He repeated this defence in a memoir begun a year or two after *Trilogy*: 'If the proposed emendations are not genuine', he wrote, 'then I claim them as mine; and there I intend to leave the question without giving myself any further trouble. . . . – Good or bad, mine or not mine, no edition of Shakespeare, while the world stands, can now be published without them: I brought them into life and light, and I am quite ready to be answerable for them.'[66] He had come, at last, to lament he had ever made the folio public. It would have been better, he concluded, to have published them as his own and to have destroyed the folio.[67] 'It is my own fault and folly that I am not now *justly* considered the first and best emendator of Shakespeare',[68] he declared. This wild overvaluation of the Perkins emendations indicates the depth of his anguish and regret.

Trilogy was published in three parts, covering the texts of Shakespeare's tragedies, comedies and history plays, each printed as he finished it and sent off as a gift to friends and former subscribers. Collier knew that 'Gift-books are generally

the most worthless in every man's library',[69] but he wanted to
set down the facts for his 'own justification' and for the
'satisfaction' of his family.[70] He was working to keep alive and
to maintain his self-esteem in the face of general condemnation of his life and career. 'I cannot get over the ground nearly
as easily and rapidly as I used to do', he wrote to his American
friend Horace Howard Furness, 'but I thank God that I can
get on at all. . . . I seldom dine out now – very seldom – if I do,
and I talk, I see, or fancy I see, a pooh-poohing disposition
upon nearly every face.'[71] Among Collier's old friends, only
Thoms remained. Henry Crabb Robinson had died in 1867,
an expected but incalculable loss. (Collier's journal would
contain many recollections of the 'worthiest and most
unflinchingly upright man I ever knew'.[72]) Peter Cunningham
had died two years later. Hazlitt had more or less dropped his
acquaintance, and Halliwell stayed at a discreet distance.
Collier saw no one; his intercourse was with a handful of
correspondents whom he had never met.

Chief among these was an Anglican curate, Joseph Wood-
fall Ebsworth, the son of a dramatist-musician whom Collier
had known in his newspaper days. Ebsworth, an avid student
of Old English Ballads and a prime mover of the newly
formed Ballad Society, thought highly of Collier's ballad
editions, particularly the early reprints produced for the Percy
and Roxburghe Societies many years before, and in the course
of preparing an edition of the Bagford Ballads in the British
Museum he wrote to Collier for assistance. 'I don't like
strangers', Collier warned him, but Ebsworth's enthusiasm
overcame Collier's hesitancy. Although they corresponded
regularly until Collier's death, they never met. 'You [are] a
man whom, unseen, I care about', Collier wrote. 'Possibly (but
I do not like to suppose it) if seen – I might not care to see
again. You might fuss and fidget me to death. On paper I like
you very much'.[73] It was therefore 'on paper' that Collier
confided in Ebsworth, and in the early months of 1874 when
the third and last part of *Trilogy* was issuing from the press, he
complained of being restive for 'something to do', some new
project to fill his time, some means to avoid as long as he could
the morbidity of age. 'I am thoroughly sick of J.P.C. and yet I
have every wish to avoid dying', he wrote.[74]

He took up the anonymous play *Edward III* (1596), convinced that it was substantially Shakespeare's. The attribution had been suggested in the late eighteenth century by Edward Capell who first noted striking textual parallels between the play, *Henry V* and Shakespeare's Sonnet 94. Collier's case cited several new parallel passages, but it was not very compelling. Nevertheless, in April 1874 he issued a pamphlet arguing that Shakespeare's authorship was 'self-evident', and two months later he published the play itself, newly edited.[75] This project encouraged a much larger one: On 4 January 1875, a week before his eighty-sixth birthday, Collier once again used the columns of the *Athenaeum* to announce 'another trifling Shakespearean experiment', a 'Third Edition' of Shakespeare, for which he needed fifty subscribers willing to pay a guinea down against the cost of five to seven shillings for each play as it was issued. Collier did not expect to live to finish the project and his programme might be terminated at any time. 'The whole money shall be spent upon print and paper', he declared. 'For the guinea, therefore, subscribers will obtain at least three entire plays, the text founded upon the best authorities' and the notes 'as brief as possible ... and avoiding all controversy.'[76] He rightly perceived a new market for Shakespeare: Horace Howard Furness, had begun the 'new Variorum Edition' in Philadelphia in 1871,[77] and several new English editions were in the offing, chief among them a third (posthumous) edition of Dyce. Collier's proposed edition was a bargain and to his gratification the subscription filled within a week of his announcement.

What followed was a remarkable demonstration of stamina in a very old man. For the next two years, once a month, wholly unassisted and with clockwork regularity, Collier edited, had printed, proofread, had bound, and personally sent off fifty-eight (the number was increased by demand) copies of each play. By the end of 1875 he had issued all the comedies; by December of the next year, all the histories and several tragedies; and by the following July he had finished the established canon and had begun to edit the best known apocrypha (*Two Noble Kinsmen*, *A Yorkshire Tragedy* and *Mucedorus*) and the poems.

In the middle of this labour, Collier was attacked yet again by Ingleby, who announced in a letter to the *Academy* that three ballads Collier had printed nearly forty years before were 'contemptible forgeries of the present century'.[78] Part of the accusation was not new: 'The Enchanted Island', a ballad first printed in *Farther Particulars* (1839, see p. 67 above), had been condemned by Hamilton in *An Inquiry* seventeen years before and Ingleby merely resuscitated the charge in order to bolster two new ones against 'The Tragedie of Othello the Moore' and 'The Atheist's Tragedy', both of which Collier had published in *New Particulars* (1836, see p. 62 above). The manuscripts of these ballads were still in Collier's possession, and Ingleby noted ominously, 'they have never been submitted to palaeographic scrutiny'. However, the *Academy* letter contained a more serious 'revelation'. Ingleby declared he had found two 'modern interpolations' in the manuscript of Henslowe's diary. One, a reference to the play 'Like Quits Like', Ingleby declared a forgery because it was written on an erasure in a handwriting unique to the diary; the second, a long entry of 20 December 1597, recording a payment of 25 shillings to 'Thomas Dickers' for a prologue to 'marloes tambelan', was made, Ingleby declared, 'with the view of furnishing the historian of the drama with an additional bit of evidence concerning the authorship of Tamburlaine.... It may very well be', Ingleby concluded, 'that the book contains other interpolations, and "thus" that "bad begins, and worse remains behind."'[79] It was an accusation for which there was no defence. Even if Collier granted (as he might have) that the disputed passages were not genuine, how could he prove they had been in the diary when he first saw it forty years before?

Publicly Collier pretended to be unaffected by Ingleby's new attack; privately he was in torment. Only his determination to complete the edition of Shakespeare kept him from slipping into a deep and consuming depression. Even so, he frequently lost heart in the project. 'What I now do is not worth one farthing an hour', he wrote in his journal, 'and perhaps then I do more harm than good.'[80] Ingleby's new charges convinced him there would be no end to the calumny – even his death would not silence his enemies. 'My memory, when I am dead, must fight its own battles; it is sure to be assailed.'[81] He charged his family to keep silent. 'It is my strict, positive, and well-considered injunction', he wrote, 'that, whatever may be said of me after my death ... not one member of my family shall say print or publish a word in my defence. If my memory cannot support and defend itself, let it fall.'[82] It was the first of many similar pleas: 'My dear Children,' he wrote a few months later, *Do not trouble yourselves about me or my Memory:* ... I know that I shall be abused abundantly and all sorts of accusations made. I do not care for one of them; nor need you. I have plenty of Enemies and unscrupulous ones. I despise them all.'[83]

This paranoia, if that is what it was, intensified his desire to complete the Shakespeare edition. His eyesight, uncertain for many years, faded periodically to near blindness, slowing his work and increasing his fear that he would become a hopeless invalid, an impossible burden to his daughter and an abomination to himself. His regimen was strict; ill one day, he worked longer the next. 'I am now in the very middle of Vol. III.', he wrote to Ebsworth. 'I fear that my enemies will call it a *muddle* and I am far from satisfied with it and with *myself* – Nevertheless, I have done the best I could for my age, and have spared neither pains nor pen.'[84] On 24 January 1878, two weeks after his eighty-ninth birthday, Collier mailed the last issue to the last subscriber.

For all his intensive labour and anxiety, Collier's 'Third Edition' was not actually 'new'. In fact, on the surface, it might seem to have had little justification other than Collier's desire to keep himself alive. But a close comparison of the new text with that of 1858 reveals a striking though unannounced difference: in this, his 'last and best' consideration of Shakespeare's text, Collier silently dropped most of the Perkins emendations he had inserted into the earlier edition in favour of the original quarto or folio text. He retained only a few of the 'best' of the Old Corrector's emendations to which he occasionally drew attention in a brief note. (Most significant of all, as noted earlier, he dropped the authentic *Titus Andronicus* emendations in favour of the corrupted First Folio readings, thereby unwittingly revealing he did not know their source.) With this, his last word on Shakespeare, Collier let his reputation rest. 'The work I was born to do', he declared, 'is done.'[85]

His life, however, was not. He was sickened by the attacks upon him, but not sickened unto death. 'What am I to do next?' he asked himself. 'Die; but . . . I hope yet to be allowed to live to undertake something else: otherwise I *shall* die.'[86] He wanted to edit a supplement to his *Bibliographical and Critical Account* (1865), but the project was blocked by lack of money, and the effect of Ingleby's and Furnivall's attacks made his approach to publishers apologetic rather than assertive: 'I have never had any business or other relations, with you,' he wrote to Chapman and Hall, publishers, 'perhaps you do not want to have any with me. If so, there is an end of the matter . . .'[87] He offered to work at the cheapest rate, virtually for nothing.

Among the publishers he approached was George Bell and Sons the successor to Bell and Daldy, who had published his edition of Spenser nearly twenty years before. Their catalogue was largely made up of cheap reprints of successful standard editions, and Bell, while not interested in a supplement to the bibliography, agreed to undertake a reprint of Collier's *History of English Dramatic Poetry* provided that Collier would expect no royalty. Collier, eager for any sort of useful work, agreed, and his only payment, he later reported, was ten free copies of the book.

Bell announced the work as a 'new edition', but the text was virtually that of 1831 brought up to date here and there with a footnote of supplemental information. Because Collier removed none of the references to the disputed manuscripts (a fault for which many were to blame him) the book became a kind of personal reassertion of his innocence. He could not have done otherwise. His 'editing' consisted of correcting galley proofs ('hard work for 90 and no encouragers', he declared) and his memory was no longer trustworthy; details that had once been clear were now cloudy. The text was long, three volumes of over four hundred pages each, and the labour tedious; he soon regretted having begun. 'I am getting on pretty well', he wrote to Ebsworth when the job was half finished, 'only so far I find it hard work at my time of life.'[88] He tired easily, and as the short winter afternoons went by, he often dozed over the printed sheets. In his own judgement he was 'sluggish and inert'; his life was running down like an unwound clock.

Nevertheless he finished the book. The reissue went virtually unnoticed by the press (it was not reviewed by any periodical or mentioned in the gossip columns) but it contributed to another controversy. It became a part of Swinburne's famous attack on Furnivall in *A Study of Shakespeare,* published a few months after *The History of English Dramatic Poetry* reappeared, an attack that ultimately precipitated the collapse of the New Shakspere Society. For a variety of personal and professional reasons, Swinburne had a deep antagonism to Furnivall and, to pique his rival, *A Study of Shakespeare* paid a generous (if somewhat involuted) compliment to Furnivall's bugaboo, John Payne Collier. Collier, Swinburne wrote in an obvious slap at Furnivall, had put all Shakespearians in his debt. To deny this, he declared, would be

shamefully deficient in that respect and gratitude which all genuine and thankful students will always be ready to offer, as all thankless and insolent sciolists can ever be to disclaim, to the venerable scholar who since I was first engaged on these notes has added yet another obligation to the many under which he had already laid all younger and lesser labourers in the same field of study, by the issue in a form fitly ennobled and enriched of his great historical work on our early stage.

This elaborately packaged praise was qualified, however; Swinburne's respect for Collier should not, he declared, 'be supposed to imply an equally blind confidence in the authority or the value' of the Perkins Folio, a book 'which has been the means of exposing a name so long and so justly honoured, not merely to the natural and rational inquisition of rival students, but to the rancorous and ribald obloquy of thankless and frontless pretenders.'[89]

In Furnivall's inevitable riposte, he dubbed the poet 'Pigsbrook', and when he subsequently attempted to use the New Shakspere Society to continue the quarrel, that organization quickly fell apart. Most of its illustrious 'vice presidents' resigned, its membership dropped, and the New Shakspere Society disbanded after slightly more than six years of

activity. It gave Collier great pleasure to know that his *old*
Shakespeare Society, much maligned in these latter days, had
lasted much longer than its 'new' successor. He did not know
Swinburne, but he was grateful, and he wrote to the poet to
express his thanks for the 'kind and handsome mention of me
and my pleasant toils upon the works of Shakespeare and his
contemporaries'.[90]

34

'I am putting my affairs in as small a compass as I can', Collier
wrote in his journal shortly before his ninety-second birthday.
'I do not like the job. I am not in any hurry to die and would
fain avoid the trouble and sorrow of preparing for it.'[91] His
'affairs' were few, not enough to occupy the hours of the last
three years of his life. If he were not an author, he was nothing.
For eighty years he had had little time for 'unproductive
thought', now he had time for nothing else. Without work to
be done, his life lost focus; without a publisher's deadline, he
slipped easily into the slow movement of undifferentiated
days. He became an observer of small unconnected events. He
chronicled the weather, the seasons passing through his
garden, the lateness of the swallows, the cold spring rain. His
only solace was reading, but that, too, was limited by his
uncertain eyesight which occasionally failed altogether and
reduced him to listening to Emma read Scott, Dickens, or
Longfellow. (Fielding, whom he admired 'beyond measure',
was 'too coarse' for her taste.) He hated the reality of his
diminishing senses; he hated the dependency it forced upon
him. 'After all my experience of reading and writing for myself
I can ill bear the change.'[92]

The restriction of age confined him mentally as well as
physically. He sometimes lost all track of time; he was often
quite quixotic. The maid reported in alarm that she had heard
him apologize to his clock for not winding it; he mislaid books
and accused his servants of theft; he was foolish with money.
At Emma's request, he readily gave her joint control of his
bank account and commended her judgement – and within
days railed that she wanted to make a 'non-entity' of him.
Slowly he forgot the world beyond the comfortable walls of his

garden and the shaded walks along the Thames. Safe from the
intrusion of the present, he slipped inexorably into the past.
He had few visitors and he wanted none. His only regular
correspondent was Ebsworth, and he had little to tell him.
How could he explain his continuing fretfulness over events
long past, events that only he remembered? How hide his envy
that others could be what he could not? 'You are of use', he
wrote to Ebsworth. 'I am of none.'[93] Emma, herself aged and
in uncertain health, cared for him with a devotion which
gratified and annoyed him – he hated to admit how helpless
he was without her care. 'I begin to fear that my corporeal
faculties will outlive my mental, that I may become an idiot a
willful idiot and a nuisance to my family by my pig-headed
obstinacy', he confided to his journal. 'I might become the
greatest nuisance to [Emma] and she without a remedy
against the old brute's tyranny.'[94]

The knots of his anxiety were not loosed by age or
forgetfulness, and the journal attests to the painful sharpness
of his mind. At ninety-two, Collier's memory was repetitious
but lucid, and his composition good. He began an autobiography and quickly filled a hundred pages: his childhood
memories were clear, but the events of his later life were
incoherent, vague and unreal. 'My memory is like ice', he
declared, 'cold, slippery and unimpressive.'[95] The memoir
finally lost all semblance of form, and Collier grew 'ashamed
both of the matter and the manner' of it.'[96] At last, he gave it
up. He had, he discovered, 'no memoirs, only memory' – a
very different thing.[97]

His journal was his only confidant. He kept it under lock
and key and addressed it regularly, filling its pages with
recollected joys and bursts of painful reminiscence, the
anguish of opportunities lost or slights suffered. His memory
was increasingly dark, and no present light could brighten it.
'It is quite sad enough to be nearly 93: but to be old and sad
too is not a comfortable condition', he wrote in July 1881. 'It is
and has been as beautiful a Summer as I ever remember, but
all along I have been in bad spirits, and never felt myself so
old.'[98] Again and again Collier recalled the fateful moments of
his life and career, reshaped as they now were by self-
concentration, a fantasy of intermingled time: and place his

father, his wife, Panizzi, Dyce, Robinson—all dead, all alive
again in Collier's ruminating memory. Crabb Robinson
('How much I owed him both by impulse and example!...I
should have been much worse but for him').[99] Had he ever
acknowledged his debt to Robinson while he lived? Why had
Robinson not sent for him at the end? His family was
attentive; 'My eldest son John and his eldest son John came to
see me and his eldest son John came to Maidenhead to see us',
he reported proudly.[100] His life and career must surely be
judged successful when he left so much behind? His marriage.
How foolish to have married before he could keep a wife and
family! And yet, marriage had saved him from 'very evil
natural propensities';[101] Louisa had saved him. Their life in
Hammersmith, their years at Riverside, the day she knew her
illness was mortal...she had accepted death more quietly
than he was likely to. But life with her had not always been
comfortable. She had belittled his projects, his literary
friendships. She hadn't liked Devonshire – the most undemanding of benefactors! Devonshire, who had been so much
more generous than Ellesmere who had deserted him before
his enemies on the 'padded British Museum Commission'.
That bitter succession! His loss of place! His plea to
Campbell – 'Impossible!' he had said, and he a friend of
twenty years! The flight to Geys, the difficulty of keeping up
appearances! And Madden dead! Panizzi, too, he had read
the other day. Had he now, at long last, outlived his enemies
at the Museum? Dyce! The confidant, the conniver who cut
him in the street! 'The more I think of it...!'[102]

And he thought of it a great deal, like a fitful sleeper held in
a dream, writing when he could, as he could, in his journal,
drawing the portrait of a long life's dying.[103] 'What can a man
do at 93 but die and get out of the way?'[104] he wrote to
Ebsworth. 'I am sick of myself', he confided to his journal,
'and other people are getting sick of me...I feel myself only
in the way.'[105] It was time for death. He dreamt of suicide, of
walking in front of a train, of drowning. Walking by the
Thames in early March 1881, he looked down at the flooding
water and had a sudden 'sinking of strength and mind', and
for a moment his life was in his hands. The moment passed,
and he walked on. 'The downhill path of life ends in a

precipice', he wrote, 'and when you are over that, it is all over with you.'[106] He was impatient, but he would follow the path to its end. 'I am writing almost in the dark in every respect', he declared. 'When if ever will it be light?'[107]

He slept fitfully much of the day and night. His dreams were vivid, filled with the clutter of life, the emptiness of death, of 'strange, ... crowded places, sometimes full of furniture – sometimes of a large hall entirely vacant.'[108] His dreams were the template of his fears. One was of the future:

I fancied I was dead and had been so for many years but that I had preserved all my living likes and dislikes. How, and why I was kept alive I do not remember, but I was kept alive and I was some 140 years old; What I was doing or why I did anything I cannot recollect, neither do I know why or where I was living but I think I had a father but I do not remember brothers or sisters. I had outlived them all. I do not remember my mother – nobody but my father and he was sharing my punishment.[109]

He felt him no anxiety – only wonder and impatience. The 'punishment' was to have outlived them all – family, friends, enemies, to have kept unsatisfied 'likes' and to be tormented, endlessly, by 'dislikes'. What end was there to any of it?

It might have been a time for Christian solace, but Collier had never been religious, even at those times of his life when death or misfortune might have urged him to seek consolation in the Church. He had simply not thought about religion very much, and his ethical rule of life was a simplistic 'Do as you would be done by. Let a man act on the maxim and then a fig for his particular tenets.'[110] Louisa had been devoutly high church and his children had followed their mother. He was, he declared, 'reckoned, if not a black sheep, a very *brown* one in my serious family.'[111] In their view, his simple belief in a 'superintending Providence' was dangerously close to agnosticism. His daughter Emma was deeply troubled by his 'lack of faith', and she assumed the task of bringing him into the Church. Collier resisted. 'I am naturally pious', he wrote in his diary, 'but people think me profane, because I speak freely and do not go to ch[urch]. All parsons are more or less humbugs, and do not believe half they preach. ... Anglo-

Catholics! I am too great an impostor myself not to know imposture when I see it and not to hate it when I find it.'[112]

Nevertheless Emma's unselfish care and deep affection touched him. She had, he knew, sacrificed her own freedom for his over the years, and as his death became increasingly imminent, he found it more and more difficult not to respond to her although he was repelled by what she demanded. 'My dear Daughter is what I call a little *stupid*stitious in her religious observances', he wrote shortly after his ninety-second birthday. And a few months later when a grand niece came to assist Emma in running Riverside, Collier noted with some discomfort that she too had 'High Church notions'. Emma sought Pycroft's help and, to a lesser extent, that of William and Henrietta. Collier loved his children, but he was not convinced by their arguments and he could not flatter them with pretended piety. He did *not*, he declared, believe in the Immaculate Conception or the Resurrection. He did *not* believe in the divinity of Jesus. Let those who could believe what they would. His faith was pragmatic. 'I believe in God because I must', he declared in his journal. 'I can discover no other solution of the great difficulty, and I believe that Christ was one of the best men, if not the best, that ever lived: he was also the wisest. All the rest is priestcraft, invention and trickery, for the sake of money only. This is my confession of faith. . . .'[113] He was, he jauntily declared to Ebsworth, 'A terrible unbeliever, and at the age of 92 wanting greatly in faith.'[114] In late fall 1881, Collier suffered several attacks of giddiness that were a warning of what was to come. His family continually remarked how well he looked, how strong. He knew better. His children continued to urge him to make a confession of faith. He thought he knew better about that too.

But his resistance weakened, bit by bit. His illness and failing eyesight made him increasingly dependent on Emma's care, and her fear of his death in sin moved him. His diary took on a confessional tone. 'When with honest eyes I look back on my career I find that I ought to be ashamed of it; but still I believe I have done some good things altho' many bad and thus I salve over my conscience', he wrote. 'It is so dark that I can hardly see a stroke that my pen makes.'[115] By Christmas he was more repentant still. 'I know my vices and

my vicious inclinations', he declared, 'and deeply and
sincerely regret them: they harmed nobody so much as
myself.'[116] On his ninety-third birthday, his view had become
more general. The world was fraught with the unpurged sins
of men. 'What a nasty excrementary creature Man is!' he
wrote. 'So much more than any beast of the field or forest.'[117]
The effects of his family's insistence were becoming apparent,
but Collier still clung to his faith in 'a superintending
Providence' which did not exact an arbitrary penance.
'Christianity is, or ought to be, cheerful', he asserted in late
January 1882.[118]

A day or two after penning that affirmation, Collier
suffered his first stroke. Within a month he was able to be out
of bed, but his body was broken, his spirit bereft, and his
eyesight virtually gone. For a while he was mindless; in
Pycroft's phrase, his 'intellect had broken'; the connecting
links of memory were discontinuous, and consciousness only
intermittent. He improved: within six weeks his mind
returned, and he was determined to live on however briefly.
Despite his blindness, he attempted to write. Years of habit
enabled him to move the pen across the paper by touch alone.
At the end of March, he wrote to Ebsworth in a scrawl, 'I
know that you will pity me from your heart's core, but this is
the best I can make of a hand-writing; I am thankful for that
and hope to improve. I am doing nothing but killing the time
as best I can. . . . I intend to practise myself in both reading
and writing: my difficulty is when I leave off to fix on again at
the right place. I have a good garden but then I know nothing
of the cultivation of vegetables or flowers, and 94 is rather late
for me to begin a science so abstruse and interesting. Altho I
cannot read your letters, I have those about me who can, and
like your literary gossip. The failing light bids me leave off
now.'[119] It was his last letter to anyone.

Quite unexpectedly, after a lapse of several weeks, he
returned to his journal on 14 May, 1882, and wrote the
'confession' that his children had urged upon him for so long.
'I am bitterly and most sincerely grieved that in every way I
am such a despicable offender', he wrote in a feeble but clearly
legible hand. 'I am ashamed of almost every act of my life.' He
signed it 'J. Payne Collier Nearly blind': and then, almost as

an afterthought, 'My repentance is bitter and sincere. I will do all in my power to amend. All my relations and friends are good, kind and pious people. It comes very late with me, but the profession is in my favour and it shall be sincere. I hope and believe I am pious as regards the treatment of my fellow creatures. J. Payne Collier.'[120] It was not a conventional confession of faith, but it would serve. His children's efforts had, at last, been rewarded.

The last entry in Collier's journal was dictated to Emma on 14 August 1882:

I have written much in verse and prose, but I can confidently say that I never produced a line, either in verse or prose that was calculated to be injurious either to morality or religion. I now close my diary because I can see to keep it no longer, and therefore use the hand of my most affectionate and serviceable daughter Emma Letitia Collier. Perhaps the above is saying a little too much – more than is [de]served. . . . My daughter is afraid that I am tiring myself by dictating and as her fears and fancies are to be indulged in, I leave off here tho' I have much still to say.[121]

John Payne Collier died of a cerebral haemorrhage at Riverside, Maidenhead, on 17 September 1883; three days later he was buried in Bray churchyard a few feet from his sister and brother-in-law. His estate was small: to his son William, he left his watch and the plain silver mug from which he had taken tea for nearly fifty years; to his daughter Henrietta, the silver inkstand he had received from his friends in America; to his son John Pycroft, the silver claret jug he had from his 'Glasgow Friends', his mother's morocco armchair, and his knee-hole desk. The remainder, including the Pelican shares he had inherited from Louisa, he left to Emma. As he had requested, his unfinished memoir was sent to Alexander Smith. The remainder of his books and manuscripts were sold at Sotheby's in August 1884. It was a large sale – one of the largest of the season. For three days Sotheby's rooms were crowded. The bidding was brisk and the prices were higher than anyone had expected.

APPENDIX

'The condemnation of John Payne Collier did not end with his death. In the years that followed, the assumption of his guilt became a certitude, and although none of his posthumous critics were as vehement as Ingleby or as vituperative as Furnivall, most agreed that any document Collier had touched was likely to be tainted.

The foregoing account has necessarily been restricted to those charges made in Collier's lifetime, but two posthumous accusations are important enough to be exceptions to this intention. The first is Sir George Warner's unequivocal declaration, first published in *The Dictionary of National Biography* in 1885 and reprinted in all editions thereafter, that he had discovered 'proof hitherto lacking that Collier was personally guilty of actual forgery.'[1] The second is Professor Giles Dawson's recent assertion that he had paleographic 'proof' that Collier had forged the Perkins Folio emendations.[2] These accusations are based on analyses of previously unsuspected manuscripts and this fact coupled with the eminence of the scholars who put them forward makes it appropriate to discuss them here.

I

In 1871, a decade after Ingleby published *A Complete View,* George Warner (1845–1936) joined the staff of the Department of Manuscripts of the British Museum. Warner, of course, had had no part in the original Museum Inquisition, but, like all of his colleagues at the Museum, he was convinced that Collier was guilty. He was also aware that Ingleby's case was largely hypothetical, and Warner was eager to find 'decisive proof' of Collier's guilt.

Several years before Collier's death, Warner was engaged by Dulwich College to catalogue its manuscripts, and in the course of that labour he found previously unnoticed 'modern forgeries' that he was certain Collier had inserted into the

Alleyn papers. In 1881 he published a catalogue of the collection[3] in which he described the 'new' forgeries and, stopping short of a direct accusation, made it clear whom he believed to be the forger. ('I cannot find that they have been published or referred to either by Mr. Collier or anyone else', he declared.[4]) He was particularly interested in six 'forged' interpolations in Edward Alleyn's unpublished diary:

As [these] were doubtless meant for use and not inserted in mere wantonness, it would be interesting to learn whether an edition of the MS. was ever contemplated and, if so, by whom. It may be laid down as a general rule that literary frauds of the kind found at Dulwich are not concocted by one person in order that the benefit of them may be reaped by another; but there may conceivably be exceptions. After Malone's death there is nothing to show whether any one used the MSS. before Mr. Collier....[5]

Although Warner clearly implied that Collier made the interpolations in the manuscript, he lacked evidence to support his belief.

Two years later, Collier died, and when his library was auctioned, Warner was sure he had found the proof he sought. Item No. 200 in Sotheby's sale catalogue was a transcript of Alleyn's diary 'in the autograph of J. P. Collier'. Warner immediately suggested to William Young, one of the governors of Dulwich College,[6] that the College might want to buy the transcript in order to compare it with the original. Young attended the sale, bought Collier's transcript (for 32 shillings), and immediately sent it to Warner to be examined. Two months later, on 23 October 1884, Warner replied:

Mr. Collier's extracts from Alleyn's Diary are extremely interesting, since they prove, as I think incontestably that the spurious interpolations in the Diary were made by Mr. Collier. These interpolations, as you will find in the Catalogue (p. xlii), are six in number, all of which, except the last (p. 183), appear in the extracts interlined. This fact, of course, taken by itself, might be used as evidence that Mr. Collier found them in the original Diary already, and copied them just as they stood. A curious circumstance, however, shows that they were not written at the same time as the rest of the contents of the several pages in which they occur, for in all cases in which the interlined words are in ink there is a 'set off' on the opposite page from these words, *and from these only* (see pp. 6, 11, 12 of

Collier's MS.). I have no doubt that Mr. Collier's method of procedure was this: having made his extracts, he first interlined the spurious words in his copy, and then turned to the original Diary and inserted them there: after which he turned over the leaf in his copy without troubling to assure himself that the ink had completely dried in the interval. Afterwards, probably some time later, when he was suspected of forgeries in other quarters, the spurious words were scored through with the pen, but the 'set off' to which I have drawn your attention is from the written letters. But there is even stronger evidence against Mr. Collier, for there are in his extracts interlined words which are not to be found in the original Diary at all. On page 175 of the Catalogue you will find a reference to the forgery 'Saw Romeo', which in the original has been partially erased as a failure. In the extracts [i.e., Collier's transcript] (p. 15) the forgery appears in the extended form, 'and saw Romeo and Juliett,' written in pencil. These words have been rubbed out (after the attempt to transfer them to the Diary was given up), but the impression made by the pencil can still be seen and read without difficulty. On the opposite page (p. 14) is another tentative forgery. Under the date 4th October (1618), over the name 'Jo. Taylor' is written in pencil (rubbed out) 'Br. Shakespeare,' the intention presumably being to endeavour to change the one name into the other in the Diary. On second thoughts, this design, I suppose, seemed too hazardous, as well it might, since Shakespeare had already been dead two years!! There is one other interlineation, 'and the Play,' in pencil, which also does not appear in the Diary. I need only add that all of these entries in the extracts are evidently in Mr. Collier's own hand, and I think I have said enough to show that the guarded language which I used about him in the Catalogue might have been infinitely stronger.

So far as I know, this letter is the only account Warner gave of his evidence and conclusion, and as such it was the basis for his assertion of 'proof' in his *DNB* biography. It was subsequently printed, with Warner's enthusiastic approval, in Young's *History of Dulwich College* (1889).[7]

The provenance of the manuscript of Alleyn's diary and the use of it by Daniel Lyson,[8] Edmond Malone and others suggest several possible sources and purposes for the 'forged interpolations' which Warner describes, but although these subjects are interesting, they have no direct bearing on the question of Warner's accusation which is based solely on his comparison of Collier's transcript with the original manuscript.

The interpolations that Warner identified in the Alleyn diary manuscript are as follows:

No. 1. 'As You Like It', interpolated into the entry for 9 April 1618;
No. 2. 'of the playhouse', 22 August 1618;
No. 3. 'theatre', 28 September 1618;
No. 4. 'saw Romeo', 30 October 1618;
No. 5. 'B. Jonson', 20 May 1619;
No. 6. 'I went to see poor Tom Dekker', 12 November 1619.

Warner's case for 'proving' that Collier made these interpolations is based on the two main assertions articulated in his letter to Young: first, Collier forged the additions in the manuscript because five of them (all except No. 6. above) appear in his transcript in a form identical to that in the manuscript, that is, as interpolations. Second, Collier made the forgeries because the only alterations in his transcript, Warner implies, are those connected with the five interpolations, and these – and only these – are offset in the transcript.

Even a cursory comparison of the manuscript with Collier's transcript (now at Dulwich College) reveals that Warner's description is grossly in error in fact and in omission. Only three – not five – of the six interpolations appear in Collier's transcript in the form they have in the manuscript. Warner's most significant error concerns No. 5, 'B. Jonson', perhaps the most important interpolation of the six. Contrary to Warner's account, this interpolation is *not interlined* in Collier's transcript (p. 21) – it is in the *body* of the text. This strongly suggests that when Collier's transcription was made the 'forgery' had already been interpolated in the manuscript, and since this interpolation does not differ significantly from the other five, it casts doubt on Warner's hypothesis concerning the sequence of the 'forgery'.

No. 4, 'saw Romeo', is another anomaly since unlike the other five it is written in pencil in Collier's transcript. Although Warner makes a subtle qualification ('in all cases in which the interlined words are in ink'), he slides over the implication: this difference suggests the note was written at a different time and possibly for a purpose different from those of the other five insertions. Thus, only three of the inter-polations might conceivably have followed the pattern of forgery which Warner describes, and I suggest that this is not enough correlation, in the absence of an explanation of the other three, to justify the elaborate hypothesis incriminating Collier.

A more serious error in Warner's description is his implication that *only* the forged interpolations were inserted in Collier's transcript and that all of these – and only these – are 'offset'. In fact, there are *many* corrections inserted in Collier's transcript, all of them clearly derived from the manuscript and all, except for the five Warner has singled out, unconnected with forgery. This is to say, there are many *bona fide* changes which Collier made in his transcript while systematically correcting it against the original. None of these corrections differs significantly in kind or execution from those corresponding to the 'forgeries' that Warner identifies, and some of them, like the suspected insertions, were made in ink which 'offset' on the opposite pages of the transcript. For example: on p. 6 of the transcript, 'all' in '& all at the Fortune' was changed to 'ale' (i.e., to '& ale at the Fortune') to correspond to the true reading in the manuscript; the link of this correction offset on p. 7. On p. 15, 'stronge' was changed to 'strange' to follow the manuscript and the ink offset on p. 14. On p. 12, 'arn' in 'Barn' is scratched and 'en' is inserted to follow the manuscript; both 'en' and the line of deletion offset on p. 13. On p. 51, 'the' is scratched and '5' is inserted to follow the manuscript; '5' offset on p. 50. There are, moreover, 'legitimate' changes inserted in the transcript which did not offset: e.g., on p. 1, 'Watt' is scratched and 'Nott' is inserted in ink to follow the manuscript but without offset, and on p. 37 'purchase' is scratched and 'personage' is inserted to follow the manuscript but without offset. On p. 10, 'and late' is inserted without deletion, to follow the manuscript. Other examples could be cited. None of these corrections is in any way suspicious; all are *bona fide* corrections of obvious errors or misreadings in the transcript. The inevitable conclusion is that the disputed corrections were made at the same time and for the same purpose.

There are, in addition, a number of pencilled editorial comments in Collier's transcript which clearly connect the transcript to Collier's edition of *Memoirs of Edward Alleyn*.

Significantly, Warner omits all reference to these notations, perhaps because they reveal the false implication of his earlier assertion that Collier had not 'published or referred to' the forged interpolations. This statement is technically 'correct', but its clear implication – that Collier had not published them because he had not published any part of Alleyn's diary – is misleading. Collier quoted extensively from the manuscript in the *Memoirs*; it was, in fact, one of his chief sources for that book. Hence Warner's suggestion that Collier may have forged the interpolations in preparation for a publication which was never issued is false, and since he refers to the *Memoirs* in his catalogue, Warner must have known it was false. If Warner's supposition concerning the purpose of the forgeries is correct, the fact that Collier did not publish the interpolations argues against his guilt since it violates Warner's own 'general rule' that such frauds are 'concocted' to be used by the forger.

The pencilled editorial notes suggest the manner of Collier's use of the diary in the *Memoirs*. For example, Collier wrote 'barge' in pencil in the margin on p. 23 of his transcript and while commenting on the diary entry, he refers to 'the Queen's barge' in the *Memoirs* on p. 152; on p. 14, he wrote 'wedding' in pencil in the margin and in the *Memoirs* he cites this entry and mentions Alleyn's wedding day on p. 153; on p. 37, he wrote 'Lewisham' in pencil in the margin and in the *Memoirs* he refers to this entry on p. 163. There are other examples. By remaining silent concerning these details, Warner distorts the apparent purpose of the transcript and implies a dishonest intention which the transcript itself does not suggest.

In the light of the foregoing, Warner's reconstruction of 'Mr. Collier's method of procedure' in forging ('having made his extracts, he first interlined the spurious words in his copy, etc.') is gratuitous. It is also illogical. If Collier made the insertions in his transcript simultaneously with the 'forged interpolations' in the manuscript as Warner describes, why did the ink of the transcript offset while the ink of the manuscript did not? The latter was not blotted but allowed to air dry; if there was time for the manuscript ink to dry before the forger proceeded to the next item, why did the ink in the transcript offset? The inevitable answer must be, the insertions in the transcript and the interpolations in the manuscript were *not* made concurrently. Well, then, perhaps Collier inserted all the 'forged interpolations' into his transcript, offsetting the ink as he went, and subsequently wrote these changes into the manuscript, allowing each to dry before going on to the next? This, too, is unlikely because it does not account for the many other *bona fide* corrections, identical in ink, form, and occasional offset, which were obviously made at the same time as the interpolated 'forgeries' and just as obviously *derived from the manuscript*. The only possible conclusion is that the insertions in the transcript must have been made *after* the interpolations in the manuscript and not before, and if that is the case, Warner's hypothesis is disproved since it rests on the assumption that the manuscript interpolations derived from Collier's transcript.

Warner's case culminates in what he sees as the strongest evidence of forgery, that concerning No. 4, 'saw Romeo':

But there is even stronger evidence against Mr. Collier, for there are in his extracts interlined words which are not to be found in the original Diary at all.... In the extracts (p. 15) the forgery appears in the extended form, 'and saw Romeo and Juliett,' written in pencil. These words have been rubbed out (after the attempt to transfer them to the Diary was given up), but the impression made by the pencil can still be seen and read without difficulty.

Unfortunately, Warner misquotes the manuscript: there is another now indecipherable word preceding 'saw' in the manuscript which he does not mention. Furthermore he has distorted Collier's note by adding a 't' to 'Juliet', perhaps to suggest a 'fabricated antique' spelling. Warner's implication is that Collier botched his transcription into the manuscript and tried to erase it, but he gives no reason for this conclusion. The reference is not more egregious than the other interpolated errors. Obviously, the 'extended form' in Collier's transcript is merely a supposition of the full title suggested by 'Romeo' in the manuscript. The partial erasure in the manuscript might well have created the uncertainty which the subsequent erasure in the transcript reveals. This pencil note does not differ from the other pencil notes – it is a comment on the manuscript and one, as it happens, that Collier did not think highly enough to use in the *Memoirs*.

Warner continues:

On the opposite page (p. 14) is another tentative forgery. Under the date 4th October (1618), over the name 'Jo. Taylor' is written in pencil (rubbed out) 'Br. Shakespeare,' the intention presumably being to endeavour to change the one name into the other in the Diary.

The pencil notation 'Mr. (not 'Br.' as Warner's letter has it) Shakespeare' is not an intended insertion; it is rather an interpretation of the manuscript 'Jo. Taylor' which is written in such a loose fashion that it looks like 'Mr. Shakespeare'. This is all that Collier's pencil note indicates; his erasure suggests that he did not think much of the suggestion. Obviously no would-be forger would have contemplated inserting Shakespeare's name in a diary begun the year after his death, and obviously Collier knew the dates as well as Warner. Warner fails to note that the transcript has many such pencil notations suggesting variant readings and identifying obscure references.[9]

Another pencil reference suggests that Collier's transcript was not initially derived from the manuscript but from another *transcript*. On p. 4 (line 3) of his transcript 'water' is underscored and 'went (L)' is written in pencil above it; and again in line 9 on the same page 'was' is underscored and '& L' written above it in pencil. The 'L' in these notes refers to Daniel Lyson who quoted from Alleyn's manuscript diary in *The Environs of London*.[10] It is clear that Collier corrected his transcript against Lyson's quotations: on p. 26 he interrupts his transcript at the description of a dinner and notes '(See Lyson for this)' after which follow two and three-quarter blank pages, space left, presumably, for a description which was never copied. This annotated comparison clearly indicates that the source from which Collier made his transcript was *not* the manuscript diary itself, for if his source had had that authority, he would have had no purpose in correcting it against the lesser authority of Lyson.

Warner's 'case' is, therefore, based on an incomplete and distorted description of Collier's transcript. He also ignores other evidence which would weaken his accusation: the six 'forged interpolations' in the manuscript are *all* in disagreement with opinions Collier held and published. Why would Collier fabricate evidence to disprove his own opinions? To be more specific: all six forgeries have theatre or drama associations, yet in the *Memoirs* Collier declared that 'Alleyn appears to have frequented theatres very little, if at all, as places of amusement . . . after the date when his Diary commences.'[10] In this opinion Collier merely echoed Malone who had seen the manuscript sometime in the 1780s and declared that it 'contains no theatrical intelligence whatsoever'.[11] In the face of Malone's statement and his own, why would Collier forge useless theatrical references into his source? Obviously the references to *As You Like It* (No. 1) and *Romeo and Juliet* (No. 4) are direct contradictions of Collier's published opinion. That Collier inserted the reference to 'B. Jonson' (No. 5) is even more ludicrous. In the *Memoirs* he specifically states that Jonson's name is *not* in the diary.[12] Why would he subsequently forge a reference which would contradict his own statement?

Finally, it is particularly ridiculous to believe that Collier would have forged the interpolation 'of the playhouse' (No. 2) into the manuscript, because he quoted this particular passage in the *Memoirs without the interpolation.*[13] His description of the original manuscript in the *Memoirs* is very complete and proves that he was quoting from the manuscript itself at the time – not from his transcript. Why would he later forge an entry into the manuscript which his own published work would call into question?[14]

Warner's accusation against Collier must therefore be seen as false: it is based on an incorrect and incomplete description of the manuscript evidence and on a series of illogical assumptions. The true circumstance is almost certainly much more simple: Collier's transcript was made from *another* transcript – probably Malone's[15] – which is now lost. Collier did not find the original manuscript of Alleyn's diary among the papers at Dulwich when he first used them around 1830. He was then writing *HEDP*, and any use he made of the diary in that book was, therefore, based on his transcript which, in the interim, he corrected against Lyson's version. However,

subsequent to the publication of *HEDP,* the original manuscript of Alleyn's diary was unearthed at Dulwich and Collier
then read it and corrected his transcript against the original.
Between the date when Malone saw the manuscript (and
presumably made his transcript of it) in the 1780s and the
date in the early 1830s when the original was unearthed at
Dulwich, someone had written the 'forged interpolations' into
the manuscript. In correcting his transcript against the
original, Collier initially inserted these additions into his copy.
Later he realized they were false and cancelled them.

This sequence is suggested by a detail which (among many)
Warner failed to note: Collier's original title for his transcript
was 'Edward Alleyn's Diary'. Later, in a different ink 'From'
was inserted before 'Edward' and 'at Dulwich College'
inserted after 'Diary'. These additions indicate that when he
first copied the diary Collier assumed it was the complete text
of the original; later, when he corrected it against the
manuscript at Dulwich, he recognized its incompleteness and
indicated that fact in his title by inserting 'From' and a
reference to his new source. If Collier had made the
unemended transcript from the manuscript itself, he would
have known it was not complete and would not, therefore,
have titled it incorrectly to begin with.

Warner's statement that his evidence 'proved' Collier
'personally guilty of actual forgery' is untrue.

II

In 1971, Professor Giles E. Dawson published what he believes
to be proof that Collier forged the Perkins Folio emendations.
Professor Dawson's argument is based on his analysis of a
manuscript commonplace book (sometimes called the 'Hall
Commonplace Book' because of a signature on its flyleaf)
which once belonged to Collier.[16] The manuscript contains
eighty-three ballads written in what appears to be a seventeenth-century hand, and of these thirty-four were published
by Collier in his edition of *Extracts from the Registers of the
Stationers' Company* in 1848 and 1849. (See p. 104 above.)

Professor Dawson's case can be briefly summarized:

> Collier forged the eighty-three ballads in the
> Hall Commonplace Book.
> Handwriting analysis proves that whoever wrote
> those ballads also wrote the Perkins
> Folio emendations.
> Therefore Collier forged the Perkins Folio
> emendations.

This argument seems to me false because its major premise is unproved; the evidence that the ballads in the manuscript are forged is weak and the argument that Collier forged them is weaker still.

Professor Dawson subscribes to the prevailing opinion against Collier in accepting Ingleby's *Complete View* and Sir George Warner's account in *The Dictionary of National Biography* (which he calls 'admirable'), and this creates an *a priori* assumption. 'I have been assuming', he declares about half-way through his article, 'that all but one of the ballads printed in the *Extracts* and most of the others were of his [Collier's] own composition.'[17] Although Professor Dawson declares that this assumption is not essential to his purpose, it is obvious that if Collier *composed* the ballads he had to have a hand in transcribing them into the manuscript. The statement admits a prejudice which effectively limits the discussion to conclusions which impugn Collier's *bona fides*. However, to convict Collier of forgery, Professor Dawson must prove beyond a reasonable doubt that Collier wrote the ballads in the manuscript – not merely that he *might* but that he *must* have done so – and this, I believe, Professor Dawson's evidence and argument fail to do.

Professor Dawson's conclusion that the ballads are forged is based on the disparity between the date at which the ballads were written into the commonplace book and the much earlier date of their presumed composition or first publication. The ballad transcriptions must have been made after 1648: roughly eighty percent of the writing in the book consists of notes unrelated to the ballads, internal dating proves these notes could not have been written before 1648, and it is clear that the ballads were copied into the manuscript *after* these notes were made, that is, after 1648. These facts are not in dispute, but Collier was slow to recognize them. In the preface to the first volume of *Extracts* (1848) he announced that the writing of the book was 'in a handwriting of the time of James I' and by implication he then attributed the ballad transcriptions to that date. However, when he published the second volume a year later, he altered his opinion, declaring that his earlier statement had been 'in too general terms' and noting that

although such is the case with respect to the greater part of it [the commonplace book], some portions are of a more remote, and others of a later date. In fact, two, if not three, handwritings are to be found in it, the earliest beginning before the year 1600, and the latest continuing until the Restoration.[18]

Collier then printed a complete list of the ballads in the manuscript, declaring they were written by an 'early scribe'.[19] His definition of 'early' can be inferred from a later comment introducing one of his illustrations, a ballad called 'A Jest of Peele and Singer' (II, 215), in which he describes the book as 'a MS. belonging to the Editor, written about the reign of Charles I...'.

The point in dispute is the effect which this late dating has on the validity of the transcriptions. The thirty-four ballads (of eighty-three in the manuscript) which Collier printed as illustrations in the two published volumes of the *Extracts* were necessarily associated with dates prior to 1588 (the last date in Vol. II), and Professor Dawson believes this is too high a concentration of early ballads in a collection made so many years after their presumed publication. He sees this concentration as too convenient to Collier's purpose, and this to him suggests they were forged.

If Collier's date [that is, Collier's original opinion] were correct – if the ballads had been written in the commonplace book in the reign of James I – we would find nothing odd in the fact that twelve of the ballads that are on datable historical subjects ... are all Elizabethan and we would scarcely notice the fact that the early poetical collections in which ten of the ballads had been printed were all published before 1588. That the entries in the Stationers' Register that correspond with thirty-four of the ballads were all made before 1588 we might think a curious coincidence but would not regard as utterly incredible.

However, the later date, i.e., mid-seventeenth century, Professor Dawson declares has

implications . . . severely damaging of [Collier's] whole case regarding the ballads. He would have us believe that a ballad collector of 1650 gathered eighty-three ballads, of which thirty-four (forty percent) had been printed, or at least entered, between 1570 and 1587 (just the period of Collier's *Extracts*) and none that were later, twelve on historical events of the reign of Elizabeth (none later), and ten that had been printed in collections before 1588 (none later).[20]

In a footnote, Professor Dawson reduces the rhetorical impact of his series by admitting that Collier's edition of the *Extracts* was *not,* as his statement in the text implies, limited to a closing date of 1587 and that Collier had, in fact, completed much of the editing of Volume III of the *Extracts* which was to cover the period 1587 to 1601. Professor Dawson might have gone a step further by noting that Collier had announced at the outset of his publication of the *Extracts* for the Shakespeare Society that he intended to edit several volumes in the series, beginning with the year 1557 and continuing as far as possible into Shakespeare's own period – that is to say, at the time Professor Dawson claims Collier was forging ballads for illustrative addenda in the *Extracts,* the scope of that edition extended at least to the year 1601. Now, there is a curious circumstance about the manuscript of Volume III: Professor Dawson admits that none of the ballad titles it contains can be 'matched with any of the eighty-three in the manuscript',[21] but if Collier forged thirty-four ballads into the manuscript to provide himself with false illustrations for the first two volumes of the *Extracts* edition, why should he not have composed more to correlate with the entries in the third volume? All three volumes were part of a single plan and there were forty-nine additional ballads with no apparent purpose in the manuscript which might have been 'used' to supply the period after 1587. If Collier forged for the first two volumes, why not for the third? Moreover, if, as Professor Dawson believes, the abrupt end to the correlation with the Registers after 1587 is suspicious, would not a clever forger – and Professor Dawson described an extremely clever forger – have avoided that suspicion by composing at least a *few* ballads to correlate with Volume III? The manuscript ballads would have looked far more like what Collier claimed they were if they had demonstrated a continuing connection with the later entries. Finally, at the very time Collier was editing the third volume for future publication – that is, at the time when he would have been most likely to have 'composed' ballad illustrations to supplement the text he was working on – he published a complete list of the ballads in the preface to Volume II ('in order that the subjects of the whole collection may be seen at once'),[22] an act which precluded any subsequent additions to the manuscript for use in Volume III. Why would Collier, if guilty, have constrained himself in this way? The absence of a correlation between Volume III and the manuscript ballads therefore argues *against* Professor Dawson's conclusions which, in any case, raise more questions than they answer.

There is a lapse in Professor Dawson's statement which, although insignificant in itself suggests another important fault in his argument. He writes that Collier 'would have us believe that a *ballad collector* of 1650 gathered eighty-three ballads, etc.' [my emphasis]. This is an error. Collier speaks of the 'scribe', the person who wrote the ballads into the manuscript; he does not call him the 'collector'. The error is not important except insofar as it reveals a penchant for believing the scribe and the collector (and the composer) are one and the same, that is, John Payne Collier, and this penchant, as I have already suggested, rests on an *a priori* assumption of Collier's guilt.

The effect of this presupposition is most apparent in Professor Dawson's second major reason for believing the manuscript ballads were forged: he produces charts to 'prove' that the thirty-four ballads which Collier printed are in an incriminating chronological order:

What can be seen at a glance ... is this: that of the first twenty-four ballads written in the manuscript (Nos. 1–24) Collier was to 'find' that seventeen corresponded with ballad titles entered in the Stationers' Register before 1570 and that the last eight corresponded with titles entered after 1575. Thus there is a roughly chronological order in the thirty-four ballads as they stand in the manuscript.[23]

Here another caveat should be made: the term 'corresponded with' might well be understood to mean 'identical to', i.e., that the ballads Collier printed were in every case the ballads which the Register identifies. This is not the case. In at least nine instances[24] the illustrations are not the ballads referred to in the Register but only very loosely analogous ones, 'specimens' included by Collier merely to elaborate his notes. It is therefore incorrect to say that in these instances (three in Dawson's list of the 'first twenty-four' and five in his list of the 'last eight') the illustrations 'corresponded' to the titles if that word implies they were identical or even necessarily of the same date. Yet this is, I believe, Professor Dawson's implication.

In addition, Professor Dawson finds five 'pairs' of ballads which appear consecutively in both the manuscript and in Collier's illustrations. This, he concludes, 'does not look like pure chance'.

If we are to believe in Collier's seventeenth-century ballad collector [note my caveat above] we must put forward a reasonable hypothesis to account for the unmistakable traces of chronological arrangement in thirty-four of the ballads as they stand in his manuscript. The assumption that he copied these from printed broadsides does not help, since the printers of ballads, fully conscious of their ephemeral nature, almost never dated their imprints. Our supposed collector would have had to be a tireless researcher to achieve even such a degree of chronological arrangement as we find. Yet with the twelve ballads about easily-dated events – Lady Jane Grey's lament, the burning of St. Paul's steeple, the great earthquake, and the others – he took no trouble to set them down in any order.

I can make no sense of this.[25]

Professor Dawson's solution is a hypothetical description of Collier in the act of forgery (I quote it at length not only to do justice to his case, but also to illustrate the way a predilection for Collier's guilt can misdirect reasonable argument):

But if instead [Professor Dawson continues] we assume that Collier himself wrote the ballads in the commonplace book we can reach a reasonable explanation of all the main features of the collection. Looking into the Stationers' Register and finding it rich in entries of popular literature, he began, in 1847, transcribing all the entries that interested him, with a view to publication. At some point during the work of editing it occurred to him that he might compose pseudo-Elizabethan ballads to fit the titles that struck his fancy as he came across them and that he could then 'find' them and print them in his notes. We cannot know whether or not he wrote the ballads in the order in which he found appropriate titles. It was obviously not in this order that he copied them into his commonplace book. . . . Presumably Collier first wrote the ballads in his ordinary hand on ordinary sheets of paper; at what stage in his work he copied them into the book appears to be inscrutable and irrelevant. When he prepared for the task of copying in his 'old' hand, though he did not sufficiently appreciate the problems of avoiding detection, he realized that the thirty-four ballads must not stand in the manuscript in the fully chronological order in which they would appear in the printed *Extracts*. It was clear to him also that his manuscript collection must not consist solely of the thirty-four ballads entered in the Stationers' Register between 1557 and 1587. There must be others with them, and these he could of course manufacture as easily as he did most of the thirty-four. It is reasonable to suppose that he had long entertained himself by writing Elizabethan ballads and that he had some of these laid away,[26] and he could write more as they were needed. Accordingly he selected a few suitable pieces, perhaps wrote some new ones, and, for verisimilitude, gathered a dozen or so from Elizabethan printed sources. These he interpolated among the sheets containing the thirty-four and shuffled them all together. The shuffling was adequate . . . or nearly so – but the interpolating was remarkably uneven. . . . The uneven interpolation, light at the beginning, heavy in the middle and at the end, does not look like chance.

Professor Dawson does not indicate how a 'chance' arrangement might differ from the pattern he describes, but he goes on to suggest two explanations for why it does not occur:

Two alternative and almost equally attractive explanations present themselves: (1) Collier was unable, till he had copied about twenty-four, to estimate how many ballads the available pages would take; (2) it may have been only after he had copied twenty-four of the ballads that he observed that the interpolation was too light and must be increased. Neither explanation accounts for the presence of the last nine superfluous ballads [at the very end of the sequence]; perhaps he merely wanted to fill up space. Since the whole eighty-three are included in a list that Collier prints in the preface to *Extracts*, II (1849), we cannot suppose any to be later additions.[27]

This hypothesis is faulty. The difficulty which the argument attempts to explain is the obvious disparity between the order of the ballads in the manuscript and the order of Collier's use of them in the *Extracts*. The apparent logic here is: if the sequence were identical, one might conclude that forgery had been committed; alternatively, following that logic, one might assume that a *lack* of pronounced congruence between the two suggests that the similarities were the product of mere chance rather than forgery.

But that is not the way Professor Dawson argues: the 'problem' as he states it is of a kind which can only prove 'forgery' – not the lack of it. On the one hand, he finds a chronological pattern which suggests forgery; on the other, he finds a *lack* of chronological pattern which suggests a clever forger who 'shuffled' his ballads to avoid a suspicious sequence. The 'evidence' is read both ways and either way it must incriminate Collier. Professor Dawson would have us believe that when Collier 'shuffled' the ballads to destroy the tell-tale chronological order he didn't know how many ballads the pages would accommodate. But why would a forger careful enough to 'shuffle' his forgeries to avoid a damning chronology be incapable – at the outset – of making the relatively simply calculation to determine the number of pages he would need to copy them? And in any case, given the loose form of the ballads as printed, why would their supposed author be unable to lengthen or shorten them to meet unforeseen exigencies of space? Why would he throw out a pattern – carefully designed to avoid suspicion – merely to interpolate many new ballads which he had no intention to publish? Certainly it could not have been to hide the dangerous 'concentration' which Professor Dawson sees – that 'fault' was already there in the first twenty-four and no subsequent pattern of interpolation, however 'loose', could change it. All in all, Professor Dawson's 'equally attractive' answers seem to me equally inadequate; both create greater difficulties than the 'problem' they seek to resolve.

The chronological ordering of the ballads does not seem to me particularly puzzling, but I think an objective view of its presumed 'difficulty' might suggest another, more likely solution which, as it happens, does not incriminate Collier.

First, I do not believe the chronology in Professor Dawson's charts is as 'unmistakable' as he does. As I have already indicated, in nine of the thirty-four instances the ballads are not identical to the Register and hence their dating cannot be inferred; the chronology is 'rough' to the point of obscurity. But for the sake of argument, let us grant the possibility that there is a slight concentration of pre-1570 ballads in the early part of the manuscript sequence and a similar concentration of post-1575 ballads in the latter part. Professor Dawson views this possibility as suspicious because, as I have noted, he makes an unsupported assumption that the person who transcribed the ballads into the manuscript was aware of their chronology, i.e., that the 'transcriber' was also the 'collector'. He thus assumes the order in which they appear must have been the result of a single collector since all of the ballads are written in the same hand. But there is no logical reason for assuming that a mid-seventeenth-century scribe was copying from *original* broadsides and ballads when he entered the pieces in his commonplace book.[28] He may well have copied from *other* manuscript collections. Indeed, given the number and variety of the ballads, a multiple source is very likely. Thus the collection may have been a transcription from several earlier manuscript ballad sources, made at different times by different collectors; the scribe need not have had any knowledge whatever of the dates of individual ballads, and their order in the Hall Commonplace Book might be merely the arbitrary sequence in which the scribe used his various sources. The chronological consistencies (and inconsistencies!) which Professor Dawson sees in the manuscript and on which he bases his case for forgery might thus be accounted for without blame. The early concentration in pre-1570 items might reflect the contents of a collection of that early period; and later chronological concentration from another made later. As Professor Dawson himself has admitted, 'if the ballads had been written in the commonplace book in the reign of James I – we would find nothing odd' in their affinities. And if they were *copied* from such a book – as it is reasonable to believe they might have been – the same judgement would apply. In the light of this, the date at which they were transcribed into the manuscript is no longer critical, and the fact that they were written after 1648 is not the damning fact which Professor Dawson has assumed. Certainly there is no longer any reason to believe that Collier copied them there.

Since Professor Dawson's major premise is not demonstrably true, we need not consider his minor one (that the manuscript ballads and the emendations in the Perkins Folio are written in the same handwriting) to disallow his conclusion (that Collier forged those emendations). However, two points might be made in conclusion. First, Professor Dawson presents a hypothetical description of Collier learning to write the 'forged seventeenth century hand':

Clearly we can ascribe to him a superior manual dexterity and perhaps superior coordination of hand and brain. Even so it was a long and taxing labor – this learning to write a new hand. I can see him bent over his task for an hour or two at a time, day after day, week after week, slowly acquiring the automatic translation of thought into written words. For when a man writes he is unconscious of the shapes of letters, or only half conscious of them, and yet they come out in his own peculiar hand. Such facility Collier obviously possessed when he wrote, with remarkable consistency, more than a hundred and fifty pages of ballads in his old commonplace book. To have stuck at the learning of that old hand he must have been strongly urged forward by an objective that was very important to him. It is not necessary to suppose that he had the Perkins folio in view from the start; in fact this is highly unlikely since he was writing the hand with at least some facility more than fifteen years before he announced the discovery of the annotations.[29]

Again, Professor Dawson would seem to have it both ways: he here announces with certainty that Collier wrote the 'hand' fifteen years prior to the Perkins Folio emendations, but a sentence or two later, the disputed document he refers to, identified only as 'one... in the Bridgewater collection' reproduced by Ingleby in *Complete View,* is said to *differ* from the ballad hand, if 'only slightly'. If it differs, however 'slightly', how can one say with certainty that Collier was 'writing [it] with at least some facility' then? The innuendo is unfortunate, particularly so as the evidence appears to be only Ingleby's facsimile and not the document itself.

But more important, Professor Dawson here admits the

almost insurmountable difficulty that any would-be forger would face in producing the ballad manuscript. This difficulty makes the supposition of Collier's guilt ridiculous, and anyone aware of Collier's life and work between 1835 and 1846 must view the suggestion with incredulity. That he devoted 'an hour or two at a time, day after day, week after week' for fifteen years during the most intensely busy period of his life in order to perfect a forger's hand for some distant unknown purpose is so unlikely it ought to shake the belief of even the most convinced anti-Collierite.

Second, Professor Dawson's culminating argument is based on imputed guilty motives:

If weakness is found in the whole argument of this paper [he writes], it will hardly be found, I think, in the paleographical part of it, and if the demonstration that it was Collier who copied the ballads into his book falls short of mathematical proof, there is another point to be thought about. If Collier acquired his manuscript volume about 1840 and it then contained the ballads, he could hardly have failed to see, three or four years after he had copied out thirty-four of the ballads, that his remarkable annotated folio, assuming it to be genuine, was in the same hand. And if he saw it, why should he not have mentioned such a very remarkable coincidence?[30]

This very hypothetical argument is based, finally, on a predilection to believe Collier a forger. Professor Dawson's paleographic evidence may or may not be weak, but it is certainly not simple or obvious: his proof requires several pages of highly sophisticated analogies based on twentieth-century knowledge and resources which no expert mid-nineteenth-century paleographer would have had – and Collier was *not* an expert paleographer. To say, therefore, that Collier 'could hardly have failed to see' the similarities because they are apparent to Professor Dawson is not very compelling, and if Collier didn't see the similarity his failure to announce it is not very suspicious. One must impute guilty knowledge to make the argument work, but if the possibility of the two hands being identical was so damning, why would the forger not alter one of them in order to make it 'differ if only slightly' from the other? And why, when the Perkins

Folio came under the scrutiny of Madden and Ingleby, did he not destroy the ballad manuscript? He had made all the use he could of it. Like so many of the arguments which have been put forward to convict Collier, Professor Dawson's rationale works only if one accepts an unlikely inconsistency: a brilliant paleographer of almost superhuman skill and cunning who is a clumsy and stupid crook. It is highly unlikely that any man could be both. I believe Collier was neither.

Professor Dawson's argument avoids the fundamental question which is not whether Collier knew the hands were the same but whether they could have been so without his having forged them. One can assume the ballads and emendations were written by the same hand without assuming that that hand was Collier's. It is entirely possible that the Old Corrector who spent hundreds of hours copying thousands of bad emendations into the Perkins Folio also copied dozens of bad ballads into the commonplace book. This is not 'a very remarkable coincidence'; even the fact that Collier came into possession of both is not remarkable when one considers the size of his collection and the variety of his purchases over forty years. That he lied about the details of acquiring the folio and was preternaturally circumspect about his use of the ballads does not prove he was a forger.

Finally, if I am correct that the arguments I have presented earlier demonstrate that Collier could not have forged the Perkins Folio emendations, and if Professor Dawson is correct that whoever wrote those emendations also wrote the ballads into the Hall Commonplace Book, it must follow that, whoever *did* write them, it was not John Payne Collier.

Notes

The following abbreviations are used in the notes:

Bodleian
: The Bodleian Library, Oxford.

An Inquiry
: *An Inquiry into the Corrections in Mr. J. Payne Collier's Annotated Shakspere Folio, 1632; and of Certain Documents Likewise Published by Mr. Collier.* By Nicholas E.S.A. Hamilton. London: Richard Bentley, 1860.

Complete View
: *A Complete View of the Shakspere Controversy, Concerning the Authenticity and Genuineness of Manuscript Matter Affecting the Works and Biography of Shakspere, published by Mr. J. Payne Collier as the Fruits of his Researches.* By Clement Mansfield Ingleby. London: Nattali and Bond, 1861.

Dyce
: The Dyce Collection, Library, Victoria and Albert Museum.

Folger
: The Folger Library, Washington, D.C.

HCR
: Henry Crabb Robinson.

HCR Corresp.
: The manuscript correspondence of Henry Crabb Robinson in Dr. Williams's Library, London.

HCR ms Diary
: The manuscript diary of Henry Crabb Robinson in Dr. Williams's Library, London.

HCR ms Remin.
: The manuscript reminiscences of Henry Crabb Robinson in Dr. Williams's Library, London.

HEDP
: *The History of English Dramatic Poetry*

Huntington
: The Henry E. Huntington Library, San Marino, California.

JDC
: John Dyer Collier.

JPC
: John Payne Collier.

JPC ms Auto.
: The memoir of John Payne Collier (ca. 1880), Folger MS. M.a. 230, Folger Library.

JPC Corresp.
: The uncatalogued manuscript correspondence of John Payne Collier, Box 1289, Folger Library.

JPC ms Early Diary
: The diary of John Payne Collier, 1811–1812, Folger MSS. M.a. 219–228, Folger Library.

JPC ms Journal
: The journal of John Payne Collier, 1873–1882, Folger MSS. M.a. 29–40, Folger Library.

Koop
: John Payne Collier papers formerly in the possession of Mrs. Cornelia Koop.

Madden ms Diary	The diary of Frederic Madden, 12 May 1859 to 13 September 1860, Bodleian MSS. Eng. Hist. C. 172 ff. 140–402 (1859) and C. 173 ff. 1–295 (1860).
Madden Papers	Miscellaneous manuscripts, letters and clippings formerly belonging to Frederic Madden, Bodleian MS. Eng. Misc. C. 96.
Morley, *HCR-BW*	Edith J. Morley, *Henry Crabb Robinson on Books and Their Writers*, 3 vols., London, 1938.
N & E I	*Notes and Emendations to the Text of Shakespeare's Plays, from Early Manuscript Corrections in a Copy of the Folio, 1632, in the Possession of J. Payne Collier,* by John Payne Collier. First edition, London: Whittaker & Co., 1853.
N & E II	*Notes and Emendations to the Text of Shakespeare's Plays...,* The second edition, revised and enlarged, by John Payne Collier, London: Whittaker & Co., 1853.
N & Q	*Notes and Queries* (London).
OMD	*An Old Man's Diary, Forty Years Ago;... 1832–1833. In Four Parts.* By John Payne Collier. London: 1871, 1872.
Reasons	*Reasons for a New Edition of Shakespeare's Works,* by John Payne Collier. London: Whittaker & Co., 1841.
Reply	*Mr. J. Payne Collier's Reply to Mr. N.E.S.A. Hamilton's 'Inquiry' into the Imputed Shakespeare Forgeries,* by John Payne Collier. London: Bell and Daldy, 1860.
Sadler	Thomas Sadler, ed. *Diary, Reminiscences, and Correspondence of Henry Crabb Robinson,* 3 vols., London: Macmillan & Co., 1869.
Shakespeare (1844)	*The Works of William Shakespeare. The Text Formed From an Entirely New Collation of the Old Editions: With the Various Readings, Notes, a Life of the Poet, and a History of the English Stage.* John Payne Collier, ed. 8 vols. London: Whittaker & Co., 1842–44.
Shakespeare (1853)	*The Plays of Shakespeare: The Text Regulated by the Old Copies, and by the Recently Discovered Folio of 1632, Containing Early Manuscript Emendations.* John Payne Collier, ed. London: Whittaker & Co., 1853.
Shakespeare (1858)	*Shakespeare's Comedies, Histories, Tragedies, and Poems.* The second edition. John Payne Collier, ed. 6 vols. London: Whittaker & Co., 1858.

Shakespeare (1878)   *The Plays and Poems of William Shakespeare, With the Purest Text, and the Briefest Notes.* John Payne Collier, ed. 8 vols. London: Privately Printed, 1875–78.

DISGRACE (pp. 1–9)

1. JPC ms Journal, 14 May 1882.
2. *Athenaeum,* 27 March 1852.
3. William Charles Macready to Mrs. Frederick Pollock, 15 March 1853, printed in *Macreadys [sic] Reminiscences and Selections from His Diaries and Letters,* ed. Sir Frederick Pollock (London, 1876), p. 693.
4. Madden ms Diary, 26 May 1859.
5. See George F. Warner's biography of JPC in the *Dictionary of National Biography* (1887) and Clement M. Ingleby, *Complete View* (1861).

I FORTUNE (pp. 10–42)

1. Frederic Shoberl, *A Biographical Dictionary of the Living Authors of Great Britain and Ireland* (London, 1816), p. 71.
2. Quoted in JPC ms Journal, 25 April 1881.
3. JPC ms Auto. p. 1.
4. Ibid., p. 7.
5. Ibid., p. 30.
6. HCR ms Remin., 1797. Cf. Sadler, i, 40.
7. *The Life of Abraham Newland, Esq. Late Principal Cashier at the Bank of England with Some Account of the Great Establishment....* London: B. Crosby & Co. 1808.
8. Jane Collier to HCR, 23 Sept. 1803, HCR Corresp.
9. JDC to HCR, 29 March 1803, HCR Corresp.
10. HCR to JDC, 27 Dec. 1803, HCR Corresp.
11. JPC ms Journal, 19 Nov. 1873.
12. See JPC's and HCR's anonymous obituary notices of Amyot in the *Gentleman's Magazine,* Jan. 1851 n.s. XXXV 3–9.
13. *N & Q,* 8 July 1854, ser. 1, X, 21.
14. See HCR ms Diary, 21 Nov. 1811; cf. HCR to Thomas Robinson, 16 Dec. 1811, HCR Corresp., printed in *Coleridge's Shakespearean Criticism,* ed. Thomas Raysor (London, 1930), ii, 228.
15. JPC ms Early Diary, 10 Oct. [1811].
16. HCR ms Diary, 10 Nov. 1812.
17. William Jerdan, *Men I Have Known* (London, 1866), p. 333.
18. HCR ms Diary, 1 Feb. 1815.
19. JPC ms Journal, 16 Jan. 1878.
20. HCR ms Diary, 24 Aug. 1816.
21. JPC's collection is now in the British Library (836 F26).
22. Shoberl was an editor of talent and shrewdness. Four years before he had founded the *New Monthly Magazine* with Henry Colburn. He had been the editor of the *Repository* since its inception in 1809 and had often been of assistance to the Colliers.
23. JPC ms Auto., p. 141.

24. London: W. Wimpkin and G. Hayden, 1819.

25. HCR ms Remin., 1818.

26. JPC ms Auto., pp. 115–16.

27. P. 12.

28. First Series, Vol. 40, col. 985–6.

29. HCR ms Diary, 16 June 1819.

30. Constable Letter Book, National Library of Scotland MS. 791, p. 83.

31. Ibid., MS. 790, p. 653.

32. A year later, James Boswell published correspondence which revealed that this source had been suggested to Malone. JPC, of course, could not have known of this correspondence when he wrote, and the discovery is therefore his own.

33. P. vii. Subsequent page references to *The Poetical Decameron* are inserted parenthetically in the text.

34. Charles Lamb to JPC, [16 May 1821], JPC Corresp.

35. HCR ms Diary, 21 July 1824.

36. JPC ms Auto., p. 127.

37. Copy in Koop.

38. Charles Lamb to JDC, [6 Jan.] 1823, *The Letters of Charles Lamb . . .*, ed. E. V. Lucas, 3 vols. (London, 1935), ii, 361.

39. HCR ms Diary, 6 Feb. 1823.

40. 'The Periodical Press', *Edinburgh Review*, May 1823, pp. 359, 358.

41. The article was published anonymously; JPC's authorship can be ascertained in the correspondence from Archibald Constable to JPC, 23 March 1822 and 4 Oct. 1822. Constable Letter Book, National Library of Scotland MS. 791, pp. 521, 625.

42. Loc. cit., pp. 360–61, 363.

43. HCR ms Diary, 28 June 1826.

44. *Fridolin, or the Road to the Iron-Foundery [sic]; A Ballad, by F. Schiller.* London: Septimus Prowett, 1824.

45. *The Fight with the Dragon; A Romance, by F. Schiller.* London: Septimus Prowett, 1825.

46. The plan called for one volume to be issued each month over a period of one year, but individual volumes sold slowly and the publication took not one but three years (1825–27). Vols. 2–9 appeared in 1825; Vol. 10 in 1826; Vols. 1, 11 and 12 in 1827.

47. Gifford died in 1826, before the Dodsley edition was completed; his edition of Ford was published in 1827; his edition of Shirley was finished some time later by Alexander Dyce.

48. The plays were: Thomas Lodge, *The Wounds of Civil War*; Robert Greene, *Friar Bacon and Friar Bungay*; Thomas Nashe, *Summer's Last Will and Testament*; and George Peele, *Edward I*. The interludes were: *The Worlde and the Chylde* (1522) and *Apius and Virginia* (1575).

49. JPC to William Carew Hazlitt, 27 Feb. 1873, BL Add. MS. 38900 f. 380.

50. Anthony Munday, *The Downfall of Robert Earl of Huntington* (1828); Anthony Munday and Henry Chettle, *The Death of Robert, Earl of Huntington* (1828); Thomas Hughes, *The Misfortunes of Arthur* (1828); Nathaniel Field, *A Woman is a Weathercock, A Comedy* (1829); and *Amends for Ladies, A Comedy* (1829); all published

by Septimus Prowett, London. Four years later these impressions were collected in *Five Old Plays, Forming a Supplement to the Collections of Dodsley and Others* (London: William Pickering, 1833). The change of publisher suggests that Pickering acquired the unsold copies of Prowett's editions and bound them together for easy remaindering.

51. *Punch and Judy, with Illustrations Designed and Engraved by George Cruikshank. Accompanied by Dialogue of the Puppet-show, an Account of its Origin, and of Puppet-plays in England.* London: S. Prowett, 1828. The immediate success of the first edition of the book led to a second in the same year. Collier supplemented the text for this edition, and he therefore may have received additional payment.

52. HCR ms Diary, 28 Oct. 1827.

53. HCR ms Diary, 2 Jan. 1828.

54. JPC ms Journal, 6 Oct. 1878.

55. HCR ms Diary, 26 Nov. 1828.

56. JPC to Jane Collier, 26 Nov. 1828, Koop.

57. HCR ms Diary, 12 Feb. 1829.

58. See Francis Bickley, *The Cavendish Family* (London: Constable, 1911), pp. 261–74, *passim.*

59. Sixth Duke of Devonshire ms Diary, 11 and 12 Oct. 1830, Chatsworth MS., Second Series, 767.454.

60. OMD, ii, 22.

II *THE HISTORY OF ENGLISH DRAMATIC POETRY* (pp. 43–68)

1. *And Annals of the Stage to the Restoration.* 3 vols. London: John Murray, 1831, hereafter *HEDP.*

2. British Library, Harleian MS. 5253.

3. 'Mask of Blackness', BL MS. Royal 17B XXXI; 'Mask of Queens', BL MS. Royal 18A XLV.

4. These papers remained in Malone's possession until his death when they passed to James Boswell the Younger who produced the posthumous 'variorum' edition of 1821 based on Malone's notes. Boswell reprinted all of Malone's excerpts from the papers and added many new ones of his own.

5. JPC to [Thomas Amyot], 23 Jan. 1830, JPC Corresp.

6. *HEDP,* iii, 88.

7. Robinson's edition of *The Works of Christopher Marlowe* (London, 1826) included *Tamburlaine* 'in deference to the received opinion' but he himself did not think the play was written by Marlowe. Three other items from Henslowe's diary printed for the first time in *HEDP* were to become infamous. These were references to Nashe's play *The Isle of Dogs* and the restraint which was placed on the company as a result of its performance. George F. Warner, *A Catalogue of Manuscripts and Muniments, of the College of God's Gift at Dulwich,* 1881, p. 160.

8. JPC to HCR, 18 Jan. 1831, HCR Corresp.

9. Jane Collier to HCR, 23 Sept. 1831, HCR Corresp.

10. Vol. 46 (1831–32), pp. 477–518.

11. 1 Aug. 1831, Vol. 33, p. 354.

12. Oct. 1831, Vol. 150, p. 329.

13. He had previously served in that post in the reign of George IV from May 1827 to Feb. 1828.

14. Dyce to JPC, 30 April 1830, JPC Corresp.

15. Ibid., 14 May 1830, JPC Corresp.

16. Ibid.

17. Alexander Dyce to JPC, 21 Aug. 1831, JPC Corresp.

18. 'The Poetical and Literary Character of the Late John Philip Kemble', *New Monthly Magazine*, 1 Feb. 1832, Vol. 34, p. 174.

19. There has been confusion concerning the date on which JPC and Amyot purchased the manuscripts and the price they paid. (See Dougald MacMillan's Prefatory Note to the *Catalogue of the Larpent Plays in the Huntington Library*, San Marino, California, 1939.) An entry in *OMD* implies that JPC bought the mss. on 11 March 1832, but that date, like many in *OMD*, is conjectural, and contemporary evidence suggests that the collection was purchased earlier, probably in late 1830: (1) In February, 1832, JPC wrote that he purchased the collection 'two years ago', i.e., in 1830 ('The Poetical and Literary Character of the Late John Philip Kemble,' *New Monthly Magazine*, Vol. 34, p. 174); (2) JPC would not have had the money to buy the mss. before his payment for *HEDP*; (3) a letter from Amyot to JPC on 15 April 1831 (BL Add. MS. 33963 f. 37) suggests that the collection had been in their possession for only a few months. The *OMD* entry gives the purchase price as £400, but in 1853 Collier said the price was £180. (See his letter to the Trustees of the British Museum, 23 Sept. 1853, cited in *Catalogue of Additional Manuscripts, Plays Submitted to the Lord Chamberlain 1824–1851*, London, 1964, p. vi.) The lower price is the more likely.

20. *The Maid of Honour*, Larpent No. 687 and *The False Concord*, Larpent No. 236. Amyot to JPC, 13 Sept. 1831, BL Add. MS. 33963 f. 39.

21. 'The Poetical and Literary Character of the Late John Philip Kemble' (cited above) and 'New Facts Regarding Garrick and His Writings', *New Monthly Magazine*, June 1832, Vol. 34, pp. 568–75.

22. For a more complete examination of this report, see Dewey Ganzel, 'Patent Wrongs and Patent Theatres: Drama and the Law in the Early Nineteenth Century', *PMLA*, LXXVI (1961), 384–96.

23. Great Britain, Parliamentary Reports (1831–32) VII, qu. 279 (hereafter referred to as *Report*).

24. Jane Collier to HCR, 8 Nov. 1832, HCR Corresp.

25. *A Catalogue of Heber's Collection of Early English Poetry, the Drama, Ancient Ballads and Broadsides... with Notices* by J. Payne Collier, Esq. London: Edward Lumley, 1834.

26. JPC to William Pickering, 19 Dec. 1833, JPC Corresp.

27. Barron Field to HCR, 17 Oct. 1835, HCR Corresp.

28. HCR ms Diary, 31 Oct. 1833.

29. HCR to Dorothy Wordsworth, 24 Oct. 1833, HCR Corresp.

30. HCR ms Diary, 20 Oct. 1833.

31. *In a Letter to Thomas Amyot, Esq.* London: Thomas Rodd, 1835.

32. *In a Letter to the Rev. A. Dyce.* London: Thomas Rodd, 1836.

33. See William Clarke, *Repertorium Bibliographicum; or, Some Account of the Most Celebrated British Libraries* (London, 1819), p. 359n., and Henry Todd, *The History of the College of Bonhommes, at Ashridge, in the County of Buckingham*. London, 1823.

34. *New Facts*, p. 6.

35. Ibid.

36. Ibid., p. 5.

37. *New Particulars*, p. 66.

38. Ibid., p. 47.

39. See JPC to William Pickering, 19 Dec. 1833, JPC Corresp., in which he describes the book (in very general terms) as a possible subject for the *Gentleman's Magazine*.

40. *The Sacrifice of Abraham... from MS. Trin. Coll. Dublin; The Harrowing of Hell... from MS. Harl. 2253; The Adoration of the Shepherds... from the Towneley MS; The Marriage of the Virgin... from MS. Cotton Vesp: D VIII; The Advent of Antichrist... from the Duke of Devonshire's MS.* A note in JPC's copy of the collected edition, now in the British Library, states that only 25 copies were printed, some of which were later made up into an omnibus volume with a new title page, *Five Miracle Plays or Scriptural Dramas*. Privately Printed, London, 1836.

41. HCR ms Diary, 10 March 1836.

42. Ibid., 24 March 1836.

43. *OMD*, IV, iii.

44. JPC to HCR, 2 Oct. 1837, HCR Corresp.

45. *A Catalogue, Bibliographical and Critical, of Early English Literature; Forming a portion of the Library at Bridgewater House*, by J. Payne Collier, London, 1837.

46. W. M. Thackeray to JPC, 22 April [1836], JPC Corresp.

47. JPC to Leigh Hunt, 3 Sept. [1838?], BL Add. MS. 38524 f. 151.

48. Charles Dickens to JPC, n.d. [1836?], JPC Corresp.

49. JPC to HCR, 22 Nov. 1837, HCR Corresp.

50. HCR ms Diary, 27 Jan. 1841.

51. JPC to Devonshire, 3 March 1840, Chatsworth MS. 17.0.

52. Ibid., 26 March 1840.

53. In a Letter to the Rev. Joseph Hunter. London: Thomas Rodd, 1839.

III *THE WORKS OF WILLIAM SHAKESPEARE* (pp. 69–107)

1. From the Prospectus, bound in with the first tract to be issued, *Historie of the Arrival of Edward IV. in England, etc.* ed. John Bruce (London, 1838), pp. 1–2.

2. *Kynge Johan. A Play in Two Parts*. By John Bale. Edited by J. Payne Collier. London: The Camden Society, 1838.

3. *The Egerton Papers. A Collection of Public and Private Documents, Chiefly Illustrative of the Times of Elizabeth and James I.* Edited by J. Payne Collier. London: The Camden Society, 1840.

4. *Old Ballads, from Early Printed Copies of the Utmost Rarity.* Now for the first time collected. Edited by J. Payne Collier. London: The Percy Society, 1840.

5. *The Pain and Sorrow of Evil Marriage, Three Humorous Tracts in Verse on the Subject of Marriage.* From an Unique Copy Printed by Wynkyn de Worde. London: The Percy Society, 1840; *The King and A Poor Northern Man: Or, Too Good To Be True.* From the Edition of 1600. Attributed to Martin Parker. London: The Percy Society, 1841.

6. *Prospectus*, issued with the first volume of the *Shakespeare Society Publications* (London, 1841), p. 1.

7. JPC to Alexander Dyce, 30 Nov. 1840, Dyce.

8. Queen Elizabeth's matrimonial plans, the affairs of the Mint, and the treatment

of Roman Catholic fugitives. His selections concerned subjects as general as the government of Ireland and as particular as the sumptuary laws governing the apparel of members of the Court. However, of all the many documents Collier published in this collection, the most famous – and ultimately notorious – was to be the account of household expenses made by Sir Arthur Mainwaring, Egerton's auditor, which recorded the costs of entertainment during Elizabeth's sojourn as guest at Egerton's estate, Harefield House, in August 1602. Among these, Collier republished the item concerning the payment to 'Burbidge's players for Othello' which he had earlier printed in *New Particulars*. See *Egerton Papers*, p. 343.

9. Many years later JPC was to describe this process: 'When I proposed to edit "Henslowe's Diary," Amyot produced from his own shelves a MS. copy of considerable portions of it, made by or for Chalmers. Upon these Cunningham (my next door neighbour) worked, Amyot and he filling up the missing pages, which were not a few, and often referring to me, where the old manager's hand was particularly illegible.' See *Athenaeum*, 21 Feb. 1874.

10. *Athenaeum*, 27 Feb. 1841, p. 166.

11. *Athenaeum*, 28 Aug. 1841, pp. 663–65.

12. *A Collection of Original Documents Illustrative of the Life and Times of Edward Alleyn, and of the Early English Stage and Drama.* London: The Shakespeare Society, 1843.

13. See Francis B. Bickley, *A Catalogue of the Manuscripts and Muniments of Alleyn's College of God's Gift at Dulwich.* Second Series (London, 1903), p. 95. JPC was allowed to keep the manuscript for two months providing he did not 'let it go out of his hands'. When it was entrusted to him, the book was carefully examined and its 'mutilations' noted; the manuscript was scrutinized when it was returned and there is no evidence that it had been altered while in Collier's possession.

14. *A dialogue bytwene the commune secretary and Jalowsy, touchynge the unstableness of Harlottes,* [attributed to Edward Gosynkyll]. London, 1844. *The Prayse of Nothing* (1585) by E[dward] D[yer]. London, 1844. A note of JPC's copy, now in the Folger Library, indicates that the cost of printing, paper and binding of 25 copies of this tract came to £12.10 and that each purchaser therefore paid 10 s. for his copy. Copies of *A Dialogue* cost 4 s.

15. A presentation copy to Sir Frederic Madden, now in the Folger Library, has the following note: 'These tracts were first castrated and afterwards entirely suppressed by the Percy Society. This is one of twenty uncastrated copies. J. Payne Collier. Dec. 1841.'

16. *The Pityfull Historie of two louing Italians, Gaulfrido and Barnardo le vayne ... translated ... by John Drout ... 1570.* London, [1844?], *A Libell of Spanish Lies Found at the Sack of Cales ... and the Death of Sir Francis Drake* by Capt. Henry Savile (1596). London, 1844, *The Merry Puck, or Robin Goodfellow* (n.d.), London, [1841?].

17. Now first collected, and accurately reprinted from the original edition. With introductory notices, by J. Payne Collier. 2 vols. London: Thomas Rodd, 1843; reissued in 1850 and again in 1875 with a few additions by William Carew Hazlitt.

18. HCR ms Diary, 6 June 1841.

19. JPC to Devonshire, 14 Feb. 1841, Chatsworth MS. 17.3.

20. *The Works of William Shakespeare*, ed. Nicholas Rowe (6 vols. London, 1709), I, Sig A2–A2^v.

21. This number does not include either *The Troublesome Reign of John, King of England* (1591) or *The Taming of A Shrew* (1594) since there was no agreement that these were versions of Shakespeare's plays.

22. Samuel Johnson, *Prefaces, Biographical and Critical to the Works of the English Poets* (10 vols. London, 1779–81), VI, 13.

23. *The Works of Shakespeare* (7 vols. London, 1733), I, xxxvii–xxxviii.

24. Ibid., I, xxxv.

25. *Shakespeare Restored: or, A Specimen of the Many Errors, as Well Committed, as Unamended, by Mr. Pope in his Late Editions of this Poet* (London, 1726), p. v.

26. Ibid., p. 138.

27. *Mr. William Shakespeare his Comedies, Histories, and Tragedies* (10 vols. London, 1767), I, 21.

28. Ibid., I, 17.

29. See Isaac D'Israeli, *Curiosities of Literature* (Ninth Edition, 6 vols., London, 1834), vi, 76–77.

30. Preface, *New Illustrations of... Shakespeare* (London, 1845), i, iv–v.

31. *Reasons for a New Edition of Shakespeare's Works Containing Notices of the Defects of Former Impressions* (London: Whittaker & Co., 1841), pp. 30–31.

32. Ibid., p. 30.

33. Ibid., pp. 7–8.

34. See, for example, JPC's note to *The Comedy of Errors*, iv, ii in *Shakespeare* (1844), ii, 153, in which he describes a substantive variation between the Bridgewater First Folio and the Devonshire First Folio.

35. The stop-press corrections in *Lucrece* (1594) led JPC to the conclusion that Shakespeare himself may have been directly involved in its publication.

36. See 'On the Earliest Quarto Editions of the Plays of Shakespeare', *Shakespeare Society Papers,* iii, 58–83.

37. See, for example, *The Grimaldi Shakspere* (London: J. Russell Smith, 1853), p. 6.

38. Introduction to *Hamlet, Shakespeare* (1844), vii, 192; JPC's contemporaries tended to denigrate the Second Quarto of *Hamlet*. Alexander Dyce, for example, virtually ignored it in favour of the First Folio text.

39. *Athenaeum,* 9 July 1842, p. 603.

40. JPC to HCR, 6 June 1842, HCR Corresp.

41. Dickens to JPC, n.d. [1841], JPC Corresp.

42. HCR ms Diary, 5 March 1844.

43. He tried to start yet another – the Aelfric Society – which failed because would-be members were unwilling to match JPC's enthusiasm with editorial labour of their own.

44. Later published as *New Illustrations of... Shakespeare.* 2 vols. London, 1845.

45. *New Illustrations,* i, 333n; i, 118.

46. Ibid., i, 73.

47. HCR ms Diary, 16 April 1844.

48. May 1844, p. 499.

49. Ellesmere to JPC, n.d. [1844], Koop.

50. *New Illustrations,* ii, 10–11.

51. JPC to Alexander Dyce, 13 Oct. 1841, Dyce.

52. Dyce to JPC, [20 March 1844], letter inserted into JPC's copy of *Shakespeare* (1844) now in the British Library (C.134 f.1).

53. *Remarks,* p. iii. Subsequent page references are inserted parenthetically in the text.

54. 24 May 1844, p. 475.

55. For example, H. N. Hudson, the American editor, notes that the arbitrary emendations of the early 'variorum' editions were no longer acceptable. He specifically mentions JPC, among others, as having 'pretty effectually put a stop to the old mode of Shakespearean editing; nor is there much reason to apprehend that anyone will at present venture upon a revival of it.' *The Works of Shakespeare*, ed. H. N. Hudson (11 vols., Boston, 1856), i, ix.

56. JPC to Forster, 3 May 1846, JPC Corresp.

57. Dyce to JPC, n.d., JPC Corresp.

58. *and Thomas, Earl of Surrey; temp 1481–1490*. London: William Nichol, 1844. The book derived from a manuscript Collier had discovered fifteen years before in the collection of the Society of Antiquaries. Since he was not a member of the Roxburghe Club, Collier was paid for his labour which included preparing the transcript and writing a long introduction.

59. See notes 14 and 16 above.

60. *A Book of Roxburghe Ballads*. London: Longman, Brown, Green, and Longmans, 1847. The Roxburghe Collection was made by John Ker, Third Duke of Roxburghe (1740-1804) and became famous at the Roxburghe sale of 1812 where it was purchased by Benjamin Heywood Bright. Bright kept his treasure to himself for two decades, but at his death in 1845 the collection was once again put on the block and purchased by the British Museum.

61. See Society of Antiquaries, *Proceedings*, II (1852), 248.

62. For details of these and other activities of JPC, see Society of Antiquaries, *Proceedings*, 1848–1856; in particular, see I (1849), 258–60, 306–7; II (1850), 53; II (1851), 137–9; III (1854), 72. See also the papers in *Archaeologia* for 1848–1856.

63. *The Marriage of Wit and Wisdom. An Ancient Interlude from a manuscript recently discovered* (1846); *Five Court Masques*, ed. from the original mss. of Ben Jonson, John Marston, etc. by John Payne Collier (Part of a volume with *Inigo Jones, A Life* by Peter Cunningham and *Remarks on Some of his* [Jones'] *Sketches* by J. R. Planché (1848)).

64. *Memoirs of the Principal Actors in the Plays of Shakespeare*. London: The Shakespeare Society, 1846.

65. See the comments of Edward Arber in the introduction to his complete edition, *A Transcript of the Registers of the Company of Stationers of London 1554-1640* (5 vols. London, 1875–1894), i, 1.

66. *Extracts from the Registers of the Stationers' Company of Works Entered For Publication Between the Years 1557 and 1570,* with notes and illustration by J. Payne Collier, Vol. I (London: The Shakespeare Society, 1848), p. vii.

67. *Extracts*, i, vii–viii. These were only part of the eighty-three ballads in his ms., a complete list of which appeared in JPC's preface to the second volume, *Extracts . . . Between the Years 1570 and 1587*. Vol. II (London: 1849), pp. viii–ix. Presumably JPC did not reprint the other forty-nine ballads because they had no counterpart titles in the Registers. Professor Giles Dawson has argued that these ballads were forgeries of Collier's composition. See Appendix.

68. In twenty-eight instalments. See *N & Q*, ser. 2, xii, 3 (6 July 1861) to ser. 3, iii, 147 (21 Feb. 1863). The transcript of the unpublished portion (i.e., 1595 to 1607) is in the Folger Library.

69. HCR ms Diary, 25 Oct. 1844 and 1 Feb. 1846. See also, HCR to Thomas Robinson, 5 Feb. 1842, HCR Corresp.

70. Ellesmere to JPC, 23 June 1848, JPC Corresp.

71. Four years earlier he had suggested JPC apply for a position in the Museum: 'The prospect might be distant, but your pretensions are such as would at least justify the attempt, and I for one would have no compunction in stating your claims as a labourer in the vineyard.' Ellesmere to JPC, 29 June 1843, JPC Corresp.

IV THE CATALOGUE CONTROVERSY (pp. 108–132)

1. Quoted in Arundell Esdaile, *The British Museum Library, A Short History and Survey* (London, 1946), p. 37.

2. *Report of the Commissioners Appointed to Inquire into the Constitution and Government of the British Museum; Together with Minutes of Evidence and Index*, Great Britain, *Parliamentary Reports* (1850), XXIV. Hereafter BM *Report.*

3. H. F. Cary in *The Times*, 17 July 1837; quoted in Esdaile, op. cit., p. 99.

4. Esdaile, op. cit., p. 58.

5. Great Britain, *Parliamentary Papers*, House of Commons (1847), XXIV, 253; cited in Edward Miller, *Prince of Librarians, The Life of Antonio Panizzi of the British Museum* (Athens, Ohio, 1967), p. 172.

6. *Report from the Select Committee on the British Museum; Together with the Minutes of Evidence, Appendix and Index*, Great Britain, *Parliamentary Reports* (1836), X, 407.

7. Madden ms Diary, Bodleian MS. Eng. Hist. C.160 f. 348.

8. On 13 July 1848. See BM *Report*, p. 234.

9. BM *Report*, Appendix No. 12, pp. 378–95.

10. 20 April 1840, p. 416.

11. BM *Report*, qu. 9705.

12. Ibid., qu. 4293.

13. *A Letter to the Earl of Ellesmere, on the Subject of a New Alphabetical Catalogue of the Printed Books in the British Museum.* Printed for private circulation only, 24 Jan. 1849, p. 18. This was followed by *A Supplementary Letter to the Earl of Ellesmere; Occasioned by Certain Interrogatories from the Keeper of the Printed Books in the British Museum.* Printed for Private circulation only, 16 April 1849. The reference to the speed of composition of *A Letter* appears in *A Supplementary Letter*, p. 6.

14. Robert Inglis to JPC, 22 Feb. 1849, JPC Corresp.

15. *A Supplementary Letter*, p. 8.

16. Ellesmere to JPC, 6 Jan. 1849, JPC Corresp.

17. Collier's style was contentious. Even the all-suffering Robinson could be angered by his manner. Collier, he wrote in his diary, was 'addicted to contradiction'. It was the more painful because unconscious. 'Tho' he does not mean it, yet he seems whenever anything is said to consider that the business of conversation is to contradict, and his manner implies thus much: "What a fool you must be if you think so!" There is a confident and vehement manner which offends.' Printed in Morley, *HCR-BW*, p. 713.

18. BM *Report*, qu. 6214.

19. Ibid., qu. 5063.

20. Ibid., qu. 5122.

21. Ibid., qu. 5123.

22. Ibid., qu. 5084.

23. Ibid., qu. 5095.

24. Ibid., qu. 5055.

25. Ibid., qu. 5052.

26. Ibid., qu. 5053.

27. After Collier completed his testimony at the end of February 1849, Panizzi published a letter to Ellesmere which imperiously demanded Collier's answers to twelve questions, none of them concerned with Collier's testimony or with the rules governing catalogue entries. Collier's reply (*A Supplementary Letter*) appeared in early April. The Commission resumed testimony in May with Panizzi's return as witness.

28. BM *Report,* qu. 9788.

29. Ibid., qu. 10016.

30. A comparison of the current British Library Catalogue with JPC's suggestions reveals that his entries are closer to present day practice than those of Jones.

31. JPC to Lord Langdale, 20 Sept. 1849, BL Add. MS. 36716. f.47.

32. BM *Report,* p. 20.

33. *Athenaeum,* 11 May 1840, p. 499.

34. Ellesmere to JPC, n.d., JPC Corresp.

35. *A Bibliographical and Critical Account of the Rarest Books in the English Language...* [ed.] J. Payne Collier (2 vols. London: Oseph Lilly, 1865), i, viii–ix. Hereafter, *Bibl. Crit. Acc.*

36. JPC to HCR, 4 March 1840, HCR Corresp.

V THE PERKINS FOLIO (pp. 133–175)

1. HCR ms Diary, 19 Aug. 1848.

2. JPC to J. W. Ebsworth, 17 July 1877, JPC Corresp.

3. HCR to Thomas Robinson, 11 Oct. 1850, HCR Corresp.

4. 'Report of the Auditors', *Tenth Annual Report of the Shakespeare Society Council* (1851), p. 12.

5. *King Edward the Fourth, Parts I and II* (1842); *The Fair Maid of the Exchange* and *Fortune by Land and Sea* (1846).

6. *The Dramatic Works of Thomas Heywood* (London: The Shakespeare Society, 1850), I, vii, viii. This edition was left incomplete and hence no plays were collected into later 'volumes'.

7. Cf. John Pearson's edition of 1874. This is typical of the treatment JPC was to receive to the end of his life and after as the result of the controversy over the Perkins Folio. Although JPC was still alive when Pearson's edition appeared, he made no public complaint of this treatment.

8. *Athenaeum,* 31 Jan. 1852, pp. 142–4.

9. 6 March 1852, p. 279.

10. 'Horatio', *Athenaeum,* 14 Feb. 1852, p. 199.

11. 'J. F. K.', *Athenaeum,* 27 March 1852, p. 363.

12. *Athenaeum,* 7 Feb. 1852, p. 171.

13. Ibid.

14. See his Preface to *Shakespeare* (1858), i, xi.

15. *Athenaeum,* 27 March 1852, p. 355.

16. 'Introduction', *N & E I*, pp. vii–viii. There was no change in this account in *N & E II*.

17. *A Few Remarks on the Emendation, 'Who smothers Her with Painting' in the Play of 'Cymbeline'* (London, 1852), pp. 6–9.

18. 22 May 1852, pp. 484–5.

19. *From Early Manuscript Corrections in a Copy of the Folio, 1632, in Possession of J. Payne Collier, Esq. F.S.A. Forming A Supplemental Volume to the Works of Shakespeare by the Same Editor, in Eight Volumes, Octavo.* London: Whittaker & Co., 1853. The 'Shakespeare Society Edition' was created by cutting the title page [A1] from Whittaker's regular trade edition and inserting two new leaves [*1, A1]: a title page that substituted the Shakespeare Society imprint for 'Whittaker & Co.' with the suppositious earlier date, '1852', and a second leaf on which was printed the usual list of members of the Council of the Shakespeare Society. (See copy in Free Library, Philadelphia.) *N & E II* is identical to *N & E I* except as hereafter described.

20. Whittaker & Co. to JPC, 24 Oct. 1856; same to the same, 22 Oct. 1856, JPC Corresp. Four years later, Whittaker complained that it still had 800 copies on hand.

21. *Fraser's Magazine*, March 1853, p. 254.

22. E.g. concerning the substitution of *sirkles* for *sickles* in *Measure for Measure* (II, ii): 'Not with fond sickles of the tested gold,/Or stones, whose rates are either rich or poor...' In the *Athenaeum* of 31 January 1852, JPC had written: 'In the two earliest folios the word in the first line is printed sickles: and "sheckels" has been of late years universally substituted as a conjectural emendation. The word of the poet was, however, I have no doubt, *circles*, – in reference to the shape which "tested gold" bore as money – and my folio of 1632 reads ... *sirkles*: thus putting an end to all difficulty arising out of the question ...' (p. 143). By the time JPC came to publish *N & E I* almost a year later, he had changed his mind: 'It is spelt *sickles* in the old copies, but the true word may be *circles*; and the manuscript-corrector of the folio, 1632, has altered "sickles" to "*sirkles*", paying no other attention to the spelling of the word. Nevertheless "shekels" may be right, and it is used, with exactly the same spelling, by Lodge in his "Catharos", 1591, sign C, where we read, "Here in Athens the father hath sufred his sonne to bee hanged for forty sickles, and hee worth four hundred talents".' *N & E I*, pp. 45–6.

23. E.g., concerning a correction in *Measure for Measure*: 'On further consideration we may be disposed to prefer an adherence to the old text....' *N & E I*, p. 504.

24. E.g., in *N & E I* he wrote that a line needed an insertion which is 'supplied in the margin of the folio, 1632, and which proves that the lines ought to run thus' (p. 295); a month or two later he changed this to 'which *seems* to prove' (*N & E II*, p. 528; emphasis added).

25. E.g., at the end of the list of emendations for *Much Ado About Nothing*, he wrote, 'It should be stated ... that most of these emendations were suggested by Hanmer, and have since been adopted by Malone and some other modern editors' (*N & E I*, p. 505).

26. E.g., in reference to an emendation in *Titus Andronicus*: in the first edition he wrote it might have been 'obtained from recitation, or even from some independent authority, written or printed. Some of the changes in this play could scarcely have been made without some such aid' (*N & E I*, p. 367). When he revised the passage for the second edition, he omitted the last sentence; he had come to believe they were all conjectures. Cf. *N & E II*, p. 372.

27. Printed in JPC's *Reply,* p. 12; reprinted in Ingleby's *Complete View,* pp. 53–4.

28. JPC to Parry, 26 April 1853, from a facsimile in *Complete View,* Plate III; whereabouts of the original unknown.

29. *N & E II,* P. iv.

30. 4 June 1853, p. 677.

31. *N & E II,* pp. v–vi.

32. March 1853, p. 245.

33. 8 Jan. 1853, p. 41.

34. 7 May 1853, p. 358.

35. 'More Improvement in the Text of Shakespeare', March 1853, p. 373.

36. *The Plays of Shakespeare: The Text Regulated by the Old Copies and by the Recently Discovered Folio of 1632, Containing Early Manuscript Emendations.* Edited by J. Payne Collier. London: Whittaker & Co., 1853.

37. Ibid.

38. 2 April 1853, p. 417.

39. *Forming an Introductory Notice to the Stratford Shakspere,* edited by Charles Knight. London, 1853.

40. *Shakespeare Vindicated,* pp. xiii–xiv.

41. Ibid., p. xi.

42. E.g., in *Shakespeare Vindicated* (1853), Singer belittled the Perkins emendation 'I understand you not: my griefs are *dull*' for 'double' (*Love's Labour's Lost,* V, ii). In 1856, he accepted it; see *The Dramatic Works of William Shakespeare,* edited by Samuel Weller Singer (10 vols. London: Bell and Daldy, 1856), II, 312.

43. 28 May 1853, p. 644.

44. *A Few Notes on Shakespeare with Occasional Remarks on the Emendations of the Manuscript-Corrector in Mr. Collier's Copy of the Folio 1632.* London, 1853.

45. Ibid., p. v.

46. Ibid., p. 69.

47. *A Few Words in Reply to the Animadversions of the Reverend Mr. Dyce on Mr. Hunter's 'Disquisition on the Tempest' (1839) and his 'New Illustrations of the Life, Studies and Writing of Shakespeare' (1845); Contained in his Work Entitled A Few Notes on Shakespeare....* London: John Russell Smith, 1853.

48. 28 May 1853, p. 644.

49. JPC to Devonshire, 31 Jan. 1845, Chatsworth MS. 17.3.

50. 2 July 1853, pp. 797–99.

51. *Observations,* p. 3.

52. *New Facts,* p. 4.

53. Ibid., p. 8.

54. (London, 1853), p. 20.

55. *Grimaldi Shakspere,* pp. 4–5.

56. Ibid., p. 16. Rumour attributed the *Grimaldi Shakspere* to Halliwell in collaboration with Frederick Fairholt, the illustrator of his *Folio Shakespeare* who was also a clever caricaturist, but although the attribution persisted, it was almost certainly wrong. (See *Athenaeum,* 20 Aug. 1853, p. 987.) It is unlikely that Halliwell would have had a hand in a parody that ridiculed not only Collier but all other

commentators – himself included. If he helped to write it, he displayed a hitherto unsuspected talent for self-parody.

57. *Grimaldi Shakspere*, p. 4.

58. Abroad, *Notes and Emendations* was pirated in both Germany and the United States. Friedrich Leo translated the book, including all of Collier's notes, into German and published it with a running commentary of his own. (*Beiträge und Verbesserungen zu Shakespeare's Dramen nach handschriftlichen Aenderungen in einem von J. P. Collier Esq. aufgefundenen Exemplare der Folio-Ausgabe von 1632*. Berlin, 1853.) Leo approved of most of the corrections, but with varying degrees of qualification. Another German scholar, Nicholaus Delius, who was then editing his own text of Shakespeare, sharply denounced *Notes and Emendations*, declaring that Collier's 'Old Corrector' was merely a blundering interpolator whose emendations were either foolish or perverse. (*J. Payne Collier's alte handschriftliche Emendationen zum Shakspere gewürdigt* von Dr. N. Delius. Bonn, 1853.) The controversy quickly crossed the Atlantic. Within a few weeks of its English publication, Collier's book was pirated in New York by Redfield and American critics reacted quickly. English journals circulated widely among American scholars, and the long, highly laudatory review in *Fraser's Magazine*, was reprinted in its entirety in the *Eclectic Magazine* in New York. Americans were sharply divided over Collier's discovery: Richard Grant White's review in *Putnam's Magazine* (October, November, 1853) was a cogent, predominantly negative, appraisal. Some of the emendations, White declared, were 'invaluable. But these, though numerous in themselves, are few indeed in comparison with those which are an outrage upon the great Dramatist' (October, 1853, p. 378). He extended this opinion in *Shakespeare's Scholar* (New York: Appleton and Co., 1854), one of the best considerations of the corrections to appear on either side of the Atlantic. However, German and American opinions of the Perkins Folio had little influence on English readers. The *Athenaeum* expressed the predominant English opinion when it declared that any question concerning Shakespeare 'must be decided, if at all, in England' (8 Oct. 1853, p. 1187).

59. See William Jaggard, *Shakespeare Bibliography* (Stratford, 1911), p. 607.

60. *An Alarum Against Userers; and . . . Forbonius and Prisceria.* London: The Shakespeare Society, 1853.

61. In particular, a new supplement to *Dodsley's Old Plays* in four volumes which would have contained plays printed by the Society in the previous ten years. See *Report of the Council of the Shakespeare Society . . . Tenth Annual Meeting . . . 26 April 1851* (London, 1851).

62. Forty-eight works bound in 19 volumes.

63. JPC to W. Wardlaw Reid, 18 March 1859, JPC Corresp.

64. HCR ms Diary, 14 Aug. 1856; printed in Morley, *HCR-BW*, p. 761.

65. *Poems by Michael Drayton from the Earliest and Rarest Editions or from Unique Copies.* Ed. J. Payne Collier. London: The Roxburghe Club. 1856.

66. He had, for example, superintended the publication of a lithographic facsimile of Devonshire's unique copy of the First Quarto of *Hamlet* (the first Shakespeare quarto reproduced *in toto* by facsimile), and he was about to do the same for Devonshire's copy of the Second Quarto of *Hamlet.*

67. See JPC's letter to *The Times*, 7 July 1859.

68. 'Dedication', *Seven Lectures on Shakespeare and Milton By the Late S. T. Coleridge/* [and]/*A List of All the MS. Emendations in Mr. Collier's Folio, 1632.* By J. Payne Collier, Esq. London: Chapman and Hall, 1856.

69. 'Introduction' to *Shakespeare* (1858), p. xi.

70. See JPC's letter to the Trustees of the British Museum cited above in note 19, p. 422 above.

71. See Ellesmere to JPC, 25 Jan. 1854, JPC Corresp.

72. Ellesmere to JPC, 21 June 1859, JPC Corresp.

VI THE ELLESMERE THEFTS AND *LITERARY COOKERY* (pp. 176–213)

1. See Madden ms Diary, 16 Jan. 1855, in which he refers to three lists, prepared for the Museum Trustees, itemizing the Ellesmere mss. he bought from Hillier, i.e., BL Add. Ch. 8481 (purchased 16 July 1853); BL Add. MS. 19631 (purchased 6 Sept. 1853) containing 27 mss.; BL Add. MS. 19632 (purchased 6 Sept. 1853) containing 22 mss.; and BL Add. MS. 19641 (purchased 19 Sept. 1853) containing 116 mss. Madden's papers in the Bodleian Library contain his own copies of these lists.

2. At a later date, probably after the whole affair was public, Madden inserted '(& which was purchased)': after 'offered me for sale'. See Madden ms Diary, 17 March 1854, Bodleian.

3. Ibid.

4. JPC to Madden, 8 Oct. 1854, Madden Papers.

5. Madden to JPC, [?] Oct. 1854, copy in the Madden Papers.

6. Hillier to Madden, [10 Oct. 1854], Madden Papers.

7. Madden ms Diary, [20 Oct. 1854].

8. Madden to JPC, 23 Oct. 1854, copy in Madden Papers.

9. JCP to Madden, 13 Nov. 1854, Madden Papers.

10. JPC to Madden, 15 Nov. 1854, Madden Papers.

11. Madden ms Diary, 28 Nov. 1854.

12. Ibid., 13 Dec. 1854.

13. Ibid., 16 Jan. 1855.

14. *The Critic*, 24 March 1860.

15. Madden ms Diary, 24 Feb. 1856.

16. Ibid., 1 March 1856.

17. 26 March 1853, p. 388.

18. *Shakespeare* (1844), ii, 37.

19. *Athenaeum*, 31 Jan. 1852, p. 143.

20. *N & Q*, 3 April 1852, ser. 1, v, 325.

21. *N & Q*, 1 May 1852, ser. 1, v, 410–11.

22. *N & Q*, 22 May 1852, ser. 1, v, 485.

23. With elaborate courtesy, Singer took issue with some of Collier's readings in *Shakespeare* (1844) and with the Perkins emendations which Collier had published. With equally elaborate courtesy ('Mr. Singer again does me injustice, I am sure most unintentionally...'), JPC corrected Singer's errors of fact. See *N & Q*, 25 Sept. 1852, ser. 1, vi, 297.

24. *N & E I*, pp. 45–6.

25. Brae to Ingleby, 6 Feb. 1854, Folger MS. W. b. 105/16.

26. *N & Q,* 19 Feb. 1853, ser. 1, vii, 178.

27. Ibid., 26 Feb. 1853, ser. 1, vii, 216.

28. Ibid., 23 April 1853, ser. 1, vii, 403.

29. Brae to Ingleby, 9 May 1853, Folger MS. W. b. 105/2.

30. *N & Q,* 21 May 1853, ser. 1, vii, 497.

31. Brae to Ingleby, 24 May 1853, Folger MS. W. b. 105/3.

32. Brae to Ingleby, 1 July 1853, Folger MS. W. b. 105/4.

33. *N & Q,* 18 June 1853, ser. 1, vii, 592.

34. Brae to Thoms, 20 Aug. 1853, Huntington MS. 27855.

35. Brae to Thoms, 30 Aug. 1853, Huntington MS. 27857.

36. Thoms to Brae, 2 Sept. 1854, Huntington MS. 27862.

37. Brae to Thoms, 4 Sept. 1853, Huntington MS. 27858.

38. Brae to Ingleby, 1 Dec. 1853, Folger MS. W. b. 105/12; and same to same, 28 Dec. 1853, Folger MS. W. b. 105/13.

39. Brae to Ingleby, ? Feb. 1854, Folger MS. W. b. 105/16.

40. Brae to Ingleby, ? May 1855, Folger MS. W. b. 105/22.

41. *N & Q,* 1, 8, 22 July 1854 and 12 Aug. 1854, ser. 1, x, 1–2, 21–23, 57–58, 117–119.

42. *N & Q,* 1 July 1854, ser. 1, x, 1.

43. Ibid., p. 2.

44. See HCR ms Diary, 21 Nov. 1811. HCR had originally intended to take notes of the lectures, 'but J. Collier having made an elaborate report, which I can hereafter refer to, I shall reserve a connected account of the whole series of lectures for a future page.' In addition, JPC's notes correspond closely with HCR's independent account which remained unpublished until long after *Seven Lectures.*

45. *Literary Cookery,* by 'A Detective' [Andrew Edmund Brae] (London: John Russell Smith, 1855), pp. 6–7.

46. Ibid., pp. 13–14.

47. Smith to Thoms, 20 November 1855, Huntington MS. 27861.

48. He later declared that he first saw the pamphlet on 21 November (the day after Smith wrote Thoms informing him the book had been withdrawn) and read it then.

49. 'Seeing the pencil date 1812 on the said Prospectus, and the same date also on my Diary, I assumed that was the true date. I had no purpose, desire, motive or intention to misrepresent the date when the said Lectures were delivered, and I verily believed when I sent the said communications for publication in "Notes and Queries" that 1812 was the year in which the said Prospectus was issued, and the said Lectures were delivered.' JPC ms draft copy dated 8 Jan. 1856, Koop.

50. Unidentified newspaper account dated 17 Jan. 1856 inserted in Ingleby's copy of *N & E I* now in the Folger Library.

51. *Shakespeare's Legal Acquirements Considered.* London, 1859.

52. See the note by Joseph Parkes in his copy of *Literary Cookery* now in the Folger Library.

53. 'Preface'. *Seven Lectures,* p. lxi.

54. Ibid., p. lxix (emphasis added).

55. Ibid., p. lxxiv.

56. Whittaker & Co. to JPC, 22 October 1856, JPC Corresp.

57. HCR to JPC, 26 Nov. 1856, HCR Corresp. printed in Morley, *HCR-BW*, p. 839; HCR ms Diary, 28 Nov. 1856; printed in Morley, *HCR-BW*, p. 763.

58. *Shakespeare* (1858), i, xxxviii.

59. *The Works of William Shakespeare.* The Text Revised by the Rev. Alexander Dyce. 6 vols. London: Moxon, 1857.

60. *Trevelyan Papers Prior to A.D. 1558* (1857); *Trevelyan Papers, Part II. A.D. 1446-1643* (1863). Part III was edited by Sir Charles Trevelyan and Sir Walter Trevelyan and collected with the first two volumes in 1872. See also John Pycroft Collier to JPC, 13 March 1857, Koop.

61. JPC to Bell and Daldy, 20 April 1857, JPC Corresp.

62. JPC to HCR, 26 Dec. 1857, HCR Corresp.

63. JPC to Bell and Daldy, 26 April 1857, JPC Corresp.

64. *Shakespeare* (1858), i, ix-x.

65. Ibid., i, xiv.

66. JPC reported to Bell and Daldy that his edition of Shakespeare was 'done and worked off', 24 March 1858, JPC Corresp.

67. E.g., *Shakespeare* (1858), i, 277, 328; v, 195.

68. 16 Jan. 1858, p. 73.

69. 1 May 1858, p. 559.

70. JPC to W. Wardlaw Reid, 22 Dec. 1858, JPC Corresp.

71. Peter Cunningham to JPC, 9 April 1858, Folger MS. y.d. 6/42.

72. *Strictures*, p. v.

73. Ibid., p. 54 and *passim.*

VII THE MUSEUM INQUISITION (pp. 214-267)

1. Ingleby published a biography of Shakespeare in 1877 and an edition of *Cymbeline* in 1886.

2. JPC to Ingleby, 14 May 1853, Ingleby Corresp., Folger MS. C.a.27.

3. *N & Q,* 9 July 1853, ser. 1, viii, 35.

4. Reported in the *Birmingham Journal,* 29 Nov. 1856, p. 2.

5. Brae to Ingleby, 11 Nov. 1856, Ingleby Corresp., Folger MS. W. b. 105/28.

6. Devonshire to JPC, 1 March 1858, JPC Corresp.

7. Brae to Ingleby, 29 March 1859, Ingleby Corresp., Folger W. b. 105/30.

8. Devonshire to Ingleby, 28 April 1859, Ingleby Corresp., Folger MS. C. a. 14; see also Ingleby's account in *The Critic,* 31 March 1860. It is significant that Ingleby changed his story when he came to write *Complete View.* In that version he said the Duke had refused him access. See *Complete View,* p. 95.

9. *The Critic,* 31 March 1860.

10. It may be significant that when Ingleby repeated the account of this event in *Complete View* some months after his *Critic* article, he pushed the time of his request back several months into the Fall of 1858. The effect of this alteration was to make Madden's period of 'delay' much longer. Ingleby changed his earlier account in other prejudicial ways; almost certainly his first version of the events is the correct one.

11. Madden ms Diary, 12 May 1859.

12. E.g., *Athenaeum*, 27 March 1852, p. 363.

13. Madden ms Diary, 26 May 1859.

14. This letter (Huntington MS 27860), dated 30 May 1859, refers to another letter which Madden claims to have sent 'two or three days ago' which he 'fears...miscarried'. There is no other evidence that the earlier note was written.

15. Madden ms Diary, 27 May 1859.

16. Ibid., 28 May 1859.

17. Ibid., 1 June 1859.

18. Ibid., 30 May 1859. This entry was probably composed at a later date; his letter to Thoms of 30 May 1859 indicates that Thoms had not yet replied to Madden's invitation.

19. Ibid., 1 June 1859.

20. Ibid., 2 June 1859.

21. Ibid., 16 June 1859.

22. See Madden's note in Bodleian MS. Eng. Misc. C.96. f. 97: 'p. 15. margin cut down – and two letters cut off.'

23. *An Inquiry*, p. ix; *Complete View*, p. 99; *The Critic*, 24 March 1860.

24. Madden ms. Diary, 17 June 1859.

25. Ibid., 19 June 1859.

26. See Perkins Folio, p. 181, col. 2, Huntington Library. For further comment on this emendation, see note 35, notes p. 441 below.

27. Madden ms Diary, 19 June 1859.

28. Ibid., 20 June 1859.

29. Ibid.

30. From a copy in Madden Papers.

31. Staunton to Madden, 29 June 1859, Madden Papers.

32. Quoted in *The Times*, 5 July 1859.

33. 'I take these Wisemen, that crow so at these set kind of fooles, *to be* no better than the fooles Zanies' (*Twelfth Night*, I, v) noted in *Seven Lectures*, p. 191; a marginal '1' (otherwise unidentified) in the same scene, not noted by Collier; and 'Oh, most pernicious *and perfidious* woman!' (*Hamlet*, I, v) noted in *Seven Lectures*, p. 259.

34. 'Look too't, I charge you; *so now* come your way[s]' (*Hamlet*, I, iii) noted in *Seven Lectures*, p. 258; and two stage directions: 'Sc. 4' in ink in the text corresponding to 'IV' in pencil in the margin (*Hamlet*, I, iv) and 'aside' in the text with the word in pencil corresponding to it in the margin (*King John*, place not identified).

35. *The Times*, 2 July 1859.

36. HCR ms Diary, 2 July 1859.

37. Ibid., 3 July 1859.

38. *The Times*, 7 July 1859.

39. HCR ms Diary, 7 July 1859.

40. Staunton to Madden, 7 July 1859, Madden Papers.

41. *N & E I*, pp. viii–ix; *N & E II*, pp. 516, 517.

42. Madden ms Diary, 7 July 1859.

43. Ibid., 5 July 1859.

44. *Athenaeum*, 9 July 1859, pp. 50–51.

45. Madden ms Diary, 13 July 1859.

46. *N & E II,* p. iv.

47. *The Times,* 16 July 1859.

48. Ibid.

49. *Bulletin,* 16 July 1859, from a clipping in Madden Papers.

50. Ingleby to Madden, 18 July 1859, Madden Papers.

51. Madden to Ingleby, 20 July 1859, Madden Papers.

52. *The Times,* 19 July 1859.

53. JPC to W. Wardlaw Reid, 20 July 1859, JPC Corresp.

54. Madden ms Diary, 19 July 1859.

55. *The Times,* 1 Aug. 1859.

56. Madden ms Diary, 28 July 1859.

57. HCR ms Diary, 28 July 1859; printed in Morley, *HCR-BW,* p. 788.

58. Madden ms Diary, 21 July 1859.

59. 'A New "Affaire du Collier"', *Saturday Review,* 23 July 1859, p. 98.

60. Madden ms Diary, 23 July 1859.

61. Ibid., 25 July 1859. It may be significant that there is no rough copy of this letter in Madden's papers; this is an unusual exception to Madden's normal practice.

62. *Athenaeum,* 6 August 1859, p. 177.

63. 'A. A. P.', *Athenaeum,* 13 Aug. 1859, p. 211.

64. Madden to Devonshire, 1 Aug. 1859, draft in Madden Papers.

65. *Athenaeum,* 10 September 1859, p. 341; 1 October 1859, p. 432.

66. Brae to Ingleby, 22 July 1859 (Folger MS W. b.105/33) and 4 March 1860 (Folger MS. W. b. 105/36).

67. *Shakespeare Fabrications,* p. [iii].

68. *Athenaeum,* 20 Aug. 1859, p. 233.

69. *Shakespeare Fabrications,* p. viii.

70. Brae to Ingleby, 11 Nov. 1856, Folger MS. W. b. 105/28.

71. *Shakespeare* (1844), iii, 309.

72. *N & E I,* p. 169.

73. *Shakespeare Fabrications,* p. 34.

74. *N & Q,* 3 July 1852, ser. 1, vi, 6.

75. *Shakespeare Fabrications,* p. 35.

76. *N & E I,* p. 68; *N & E II,* p. 68.

77. *Seven Lectures,* p. 168.

78. *Shakespeare Fabrications,* p. 47. JPC indicated in *N & E I* that *Johnson* had suggested 'importable' – hence JPC was likely to take this reading as the first; the correction of 'i' to 'u' was in text, not on the margin and hence easily overlooked; in any case, JPC's use of the Perkins emendations was selective in 1858.

79. *Shakespeare Vindicated,* p. 146; quoted in *Shakespeare Fabrications,* p. xx.

80. *Shakespeare* (1844), ii, 431.

81. Brae to Ingleby, 22 July 1859, Folger MS. W. b. 105/33.

82. JPC to W. Wardlaw Reid, 19 Sept. 1859, JPC Corresp.

83. HCR ms Diary, 27 Sept. 1859; printed in Morley, *HCR-BW,* p. 791.

84. *Athenaeum,* 20 Aug. 1850, pp. 233–35.

85. Madden ms Diary, 16 Sept. 1859.

86. Undated clipping in Madden Papers.

87. Madden ms Diary, 12 Sept. 1859.

88. Ibid., 18 Oct. 1859.

89. Ibid., 15 Oct. 1859.

90. Ibid., 11 Oct. 1859.

91. Ibid., 25 Oct. 1859.

92. *Fraser's Magazine,* Jan. 1860, pp. 53–64.

93. Madden ms Diary, 17 Nov. 1859.

94. *Athenaeum,* 1 Oct. 1859, p. 432.

95. HCR ms Diary, 8 Nov. 1859; printed in Morley, *HCR-BW,* p. 792.

96. Madden ms Diary, 5 Dec. 1859.

97. Ibid., 7 Dec. 1859.

98. Ibid., 1 Jan. 1860.

VIII *AN INQUIRY* AND *A REPLY* (pp. 268–323)

1. *An Inquiry,* p. ix.

2. Ibid., pp. 20–21.

3. Ibid., p. 1; cf. *The Times,* 2 July 1859.

4. E.g., in *Hamlet,* IV, vii, the Second Folio text reads 'An Iemme of all *our* Nation'. The Perkins emendation changed 'our' to 'that'; Collier read it as 'the' and so printed it in *Seven Lectures,* p. 261 (see *An Inquiry,* pp. 50–51). There were many others in *Seven Lectures* which Hamilton either did not see or did not record: e.g., in *Henry VI, Part II,* IV, ix, the Second Folio text reads 'I pray thee, Buckingham, go and meet him.' Perkins inserted 'thou' between 'go' and 'and'; Collier read it as an insert of 'then' between 'Buckingham' and 'go'. See *Seven Lectures,* p. 223.

5. *An Inquiry,* p. 85.

6. Ibid., pp. 71–2.

7. Ibid., p. 94.

8. *Memoirs of Edward Alleyn,* p. 13.

9. *An Inquiry,* p. 95.

10. *HEDP,* i, 207.

11. *An Inquiry,* p. 103.

12. *The Critic,* 11 Feb. 1860, p. 166.

13. *The Literary Gazette,* 18 Feb. 1860, p. 197.

14. HCR ms Diary, 15 Feb. 1860; printed in Morley, *HCR-BW,* p. 794.

15. Wellesley to JPC, 13 August 1859, printed in *Athenaeum,* 18 February 1860, p. 231 (repeated pp. 237–8).

16. Ibid., p. 238.

17. Ibid.

18. Ibid., p. 239.

19. Ibid.

20. Ibid., p. 233.

21. Ibid., p. 239.

22. HCR ms Diary, 19 Feb. 1860; printed in Morley, *HCR-BW*, p. 795.

23. Madden ms Diary, 23 Feb. 1860.

24. Ibid., 27 Feb. 1860.

25. Madden to Wellesley, 20 Feb. 1860, copy in Madden Papers.

26. Wellesley to Madden, 20 Feb. 1860, Madden Papers.

27. Wellesley to Madden, 23 Feb. 1860, Madden Papers.

28. Madden ms Diary, 20 Feb. 1860.

29. *The Spectator*, 25 Feb. 1860, p. 187.

30. *The Critic*, 25 Feb. 1860, p. 229.

31. *Athenaeum*, 25 Feb. 1860, p. 269.

32. *Athenaeum*, 18 Feb. 1860, p. 238.

33. *The Critic*, 3 March 1860, p. 265.

34. *Athenaeum*, 10 March 1860, p. 341.

35. *Mr. J. Payne Collier's Reply to Mr. N. E. S. A. Hamilton's 'Inquiry' into the Imputed Shakespeare Forgeries* (London: Bell and Daldy, 1860).

36. *Reply*, pp. 19, 23–24.

37. Ibid., pp. 24–25.

38. Ibid., pp. 28–30.

39. Ibid., p. 63.

40. Ibid., p. 32.

41. Ibid., p. 46.

42. Edmond Malone, *An Inquiry into the Authenticity of Certain Miscellaneous Papers and Legal Instruments . . . .* London, 1796.

43. *Reply*, p. 55.

44. Ibid., p. 71–2.

45. Madden ms Diary, 17 March 1860.

46. Hamilton to Madden, 16 March 1860, Madden Papers.

47. Staunton to Madden, 21 March 1860, Madden Papers.

48. Lowe to Madden, 17 March 1860, Madden Papers.

49. *The Times*, 19 March 1860; reprinted in *Athenaeum*, 24 March 1860, pp. 411–12.

50. Fair copy in Madden Papers.

51. Lowe to Madden, 21 March 1860, Madden Papers.

52. *The Critic*, 24 March 1860, p. 359.

53. Ibid., 31 March 1860, p. 389.

54. Ibid., 7 April 1860, p. 421.

55. Madden ms Diary, 6, 17 June 1859.

56. Ibid., 19 June 1859.

57. JPC to Sotheby, 1 April 1860, JPC Corresp.

58. *N & Q*, 24 March 1860, ser. 2, ix, 214.

59. Madden to Thoms, 26 March 1860, copy in Madden Papers.

60. See Madden ms Diary, 20 April 1860.

61. Review of *Reply*, *Literary Gazette*, 24 March 1860, p. 371.

62. Madden to Staunton, 24 March 1860, copy in Madden Papers.

63. Staunton to Madden, 26 March 1860, Madden Papers.

64. Madden ms Diary, 28 June 1860.

65. Ibid., 18 March 1860.

66. Ibid., 21 March 1860.

67. Ibid., 23 March 1860.

68. Ibid., 28 March 1860.

69. Ibid., 20 April 1860.

70. Ingleby to Madden, 7 April 1860, Madden Papers.

71. Madden ms Diary, 21 Feb. 1860.

72. Ibid., 29 March 1860.

73. Madden to Wright, 18 March 1860, copy in Madden Papers.

74. Madden ms Diary, 23 Feb. 1860.

75. Ibid., 19 March 1860.

76. *Athenaeum*, 31 Jan. 1852, p. 142.

77. *N & E I*, p. vi.

78. Madden ms Diary, 29 March 1860.

79. Madden's letters to Hamilton make it clear, however, that Hamilton, not Madden, found the catalogue entry. See Madden to Hamilton, 4 April 1860, Madden Papers.

80. Madden ms Diary, 5 April 1860.

81. 'The Alleged Shakespeare Forgeries', *Edinburgh Review*, April 1860, p. 454.

82. Ibid., p. 477.

83. Ibid., p. 455.

84. Ibid., p. 458.

85. Ibid., pp. 460–61.

86. Ibid., p. 475.

87. Ibid., p. 486.

88. Madden to Staunton, 8 April 1860, copy in Madden Papers.

89. Madden ms Diary, 20 April 1860.

90. Madden to Ingleby, 11 April 1860, copy in Madden Papers.

91 *Birmingham Post*, 14 April 1860; quoted in *Athenaeum,* 21 April 1860, p. 547.

92. From a clipping in Madden Papers.

93. Ingleby to Madden, 18 April 1860, Madden Papers.

94. Madden to Ingleby, 19 April 1860, copy in Madden Papers.

95. Ingleby to Madden, 20 April 1860, Madden Papers.

96. Madden ms Diary, 21 April 1860.

97. Madden to Ingleby, 23 April 1860, copy in Madden Papers.

98. *The Critic,* 28 April 1860, p. 515.

99. Ingleby to Madden, 27 April 1860, Madden Papers.

100. *Saturday Review,* 21 April 1860.

101. Madden ms Diary, 27 April 1860.

102. *Saturday Review,* 21 April 1860.

103. HCR ms Diary, 22 April 1860; printed in Morley, *HCR-BW*, p. 797.

104. *The Plays of Shakespeare*. London: George Routledge & Co., 1858. Despite the date on the title page, this work had been appearing in monthly parts since November 1857. The final instalment was dated April 1860.

105. *Athenaeum*, 13 Oct. 1860, p. 475.

106. *Athenaeum*, 11 Aug. 1860, p. 197.

107. JPC to Robert Balmanno, 18 May 1860, JPC Corresp.

108. *Athenaeum*, 13 Oct. 1860, p. 475.

109. JPC to Sotheby, 15 Nov. 1860, JPC Corresp.

110. JPC to Robert Balmanno, 28 Dec. 1860, JPC Corresp.

111. JPC to Sotheby, 15 Nov. 1860, JPC Corresp.

IX *A COMPLETE VIEW* (pp. 324–355)

1. *Complete View*, p. 2.

2. The writer was Holcombe Ingleby. See *DNB*, XXVIII, 436.

3. *Complete View*, p. 316.

4. See Brae to Ingleby, 24 May 1853, Folger MS. W.b. 105/3.

5. *Complete View, p. 2.*

6. Ingleby to Madden, 4 April 1860, Madden Papers.

7. Madden to Ingleby, 6 April 1860, copy in Madden Papers.

8. *Complete View*, p. 317.

9. Ingleby to Madden, 6 June 1860, Madden Papers.

10. Madden ms Diary, 27 June 1860.

11. *Complete View*, pp. 51–2.

12. Ibid., p. 119.

13. Ibid., pp. 67–8.

14. Ibid., p. 66.

15. Ibid., p. 65.

16. Ibid., p. 95.

17. See John Forster to JPC, 10 Nov. 1855; same to same, 12 Feb. 1856, JPC Corresp. See also 'An Edinburgh Reviewer' [Herman Merivale] in *Athenaeum*, 25 Aug. 1860, p. 257.

18. See p. 299 above.

19. *Complete View*, p. 99.

20. Madden ms Diary, 28 May 1860.

21. *Complete View*, pp. 99–100.

22. Ibid., p. 114.

23. Ibid., p. 320–21.

24. Ibid., p. 303.

25. *An Inquiry*, p. 84n.

26. *Complete View*, p. 311.

27. Ingleby ought to have learned caution from Hamilton. In *An Inquiry*, Hamilton had demanded that Collier 'produce' a document concerning Shakespeare's *Richard II* that JPC had cited in 1856. Hamilton implied that the manuscript did

not exist, but within weeks of the charge, the document was found in the State Paper Office (where it belonged) and proved to be genuine.

28. *Complete View*, pp. 325–6.

29. *Athenaeum*, 22 Dec. 1860, p. 874.

30. *London Review*, 2 March 1861, p. 237.

31. *The Critic*, 7 Jan. 1862, p. 8.

32. *London Review*, 2 March 1861, p. 237.

33. E.g., *A Winter's Tale*, Perkins Folio, p. 290; *Antony and Cleopatra*, Perkins Folio, p. 372; *Romeo and Juliet*, Perkins Folio, p. 82; *The Tempest*, Perkins Folio, p. 15; and *Henry IV, Part 2*, Perkins Folio, p. 93.

34. Madden's note, made while he was examining the Perkins Folio for the first time in the British Museum (Bodleian MS. Eng. Misc. C. 96, f. 92, mentioned on p. 225 above), reveals that he himself discovered at least one of these cuts. Since this clearly disproves his later contention that all the notes were made after binding, either he failed to connect this important detail with his conjecture about the date of the rebinding (and thus overlooked presumptive evidence of Collier's innocence) or he later suppressed his discovery knowing it might have the effect of exonerating Collier.

35. A glaring example of this is the stage direction in *Richard III*, I, iv, in which, after attacking Clarence in the Tower, the two murderers, in the emendation of the Old Corrector, are made to 'exit with the dead bodie', a substitution for the standard stage direction 'exit with the body'. This emendation was one of those which Ingleby said had a pencil note lying directly beneath the ink. The 'correction' is ludicrous: Clarence is not dead when his assassins exit with his body since he is being dragged off to be drowned in the abominable butt of malmsey. The 'corrector' who wrote this note demonstrated an ignorance which would destroy any claim to authority and discredit other corrections made in the same hand. Collier knew this as well as anyone, and it is significant that this emendation never appeared in any of his published lists. In all subsequent editions of the play (i.e., 1853, 1858, 1878) he ignored the Old Corrector and printed 'exit with the body'.

36. *Shakespeare's Titus Andronicus. The First Quarto 1594.* Reproduced in facsimile from the unique copy in the Folger Shakespeare Library with an introduction by Joseph Quincy Adams. New York: Charles Scribner's Sons. 1936.

37. I.e., 'mistership' (Q2, Q3, F1, F2) is 'mistriship' in Q1 (H3 recto line 3) and is so changed in Perkins; 'haile *to* Romes' (Q2, Q3, F1, F2) is 'Haile Romes' in Q1 (K4 recto line 13) and 'to' is deleted in Perkins; 'friend' (Q2, Q3, F1, F2) is 'friends' in Q1 and so changed in Perkins; 'Why now Lord?' (F1, F2) is 'Why how now Lords' in Q1 (C3 verso line 11) and Q2 and 'how' is inserted in Perkins; 'bosome' (F1, F2) is 'bosomes' in Q1 (G1 verso line 11) and Q2 and is so changed in Perkins.

38. On K4 recto, line 31, 'storie' was partly defaced thus making its meaning unintelligible to the typesetter of Q2 and he therefore substituted the word 'matter' along with several lines of doggerel. The Old Corrector made no change here, apparently rejecting 'storie' in order to keep the inserted verse.

39. My examination of the Perkins Folio confirms the fact that the twelve examples cited by Hamilton and Ingleby are the only ones in the book.

40. Hamilton to Madden, 19 March 1860, Madden Papers. 'I think that Maskelyne washed away ink either from *three* or perhaps *four* words or parts of words.'

41. I.e., 'parting' in *Love's Labour's Lost*, Perkins Folio, p. 143 (Ingleby facsimile No. 6, opposite p. 112 in *Complete View*); 'mistaking' in *Coriolanus*, Perkins Folio, p. 56 (Ingleby facsimile No. 18, in the same place).

42. See Madden to Ingleby, 20 July 1859, Folger MS, C.a. 14. f.3.

43. *Shakespeare Vindicated*, p. xii.

44. *N & E I*, p. 96.

45. *The Dramatic Works of William Shakespeare, the Text Carefully Revised with Notes* by Samuel Weller Singer (10 vols., London, 1856), II, 313.

46. The facsimiles printed in Hamilton are reproduced because the Perkins Folio no longer clearly shows many of the pencil marks. The lithographic facsimiles of F. N. Netherclift were not thought to be particularly accurate even when they were printed and were condemned for showing more than was apparent to some observers of the folio. Certainly the lithographer was under heavy pressure to 'find' coherent pencil evidence to support the Museum's contention. Even so, it would be unjust to assume the marks he reproduced were never there. It is, simply, impossible to recapture what may have been in the book in 1859 except through the evidence he gave.

X MEN'S EYES (pp. 357–395)

1. Palgrave to Ingleby, 14 Jan. 1861, Folger MS. C.a.14.

2. JPC to William Carew Hazlitt, 19 May 1866, BL Add. MS. 38899, f. (see below n. 5 etc) 38.

3. Two of Hazlitt's most valuable projects, *Dodsley's Old Plays* (1874–76) and *Shakespeare's Library* (1875), were to be new editions of works that Collier had published many years before, but in both Hazlitt was almost slavish in retaining all of Collier's introductions and editorial notes.

4. W. Carew Hazlitt, *Four Generations of a Literary Family* (2 vols. London, 1897), II, 21.

5. JPC to Hazlitt, 16 Aug. 1866, BL Add. MS. 38899, f. 95.

6. JPC to Hazlitt, 23 Nov. 1866, BL Add. MS. 38899, f. 184.

7. JPC to Hazlitt, 28 Nov., 1866, BL Add. MS. 38899, f. 192.

8. JPC to Hazlitt, 7 March 1867, BL Add. MS. 38899, f.282.

9. Published in 28 instalments: 6 July 1861 (*N & Q*, ser. 2, xii, 3ff) to 21 February 1863 (*N & Q*, ser. 3, iii, 145ff). As with the earlier editions, this transcript included only titles of works of poetry, drama, tracts, travels and light literature. The volumes issued to the Shakespeare Society members covered the entries in Registers A and B from 1557 to 1587. The extracts published in *N & Q* completed the listings of Register B which ended in 1595. Collier's transcript continued into Register C, but he never published this portion, possibly because he knew it was soon to be superseded (in 1875) by Edward Arber's edition of all the Stationers' Registers.

10. *The Works of Edmund Spenser.* 5 vols. London: Bell and Daldy, 1862. For JPC's expectations see his letter to Francis Child, 2 May 1861, Harvard. Half a century later, his preeminent successor, Ernest de Selincourt, was to call it 'the most accurate that had as yet appeared' and despite some reservations, was to declare Collier's emendations 'both which he accepted himself and those merely offered as suggestions... brilliant and scholarly' (*The Poetical Works of Edmund Spenser* (3 vols. Oxford, 1910) I, 509).

11. The Aldine edition of 1866 and another by Bickers and Son, 1873.

12. *Athenaeum,* 18 Jan. 1862, p. 73.

13. *Westminster Review,* Jan. 1867, n.s., XXX, 149.

14. Child who adopted Collier's text when he republished his edition of Spenser's poems in 1864 gave JPC full credit; most editors, however, have belittled Collier for what they call his inconsistency and errors in transcription, faults they ignore in Todd as well as in Collier's numerous nineteenth-century successors.

15. HCR ms Diary, 22, 23 Oct. 1863; printed in Morley, *HCR-BW,* p. 808.

16. JPC ms Late Diary, 14 Dec. 1880.

17. *Athenaeum,* 26 April 1862, p. 563.

18. JPC to Hazlitt, 11 March 1867, BL Add. MS. 38899, f. 283.

19. JPC ms Journal, 22 March 1874.

20. Among them, all of his black-letter ballads which, added to those Ouvry already owned, made his one of the finest private ballad collections in England.

21. JPC to Hazlitt, 7 Oct. 1865, BL Add. MS. 38898, f. 301.

22. JPC to Henry Brown, 3 Nov. 1869, JPC Corresp.

23. *Bibl. Crit. Acct.,* i ix.

24. JPC to Hazlitt, 9 Nov. 1869, BL Add. MS. 38900, f. 429.

25. Collier claimed to have discovered the unique first edition (i.e., first edition, first issue) of *Tottel's Miscellany* at the Bodleian. (Heretofore, the second issue had been assumed to be the first.) He announced his find in the *Athenaeum* (17 Dec. 1864) and enlarged his claim in *N & Q:* 'What purported to be *the first edition* was reprinted by Dr. Sewell in 1717, and by Bishop Percy, Dr. Nott, and Sir Harris Nicolas afterwards; but I discovered a copy which showed that they were all in error, and that the second edition had been all along mistaken for the first, which differs in many essential particulars, and clears away many corruptions. Nobody had ever heard of this *first edition,* and I reprinted it in three parts. ...' (*N & Q,* ser. 3, x, 224.)

Hyder E. Rollins has disputed this claim in his definitive edition of *Tottel's Miscellany* (Harvard, 1929): 'Collier boasts of having "discovered" *A* [first issue of 1557 edition] whereas [Thomas] Park, [Henry] Bohn, and [William Carew] Hazlitt certainly knew that it preceded *B* [second issue of 1557]..., while [George] Nott had studied it carefully and in his edition ... reprinted its thirty unique poems' (II, 58).

The disagreement is not in itself important, but it suggests the grudging way in which Collier's work has been treated by his successors. In point of fact, there is no evidence that Park knew of the first issue and Rollins himself gives evidence (II, 41) proving that Park thought the second issue was the first; Hazlitt acknowledged that his source was Collier (see *Hand-Book to the Popular, Poetical and Dramatic Literature of Great Britain* (London, 1867, p. 585); Nott's edition of 1814, unpublished and extant only in four incomplete copies in the British Library, was derived not from the first but from the second issue of Surrey's poems, and Rollins's inference that Park's emendations in one of those copies prove he knew the first issue is not conclusive (there were other possible sources for the poems he reprinted) and is, in any case, beside the point. The only real claimant to prior discovery is Bohn who cited the first issue in his revision of Lowndes's *The Bibliographer's Manual of English Literature* (IX, 2547-8) published in October 1863 (see *Athenaeum,* 3 October 1863). This was fully a year before Collier's announcement, and this may therefore have been Collier's source. However, it is equally possible and more probable, that Bohn's source was Collier (rather than the other way around): although he cited the unique first issue copy at the

Bodleian, Bohn quoted the title page of the *second* issue, an error which suggests that he had not seen the book himself and was writing from hearsay, i.e., from his correspondent, Collier. Collier had seen the book and was the first to reprint its title page correctly (in *Bibl. Crit. Acct.*).

Collier's claim of 'discovery' is certainly contested by Bohn's reference, incorrect though it was, but there is no question that Collier was the first to reprint the whole of it correctly. In the light of all this – and the importance of the discovery – Rollins's comments *contra* Collier seem a bit niggardly.

26. Hyder Rollins strongly disagrees. In his edition of *The Paradise of Dainty Devices* (Harvard, 1927), he praises Brydges and condemns Collier. Although Brydges apparently never saw the original text and printed his version from a transcript made by George Steevens (dead ten years when Brydges's reprint appeared) into which he inserted, arbitrarily, new poems from later editions (producing a conglomerate text with no clear relation to any edition), Rollins praises his work: 'The defects of his [Brydges's] editing must be passed over in charity and gratitude. After all, to have produced a scholarly work that has lasted undisturbed for more than a century is an achievement so remarkable as to arouse one's envy' (p. xxxvi). For Collier, on the other hand, Rollins has only scorn, declaring, 'Collier's reprint is now hard to find, and when found, costs more than it is worth' (p. xxxvii).

Collier's reprint was based on a transcript of a second edition which he carefully collated with the original. Like all known copies, Collier's original was defective, lacking six leaves, and to fill this lack he copied twelve pages from the Bodleian copy of the first edition (which was even more defective) and inserted them between square brackets in his text. This produced an eclectic text (Collier announced it as such), but even with this fault, it was the most complete reprinting of either the first or second edition available until Rollins's own. Yet Rollins condemns Collier out of hand: 'It would be impossible to find elsewhere a reprint that, however innocently, gives a false notion of its original' (p. xxxvii). One need not be a Collier partisan to appreciate that Rollins has misstated Collier's purpose and incorrectly represented his edition. (He also misdated it and confused the particulars of its publication.) See JPC to Hazlitt, 19 Oct. 1867, BL MS. 38899, f. 471.

27. *Athenaeum,* 28 July 1866, p. 113.

28. New York: David G. Francis and Charles Scribner & Co., 1866.

29. Tradition has it that after several years an order was issued banning any new tract by Nashe or Harvey and ordering those already published to be destroyed. Whether that order was given is not known, but the pamphlet war stopped and the copies became scarce. Although many copies of the original publications were printed, very few survive; some exist in only one or two copies and none in more than six. Sir Egerton Brydges had published three of Harvey's tracts and one of Nashe's in *Archaica* (1815), and Greene's *A Quip for an Upstart Courtier* (which apparently started the quarrel) had appeared in the *Harleian Miscellany* (1745).

30. *Athenaeum,* 27 Feb. 1869, p. 311.

31. JPC to Hazlitt, 6 Feb. 1868, BL Add. MS. 38900, f. 51.

32 *Broadside Black-letter Ballads, Printed in the Sixteenth and Seventeenth Centuries,* 1868, pp. 130. *Twenty-Five Old Ballads and Songs: from manuscripts in the possession of J. Payne Collier, Octogen. A Birthday Gift,* 1869, pp. 56. *A Few Odds and Ends, for Cheerful Friends. A Christmas Gift,* 1870, pp. 52. The last was a collection of his own poetry.

33. JPC to William Hazlitt, the Younger, 29 Feb. 1868, BL Add. MS. 38900, f. 69.

34. JPC to Alexander Smith, 29 March 1868, JPC Corresp.

35. *The Players Scourge, or Actors Tragaedie,* p. 700.

36. Sign. aa3 recto.

37. *Dodsley's Old Plays* (1825), viii, 4.

38. *HEDP,* ii, 443.

39. *Memoirs of Edward Alleyn,* p. 40.

40. See Laing's introduction, p. ix.

41. Ibid., p. xxiii.

42. P. 1.

43. *Bibl. Crit. Acct.,* i, 465.

44. *Was Thomas Lodge an Actor? An Exposition Touching the Social Status of the Playwright in the Time of Queen Elizabeth* (London, 1867), p. 14; quoted in Frederick Furnivall's edition of *The Fraternitye of Vacabondes* (London: Early English Text Society, Extra Series, IX, 1869), p. xxv note.

45. See *Henslowe Papers,* ed. Walter W. Greg (London, 1907), p. 46.

46. *DNB,* Suppl. II, 65.

47. Introduction to *The Leopold Shakspere,* London: Cassell Petter & Galpin, 1877. The text of the edition was that of Delius.

48. See *Athenaeum,* 13 March 1869, p. 377; 10 April 1869, p. 508; and 17 April 1869, p. 541.

49. Pp. xxiv–xxvi.

50. See *Bibl. Crit. Acct.,* i, 327.

51 The *Fyrst Boke of the Introduction of Knowledge Made by Andrew Borde* . . . Ed. F. J. Furnivall (London: Early English Text Society, 1870), p. 71.

52. *The Dramatic Works of John Crowne.* 'Dramatists of the Restoration' Series. (4 vols. Edinburgh: William Paterson, 1873); JPC to James Maidment, 19 June 1873, JPC Corresp.

53. It was a curious relationship. They were to become very close friends and even collaborated in editing an early Elizabethan play (*The Female Rebellion, A Tragicomedy* . . . Privately printed from a MS. in the Hunterian Museum. Glasgow, 1872) but they met only once, nearly ten years after Smith's first letter and shortly before Collier's death. Collier preferred it that way, he said; 'on paper' he could like a correspondent, but once met, he might not want to see him again. He did not want to run the risk of disappointment, and for ten years they were 'faceless correspondents'. When they met at last, Collier thought Smith 'a nice unpretentious man', but they never saw one another again.

54. Written by Reginald Poel, Thomas Cromwell, Michael Throckmorton, and Thomas Starkey. Copied from the originals. London, 1871.

55. Furnivall's fervour is apparent in his Prospectus: 'I hope for a thousand members – many from our Colonies, the United States, and Germany; so that the Society may be a fresh bond of union between the three great Teutonic nations of the world. . . . I hope also that every Member of the Society will do his best to form Shakspere Reading-parties, to read the Plays chronologically, and discuss each after its reading, in every set of people, Club or Institute, that he belongs to: there are few better ways of spending three hours of a winter evening indoors, or a summer afternoon on the grass.' 'Founder's Prospectus of the New Shakspere Society', p. 10, printed in *Shakspere Allusion-Books,* Series IV, Part I, ed. C. M. Ingleby. London: The New Shakspere Society, 1874.

56. *The Academy,* 17 Jan. 1874, p. 66.

57. *The Academy*, 24 Jan. 1874, p. 95.

58. *Athenaeum*, 14 Feb. 1874, p. 226.

59. *Athenaeum*, 21 Feb. 1874, p. 257.

60. *Athenaeum*, 28 Feb. 1874, p. 293.

61. *Athenaeum*, 9 May 1874, p. 630.

62. One volume, numbered '14' (July 1874 to June 1876) is unaccountably missing from the series now part of the Folger Library MS. M.a. 29–40.

63. *Trilogy. Conversations Between Three Friends on the Emendations of Shakespeare's Text Contained in Mr. Collier's Corrected Folio, 1632.* In Three Parts. For Private Circulation Only. (London, 1874), ibid. See JPC ms Journal, 14 July 1873.

64. Ibid.

65. *Trilogy*, Part I, pp. v–vi.

66. JPC ms Autobiography, p. 147.

67. See the New Variorum *Coriolanus* (Philadelphia, 1928), p. 590. This edition printed a long section of *Trilogy* (pp. 589–95).

68. JPC ms Journal, 21 Nov. 1877.

69. Ibid., 10 June 1873.

70. Ibid., 1 Oct. 1873.

71. JPC to H. H. Furness, 17 Nov. 1876, the Houghton Library, Harvard.

72. JPC ms Journal, 6 May 1878.

73. JPC to Ebsworth, 14 March 1878, 16 March 1879, JPC Corresp.

74. JPC ms Journal, 19/20 March 1881.

75. *King Edward the Third: A Historical Play Attributed by Edward Capell to William Shakespeare, and Now Proved to be his Work* by J. Payne Collier. Reprinted for Private Circulation Only. London, 1874.

76. *Athenaeum*, 9 Jan. 1875, p. 52.

77. Furness, a friendly correspondent of Collier, avoided pronouncing judgement on Collier's 'forgeries' and credited the Perkins Folio in his notes as a valid source of *conjectural* emendation.

78. *The Academy*, 1 April 1876.

79. Ibid., p. 313.

80. JPC ms Journal, 10 March 1877.

81. Ibid., 13 Jan. 1878.

82. Ibid., 3 April 1877.

83. Ibid., 13 March 1879.

84. JPC to Ebsworth, 15 Feb. 1879, JPC Corresp.

85. Echoing Chapman's line from 'The Translator's Epilogue' to Homer.

86. JPC ms Journal, 24 Jan. 1879.

87. JPC to Chapman and Hall, 20 Aug. 1877, JPC Corresp.

88. JPC to Ebsworth, 16 Oct. 1878, JPC Corresp.

89 *A Study of Shakespeare.* Third Edition (London, 1895), pp. 127–28.

90 JPC to Swinburne, 26 Jan. 1880, Berg Collection, New York Public Library.

91. JPC ms Journal, 14 Dec. 1880.

92. Ibid., 1 Jan. 1882.

93. JPC to Ebsworth, 19 Oct. 1881, JPC Corresp.

94. JPC ms Journal, 28 Oct. 1882.

95. Ibid., 6 Sept. 1881.

96. Ibid., 3 July 1880.

97. Ibid., ? Jan. 1882.

98. Ibid., 30 July 1881.

99. Ibid., 6 May 1878.

100. Ibid., 27 Nov. 1880.

101. Ibid., 27 Oct. 1879.

102. Ibid., 8 May 1877.

103. Ibid., 22 Oct. 1878.

104. JPC to Ebsworth, 7 Jan. 1881, JPC Corresp.

105. JPC ms Journal, 27 March 1880.

106. Ibid., 10 Dec. 1877.

107. Ibid., 12 Oct. 1881.

108. Ibid., 21 Sept. 1881.

109. Ibid., 24 March 1880.

110. Ibid., 28 May 1881.

111. Ibid., ? July 1881.

112. Ibid., 24 June 1876.

113. Ibid., 12 Oct. 1879.

114. JPC to Ebsworth, 8 Aug. 1880, JPC Corresp.

115, JPC ms Journal, 7 Dec. 1881.

116. Ibid., 23 Dec. 1881.

117. Ibid., 11 Jan. 1882.

118. Ibid., 24 Jan. 1882.

119. JPC to Ebsworth, ? March 1882, JPC Corresp.

120. JPC ms Journal, 14 May 1882.

121. Ibid., 14 Aug. 1882.

APPENDIX (pp. 396–416)

1. *DNB* (1959), IV, 808–9.

2. 'John Payne Collier's Great Forgery', *Studies in Bibliography,* Papers of the Bibliographical Society of Virginia, Vol. 24 (1971), pp. 1–26. Hereafter Dawson.

3. *A Catalogue of the Manuscripts and Muniments of the College of God's Gift at Dulwich.* London, 1881. Hereafter *Catalogue.*

4. *Catalogue,* pp. xlii–xliii.

5. Ibid., p. xlvi.

6. He did so through Robert Douglas, an associate at the British Museum. Why Warner did not write to Young directly is not clear.

7. II, 341.

8. Lyson used the manuscript while writing *The Environs of London...* (2 vols., London, 1792) and quoted from it *in extenso*, pp. 97–100.

9. E.g., on p. 1, Collier inserted a line in pencil, 'Proprietor of the Red Bull' to

identify an obscure reference; on p. 2, he wrote in pencil 'This entry in every quarter', a reference to other parts of the diary; and so on.

10. *Memoirs,* p. 155.

11. *The Plays and Poems of William Shakespeare ... by the Late E. Malone....* Edited by James Boswell (21 vols., 1821), I, Part 2, p. 221.

12. 'Considering that dramatic poets were so numerous about this period, and a little earlier, and that Alleyn must necessarily have been acquainted with many of them, we are surprised not to see such men as Jonson ... among the persons occasionally entertained at Dulwich; but we find none such, and Alleyn does not seem, in this respect to have kept up his connection with the stage' (p. 154).

13. See *Memoirs,* p. 106.

14. The manuscript is now Folger Library Ms. V.a. 339.

15. Malone made a practice of copying manuscripts he used (see his transcript of Henslowe's manuscript diary now at Dulwich). Malone saw the Alleyn diary in the 1780s and it was also seen by Lyson in the 1790s (as I have noted above), but as Collier's comparison of his transcript to Lyson's would suggest, Lyson could not have been his original source.

16. Dawson, p. 16.

17. *Extracts,* ii, vii.

18. *Extracts,* ii, viii.

19. Only one other illustration in Vol. II refers to the date of the manuscript and it is consistent with Collier's statement here: Collier printed a ballad called 'The Choice of Friends' (II, 189) in conjunction with an unrelated 1584–85 entry in the *Register,* declaring that the manuscript copy was 'of about sixty years later date', i.e., about the mid-seventeenth century.

20. Dawson, pp. 13–14.

21. Dawson, p. 13, footnote.

22. *Extracts.* II, viii.

23. Dawson, p. 15.

24. I.e., following Professor Dawson's numbering (which unaccountably differs slightly from Collier's), Nos. 12 (printed at I, 129), 17 (I, 130), 22 (I, 104), 32 (I, 40), 63 (II, 35), 65 (II, 216), 69 (II, 30), 71 (II, 43), 73 (II, 125).

25. Dawson, p. 15.

26. I know of no evidence to support either of Professor Dawson's suppositions.

27. Dawson, pp. 15–16.

28. It should be noted here that Collier was himself vague on this point. However, whether Collier assumed the transcriber used original versions is not germane to my consideration which is not to prove Collier's suppositions correct but rather to show that Professor Dawson's case is not convincing. The possibility that Collier was wrong in his hypothesis concerning the origin of the manuscript ballads does not make Professor Dawson right in his. There are more than two alternatives, as I think my argument shows.

29. Dawson, pp. 24–5.

30. Dawson, p. 26.

Index